Communications
in Computer and Information Science   1694

More information about this series at https://link.springer.com/bookseries/7899

Rubina Polovina · Simon Polovina ·
Neil Kemp (Eds.)

Measuring Ontologies for Value Enhancement: Aligning Computing Productivity with Human Creativity for Societal Adaptation

First International Workshop, MOVE 2020
Virtual Event, October 17–18, 2020
Revised Selected Papers

 Springer

Editors
Rubina Polovina 🄳
Systems Affairs
Toronto, ON, Canada

Simon Polovina 🄳
Sheffield Hallam University
Sheffield, UK

Neil Kemp
Kemp & Associates, Inc.
Ottawa, ON, Canada

ISSN 1865-0929 ISSN 1865-0937 (electronic)
Communications in Computer and Information Science
ISBN 978-3-031-22227-6 ISBN 978-3-031-22228-3 (eBook)
https://doi.org/10.1007/978-3-031-22228-3

Preface

Recent multi-scale global social changes have amplified the interest in sharing the data-information-knowledge-wisdom (DIKW) space, including, but not limited to pandemics, economic crises, climate change, racial issues, and armed conflicts. These new (and old) challenges have raised awareness of the complex set of crucial political, social, economic, technological, environmental, psychological, or cultural problems humanity faces that need solving. The latest social changes impact all segments of societies: public and private sector organizations, the political sphere, the public sphere, communities, and individuals. And as some societies create scenarios that would benefit only them, other societies worldwide look for solutions to avoid devastating socioeconomic costs and apocalyptic scenarios. From this arises the intriguing question of how DIKW sharing via social technologies may unleash both (individual and collective) human creativity and contribute to human adaptability to find solutions for these complex sets of crucial and all-pervasive problems that humanity faces and that need solving. The implied suggestion is that there are ways to improve human adaptation by employing DIKW technologies that could rapidly find creative solutions for the grand challenges confronting humanity.

The awareness of the above challenges and associated risks brings new dimensions to our research. One of our assumptions is that the solutions to these problems cannot be achieved by advancing only one field; a transdisciplinary approach and the collaboration of people from various domains are necessary to face these challenges, which imposes yet another challenge for DIKW sharing.

Besides research on DIKW sharing and transfer among public and private sector enterprises, mass media, or public arenas with a promise to resolve the above-described complex problems, there is also significant research on DIKW sharing via social media, such as the impact of scientific research via social media, and, also on exposure to political ideology via social media. There are pluralisms of these values. For example, it is noted that the activities of DIKW sharing also involve individuals who commit time, effort, intellectual capital, and other resources to take risks to share DIKW without any clear benefits to them essentially. Technical and legal questions aside, we are witnessing the broader phenomenon of how individuals interact with DIKW, raising questions of motivation and ethics that influence or affect the decision to share DIKW and the actual activity of sharing. Additionally, misinformed DIKW sharing occurs daily in formal, informal, unauthorized (or sometimes outright illegal) communities. These experiences can nonetheless be used to research the nature of the DIKW sharing activities, their motivation, and their impact beyond traditional value-seeking. Fundamentally, DIKW sharing is a property of being human. Finding satisfaction in altruism, enjoyment in helping others, and self-effectiveness are important motivational determinants.

The grand challenges humanity faces have emerged in the context of DIKW representation in artificial intelligence (AI), involving the logical manipulation of increasingly large information sets (e.g., the Semantic Web, bioinformatics, and so on). Improvements in storage capacity and performance of computing infrastructure have also affected the nature of DIKW representation and reasoning systems, shifting their focus towards representational power and execution performance (e.g., natural language processing). In other words, DIKW representation and reasoning research has faced the challenge of developing DIKW representation structures optimized for large-scale reasoning.

In general, we are witnessing the emergence of the global DIKW space, which calls for creating a meta-level space through which other transdisciplinary DIKW segments may be integrated to cohere the DIKW space at a higher level. Hopefully, the emergence of this meta-level space will overcome the knowledge economy's fragmentation, commodification, and instrumentalism based on current societal premises.

The development of effective techniques for DIKW representation and reasoning (a crucial aspect of successful intelligent systems) and different DIKW representation paradigms, as well as their use in dedicated reasoning systems, have been extensively studied in the past. However, nowadays, they are facing the question of whether they may effectively mitigate the future risk of the grand challenges discussed above. These techniques must overcome the monologic, facilitate multi-perspectivity, and enable integration through integral and holistic paradigms and overlapping dimensions. These techniques cannot rely on fixed concepts alone. The techniques that allow concept vitality and imagination, creativity, and higher-order thinking require DIKW from multiple perspectives. These perspectives reveal their integral interconnectedness through our creative artfulness, multiple intelligences, and lines of abilities and thus must be explored. In addition, it is important to integrate DIKW technologies and the humanities to unleash human creativity and imagination.

Measuring Ontologies for Value Enhancement (MOVE) is a community of researchers and practitioners that aims to inspire research and discussion on the above-described topics. Therefore, MOVE's mission is to advance the research into the creation, evaluation, advancement, and measurement of DIKW spaces, thereby bringing value to our human understanding of, and interaction with our environments. Most importantly, MOVE brings together scientists and practitioners to exchange novel ideas and experiences in developing and evaluating DIKW-intensive systems, both digital and social. The community events (e.g., workshops, lectures, talks) have provided broad forums for reporting and discussing scientific progress on different challenges in advancing the development of DIKW-intensive systems, evaluation, and distribution of societal knowledge. The community is determined to ensure that the MOVE research facilitates the fair distribution of DIKW. In addition, the MOVE community encourages online discussions and explores ways of enriching online human interaction.

We focus on research of the DIKW space, including through computer-mediated methods represented by its ontologies. That is, the MOVE research includes, but is not limited to, the following:

- Ontologies as a medium that enables comparing and measuring the DIKW space
- Ontologies and their convergence or divergence with the values that motivate and determine DIKW sharing
- Properties and dynamics of ontologies shared via social technologies in their relation to human adaptation
- Formal ontologies and their applications
- Ontology-driven systems development

- DIKW representation methods
- Ontologies for open data, open platforms, open source
- Societal DIKW systems
- Ethics of DIKW sharing

This first MOVE publication contains selected and extended papers from the inaugural MOVE 2020 workshop, held in conjunction with the 23rd ACM Conference on Computer-Supported Cooperative Work and Social Computing (CSCW 2020). The publication culminates the (spirited) workshop round-table discussions at MOVE2020. We identified that the community needed to engage with the present-day challenges, including the separation of fake versus actual knowledge, enabling fair knowledge sharing, advancement of knowledge-sharing methods, and how to put the specialized knowledge pieces together.

The first two papers deliberate on the complexity of knowledge-intensive societal endeavors, particularly on the dynamics of these systems. The second group of papers bring forward methods for modeling ontologies, recognizing inconsistent ontologies, creating ontologies of explanations, and creating ontologies for worldviews to advance (digital) ontologies for the humanities. The third group of papers is about enterprise ontologies, merging enterprise architecture development and formal concept analysis, and strategy ontology. The fourth group of papers is dedicated to knowledge discovery and innovations. There are two papers on collaboration-facilitated knowledge mapping and knowledge discovery, and collaboration for sensemaking and innovations. Furthermore, there are two papers on using a trusted data source to advance research on social determinants, inequalities, and the underuse of social prescriptions for mental health. The last paper explores how a particular domain ontology of FinTech may be shared with the broadest audience in a seemingly informal and intuitive way.

The above papers reflect the post-inaugural workshop activity. Five of the 13 workshop presentations involving 19 authors were turned into seven extended and revised full papers for the MOVE publication. Furthermore, our community engaged with key authors, writing about the topics mentioned above, in relationed to aligning computing productivity with human creativity for societal adaptation. This community engagement resulted in further discussions during 2021 and early 2022. We invited these authors to submit their full papers pertinent to the topics above. We were offered six original papers, from which, after the review, we accepted five. We were happy that two of these invited papers were written by our younger colleagues since one of our goals is to promote research results without limitations regarding age, geopolitical borders, or other divisive interests. This allowed the community members to gain new insights and inspiration.

All MOVE workshop selected papers and invited papers underwent a rigorous single-blind review process with at least two independent reviewers per paper. The papers were reviewed for their originality, significance, rigor, and applicability. Where MOVE chairs submitted a paper, another chair who was not a paper co-author was asked to organize the peer-review process without disclosing the names of the reviewers to the authors. The reviewer chair contacted at least two more reviewers. Thus, such the papers received at least three independent reviews.

We thank all our reviewers for their hard work and valuable comments.

Finally, special thanks go to all contributing authors. The MOVE 2020 workshop would not have been possible without the dedicated involvement of the contributing authors. Although we come from multiple backgrounds (including computer science, AI, philosophy, and medicine), we worked together and inspired each other.

October 2022   Rubina Polovina
                                                      Simon Polovina
                                                      Neil Kemp

Organization

Program Committee Chairs

Rubina Polovina   Systems Affairs Inc., Canada
Simon Polovina   Sheffield Hallam University, UK
Neil Kemp   Kemp & Associates Inc., Canada

Program Committee

Jamie Caine   Sheffield Hallam University, UK
Giulia Felappi   University of Southampton, UK
Felix Hovsepian   Blue Manifold, UK
David Jakobsen   Aalborg University, Denmark
Anant Jani   University of Oxford, UK
Aidin Kerim   Ontario Public Service, Canada
Wim Paul Remi Laurier   Université Saint-Louis, Belgium
Pana Lepeniotis   Data Clarity Ltd, UK
Aldo De Moor   Community Sense, The Netherlands
Suzana Stojakovic-Celustka   InfoSet, Croatia
Ragupathi Sundararaj   Ontario Public Service, Canada
Anders W. Tell   Ecru Consulting, Sweden

Organizers

Rubina Polovina   Systems Affairs Inc., Canada
Simon Polovina   Sheffield Hallam University, UK
Neil Kemp   Kemp & Associates Inc., Canada
Ken Pu   Ontario Tech University, Canada

Contents

Complexity of Knowledge-Intensive Endeavors

On Understanding and Modelling Complex Systems, Through a Pandemic 3
  Rubina Polovina

Towards Endeavor Architecture to Support Knowledge Dynamics
of Societal Adaptation 21
  Rubina Polovina and Simon Polovina

Ontology Modeling

Towards Detecting Fake News Using Natural Language Understanding
and Reasoning in Description Logics 57
  Adrian Groza

Towards an Ontology of Explanations 73
  Adrian Groza and Mihai Pomarlan

Formal, Measurable Ontologies for Worldviews 86
  David Jakobsen and Simon Graf

Enterprise Ontologies

Underpinning Layered Enterprise Architecture Development with Formal
Concept Analysis 101
  Matt Baxter, Simon Polovina, Neil Kemp, and Wim Laurier

Advancing Strategy Ontology 114
  Jamie Caine

Knowledge Discovery and Innovations

Participatory Collaboration Mapping of Design-Enabled Urban
Innovations: The MappingDESIGNSCAPES Case 171
  Aldo de Moor, Evi Papalioura, Evi Taka, Dora Rapti, Annika Wolff,
  Antti Knutas, and Tomas te Velde

Collaborative Sensemaking of Design-Enabled Urban Innovations: The
MappingDESIGNSCAPES Case   203
Aldo de Moor, Evi Papalioura, Evi Taka, Dora Rapti, Annika Wolff,
Antti Knutas, Tomas te Velde, and Ingrid Mulder

A Novel Ontological Approach to Track Social Determinants of Health
in Primary Care   227
Dylan McGagh, Anant Jani, John Williams, Harshana Liyanage,
Uy Hoang, Cecilia Okusi, Julian Sherlock, Filipa Ferreira,
Ivelina Yonova, and Simon de Lusignan

A Novel Ontological Approach to Estimate Inequalities and Underuse
of Social Prescriptions for Mental Health in Primary Care in England   241
Anant Jani, Harshana Liyanage, Cecilia Okusi, Julian Sherlock,
Uy Hoang, Dylan McGagh, John Williams, Filipa Ferreira,
Ivelina Yonova, and Simon de Lusignan

FinTech and Its Implementation   256
Suzana Stojakovic-Celustka

Author Index   279

Complexity of Knowledge-Intensive Endeavors

On Understanding and Modelling Complex Systems, Through a Pandemic

Rubina Polovina(✉) (iD)

Systems Affairs, Toronto, ON, Canada
rubina@systemsaffairs.com

Abstract. The Upper Modelling Framework (UMF) is an upper ontology that sheds light on the relationships and dependencies within complex domains and demonstrates an intuitive approach to explaining domain complexity. It also considers the multiple facets (or dimensions) of the universe of discourse to illustrate how this ontological framework may be used to break down the domain complexity, understand it, and synthesize it into a model of principles. Using a pandemic as a case study, the expressiveness of the framework is illustrated, including how the UMF may guide sharing of the Domain-Information-Knowledge-Wisdom (DIKW) continuum. The findings contribute to a new way of studying complex domains by considering and supporting cognitive activities (e.g., thinking, reasoning) carried out by the participants (i.e., agencies) and developing epistemic relationships among them.

Keywords: Upper ontology · Systems modelling · Social ontology · Pandemic · Upper modelling framework

1 Introduction

Humanity faces a complex set of crucial and all-pervasive problems (political, social, economic, technological, environmental, psychological, and cultural) that need solving. Gell-Mann (1995, 2013) pointed out that the solutions cannot be achieved by advancing only one field; collaborating with people from various domains is necessary to address these challenges.

One method of overcoming the complexity of a discourse of interest and enabling the collaboration of people from various domains was the introduction of multiple perspectives. For example, Enterprise Architecture (EA), which has been traditionally used by Information and Communications Technology (ICT) communities, organizes a set of perspectives (or views) representing the different points of view of different participants (Zachman, 2011). However, Lapalme (2012), Lapalme et al. (2016) pointed out the insufficiencies of most EA frameworks in modelling complex adaptive systems, particularly regarding modelling social actions. Moreover, Mowles (2014) identified another challenge: the evaluation of complex social actions, seeing non-linearity in the social as the norm rather than an exception, and what the evaluators may do to assert that social interventions work.

© Springer Nature Switzerland AG 2022
R. Polovina et al. (Eds.): MOVE 2020, CCIS 1694, pp. 3–20, 2022.
https://doi.org/10.1007/978-3-031-22228-3_1

To overcome those shortcomings, we offer the Upper Modelling Framework (UMF), which originated in systems science (Polovina and Wojtkowski, 1999), as an upper ontological framework to facilitate the modelling of complex domains. We wish to draw attention to the principles of complex systems models, which are the foundation for the perspectives as seen from various points of view:

(i)   the holistic model that integrates individual perspectives
(ii) the sets of models that comprise unique points of view (i.e., perspectives)
(iii) the models (i.e., artefacts) of the specific perspectives.

In the context of this paper, "models" are understood as vessels that carry DIKW about the universe of discourse Frigg and Hartmann (2020). In other words, they represent the DIKW of a complex endeavour. These models enable discourse, explanations, learning, the creation of systems, and the observation of interactions with the systems' environment (e.g., changes).

This paper is structured as follows: First, we elaborate on the UMF as an upper ontological framework for systems modelling. The UMF is offered as a framework that may facilitate the emerging need to model rapid and wide-scale societal changes (e.g., pandemics, economic crises, racial issues, environmental issues), their concepts, and their complexity. Second, we illustrate the expressiveness of the UMF and its potential to break down the complexity of the universe of discourse. Third, we show how the UMF may be used to facilitate breaking down the complexity of a social phenomenon, namely, the COVID-19 pandemic. In this case study, we discuss the monitoring and planning of the social endeavour that should inform decision-making (i.e., the pandemic response). Finally, we offer our concluding remarks, including the forward-looking statement.

2   The Upper Modelling Framework (UMF)

The Upper Modelling Framework (UMF) was originally proposed by Polovina and Wojtkowski (1999) to contribute to the discussion of systems modelling and to illustrate gaps between object-oriented modelling and models that human minds create. Object-oriented modelling represents an object as a bundle of properties and methods. Objects created in the human mind depend on the modeller's cognizance and reflect the modeller's social relationships and dynamics. At this point, we will define an object by paraphrasing Merriam-Webster's definition of an object (i.e., "something mental or physical toward which thought, feeling, or action is directed" Object (2022)). An object is anything that may engage any faculty of someone's mind or anything and everything that may be distinguished from the observed domain.

Polovina and Wojtkowski (1999) took into consideration cognitive activities carried out by the modellers (e.g., thinking, reasoning, learning, abstraction, deduction), their universe of discourse, and the models' principles (or dimensions), created objects and relationships among the objects. They presented these cognitive activities from an intuitive point of view. The term "system" was applied to encompass social, technical, physical, and natural systems or any combination.

The purpose of the UMF is to facilitate the modelling of complex domains, their rules; the complexity of the universe of discourse; and cognitive activities that generate knowledge flows, explanations, and the creation and transformation of the models.

2.1 Four Spheres of the Model Existence

The UMF distinguishes four spheres or levels of the model's existence (the terms "spheres" and "levels" are used interchangeably): principal, conceptual, formative, and manifestation spheres (Fig. 1). The foundation for this separation is based on insight gained by observing the modeller's cognitive activities (e.g., thinking, reasoning) and the modeller's universe of discourse, as described in the following text.

Cognitive activities (of modelling) with a tendency to generate or impact a system may be initiated by determining the essential idea the system enacts. The determination of the crucial idea occurs at the highest sphere of the system's existence, the principal sphere, which presents the system's most abstract (i.e., principal) representation. In the next sphere, the universe of discourse (i.e., domain) is conceptualized, which initiates the formation of the concept, and is denoted as a prototype. At the third sphere, prototypes are particularized, concretized, and may be constrained until desired forms are obtained. These forms will serve as moulds (of ideas) at the lowest sphere of the system instantiation, the physical sphere, where the actual manifestation of instantiation occurs—the abstract (forms of) ideas are becoming a reality. This is a typical, top-to-bottom knowledge transformation flow; from abstract spheres (i.e., principal, conceptual, formative) to

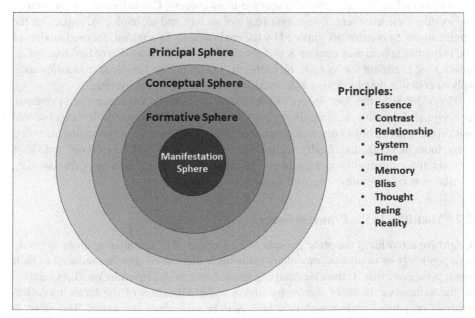

Fig. 1. Four spheres (or levels) of the model's existence and ten modelling principles of the Upper Modelling Framework (UMF).

the instantiated manifestation in the physical sphere. The process is denoted as systems generation.

At the same time, cognitive activities may also be triggered by stimuli coming from the physical world (e.g., sensing the environment). Selected stimuli may be put into context to create information. This information may be examined (e.g., summarized) at the lowest level (i.e., formative sphere) and moulded until a concept can be recognized and further abstracted to its essential idea (at the highest level of its existence in the principal sphere). Thus, the cognitive activities and knowledge transformation may also follow bottom-up patterns: from the physical sphere towards higher levels of abstraction.

It is notable as well that cognition and DIKW transformation do not necessarily follow any sequential order: system changes may be initiated at any level, and changes may be directed either towards its instantiation in the physical world or towards higher levels of abstraction, depending on what opportunities for change are presented.

Since every modeller may have their own interpretation of the universe of discourse (i.e., their own world), then, depending on the modeller's world (e.g., individuality, knowledge, preferences, creativity, social relationships, bias), multiple interpretations of the UMF spheres may exist. It is up to the modellers and their social circles to decide the universe of discourse and to set its boundaries. To make this framework operational, however, less ambiguous, and more pragmatic distinctions need to be established for the sake of communication and DIKW generation among the participants (e.g., community).

For example, a pragmatic interpretation for system development may be that the principal and conceptual spheres contain abstract models of the universe of discourse. The modellers express their view of reality, either an existing or desired vision, focusing on understanding the universe of discourse in its entirety. Considerations may include the system's environment, integration (e.g., of society and technology), impact on the environment, or constraints imposed by the environment. In contrast, focused models of the formative sphere may contain actionable DIKW with the intention of building, maintaining, or changing the system, including its environment. Finally, the manifestation sphere contains the physical, instantiated implementation of the system.

In addition to the four spheres or levels of the model's existence (i.e., principal, conceptual, formative, and manifestation), ten main modelling principles are observed within the spheres: object essence, contrasted object, relationship, system, time, memory, bliss, thought, being, and, finally, reality. These principles may also be considered views or modelling dimensions that enable recursiveness and the generation of fractals (i.e., similar pattern structures across all spheres.)

2.2 Modelling in the Principal Sphere

Cognitive activities of the principal sphere are focused on differentiating ideas. Working independently or in groups, modellers refine their ideas until they are reduced to their main principles, that is, the ideas that capture only the most important qualities relevant to the endeavour. In other words, by fusion and clarification of the ideas, modellers abstract only those ideas which they believe to be relevant to the model. Therefore, at this level of existence, the ideas, reduced to their principles, may exist without any form, individuality, instance, or manifestation. Sometimes, modellers have no names for their ideas but only a recognition that they are important for the discourse and endeavour.

The new reality cannot be generated from scratch, disconnected from the existing world. Instead, the new reality will arise from modellers' intentions as well as from the objectively existing world (Polovina and Wojtkowski, 1999). This new reality will be influenced by modellers' thinking and active, iterative, and creative activities. It will also echo social relations and dynamics (Table 1).

Table 1. Model properties in the four spheres (or levels) of the model's existence

Principal Sphere	• Objects do not have crisp boundaries
Conceptual Sphere	• Objects receive their first forms (or prototypes). Formal paradigms known to humankind also reside here • If cognitive processes are moving up (from the formative spheres), formal paradigms are created in this sphere
Formative Sphere	• Prototypes are particularized, concretized, and constrained until satisfactory forms are obtained • Models may also be unrefined and concrete observations of phenomena in the manifestation sphere
Manifestation Sphere	• Forms are instantiated • Models are also made by perceiving the physical world (i.e., reality)

Resolving the Main Principles. The pure fact that the modeller directs their attention to a particular object means the modeller is discriminating between the "rest" of the observed domain in favour of the recognized (or realized) object. For us, this object recognition consists of two steps: first, choosing the relevant object; and second, determining its essence, which identifies the reason for the object's presence in the model. Determining the essence of an object implies the idea of another object that is contrasted with the first one. Now the idea of two contrasted (or compared) objects implies the idea of betweenness. The modeller discriminates between the two objects and determines the essence of their relationship. Thus, relationships are objects with the primary quality of connecting or disconnecting other objects.

The three main principles of essential and contrasting elements and the relationships between them are therefore identified as essentially disjointed possibilities. At the same time, however, they imply something that exists as a connected whole, which leads to the notion of the fourth principle; that is, the notion of a system: it is a complex but ordered whole. Now that the system has its structure, it can be decomposed and viewed either holistically or as connected elements.

Within the previously defined principles of essential and contrasted objects, relationships, and systems, no change is possible without the notion of motion—nothing could happen without the idea of dynamics, which implies the idea of time. Now that time (discrete or continuous) is introduced, relationships among system elements may be considered static or dynamic. Static relationships are expressed in system structure and similarities with other elements or origins. Depending on the complexity of the causality of the universe of discourse, events and sequences of events may sometimes be considered dynamic relationships because they exist only at the moment they occur. Now that time has been introduced; the object may have a past, present, and future. Such an object has the capacity for experience or memory.

Now when the object may remember, the object may have a notion of bliss, which may be concretized as a capacity to differentiate positive versus negative experiences or learn what is desired versus what is undesired. In other words, the object may gain an ability to recognize the opposites, that is, their similarities and differences. For example, for an ICT system, it may mean that the system can distinguish its fully functioning states versus the states in which the integrity of the system has been compromised because of security, privacy, or safety breaches. This principle is significant for AI, because its concretizations include a capacity to recognize ethical versus unethical.

This leads to the concretization of the eight principles of thought. That is, the object may now have goals and the capacity to plan and strategize. This leads to the next principle of coming into being, and the object may take an initiative and launch an action.

We have previously described the essential notion of a system—it is an object that consists of interrelated elements (which are also objects) that form a unified whole. That is, by applying the ten main UMF principles, we may describe a system with its structure, notion of time, memory, a capacity to evaluate its experience, and a capacity to learn and exhibit goal-oriented behaviour. That is, the system may take action and exhibit behaviour that may change both itself and its environment. Thus, the system is embedded in reality, and its impact on its environment may characterize it.

2.3 Conceptual Sphere

Visions of the new and desired reality are born in the conceptual sphere, in which modellers construct their own visions of the future reality. However, if there is more than one modeller in the group, their visions may not necessarily converge. These first blueprints of systems are denoted as prototypes. The conceptual sphere also contains all methodologies, methods, paradigms, formalisms, and other patterns that modellers have at their disposal. All of these enable recognition of the building blocks of the new and desired reality. The choice of the specific building blocks depends on the principles resolved on the previous level.

By no means does this imply that the vision of the new reality is created in a vacuum. Instead, the new system will impact the existing environment (i.e., reality) and vice versa: the existing environment will impact the newly envisioned system. Constraints from both sides limit the new system; for example, the complexity and depth of a modeller's tacit knowledge (as a part of the modeller's world) limits their vision of the new system and their ability to formalize them and predict the impact on the existing systems (e.g., environment). At the same time, constraints coming from the existing systems (e.g., infrastructure) also limit the new desired system (i.e., new reality).

In this dynamic process, modellers may move through all four spheres. Sometimes, cognitive activities may start in the principal sphere and proceed through the conceptual and formative spheres to the manifestation sphere (i.e., reality). Still, they can also move back and forth between the spheres. In our example, modellers will have to assess the existing ways of communication and qualities of discourse, understand their deficiencies, and introduce changes per the new visions. In practice, the modellers will need to start in the formative sphere, process their observations of the existing system (in the manifestation sphere), and then go back to the conceptual sphere to identify missing blocks of communication, create new ones, incorporate them into the new design, and materialize them into reality.

2.4 Formative Sphere and Manifestation

An appreciable form of the system is produced in the formative sphere. Here, the form receives characteristics in terms of quantities, dimensions, and design, establishing it as a specific system. Concepts that individualize the system are given at this time. The system that is conceptualized at the highest level becomes the ideal vision and is formed in this sphere to meet specific requirements. In the formative sphere, the modellers make efforts to formalize further and complete the system description that will be instantiated in the manifestation sphere (i.e., in reality).

A form is a descriptor, so the conceptualized vision can be realized (i.e., instantiated). A form is the main concept of the formative sphere. A form will be manifested in reality, and the "embodiment" will closely resemble the original form and concept, depending on constraints that influence cognitive activities (i.e., modellers' worlds), as well as the creation and emergence of the new system.

The modellers may or may not be aware of the constraints that govern the limits of their visions. For example, one approach to modelling is to create a purely idealized vision at the conceptual level without assigning any constraints at this level, particularly if limitations have not been resolved in the principal or conceptual spheres. Here, the constraints are that variable factors will be specified in the formative sphere. Those limiting factors might be budgets, benevolent or malevolent relationships, liabilities, or legacy infrastructures. Constraints can also be used to determine the properties of the new systems, validity, feasibility of DIKW invested into the vision, or infer DIKW that is not directly available. Constraints may also be added to protect the integrity of the vision (e.g., copyright, various security controls, privacy protection, and safety measures).

3 The Main Modelling Principles or Modelling Dimensions

The UMF principles may be used as dimensions to classify models and modelling paradigms in Information and Communication Technology (ICT) and Artificial Intelligence (AI), as shown in Table 2.

Table 2. The main modelling principles (or ten modelling dimensions)

Modelling principles	Description	Examples of cognitive processes and formal paradigms
Essence	• Object recognition • Determining the essence (i.e., why it is relevant in the model)	• Object identification • Image recognition
Contrast	• Associated/disassociated objects • *Now the idea of two objects implies the "betweenness."*	• Environment from which the first object is "carved out." • Sets of objects
Relationship	• Connects or disconnects • Hierarchical or anarchical, part-of or kind-of • *Now the essential and contrasted objects, and the relationships between them, are identified as essentially disjointed possibilities*	• Entity-relationship modelling • Semantic modelling • Nestedness
System	• First notion of the system—consists of the parts, but it is a whole • *Now the system may have its structure, but nothing can move yet*	• Relational database schema that is time-invariant • Modularity
Time	• Discrete, continuous • Events, sequences • Relationships may be static or dynamic • System dynamics • *Now objects may have a past, present, and future*	• Attributed finite state automata • Formal grammars • Finite automata
Memory	• Storing and retrieving information • *Capacity for experience*	• Push-down automata (remembering their recent paths) • Big data
Bliss	• *Capacity to evaluate and discriminate* (e.g., bliss vs pain, desired vs undesired, good vs evil, true vs false)	• Being able to recognize security, privacy, or safety breaches

(continued)

Table 2. (*continued*)

Modelling principles	Description	Examples of cognitive processes and formal paradigms
Thought	• Power of *intentionality* (to be "about" something) • Capacity for planning • *Independent behaviour* • Interpreting, inferring, analyzing, deducing, and other thinking skills	• Expert systems • Agent technologies
Being	• Coming into being • Distribution • Emerging properties (that the parts do not have on their own) • Capacity to interact with a wider whole • Adaptation	• Multi-agents that can learn from interactions (e.g., their population may increase over time, they may compete amongst themselves) • Distributed AI • Artificial life
Reality	• Embedded into the environment • Capacity to evaluate other complex systems • *Capacity to intervene and deliberately change the environment*	• Multi-agents that can change the environment (i.e., being aware of the impact and adapting accordingly) • Evaluate order vs disorder

4 Modelling Pandemic DIKW Flows

In December 2019, the first unknown pneumonia cases were detected in Wuhan, China and reported to World Health Organization (WHO). Soon after, in January 2020, Chinese authorities reported that the novel coronavirus had caused the disease, and the first deaths caused by severe pneumonia were announced. Chinese authorities and health organizations could not stop the outbreak. Multiple cases had been reported in Asia, and the first case the US.

We could not find trustworthy information on the novel virus at that time. It was unclear how fast the disease spread and how infectious it was. There was no international consensus on how to prevent the spreading of the virus—for example; there was no consensus if health workers and the general public should wear medical masks or not (Eikenberry et al., 2020). Furthermore, collaboration among the media organizations, governments and health organizations was uncertain. For instance, CNN declared the world pandemic before WHO (Gupta, 2020).

Concerned citizens worldwide reached out on social media to warn the rest of the world about the danger. For example, Dr Wenliang was targeted by Chines police because of his attempts to warn the public of new pneumonia via social media. He later died of the disease. Soon after, it became evident that biopolitics presided over all communications in the public sphere and among the involved organizations (CNN Editorial Research, 2022).

At the same time, numerous concerned citizens, frustrated by inadequate government responses around the world, started to educate the public about the new disease. For example, a Saskatoon student, unable to find a centralized tracker for the novel coronavirus, launched his own (Kessler, 2020). On the other side of the globe, Campbell (2022) started a YouTube channel to educate the public about the disease.

The debate on the virus's origin has been ongoing from the beginning of the pandemic. According to WHO SAGO preliminary report (2022), we still cannot determine the virus's origin. According to one of The Lancet Microbe's editorials (2022), "the potential problem here is the conflict between scientific and political approaches".

In early 2020, we understood that the whole world was going to be involved, so we started observing the development of the pandemic, aware of its high complexity. To break down the complexity of the phenomenon, we observed the pandemic from the UMF prism and made the following general assumptions.

Since a pandemic is prevalent over the whole society (or the whole world), we assume that the societal endeavour intends to engage and empower all segments of society to adapt and respond. In addition, since the etiologic agent (i.e., infectious substance) is novel and fast spreading, and with a significant mortality rate, timely sharing of relevant DIKW across all segments of the society may be crucial, or the society may be doomed (Callaghan, 2016, 2020). The following case study will illustrate how the UMF may facilitate the modelling and evaluating the DIKW relevant to the COVID-19 pandemic and other pandemics.

We have been observing the COVID-19 pandemic and DIKW flow relevant for the societal response. Identification of the objects relevant to the endeavour may start at any point. We began by identifying agencies that participate in the DIKW generation and sharing, moved to determine the first principles, returned to refine the agencies (Table 3 and Fig. 2), and continued refining the first level of the model until we were satisfied with the model of the pandemic principles (as described in Table 4). Through this process, we realized the importance of separating relevant DIKW from fake DIKW, including the dynamics of the DIKW generation and sharing among the agencies. While discussing these principles, a need to monitor and evaluate the societal DIKW system emerged as a new concept and possible research field.

Table 3. Agencies of the COVID-19 pandemic

Agencies	Description and examples
Political Parties	Societal political parties (e.g., Democrats and Republicans, Conservatives and Liberals, Communist parties)
Governments	Political elements of governments (e.g., elected governments at various levels, such as federal, state, provincial, or municipal governments)
Bureaucracies	Bureaucratic apparatus that supports the governing politicians, policies, and programs and provides government services
Media	News media organizations, social media providers, content creators (on social media)
Private Sector	Directly involved organizations (e.g., vertical industries and sectors, such as the pharmaceutical industry, or impacted organizations, such as transportation)
International Organizations	Organizations funded by more than one government (e.g., World Health Organization)
Science, Research, and Education	Universities, colleges, institutes
Hospitals	Networks of hospitals funded by governments and/or private sector organizations
Organizations that support vulnerable populations	Long-term care homes, shelters, refugee camps
Communities	Local communities, groups of hacktivists and activists, online communities
Individuals	Citizens

In short, the first (principal) level is determined by selecting the drivers that we found relevant for enabling a rapid response to the pandemic. We did not discuss the formal paradigms at the principal level, as the choice of the formal apparatus should be resolved at the second level; that is, in the conceptual sphere, where an initial social ontology of the pandemic should emerge. This initial social ontology would be refined at the third level (in the formative sphere) so that it can be implemented in society (manifestation level). In this way, the UMF serves as an upper ontology that facilitates the creation of a domain ontology, in this case, a social ontology of the pandemic.

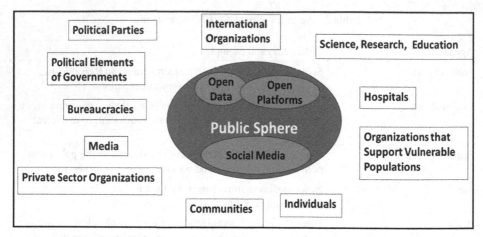

Fig. 2. Agencies within the COVID-19 pandemic that share knowledge via the public sphere.

5 Forward-Looking Statement

We used the Upper Modelling Framework (UMF) to structure our observations of the COVID-19 pandemic. Observing the development of the pandemic and decision-making about the pandemic response revealed multiple limitations. The decision-making had been bounded by a lack of knowledge (on the novel disease and the pandemic spread), decision-makers limited cognitive capabilities, limited economic means to deal with the pandemic, geopolitical interests, and possibly many other factors. We focused on observing knowledge flows through society and identified the main factors relevant to the pandemic response. As a result of our study, a new model of a societal knowledge system emerged, which may serve as a logical starting point for the creation of a multifaceted pandemic social ontology.

In this way, we contribute to establishing global and societal knowledge meta-modelling. We demonstrated how the UMF-guided principal model facilitates complex thinking that Gidley (2013) defined as that which "involves the ability to hold multiple perspectives in mind while at the same time being able to meta-reflect on those per-spectives and the potential relationships among them." In addition, the natural language, diagrams, and ideas could be intuitively grasped are deliberately used to encourage the collaboration of people from heterogeneous domains. This facilitates solving problems that are too complex to be solved by advancing only one field (Gell-Mann, 2013).

In this pandemic case study, we tackled the model of the principles only to limit the discourse of interest and to enable an intuitive evaluation of the epistemic relationships among the agencies and the DIKW dynamics of the pandemic. The principal model may also guide the creation of models in the conceptual and formative sphere, and ultimately, these models may be used to change the reality of the outcomes of this or future pandemics.

Table 4. The observed modelling principles of DIKW sharing during the COVID-19 pandemic

Modelling principles	Description	Examples of cognitive processes and formal paradigms
Essence	• Pandemic • *True DIKW* • *False DIKW*	• No consensus on the pandemic definition
Contrast	• Scientific and relevant DIKW • Agencies	• Early DIKW on the disease-causing agent has not been shared • Could the relevant DIKW have been shared earlier to adapt to the situation better and faster? Who has been sharing knowledge during the pandemic? • Associative thinking may continue to identify the agencies (see the principle of being)
Relationship	• Interfaces (social and digital) • DIKW flow between two agencies	• Agencies are connected via their interfaces • Agencies' determinants are capacities to generate and use DIKW • Agencies' capacity to share and transfer DIKW determine DIKW flows
System	• Societies • Geopolitical systems • *Societal DIKW system*	• Society as a Complex Adaptive System (CAS) consists of its agencies that are also CASs • Society is also determined by its geopolitical system • The societal response to the pandemic is determined by the DIKW structure
Time	• Rapid spread	• The timeframe has been dictated by the disease-causing agent
Memory	• Historical DIKW • Experience	• Experience from the previous pandemics • Experience, such as DIKW of the behaviours and roles played by the agencies in the past (e.g., medical mask-wearing)

(continued)

Table 4. (*continued*)

Modelling principles	Description	Examples of cognitive processes and formal paradigms
Bliss	• Competing messages (e.g., political messages) • *True (effective and scientific) DIKW vs fake (dangerous and pseudoscientific) DIKW*	• Sharing of the true DIKW compromised by political doctrines and ideologies, conspiracy theories, misinformation, fake knowledge, propaganda, etc • Behaviour and outcomes desirable to one agency (i.e., in this case, a group of people) are not necessarily desirable to others • *This appears to be an inherent and inescapable property of social systems that has an impact on social technologies and the implementation of methods for recognizing fake DIKW*
Thought	• Increase flow of true DIKW • Separate true DIKW from fake DIKW • Measure DIKW flow • Other strategic principles relevant for true DIKW flow	• An initial strategy may be to evaluate and improve the flow of true DIKW through society. This implies the necessity to separate true DIKW from fake DIKW • *Going back to the principle of bliss and essence—methods for recognizing fake DIKW are necessary*
Being	• Agencies including: elected governments, bureaucracies, political parties, international organizations, scientific organizations, healthcare organizations, organizations that support vulnerable populations, private sector organizations, media, public sphere, communities, and individuals • DIKW flow/network	• Agencies have strategies, goals, DIKW, interfaces, capacities to generate and use true DIKW, vulnerabilities to fake DIKW, and engagement in the deliberate and/or unintentional dissemination of fake DIKW • The agencies relevant for the pandemic response are networked by the DIKW flow • The emergence of the societal DIKW flow/network with its structure and dynamics consistutes the societal DIKW system

(*continued*)

Table 4. (*continued*)

Modelling principles	Description	Examples of cognitive processes and formal paradigms
Reality	• New reality • Societal DIKW system with its structure and flow/network (social and technology)	• The emergence of a new reality; in this case, (un)successful mitigation of the pandemic • Managed societal DIKW flow/network (e.g., global) • Measuring outcomes • Desired DIKW flow may include: top-down and bottom-up flow, inclusiveness, openness, integration, individualism, collaboration, adaptiveness, dealing with opportunism, and emergence (of a positive outcome) (Polovina and Polovina, 2022)

Our approach was holistic (as we considered the societal knowledge systems) but also allowed further fragmentation (e.g., further specialized research of epistemic interfaces between research institutions and governments or specialized research of epistemic relationships among research organizations and private sector organizations).

In addition, from the same principles, we could intuitively capture, model, and evaluate the complexity of the endeavour (Table 5). For example, one of the factors that generate the complexity was embedded into the essence of the observed model; that is, the lack of formal definitions (and formal apparatus) of knowledge; formal definition of "true," scientific, and relevant knowledge (i.e., episteme), but also lack of formal definition of "fake" knowledge represented by pseudoscientific assertions, propaganda, or conspiracy theories. At the same time, it has been acknowledged that the pandemic was caused by a highly contagious disease, and consequently, all elements of society had to respond, adding other degrees of structural complexity and complexity to the epistemic relationships among the agencies (i.e., their interfaces). Furthermore, all social agencies must work together, which implies a high degree of dynamic complexity.

The ideas outlined in the model of the principles (Table 4) may be further conceptualized and formalized in the conceptual and formative spheres, as we described in the section on Conceptual Sphere (2.3). However, further conceptualization implies the use of paradigms specific to their fields; that is, specialized knowledge will be required, which, in turn, implies fragmentation among the agencies. This emphasizes the importance of the principal model; that is, it enables us to put together all the elements of the endeavour but also guides the choice of the paradigms to be used in the conceptual and formative spheres, which leads us toward the concept of endeavour architecture (Polovina and Polovina, 2022)—the architecture of a sincere human attempt, a determined or assiduous effort towards a specific goal. Ultimately, we need to move beyond enterprise

Table 5. Factors that generate complexity in the principal model of the pandemic

UMF Principles	Factors that generate complexity
Essence	• Lack of formal definition of "true" knowledge • Lack of formal definition of "fake" knowledge • The relatively new and unresearched idea of a global and societal knowledge system (Gidley, 2013)
Contrast	• An overabundance of ideas that might have been associated with the pandemic (because many, if not all, elements of the society are involved) made it difficult to determine what was relevant
Relationships	• Multifaceted epistemic relationships among agencies necessary to respond to the pandemic (e.g., epistemic relationships between the research organizations and the governments differ from the epistemic relationships among the research organizations and the private sector organizations)
System	• Multiple heterogeneous elements of society (e.g., from political parties, private and public sector organizations, and media down to the individuals) and their disparities complicate the structure of the (knowledge) system
Time	• Rapid response (i.e., knowledge generation) was required to save lives
Bliss	• Lack of formal methods to separate "true" knowledge from "fake" knowledge
Memory	• Relatively little DIKW about the novel disease and limited experience with the disease's potential to cause the global pandemic
Thought	• Multiple conflicting geopolitical, biopolitical and societal interests and strategic directions
Being	• A relatively new field of modelling global or societal knowledge systems that have just started emerging (Gidley, 2013) • All elements of society must work together
Reality	• Difficulties obtaining feedback (e.g., data on the spread of the pandemic)

architecture (i.e., architecture of a company, business, organization, or other purposeful endeavours).

Various elements of endeavour architecture may be included, for example, formal models for the evaluation of systems' complexity (Clark and Jacques, 2012; Franco et al., 2022). Moreover, an ontology-driven approach may enable further formal conceptualization. For example, Groza (2022) discussed how description logic might be used to recognize inadequacies of the COVID-19 ontologies. Baxter et al. (2022) explored an enterprise ontology to improve epistemic relationships. An ontology of explanations (Groza and Pomarlan, 2022) may be used to improve agencies' interfaces. Furthermore, methods for knowledge discovery, like the one described by de Moor et al. (2022), may be used to identify DIKW sources.

However, we do not expect that balancing the conflict between scientific and political approaches will be resolved in the near future, if ever. For example, Patel et al. (2021) called the governments to pause Twitter censorship because they found that the diffusion of scientific research papers via Twitter has a positive correlation with the outcome. At the same time, Haman (2020) found that the political leaders gained more followers on Twitter since the pandemic started; that is, it seems that citizens were interested in the latest update from their leading politicians. Thus, we anticipate that this potential conflict and duality (i.e., science and politics) will be an important element of endeavour architecture.

With this research agenda, we aim to advance the modelling of societal and global knowledge that includes pluralism of complex cognitive activities, such as creative and critical thinking, problem-solving, concept development, conflict resolution, moral and ethical reasoning, dealing with dichotomies and paradoxes, and ultimately, adaption to various societal challenges. Moreover, we are bringing forward modelling paradigms (such as the UMF, ontology-driven systems development, and endeavour architecture) that merge intuitive and formal modelling to enable experts from multiple domains to collaborate and integrate their research results to find solutions to complex societal problems.

References

Baxter, M., Polovina, S., Kemp, N., Laurier, W.: Underpinning layered enterprise architecture development with formal concept analysis. In: Polovina, R., Polovina, S., Kemp, N. (eds.) Aligning Computing Productivity with Human Creativity for Societal Adaptation,. The 1st Measuring Ontologies for Value Enhancement (MOVE) Workshop at the 23rd ACM CSCW2020, revised selected papers. CCIS 1694. Springer Nature Switzerland (2022). https://www.springer.com/series/7899/books

Callaghan, C.: Disaster management, crowdsourced R&D and probabilistic innovation theory: toward real-time disaster response capability. Int. J. Disaster Risk Reduction **17**, 238–250 (2016). https://doi.org/10.1016/j.ijdrr.2016.05.004

Callaghan, C.: The Physics of a Coronavirus Pandemic: How to avoid Impending Apocalyptic or Dystopian Economic. SSRN (2020). https://papers.ssrn.com/sol3/papers.cfm?abstract_id=3567585

Clark, B.J., Jacques, R.D.: Practical measurements of complexity in dynamic systems. Procedia Computer Science **8**, 14–21 (2012)

Cambell, J.: Dr John Campbell. YouTube channel, https://www.youtube.com/c/Campbellteaching, last accessed 14 September 2022

CNN Editorial Research. Covid-19 Pandemic Timeline Fast Facts, CNN Health. https://www.cnn.com/2021/08/09/health/covid-19-pandemic-timeline-fast-facts/index.html, last accessed 12 September 2022

Eikenberry, E.S., et al.: To mask or not to mask: Modelling the potential for face mask use by the general public to curtail the COVID-19 pandemic. Infectious Disease Modelling **5**, 293–308 (2020). https://doi.org/10.1016/j.idm.2020.04.001

Franco, J.P., Doroc, K., Yadav, N., Bossaerts, P., Murawski, C.: Task-independent metrics of computational hardness predict human cognitive performance. Sci Rep **12**, 12914 (2022). https://doi.org/10.1038/s41598-022-16565-w

Frigg, R., Hartmann, S.: Models in Science. In: Edward, N.Z. (ed.) The Stanford Encyclopedia of Philosophy (Spring 2020 Edition), https://plato.stanford.edu/archives/spr2020/entries/models-science

Gell-Mann M.: A Crude Look at the Whole. Talk given at Nanyang Technological University, Singapore (4 March 2013). https://www.paralimes.org/tag/murray-gell-mann/

Gell-Mann, M.: What is Complexity? (1995). http://complexity.martinsewell.com/Gell95.pdf

Gidley, J.: Global knowledge futures: articulating the emergence of a new meta-level field. Integral Review **9**(2), (June 2013)

Groza, A.: Towards detecting fake news using natural language understanding and reasoning in Description Logics. In: Polovina, R., Polovina, S., Kemp, N. (eds.) Aligning Computing Productivity with Human Creativity for Societal Adaptation. The 1st Measuring Ontologies for Value Enhancement (MOVE) Workshop at the 23rd ACM CSCW2020, revised selected papers. CCIS 1694. Springer Nature Switzerland (2022). https://www.springer.com/series/7899/books

Groza, A., Pomarlan, M.: Towards an ontology of explanations. In: Polovina, R., Polovina, S., Kemp, N. (eds.) Aligning Computing Productivity with Human Creativity for Societal Adaptation,. The 1st Measuring Ontologies for Value Enhancement (MOVE) Workshop at the 23rd ACM CSCW2020, revised selected papers. CCIS 1694. Springer Nature Switzerland (2022). https://www.springer.com/series/7899/books

Gupta, S.: Why CNN is calling the novel coronavirus outbreak a pandemic. CNN Health (2020). https://www.cnn.com/2020/03/09/health/coronavirus-pandemic-gupta/index.html, last accessed 12 September 2022

Haman, M.: The use of Twitter by state leaders and its impact on the public during the COVID-19 pandemic. Heliyon 6(11) (2020). https://www.sciencedirect.com/science/article/pii/S24058 44020323835, last accessed 30 September 2022

Kessler, R.: University of Saskatchewan student launches COVID-19 tracker to graph coronavirus cases. Global News Health (2020). https://globalnews.ca/news/6705571/usask-student-covid-19-tracker/

Lapalme, J.: Three Schools of Thought on Enterprise Architecture. IEEE Computer Society (2012)

Lapalme, J., Gerber, A., Van der Merwe, A., Zachman, J., De Vries, M., Hinkelmann, K.: Exploring the future of enterprise architecture: A Zachman perspective. Computers in Industry 79, 103-113 (June 2016)

Object. Merriam-Webster.com Dictionary, Merriam-Webster, https://www.merriam-webster.com/dictionary/object, last accessed 13 September 2022

de Moor, A., et al.: Participatory collaboration mapping of design-enabled urban innovations: the MappingDESIGNSCAPES case. In: Polovina, R., Polovina, S., Kemp, N. (eds.) Aligning Computing Productivity with Human Creativity for Societal Adaptation. The 1st Measuring Ontologies for Value Enhancement (MOVE) Workshop at the 23rd ACM CSCW2020, revised selected papers. CCIS 1694. Springer Nature Switzerland (2022). https://www.springer.com/series/7899/books

Mowles, C.: Complex, but not quite complex enough: The turn to the complexity sciences in evaluation scholarship. Evaluation 20(2), 160–175 (2014)

Patel, V.M., Haunschild, R., Bornmann, L., Garas, G.: A call for governments to pause twitter censorship: using twitter data as social-spatial sensors of COVID-19/SARS-CoV-2 research diffusion. Scientometrics 126, 3193–3207 (2021). https://doi.org/10.1007/s11192-020-03843-5

Polovina, R., Polovina, S.: Towards Endeavor Architecture to Support Knowledge Dynamics of Societal Adaptation (2022). In: Polovina, R., Polovina, S., Kemp, N. (eds.) Aligning Computing Productivity with Human Creativity for Societal Adaptation. The 1st Measuring Ontologies for Value Enhancement (MOVE) Workshop at the 23rd ACM CSCW2020, revised selected papers. CCIS 1694. Springer Nature Switzerland (2022). https://www.springer.com/series/7899/books

Polovina, R., Wojtkowski, W.: On the Nature of Modelling and Object Orientation. In: 4th Systems Science European Congress Proceedings, pp. 679–688. Valencia Spain (1999)

The Lancet Microbe: Searching for SARS-CoV-2 origins: the saga continues. Editorial, The Lancet Microbe 3(7), E471 (2022). https://doi.org/10.1016/S2666-5247(22)00161-6

WHO SAGO: WHO Scientific Advisory Group for the Origins of Novel Pathogens (SAGO): preliminary report, 9 June 2022. Geneva: World Health Organization (2022). https://cdn.who.int/media/docs/default-source/scientific-advisory-group-on-the-origins-of-novel-pathogens/sago-report-09062022.pdf, last accessed 20 September 2022

Zachman, A.J.: Yes, "Enterprise Architecture is Relative" BUT it is not Arbitrary. Zachman International (n.d.). https://www.zachman.com/ea-articles-reference/57-eanotarbitrary

Towards Endeavor Architecture to Support Knowledge Dynamics of Societal Adaptation

Rubina Polovina[1]([✉]) [iD] and Simon Polovina[2] [iD]

[1] Systems Affairs, Toronto, ON, Canada
rubina@systemsaffairs.com
[2] Sheffield Hallam University, Sheffield, UK
s.polovina@shu.ac.uk

Abstract. To facilitate societal adaptation, we need to establish the principles of Endeavor Architecture (EnA) in addressing the limitations of Enterprise Architecture (EA). To support the social perspectives that EnA adds, we propose establishing EnA directions and requirements, particularly epistemic relationships among the agencies. Furthermore, we assert that EnA must be open to new paradigms and technologies to facilitate societal adaptation. EnA also must accelerate data, information, knowledge, and wisdom transformation, integration, and sharing. We illustrate how the Upper Modelling Framework (UMF), an open, system-oriented upper ontology, along with ten principles of knowledge dynamics, may serve as a framework that sets the direction of EnA beyond EA.

Keywords: Endeavor architecture · Enterprise architecture · Upper ontology · Knowledge sharing

1 Context and Motivation for Establishing Endeavor Architecture

Societal changes (e.g., economic crises, climate change, racial issues, pandemics, escalating armed conflicts) painfully remind us that all elements of society, societal endeavors, and enterprises (big or small, private or public, profit or nonprofit) must be able to adapt to wide-scale, rapid and disruptive societal changes. These complex societal changes include all-pervasive problems (political, social, economic, technological, environmental, psychological, and cultural) that humanity faces and needs solving. Murray Gell-Mann (2013) pointed out that the solution to these problems cannot be achieved by advancing only one field; the transdisciplinary approach and collaboration of people from various domains are necessary to face these challenges. With this paper, we contribute to the discussion that has its goal inauguration of the new manner of study of complex domains and further articulation of the new meta-level studies of global Data-Information-Knowledge-Wisdom (DIKW) space (Gidley 2013). The expectations are that these studies will support societal adaptation by integrating understanding complexity, problem-solving, innovation, discovery, and research. These changes are pertinent to Endeavor Architecture (EnA), hence how we need to create it, thereby setting the foundation of EnA.

© Springer Nature Switzerland AG 2022
R. Polovina et al. (Eds.): MOVE 2020, CCIS 1694, pp. 21–54, 2022.
https://doi.org/10.1007/978-3-031-22228-3_2

This paper is organized as follows. First, we describe the context and the motives for establishing EnA to facilitate adaption (or evaluation of adaptational and transformational capacity). In that context, we focus on the development of cities, the rise of their citizens, rapid and widespread societal changes (e.g., pandemics), and Artificial Intelligence (AI) impacts as AI enters the mainstream, as they are all increasing the complexity of societal endeavors. Then we briefly describe Enterprise Architecture (EA)–a tool used by ICT and ICT-management communities to model and overcome the complexity of ICT-intensive enterprises. We discuss EA's limitations and elaborate on the necessity to introduce Endeavor Architecture (EnA) to model complex societal changes and facilitate societal adaptation (or evaluation of the capacity for adaptation). We also introduced the Upper Modelling Framework (UMF) to serve as an upper ontology of EnA. We elaborate on the DIKW dynamics (supported by the UMF) that facilitate societal adaptation as new directions and principles for the creation of EnA. We illustrate how EnA's four functions and ten principles of DIKW dynamics may be used to guide the evaluation of DIKW in relation to the adaptation and transformation of societal agencies. At the end, we answer some of the elementary questions of EnA and outline our research agenda in the forward-looking statement.

2 Environmental Adaption

In articulating our motives, we begin by defining environmental adaptation as an effort of an agency (which may be a society, an individual, any group, or any organization) triggered by specific events that are being translated into actions that aim to reduce the distance between the agency and its environments (e.g., economic, natural, civil liberty, health) in a satisfactory way. In this context, acceptable environmental adaptation is a variable term and may mean anything from bare survival to thriving in new environments.

Human societies have adapted to environmental changes throughout their existence. Environmental adaptations vary according to the system and environment in which they occur. At the point when the environmental changes become insurmountable, adaptation may happen at multiple (overlapping) levels:

- Social: an individual's or group's behavior changes to conform with the prevailing system of norms and values in their social environment, e.g., group, class, collective. It is reinforced by social control, which includes social pressure and state regulation.
- Cultural: an individual or group tries to gain knowledge or change behavior that enables them to adjust, survive, and thrive in their environment. The scale of culture changes depends on the extent of the environment changes. It could vary from slight modifications in livelihood systems (technology, productive and procurement activity, mode of life, and so on) to the principal transformation of the whole cultural system, including its social, ethnic, psychological, and ideological layers.
- Organizational or Enterprise: intentional decision-making leading to observable actions that aim to reduce the distance between an organization and its economic and institutional environments
- Societal: Interplay between cultural and other societal-scale changes, including economies, infrastructures, public and political spheres with mass social outcomes

We tailored these definitions informed by research on organizational adaptation (Smit et al. 2001; Sarta et al. 2020), relationships between social learning and adaptation (Boyd et al. 2011; Richerson and Boyd 2020), adaptation related to climate change (Simonet and Duchemin 2010; Few et al. 2017; Phuong et al. 2017), adaptation as understood in semantic web-technologies (Tran et al. 2006), and studies in genetic adaptation (Orr 2005).

We also acknowledge the interdependencies of the environment, for example, the interplay of premature mortality (i.e., health) and socioeconomic inequalities (Shahidi et al. 2020). Furthermore, we do not separate the agency from its environments; to be successful, the agency's adaptation must be satisfactory for the environments from which it has evolved and emerged (e.g., climate changes). Besides, evaluating societal adaptation's actions, outputs, and outcomes implies ethical considerations (Lacey et al. 2015). Ethical considerations are also implied in the societal use of technology (particularly emerging technologies) in anticipation that these technologies will improve the outcomes, but they carry risks (Heintz et al. 2015; Kendal 2022).

Our definition distinguishes adaptation from generic strategic change. It refocuses adaptation research around a specific type of intentional change aimed at increasing convergence between the agency and (some of) its environment(s). Equipped with this definition, we may distinguish adaptation from its motives and triggers (e.g., pursuing change, responding to environmental pressure) and results that may be expressed as outputs, outcomes, or consequences (e.g., performance, survival). Ultimately, we cannot assume that every change is necessarily adaptive and not every adaptive move is necessarily successful—changes imply risk that sometimes may lead to maladaptation (Boyd et al. 2011).

Similarly, as a result, our discussion guides readers toward consistent uses of adaptation that can resolve certain ambiguities and promote new insights in relation to DIKW dynamics for both disciplinary and interdisciplinary research (McMahan and Evans 2018). We assert that to facilitate societal adaptation, all societal agencies must stay open to new knowledge and technologies, stimulate research, innovation, and adaptation to the ecological environment, but also find ways to deal with forces that might oppose the development of societal and individuals' wellbeing.

Our discussion focuses on evaluating and creating environments where adaptation can occur and from which adaptation may emerge. We bring forward the necessity of rethinking and evolving models and practices to support societal adaptation and facilitate innovation during rapid and widespread periods of change. Enterprise Architecture (EA) has been one of these models used by ICT communities to overcome the complexity. However, we discuss the deficiencies of EA. We are proposing Endeavor Architecture (EnA) to emphasize the gap between an endeavor (i.e., a sincere attempt, a determined or assiduous effort towards a specific goal) and an enterprise (i.e., a company, business, organization, or other purposeful endeavors.) We elaborate on four functions that support ten principles for evaluating DIKW dynamics as they are necessary to facilitate adaptation. In other words, we propose new requirements and directions for EnA to explore societal adaptation, particularly DIKW flows of adaptation. We begin by using urban development examples to illustrate the necessity of establishing and evolving EnA to facilitate the emergence of new enterprises and endeavors and dealing with urban development complexity.

2.1 Urban Development

According to The World Bank (2020), some 55% of the world's population (i.e., 4.2 billion inhabitants) live in cities. If this trend continues, by 2050, with the urban population more than doubling its current size, nearly 7 of 10 people worldwide will live in cities. This phenomenon has attracted multifaceted research and the creation of the Smart City concept. However, still, the analysis of the smart city literature revealed ambiguity of the relevant ideas of the interdisciplinary science of smart cities (Mircea et al. 2017)—global language norms and clarity of concepts have yet to be achieved (Moir et al. 2014; Lom and Prybil 2021; Mora et al. 2020). Although it appears that integrated ICT infrastructure is a common denominator for all smart cities, the opinions on ICT prominence and level of sophistication and innovation in smart cities vary. For example, according to Giffinger et al. (2007), ICT is not that crucial. On the other hand, other authors (Hall et al. 2000; Harrison et al. 2010; Harrison and Donnelly 2011; Mircea et al. 2017) recognized it as one of the fundamental factors. Furthermore, a school of thought is that an ever-evolving and innovating ICT plays an essential, perhaps even leading role, in a smart city (Toppeta 2010; Washburn et al. 2010; Batty et al. 2012; Chourabi et al. 2012). Ultimately, the concept of city collective intelligence (Mohanty et al. 2016) was accentuated and empowered by integrating city infrastructures (e.g., social, ICT, business.) Chourabi et al. (2012) considered ICT the "inner" and "meta-factor" of smart cities. Since it has the potential to impact each of the other "inner" factors (i.e., management and policy) and all seven "outer" factors (i.e., governance, people and communities, natural environment, infrastructure, and economy), they reasoned those innovations must happen across all smart city factors to ensure success.

Thus, there is a need for meta-paradigms; that is, sets of concepts and propositions that sets forth the phenomena with which a discipline is concerned that have expressiveness to integrate all factors of urban development, perpetual innovation in all domains, interdisciplinary collaboration, technology, and collective intelligence. Particularly, there is a need to create meta-paradigms whose discourse of interest is an endeavor that is influenced by multiple (or all) societal agencies, rather than driven by the interests of the (public or private) enterprises. For example, the COVID-19 pandemic impacted all elements of society; elected governments, bureaucracies, political parties, international health organizations, scientific organizations, healthcare organizations, organizations that support vulnerable populations, private sector organizations, public sphere and media, communities, and individuals. To facilitate observation of the pandemic, Polovina (2022) used the UMF as an upper-ontology that helped break down the discourse of interest and create new concepts of societal knowledge.

2.2 Complexity

However, Nam and Pardo (2011) warned of an omnipresent risk generated by complexity and innovation, emphasizing that organizational and policy innovation must match technological innovation. Other authors acknowledged risk too. For example, Dawes et al. (1999) established that ICT innovations are more rapid than management and organization innovations and that policy innovations are even slower than organizational ones. Chourabi et al. (2012) reasoned that the "meta-factor" ICT success positively impacts all other smart city factors. However, the risk of ICT failure may increase all other risks. In addition, due to unanticipated events of complex endeavors (e.g., when new information flows are created), ethical and moral questions may emerge (Cecez-Kecmanovic and Marjanovic 2015).

Consequently, the importance of applying adequate methods for reducing complexity and mitigating risk has been recognized (Kakarontzas et al. 2014). Needs for new methods had been identified (Dawes et al. 1999), including a need to pay attention to "unforeseen consequences and unanticipated effects which were ignored because the systems in question were treated to immediate and simplistic terms" (Batty et al. 2012).

Again, there is a need for meta-paradigms that reduce complexity, for example, by introducing only crucial concepts from multiple domains and creating new, condensed, and optimal discourses of interest pertinent for DIKW-intensive societal endeavors. We brought forward the UMF (Polovina and Wojktowski 1999) as an upper ontology to facilitate our research by breaking down the discourse of interest according to its main principles (i.e., object essence, contrasted object, relationships, system, time, memory, bliss, thought, being, reality). This breakdown further enables the identification of the main generators of the endeavor complexity (e.g., structural complexity, the complexity of DIKW dynamics), and in that way, facilitates the management of complexity risk (Polovina 2022).

2.3 Wide-Spread and Rapid Societal Changes

Moreover, the recent COVID-19 pandemic reminded us of a need to collaborate across the globe and share data, information, knowledge, and wisdom to respond to the pandemic and other rapid and widespread societal changes (Polovina et al. 2020a, b; Singer-Velush et al. 2020) emphasizing the importance of ecological adaptation. Other authors also warn us of the necessity to mitigate the risks that societies worldwide face (Callaghan 2016, 2020). Furthermore, these recent developments accelerate fine-tuning of Enterprise Risk Management (ERM); as Andersen pointed out that when actual developments take an enterprise by surprise and organizational decision-makers must deal with influences from unexpected events–like pandemics and climate effects–formal control-based guidelines and practices are insufficient as they are only convenient and make the decision makers feel safe but provide a false sense of security (Andersen et al. 2021; Continuity Central 2022).

In our case study of the COVID-19 pandemic (Polovina 2022), we looked at the pandemic through the UMF as a prism and identified societal agencies that participate in the societal endeavor (i.e., response to the pandemic) and created the model of the pandemic principles in relation to DIKW sharing. The next step might be to look at the DIKW flows among these agencies; that is, the principles of DIKW dynamics described in this paper may further facilitate the evaluation of the societal DIKW dynamics in relation to the pandemic response and support subsequent decision-making (e.g., to strengthen social and technological interfaces between research organizations and governments).

2.4 Artificial Intelligence (AI)

Furthermore, as Artificial Intelligence (AI) enters the mainstream, Vinuesa et al. (2020) pointed out that AI may have a positive impact on 82% of the United Nations (UN) Sustainable Development Goals targets. These targets include poverty reduction, quality education, clean water and sanitation, and affordable and clean energy. However, according to the same source, AI technologies may inhibit 38% of the targets, including high energy consumption, due to the massive computational resources required for AI. There is also a concern that AI may trigger inequalities that inhibit poverty reduction. Furthermore, AI may enable nationalism, hate towards minorities, and biased election outcomes damaging social cohesion, democratic principles, and even human rights. Dignum (2018) called for responsible AI, which requires social values, moral deliberation, and methods to link moral values to systems requirements in traditional systems development.

The UMF is an upper ontology (or meta-paradigm) that facilitates the integration of ICT and AI paradigms by classifying their expressiveness according to the UMF principles (Polovina 2022). Moreover, the UMF facilitates the generation of EnA instances whose domains may be any human endeavors (e.g., enterprise, societal, global). Last but not least, EnA principles allow the creation and evaluation of pluralistic perspectives (e.g., ethical, risk, impact on the environment).

3 Enterprise Architecture

ICT communities have traditionally used EA to overcome the complexity of ICT-intensive endeavors. For example, Nam and Pardo (2011) proposed EA as an organizational and managerial strategy for encouraging innovation in urban interoperability initiatives. However, Gong and Jannsen (2019) pointed out that poorly understood EA value claims are used to justify EA initiatives, often without empirical verification. Kaisler and Armour (2005) identified multiple EA challenges, including insufficient motivation for EA modeling techniques.

At the same time, Gell-Mann (1995, 2001, 2013), who researched complexity, pointed out that the solution to the world problems: pandemics, climate changes, widespread economic crises) cannot be achieved by advancing only one field; the collaboration of people from various domains is necessary for these challenges. Moreover, Mowles (2014) identified another challenge; evaluation of complex social actions, seeing non-linearity in the social as the norm rather than an exception, and what the evaluators may do to assert that social interventions work. Significantly, Lapalme (2012) La Palme et al. (2016) pointed out most EA frameworks' insufficiencies in modeling complex adaptive systems.

Furthermore, it has been noted that although numerous authors extensively wrote about the EA principles, frameworks, and management, it is significantly more difficult to find empirical evidence that supports the promises of EA (Gong and Janssen 2019).

Since potential failures of endeavors to adapt to widespread, sudden, and disruptive societal changes (e.g., pandemics, climate change, natural disasters, armed conflicts) include human lives, public health, social justice, and taxpayers' money, we cannot avoid ethical questions on EA applicability and implementation. Therefore, we offer a brief analysis of the EA limitations.

3.1 Evolution of Enterprise Architecture

In the 1980s, John Zachman advanced the idea of EA by describing enterprises as "a set of architectural representations produced over the process of building a complex engineering product representing the different perspectives of the different participants" (Zachman n.d.). The motivation for Zachman's EA framework was "for rationalizing the various architectural concepts and specifications to provide clarity of professional communication, to allow for improving and integrating development methodologies and tools, and to establish credibility and confidence in the investment of systems resources" (Zachman 1987). Zachman's framework models any social or technical system consisting of people only, people and computer systems, or computer systems only (Sowa and Zachman 1992). That is, all types of enterprises, from consortia of companies or governments, commercial organizations, business firms, and social ventures, to start-up businesses and undertaken projects (or to be undertaken.)

Even in those early days of ICT architecture, it has been noted that ICT architecture needs to be put in the context of a broader business context (Hammer & Company 1986). Later, the authors, such as Tapscott and Caston (1993) or Ross and her colleagues (2006), argue that EA has a broader position than ICT, EA still stayed deeply rooted in a business context.

As predicted by Zachman (1987), not only did the evolution of EA, both as a concept and organizational activity, result in heterogeneous EA frameworks, but also heterogeneous EA schools of thought and communities of practice emerged (Lapalme 2012; Lapalme et al. 2016).

- Enterprise ICT Architecting—models ICT of an enterprise only; the universe of discourse is the enterprise-wide ICT platform.
- Enterprise Integrating—integrates all enterprise factors (e.g., governance structure, production, ICT capabilities); the universe of discourse is the enterprise as a whole
- Enterprise Ecological Adaptation—models the enterprise and its environment, including relationships between the two. The universe of discourse is the whole enterprise in which innovation is understood as an adaptation to its environment. In addition, the universe of discourse includes the way the enterprise impacts its environment.

4   Four Functions of Endeavor Architecture

To explore the properties of EA and EnA in relation to environmental adaptation, we identified four architecture functions (relevant to adaptation). The report informed us of the environmental adaptation Smith et al. prepared (2001). The authors identified technology and research as the factors relevant to the adaption response. The integration function relates to the multiple communication and educational response options, i.e., diffusion of DIKW in our context.

Table 1. Four architecture functions relevant to adaptation

Architecture Function	Description
Development	Advancement and development of digital technologies (e.g., ICT and AI)
Integration	Communication and sharing of acquired DIKW (i.e., integration of societal agencies across human and digital interfaces)
Environmental Adaptation	Facilitation of agencies' innovation and adaptation to the environment, purposeful or accidental. Both development and integration support environmental adaptation
Research	Generation of new scientific DIKW (i.e., quest for new knowledge and conclusions) and technologies necessary to adapt to (immediate or future) environmental changes and address complex phenomena, in general

5 Exploring the Limitations of EA

We evaluated how the EA authors addressed four architecture functions (if they addressed them at all) in the following table. We also included some EA standards and tools (Table 3).

The domain of EA is an enterprise in its organized professional and administrative form in which people work and interact with institutional authority. This relates to Habermas's "system" of predefined situations, or modes of coordination, in which the demands of communicative action are relaxed in this way within legally specified limits (Bohman and Rehg 2017). That is, the system that comprises common patterns of strategic action that serve the interests of institutions and organizations (Baxter 2013). In other words, EA concerns are neither communities, citizens of urban or rural areas, individuals, and their interactions, nor other elements that relate to Habermas's lifeworld – facets and patterns of our social and personal life outside of institutions and organizations. Neither EA concern is the public domain, which relates to Habermas's public sphere–the domain of social life where public opinion can be formed and all citizens can access (Habermas 1991). In other words, environmental adaptation in EA is limited to the enterprise's adaptation to its environment.

During disruptive, widespread societal changes (e.g., pandemics, natural disasters, armed conflicts, hardships), these worlds can collide, exposing an individual (or citizens, groups, or other societal elements) to tremendous pressure. Under this pressure, these societal elements must adapt or face doomed outcomes. Therefore, we reject the concept of having the enterprise, lifeworld, and public domain separated. This does not mean that we reject reductionism in general. Still, we acknowledge that reducing complex realities to specific (simplified) views may ideally be purposeful in some situations but not in all situations. Neither do we limit the number of views (i.e., worlds). Still, we acknowledge that the models (of complex realities) should be determined by their purpose–contribution to solving the problems at hand, ultimately leading to the most optimal adaptation. There will be situations where simplified models will lead to the

Table 2. EA authors and their positions concerning four functions relevant to societal adaptation (i.e., development, integration, ecological adaptation, and research)

EA authors	Architecture functions addressed
Finkelstein (2006)	**Development:** ICT development, particularly data-oriented **Integration:** Integration of enterprise data, aligning business and ICT, integration of enterprise functions via data (i.e., through an ICT platform by using XML and Web Services) **Enterprise adaptation:** Adaptation limited to data-oriented methods
Martin (1995)	**Integration:** Enterprise integration is achieved by implementing organizational management methods, such as strategic visioning, human and culture development, ICT development, enterprise redesign, value-stream reinvention, procedure and redesign, and Total Quality Management methods **Enterprise adaptation:** The enterprise capabilities limit environmental adaptation (i.e., to get the right enterprise strategic vision and transform accordingly)
Frosch-Wilke and Tuchtenhagen (2016)	**Development:** ICT development, particularly Business Intelligence (BI)
Hanschke (2010)	**Development:** ICT process-based management achieves enterprise integration (of ICT into the enterprise). Focused on ICT strategic management
Op't Land et al. (2009)	**Integration:** Integration of EA management with enterprise management
Perks and Beveridge (2003)	**Development:** ICT development (used TOGAF as its foundation) **Integration:** Integration with enterprise management (primarily aligning ICT and business)
Ross et al. (2006)	**Integration:** Integration of ICT and enterprise strategy **Enterprise adaptation:** Advancing enterprise strategy and environmental adaptation

(*continued*)

Table 2. (*continued*)

EA authors	Architecture functions addressed
van Steenbergen et al. (2008)	**Integration:** Integration of EA management and enterprise management (i.e., assessing EA maturity)
Giachetti (2010)	**Integration:** Advancing enterprise systems design and integration of its functions by describing enterprise engineering methods (e.g., strategizing, process modeling, information modeling, organizational modeling) **Enterprise adaptation:** Advancing enterprise strategy and environmental adaptation
Gharajedaghi (2006)	**Integration:** Advancing enterprise system design and integration of its functions **Enterprise adaptation:** Advancing environmental adaptation. Raising awareness of socio-cultural enterprise facets and self-organizations and acknowledging the need for innovations and the importance of social aspects of an enterprise **Research:** Encourage holistic research of social systems and use systems science as a logical starting point for enterprise design, emphasizing that (enterprise) systems design cannot be separated from the system's principles. Encourages research of systems concepts (e.g., openness, purposefulness, multidimensionality, emergent enterprise properties)
Hoogervorst (2009)	**Integration:** Establishes enterprise (as a system) design and its integration with enterprise governance. Integration with enterprise strategy. View an enterprise as a socio-technical system

(*continued*)

Table 2. (*continued*)

EA authors	Architecture functions addressed
Zachman's enterprise architecture framework (Zachman 1987, 2011, 2019; Sowa and Zachman 1992; Kappelman and Zachman 2013)	**Development:** Classification of ICT paradigms **Integration:** Establishes enterprise (as a system) and its integration with enterprise governance **Enterprise adaptation:** Zachman's enterprise ontology establishes an understanding of the EA domain and facilitates environmental adaptation (by modeling an enterprise and its context) **Research:** Zachman's enterprise ontology (as an upper ontology) may facilitate research of new paradigms, for example, by proving that new concepts are outside of the domain defined by Zachman's ontology
Jan Dietz (Dietz 1999); Dietz and Mulder 2020a, b))	**Development:** Design and Engineering Methodology for Organizations (DEMO) developed in the 1990s, focuses on the requirements determination for software development **Integration:** Integration with management **Enterprise adaptation:** DEMO may facilitate organizational adaptation to the environment from the management point of view

optimal solution, but there will be situations where only holistic views (and synthesis of views) will work. Instead of relying on the prescriptive nature of architecture, we acknowledge that there are times and situations when societies must exert efforts and collective intelligence to develop new solutions.

6 Endeavor Architecture

We, therefore, introduce the concept of Endeavor Architecture (EnA) to enhance the discourse of interest (from enterprises) towards more complex domains where enterprises, the lifeworld, and the public sphere are not separated. This unavoidably shifts focus towards general intelligence (which comprises different cognitive abilities and allows intelligent beings to acquire knowledge and solve problems). Artificial General Intelligence (AGI) models general intelligence. There are numerous theories of intelligence and intelligence types. Still, for this article, the most important abilities are general ability (also referred to as 'g'), an overarching ability that is theorized to be relevant to and involved in an extensive variety of cognitive tasks (Sternberg 2012). That is, the concept of general intelligence proposes that one intelligence is measured

Table 3. EA standards and tools, and their relation to four functions relevant to societal adaptation (i.e., development, integration, ecological adaptation, and research)

EA standard/tool	Architecture functions addressed
TOGAF (The Open Group 2022)	**Development:** In the context of governance only **Integration:** Primarily integrate ICT and ICT governance and support alignment with other enterprise functions, such as strategic management. It includes gap management in relation to alignment to other enterprise functions (e.g., financial, human resources) **Enterprise adaptation:** Supports Business Transformation Readiness Assessment
ArchiMate (The Open Group 2019)	**Development:** In the context of governance only **Integration:** This is an enterprise architecture modeling language. It facilitates the integration of business, business processes, technology, and governance
Enterprise Architect (Sparx Services)	**Development:** Strong support for UML (Unified Modeling Language) and round-trip engineering that synchronize related software artifacts, such as source code, models, configuration files, and even documentation **Integration:** Supports ArchiMate, TOGAF and some other EA standards. IT also integrates ICT development and ICT governance. Since it is extended with EA frameworks, it can fully support ICT integration with management and business **Enterprise adaptation:** Multiple modeling diagrams may be used to model environmental adaptation **Research:** Being an open tool and since that can integrate all levels of ICT development with other enterprise facets, it may be used to support research activities
Essential Project (Enterprise Architecture Solutions)	**Development:** Conceptual, logical, and physical layers based on ontology and a meta-model **Integration:** Integration of ICT and management, with a support layer for management (e.g., strategy) **Enterprise adaptation:** End-user views of environmental adaptation from an extended metamodel **Research:** Open-Source choice enables the community to conduct their research and development

by a 'g factor' that underlies performance in all cognitive domains. The performance comprises performances in different but interrelated cognitive tasks, all contributing to the 'g factor'.

At this point, we must mention that the early work of Zachman (1987) and Sowa (Sowa and Zachman 1992) contained some considerations of general intelligence, such as defining the views of the Zachman EA Framework by using primitive interrogatives (i.e., What, How, When, Who, Where, and Why) and using some concepts of upper ontologies (i.e., objects). Still, as previously discussed, the primary discourse of interest has been deeply rooted in enterprises and limited to business and organizational domains.

Now we will return to the four functions that facilitate adaptation (Table 1). These are: (i) advancement and development of digital technologies (e.g., ICT and AI), (ii) communication and exchange of acquired DIKW (i.e., integration of societal agencies across human and digital interfaces), (iii) facilitation of agencies' innovations and adaptation to the environment, purposeful or accidental (i.e., environmental adaptation), and (iv) research and generation of new scientific DIKW (i.e., quest for new knowledge and conclusions) and technologies, as necessary for adaptation to environmental changes, including societal changes and addressing complex phenomena, in general. The following table illustrates the need to establish Endeavor Architecture (EnA) practices to support these four functions.

Table 4. Endeavor Architecture (EnA) properties and examples relevant for societal adaptation

Function	Endeavor architecture (EnA) properties and examples
Development	Everything that is represented by EA plus the development and implementation of new technologies (e.g., new programming languages, new platforms, new knowledge representation methods, AI modeling) This implies the following: • Openness to accept novel scientific and technological paradigms (e.g., AI paradigms) • Classification of ICT and AI paradigms (e.g., by using Upper Modelling Framework (Polovina 2022)) Examples: • Development of digital technologies for new types of organization and management (e.g., new alliances and establishing new knowledge flows among agencies) • Development of digital technologies that explore and support societies and broader alliances (e.g., global endeavors that transcendent geopolitical boundaries) • Development of technologies that might reduce social conflicts in public discussions (Heng and de Moor 2003) • Development of methods (e.g., ontologies) that may facilitate the emergence of collective intelligence among individuals and groups focused on the advancement and development of ICT, such as groups of developers in an organization, open-source (code) communities, or city hackathons

(*continued*)

Table 4. (*continued*)

Function	Endeavor architecture (EnA) properties and examples
Integration	Everything that is facilitated by EA plus the sharing of the DIKW space, including the dynamics of its sharing among societies and their elements, such as social groups, movements, minorities, and broader formal and informal alliances Examples: • Implementation of platform and infrastructure that facilitate DIKW sharing of smart cities • Creation of social ontologies to evaluate societal response to pandemics (Polovina 2022)) • Creation and development of ontologies that support various domains, and ultimately integration of those ontologies. Including EA ontologies (Baxter et al. 2022) • Exploring domain ontologies and ways to communicate with broader audience, such as FinTech (Stojakovic-Celustka 2022) • Domain modeling (e.g., city utilities, traffic, finance) often takes some forms of knowledge repositories or reference models, making its implicit knowledge explicit. Typically, these models are made reusable to realize their value • Undertaking activities that develop human interfaces among certain societal groups (e.g., scientific communities and government) • Undertaking activities that develop technological interfaces among systems (e.g., developing trust (Groza and Pomarlan 2022)) • Implementation of ontologies that facilitate DIKW sharing among various communities (e.g., health ontologies for sharing health information among medical practitioners and patients) • Exploring DIKW patterns (e.g., propaganda patterns that may be propped up by any element of a society)
Environmental adaptation	Everything facilitated by EA plus facilitation of efforts to encourage implementation of scientific innovations and monitor their impact (e.g., on citizens' social lives, environment) Examples: • Endeavors that deliberately facilitate inadequate government policies (e.g., environmental policies), such as organizing government propaganda to cover up fundamental inadequacies • Endeavors organized by citizens to reveal inadequate government policies (e.g., environmental policies) • Modeling and creating endeavors that oversee environmental changes by mobilizing multiple societal elements (e.g., citizens, organizations, governments). The new DIKW obtained may not comply with what is publicized (e.g., posted by governments or marketed by various organizations (Global Forest Watch 2022) • Open Data • Open Platforms (e.g., Global Forest Watch 2022) • Endeavors facilitate the integration of scientific innovations, societal agencies, and digital technologies (Olan et al. 2022). Developing human interfaces that enable these integrations and therefore making them available to various elements of the society • Facilitating collaboration, knowledge discovery and sensemaking across multiple organizations (de Moor et al. 2022a, b) • Exploring DIKW sources and use them to advance research in other fields (e.g., exploring health-related data (Jani et al. 2022; McGagh et al. 2022)) • Exploring societal health issues through social media mining • Exploring the impact of social media on adolescents (Kelly et al. 2018)

(*continued*)

Table 4. (*continued*)

Function	Endeavor architecture (EnA) properties and examples
Research	Searching for DIKW is necessary to adapt to societal changes and address complex phenomena in general. In this way, we are changing EA's discourse of interest and moving it from business domains toward general intelligence and Artificial General Intelligence (AGI). We also do not separate enterprise, lifeworld, and public domains, which add complexity to the research necessary to support the endeavor. It is also noticeable (from these examples) for architecting endeavors that we need to consider research that comes from various faculties of science, as noted by Gell-Man (2013)
	Examples:
	• Creation of new concepts to serve as determinants of societal capabilities (e.g., smart city success factors (Chourabi et al. 2012))
	• Advancing organizational concepts by using ontology-driven methods (e.g., advancing strategy ontology (Caine 2022)
	• Research on the limitations of the existing paradigms and the creation of new paradigms
	• Exploring new organizational and societal transformational initiatives (e.g., undertaking an initiative to enhance the capacity of the government to use scientific innovations)
	• Exploring methods to verify the consistency and success of government policies
	• Exploring methods for social media mining (Xiong et al. 2022)
	• Research on social media design that mitigates the risk of harming their users
	• Research on social media political influence
	• Research on methods to identify false knowledge
	• Creating methods that facilitate competencies on social networks
	• Explore individual views, 'citizens' experiences, and similar that support adaptation to societal changes
	• Research on collective intelligence
	• Research on collective emotion (Lan et al. 2022)
	• Research on general intelligence and Artificial General Intelligence (AGI) (Latapie et al. 2021)
	• Exploring social media's impact on political activities and geopolitical development, in general (Lan et al. 2022)
	• Research on knowledge patterns in the humanities (Jakobsen and Graf 2022))
	• Research on relationships among big data and ethnographies (Hong et al. 2022)
	• Research of DIKW patterns and DIKW diffusion (e.g., propaganda patterns that may be propped up by any element of a society)

7 Influences on Endeavor Architecture

We started by exploring some societal drivers that generate societal changes and impose societal adaptation. Then we explored the limitation of Enterprise Architecture (EA), which was recommended for modeling complexity, and concluded that we need to enhance the discourse of interest and include other societal facets (i.e., enterprises, lifeworld, and public domain) to be able to respond to widespread and abrupt societal changes (e.g., economic crises, climate change, racial issues, pandemics, escalating armed conflicts).

We asserted that it is necessary to introduce the concept of Endeavor Architecture (EnA) to model the complexity of societal changes that trigger societal adaptation. That is, if we apply the definition of adaptation (Sect. 2), EnA reduces the distance between an agency and its environment by reducing the complexity of the endeavor and by facilitating the creation and development of the solutions.

Thus, EnA is not prescriptive; that is, EnA may use any available paradigms to create and organize its models. EnA may also include meta paradigms (i.e., sets of concepts and propositions that set forth the phenomena with which a discipline is concerned). This enhances our discourse of interest and moves it toward general intelligence and Artificial General Intelligence (AGI). At the same time, it makes it open to research and accepts new paradigms (Table 4).

Therefore, at this point, we will introduce the Upper Modeling Framework (UMF), a system-oriented framework, and an upper ontology to shed light on relationships and dependencies of the drivers for societal adaptation within complex domains, i.e., societal endeavors.

7.1 Upper Modelling Framework

The Upper Modelling Framework (UMF) was initially proposed by Polovina and Wojtkowski (1999) to study models (i.e., objects) that human minds create, which not only depend on a modeler's cognizance but also reflect the modeler's social relationships and dynamics. It is also a study in Artificial General Intelligence (AGI) (Goertzel 2014; Yaworsky 2018), inspired by general human intelligence. The UMF facilitates modeling complex domains; its rules, complexity of the universe of discourse, and cognitive activities generate knowledge flows, explananda, creation, and transformation of the models. An object is defined as anything that may engage any faculty of someone's mind or anything and everything distinguished from the observed domain. A model is understood as a "vessel" that contains a chunk of knowledge. Polovina and Wojtkowski (1999) considered cognitive activities carried out by the modelers (e.g., thinking, reasoning, learning); their universe of discourse; the 'model's principles (or dimensions), created objects and relationships among the objects, and presented these cognitive activities from an intuitive point of view. The term "system" "was applied to encompass social, technical, physical, and natural systems, or any combination.

7.2 Four Sphere of MODel's Existence

The UMF distinguishes four spheres of the model's existence: principal, conceptual, formative, and manifestation spheres (Fig. 1). The foundation for this separation is based on insight gained by observing the modeler's cognitive activities (e.g., thinking, reasoning) and the modeler's universe of discourse, as described in the following text.

Cognitive activities (modeling) with a tendency to generate or impact a system may be initiated by deciding the essential idea the system enacts. The essential idea's determination occurs at the highest sphere of system existence, the principal sphere, which presents the system's most abstract (i.e., principal) representation. In the next sphere, the universe of discourse (i.e., domain) is conceptualized, which initiates the concept's formation, thus denoted as a prototype. Prototypes are particularized, concretized, and constrained in the third sphere until desired forms are obtained. These forms will serve as molds (of ideas) at the lowest sphere of the system instantiation. In the physical sphere, where the actual manifestation of instantiation occurs – the abstract (forms of) ideas are becoming a reality. Thus, a typical, top-to-bottom knowledge transformation flow occurs; from abstract spheres (i.e., principal, conceptual, formative) to the instantiated manifestation in the physical sphere. The process is denoted as systems generation.

At the same time, cognitive activities may also be triggered by stimuli from the physical world (e.g., sensing the environment). Selected stimuli may be put into context to create information. This information may be examined (e.g., summarized) at the lowest level (i.e., formative sphere) and molded until a concept can be recognized and further abstracted to its essential idea (at the highest level of its existence in the principal sphere). Thus, the cognitive activities and knowledge transformation may also follow bottom-up patterns: from the physical sphere to higher levels of abstraction. Also, cognition and knowledge transformation do not necessarily follow any sequential order: changes may be initiated at any level, and changes may be directed either towards their instantiation in the physical world or towards higher levels of abstraction, depending on what opportunities for change are presented.

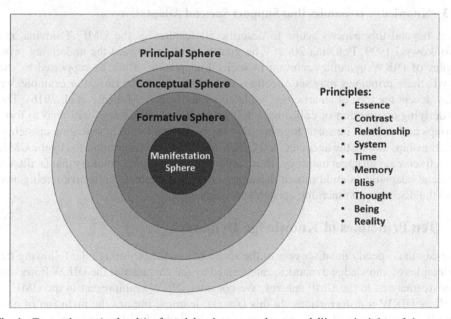

Fig. 1. Four spheres (or levels) of model existence and ten modelling principles of the upper modelling framework (UMF)

Since every modeler may have their interpretation of the universe of discourse (i.e., their world), then, depending on the modeler's world (e.g., individuality, knowledge, preferences, creativity, social relationships, bias), multiple interpretations of the UMF spheres may exist. It is up to the modelers and their social circles to decide the universe of discourse and set its boundaries. However, to make this framework operational, less ambiguous, and pragmatic distinctions must be established for communication and knowledge generation among the participants (e.g., community). For example, a pragmatic interpretation for system development may be that the principal and conceptual spheres contain abstract models of the universe of discourse. The modelers express their view of reality, either existing or desired vision, focusing on understanding the universe of discourse in its entirety. Considerations may include the system's environment, integration (e.g., social and technology), impact on the environment, or environmental constraints.

In contrast, focused models of the formative sphere may contain actionable knowledge to build, maintain, or change the system, including its environment. Finally, the manifestation sphere contains the physical, instantiated implementation of the system. In addition to four spheres or levels of the model's existence (i.e., principal, conceptual, formative, and manifestation), the ten main modeling principles are observed within the spheres: object *essence, contrasted* object, *relationship, system, time, memory, bliss, thought, being* and, finally, *reality*. These principles may also be considered views or modeling dimensions that enable recursiveness and generation of fractals (i.e., similar pattern structures across all spheres (Polovina 1999; Polovina and Wojtkowki 1999)).

7.3 Knowledge Dynamics that Support Societal Adaptation

It is beyond this paper's scope to describe all features of the UMF (Polovina and Wojtkowski 1999; Polovina 2022). The goal is to bring forward the underlying principles of DIKW dynamics relevant to societal adaptation. Thus, as supported by the UMF, these principles may set directions and requirements for EnA. For example, we may accept the idea of smart cities' collective intelligence (Mohanty et al. 2016). The underlying assumption of collective intelligence is that the citizens will tend to form groups and strive to be smart together. Discovery and modeling of emerging epistemic relationships among the agencies, and DIKW transformation are supported by the UMF, which serves as an upper ontology. Thus, any subsequent domain ontology that facilitates societal adaptation should inherit these properties and facilitate collective intelligence and the discovery of emerging epistemic relationships.

8   Ten Principles of Knowledge Dynamics

We can thus specify the discovery of the above relationships through the following ten principles of knowledge dynamics, categorized by the character of the DIKW flows and transformations in the UMF spheres. We consider DIKW omnipresent in the UMF as well as DIKW transformations. In this context, learning implies the inclusion of new DIKW, and it is associated with an agency (e.g., individual learning, organizational learning).

8.1 Top-Down

A modeling approach starts at the higher level of abstraction, that is, by establishing the principles and moving towards creation, followed by formation, and finalized by instantiation of a system. This flow relates to cognitive activities that lead to the materialization of an abstract idea. The rows of the Zachman Framework (Zachman 2015) and TOGAF (The Open Group 2022) are described in this way. This top-down knowledge movement is typical for corporations and governments, where most initiatives and articulation of an enterprise are expected to start with the executives.

8.2 Bottom-Up

As societal adaptation invites new forms of organization—not all endeavors are expected to follow traditional patterns in which initiatives and articulation of the system start from the top. For example, suppose we assume that the citizens want to achieve a "higher quality of work, study, life, and social relations" (Toppeta 2010), then, as the first step. In that case, the citizens' participation must be increased (Vacha et al. 2016). To shape the endeavor, their ideas must flow via various channels (Knauss et al. 2012). It is thus a DIKW generation that is bottom-up, which resembles abstraction. Another example includes city sensors, which send data from the physical world to be processed and transformed towards higher levels of abstraction (i.e., UMF formative sphere). One of the requirements may be to recognize new patterns (for which the system has not been designed) and changing models of the UMF conceptual sphere (e.g., detecting new patterns of water pollution).

8.3 Inclusion

We concur with Quick and Feldman (2011), who favor public endeavors to engage in problem-solving. Inclusion also implies that someone has been excluded in the past, but now, they may bring new actionable knowledge to problem-solving. Since many of these groups cannot have in-depth knowledge of modeling and technology, the EnA methods must be relatively intuitive and flexible to encourage problem-solving. Otherwise, insisting on formal modeling may pose a cognitive burden for the participants. For example, it might be necessary to develop and share models that include both elements from the conceptual and formative sphere to encourage inclusion as a principle (i.e., formal or semi-formal vocabularies of terms covering a specific domain and shared by the communities of the users.) Moreover, it is necessary to enable assigning the meaning to these models, resolving semantic ambiguity among modeling paradigms.

8.4 Individuation

Enabling the manifestation of a person's potential, improving quality of life, and realizing dreams and aspirations may also positively impact problem-solving. A different conception of individuation (Gaß et al. 2015) calls for the synthesis and productivity of technologies. For example, generating code from executable specifications (Polovina and Wojtkowki 2002) and orchestrating cloud SaaS services may enable individuals to realize their ideas in relatively short periods. In this case, complex DIKW transformations are hidden from the individual, although these transformations may happen at all UMF levels.

8.5 Openness

When previously excluded groups or individuals can bring forward their problem-solving ideas, the endeavoring organization (formal or informal) opens to these new ideas, discoveries and paradigms, no matter how outrageous or disruptive they appear. We are not limited to technological discoveries but all society's agencies—new ideas will be born in organizations, environmental projects, new forms of government, and elsewhere. Ultimately, all agencies will need appropriate venues to validate new paradigms (e.g., validation of scientific knowledge (Munafò et al. 2017).) Thus, EnA must stay open to new concepts, ontologies, paradigms, or technologies, including changes in the EnA foundation itself. Thus, all four spheres of UMF models must stay open.

8.6 Integration

If burdened by legacy systems, standards, and complex planning, technology infrastructure may needlessly complicate EnA. Such an infrastructure may not be open enough to new technologies and paradigms. The same is true for social norms and stereotypes. Instead, to encourage the integration of new paradigms, these legacy infrastructures and stereotypes may constrain new endeavors and prevent seamless integration of various communities and groups of citizens striving to engage in problem-solving and bringing new, sometimes disruptive solutions. Indeed, the need for integrating interdisciplinary research into the ecosystem has been highlighted (Knauss et al. 2012), which increases the complexity of social interaction and calls for research methods that enable contact points between social and digital. Notably, it will be essential to reconcile the semantics of multiple models. EnA needs to separate the perspectives and facilitate their integration and synthesis, for example, by embracing methods that integrate EnA artefacts. Again, these transformations impact all four UMF spheres.

For example, multi-jurisdictional endeavors that require coordinated efforts of provincial government and municipalities might encounter numerous operational risks due to too cumbersome and bureaucratic business processes. This may only discourage the integration of city groups. For instance, legislation for the use of a pesticide may exist. Still, the collaboration between the municipal and state government may be inadequate to the point that the citizens are left to their own means to fight the use of pesticides on their properties without their consent.

In another example, the city of Melbourne, Australia, assigned trees email addresses so citizens could report problems (Blakemore 2015). In addition to reporting problems, people started writing thousands of love letters to their favorite trees. As this Melbourne case shows, emotional attachments to the city trees are essential for the citizens' well-being. The feedback received (i.e., citizens' appreciation for individual threes) should be quickly integrated into the city policies and regulations.

8.7 Opportunism

Integrating physical, technological, and social systems create a new space (and cyberspace) for numerous threat agents and potential negative tendencies. For example, micro-opportunism includes an unethical appropriation of one's authentic knowledge by the community (or vice-versa) and micropolitics. Macro-opportunism may include national security threats and macro politics. There is a broad range of threat agents—from malicious individuals to organized crime and terrorists who attempt to misuse the system's vulnerabilities. These threat agents may even form informal or semi-formal alliances with legitimate participants. They together emerge as a new, unanticipated, threatening form of collective intelligence. EnA needs to include perspectives and methods to deal with these negative tendencies (e.g., recognition of false knowledge (Conroy et al. 2015; Groza and Pop 2020; Groza 2022; Groza and Pomarlan 2022). Again, all UMF spheres are impacted.

8.8 Collaboration

So far, we have discussed how citizens may get included in problem-solving, decision-making, and all societal activities, which leads us to collaboration—two or more agencies working together to achieve something. However, in an older research paper on demography and diversity in organizations, Williams and O'Reilly (1998) concluded that diversity might impede group functioning. Most importantly, these authors pointed out the importance of distinguishing two types of group performance. They are idea generation (i.e., creativity) and the implementation of the ideas that might be differently impacted by diversity; that is, creativity may be boosted by diversity; in contrast, implementation of the ideas may be weakened by diversity. If a group cannot intuitively find a way to accommodate the diversities in complex problem solving (e.g., organizational, educational, and cultural), the separated EnA views may further emphasize diversity. The result may be a negative impact on the collective intelligence of the group. In other words, it seems as if collective intelligence must be in place should the group want to take advantage of EnA, not the other way around.

We still lack a deep understanding of all the intricacies of collective intelligence and collaboration. For example, newer research, particularly in dispersed groups that communicate via technology platforms, showed that communication that boosts collective intelligence occurs on different levels. Chikersal et al. (2017) pointed out that synchrony of facial expressions is essential and predicted that technologies enabling participants to see their faces may boost collective intelligence. Furthermore, they found that synchrony of electro-dermal activities and heart rates are associated with group satisfaction rather than performance. They also reinstated that a significant relationship between collective intelligence and group satisfaction was not observed (Woolley et al. 2015; Chikersal et al. 2017). Therefore, it is necessary to further collective research intelligence (Søilen 2019), and in parallel, EnA needs to explore, discover, and establish less obvious epistemic relationships in agencies supporting collective intelligence. Although the UMF is generic, it allows exploring epistemic relationships across all its spheres, and may guide the research of phenomena, such as collective intelligence (Polovina 2022).

8.9 Adaptiveness

Previously, we defined adaptation as an effort of an agency (which may be a society, an individual, any group, or any organization) triggered by specific events that are being translated into (spontaneous or deliberate) actions that aim to reduce the distance between the agency and its environments (e.g., economic, natural, civil liberty, health) in a satisfactory way. In other words, the challenge is to obtain (and enable) technology and create (or participate) in an endeavor needed to adapt. In this paper, we are discussing the dynamics of DIKW sharing for adaptation; that is, establishing epistemic relationships among agencies. These epistemic relationships may be obvious (e.g., as in top-town manage enterprises), or less apparent (e.g., as bottom-up DIKW flows in enterprises), or even latent (e.g., as DIKW flows among individuals or informal groups). This study's contribution is synthesizing observations from a wide range of studies to describe the principles of DIKW dynamics relevant to societal adaptation.

An example of a less apparent epistemic relationship between technology and organization is articulated as a tendency that (i) technology of a complex system and (ii) organizational structure (which produces or maintains the system) mirror each other. Colfer and Baldwin (2016) connected this epistemic relationship with an organization's ability to innovate and adapt to environmental changes. The conclusions of their study may be summarized as follows:

- If a technological system is changing and complexity is increasing rather slowly, mirroring (of the technology architecture), and organization may be common and cost-effective.
- If technologies are changing and complexity is increasing, integration (into an enterprise) may require broader DIKW than necessary to manage the technological system components only. In this case, too rigid mirroring may be a "trap" because there is no potential for innovation and research. Partial mirroring, which allows for research and innovation beyond the technological system's boundaries may be a solution. For example, mirroring may be broken by establishing relational contracts among organizations to acquire new DIKW.
- If technologies are changing rapidly and complexity increases, mirror braking may be inevitable. Besides strategic investments in relational contracts beyond the existing organization, high levels of communication and collaboration among allies may be necessary to obtain new DIKW. When technical interdependencies are growing, preemptive modularization and implementation of patterns that may reduce technological and organizational complexity may be explored.
- In open, collaborative endeavors, technology may boost new organizational patterns, such as various transient organizational structures or stigmergic endeavors. New models are anticipated yet to be developed, as underlying technologies remain dynamic and innovative.

Therefore, EnA must support discovering and exploring new epistemic relationships (among the agencies) and adapt as necessary.

8.10 Emergence

Under this emergence principle, new forms of agencies (e.g., governments, organizations, communities, movements) are anticipated. They can be highly organized due to various undelaying technologies and exhibit collective intelligence properties that individual agencies could not achieve. On the one hand, these new organizations may more efficiently manage physical systems (including their environment) due to numerous sensors, integration of physical (including live (Raphael and Posland 2019)), digital and social, and vast volumes of data collected. On the other hand, the threat agents will also organize. They will use new technologies and integrated networks and explore vulnerabilities in a way that could not be anticipated. In other words, as new forms of legitimate endeavors emerge, new alliances of threat agents or (not long ago unlikely) alliances of threat agents and legitimate enterprises may also emerge. Thus, recognizing emerging patterns that have not been predicted in the original technological, enterprise, and societal systems design may become crucial for societal adaptation and design endeavors to respond to the merging situations. Ultimately, EnA should enable these perspectives. The UMF allows for the creation of new perspectives.

9 Discussion

At this point, we will address further questions pertinent to EnA.

9.1 Why Do We Need EnA, and Why is EA Unsatisfactory?

EA is firmly rooted within the enterprise domain, as demonstrated in Table 2. For example, TOGAF is intended for "small, medium, and large commercial businesses, as well as government departments, non-government public organizations, and defense agencies" (The Open Group 2022). Therefore, an EA domain (i.e., the discourse of interest) may include any businesses, groups of countries, governments, or governmental organizations (such as militaries) working together to create common or shareable deliverables or infrastructures. An EA domain may also be a partnership and alliance of businesses working together, such as a consortium or supply chain.

EnA discourse of interest is broader and may include any elements of societies; individuals or groups, organizationally differentiated (e.g., communities) or undifferentiated (e.g., demographics that describe populations and their characteristics). Furthermore, we are not imposing any limitations on the UMF discourse of interest. Ultimately, the UMF may be used to model any system, social, technical, natural, or any combination of these. Thus, we need EnA to model or evaluate models of societies, global and isolated phenomena and undertakings, social changes, and similar.

Most importantly, by including the UMF, we highlight the importance of general intelligence in human endeavors, as they are crucial for adaptation.

For example, Reader et al. (2011) "highly correlated composite of cognitive traits suggests social, technical and ecological abilities have coevolved in primates, indicative of an across-species general intelligence that includes elements of cultural intelligence". Furthermore, they argue that the abilities observed in primates, such as discovering novel solutions to environmental or social problems, learning skills and acquiring information from others ('social learning'), using tools, extracting concealed or embedded food, and engaging in tactical deception are ecologically relevant measures of behavioral flexibility. They pointed out that human intelligence may greatly rely on language or another uniquely human capability.

Richerson and Boyd (2020) researched connections between individual intelligence, learning capacity and cultural adaptation. They argued that when a "new desirable innovation is rare… the role of individual learning is maximal. In a recently changed environment, many individuals may use individual learning/creativity to adapt relatively rapidly". Thus, individual learning is important for cultural adaptation, and "human life history is adapted to exploit the adaptive advantages of culture"; that is, individual learning and cultural learning are complementary. Boyd et al. (2011) also indicated that social learning is essential for human adaptation.

Therefore, we include the UMF as a meta-paradigm of AGI into EnA, as it appears that general intelligence has been in the human lineage for a long time, and it may be one of the underlying factors of human adaptation.

9.2 How EnA Differs from EA, and Whether is It Supposed to Incorporate or Replace It?

EnA is also not prescriptive in that it does not call for artifacts or actions that are not directly related to problem-solving. Therefore, if any of the existing EA models or frameworks may resolve the problem at hand, there is no reason not to use them. However, if the problem at hand calls for more-expressive modeling, EnA may guide modelers to choose better-suited paradigms and create artifacts of that EnA instance.

For example, good indications that the modelers may need to choose paradigms beyond the traditional EA paradigms (e.g., Zachman's EA Framework (Zachman 2008) or TOGAF (The Open Group 2022)) may be:

- Societal or organizational transformations that call for profound cultural changes and affect the fabric of a society or an enterprise (e.g., enhancing a capacity of a government to use scientific research)
- All-pervasive and wholistic societal changes, such as transformation that require integration of enterprises, people's lifeworld (e.g., citizens and communities), and public sphere, including traditional and social media (Polovina 2022)
- An overarching context of human endeavor where the scope of transformation is bigger than a single enterprise and may include society as a whole or global endeavors, such as a response to natural disasters, pandemics (Polovina 2022), or global economic crises.
- When multiple segments of society are involved (e.g., environment, economy, health), and the solutions require collaboration across multiple sectors.
- To identify gaps between fundamental and applied science or a theory and its applications (e.g., the Enterprise Risk Management (ERM) field is dominated by the private sector, but it is necessary to outline ERM for the public sector (Continuity Central 2022; Andersen et al. 2021)).
- Strategic elements and communications that are less signified (if addressed at all) in EA (e.g., privacy (Cavoukian 2011) or safety architecture (Stewart et al. 2021)).

9.3 Why Do We Need UMF, and How Does It Differ from Other Upper Ontologies?

Being an upper ontology, the UMF facilitates the generation of domain ontologies. In other words, the UMF discourse of interest is general intelligence, and it contains generic semantics, such as principles, objects, relationships, systems, and similar. Therefore, the UMF may facilitate the creation of EnA instances and, ultimately, an overarching EnA ontology.

In this context, an EnA ontology is considered a domain ontology whose discourse of interest contains semantics pertinent to human endeavors. For example, an EnA ontology includes four functions of EnA in relation to adaptation (Table 1) and the principles of DIKW dynamics pertinent to an endeavor, (e.g., human collaboration, individuation, dealing with opportunism). EnA may also include other domain ontologies, such as EA frameworks, to facilitate the modeling of enterprise architectures of an endeavor.

However, an EnA ontology also includes the UMF. It may include other paradigms of AGI because general intelligence is important for EnA, especially when EnA must facilitate solving complex and important societal problems. At that point, ethical considerations and sound judgment are unavoidable, as Habermas (Habermas 2003) pointed out: "No science will relieve common sense even if it is scientifically informed, of the task of forming a judgment...."

The UMF differs from other upper ontologies (GUA n.d.) because it does not contain enterprise semantics. For example, Zachman's EA Framework (Zachman 2015) contains Executive Perspective, Business Management Perspective, and Architecture Perspective. In contracts, the UMF discourse of interest is general intelligence, and its discourse of interest contains generic terms, such as object, relationships, and similar. The UMF also does not limit DIKW flows through its four spheres-DIKW may move in all directions. In contrast, the Zachman EA Framework implies top-to-bottom movements (Zachman 2015). Furthermore, the UMF allows the creation of new perspectives in EnA (e.g., strategically important safety view and architecture) and the creation of artifacts that contains DIKW from different spheres to facilitate human creative thinking.

9.4 What Are the Requirements for Good EnA, and How Can Approaches Be Evaluated?

Ideally, EnA will provide a simple (or seemingly simple solution) for a complex problem. For example, the EnA models may intuitively break a complex domain and identify the observables that will become measurable and manageable. Furthermore, a complex pandemic response may be broken down, and the interfaces among the involved agencies may be identified. These interfaces may be observed as we advance, and DIKW flows may be evaluated. That is, new observables may also be determined as necessary, such as the societal capacity to share knowledge (Polovina 2022). Ideally, the EnA should be modeled in a way that is (relatively) easily observed and tested, although the discourse of interest may be complex.

However, the models of EnA are not predetermined but rather problem-solving oriented. That is, the set of chosen EnA models (and their organization) is context-dependent. For example, the model of the EnA instance principles may be an informal diagram of the involved agencies. Still, it can also be a computer simulation of the interaction of the involved agencies. Whatever suits the agencies better helps them reduce the complexity and guides them towards the solution. We assume the modeling includes ethical considerations, and the solution should also be acceptable for all affected agencies and their environment.

Last but not least, we aim to encourage problem-solving that allows adaption of pluralistic societies in a manner that is acceptable for all elements of the society, rather than encourage single-sided adaption by imitation that may turn into maladaptation for some elements of the society.

9.5   How EnA Differs from Other Societal Approaches Such as KAOS, or Linguistic Approaches Such as DEMO?

Knowledge Acquisition in Automated Specification (KAOS) methodology focuses on modeling goal-oriented agents (Lapouchnian 2005). Thus, from the UMF point of view, KAOS is a domain ontology whose domain is the intersection of an organization (including social aspects), agent-oriented technology and requirements acquisition, and particularly goal-oriented agents. For example, if the models of the UMF principles call for a goal-oriented agent methodology, the modelers may incorporate KAOS models in their instance of EnA. However, suppose during the creation of the UMF principles, the modelers realized that they needed need to focus on the properties of the societal DIKW systems and the qualities of DIKW itself. In that case, other approaches may be chosen or researched. That happened when we modeled the societal pandemic response (Polovina 2022). We realized we needed methods to evaluate the overall societal DIKW system, particularly to separate "true" knowledge from "fake" knowledge. Thus, we needed the paradigms that may support these distinctions. The importance of the UML principles is to facilitate this discovery and lead the modeler to choose the conceptual paradigms that better suit their intentions.

Similarly, from the UMF point of view, Design and Engineering Methodology for Organizations (DEMO) (Dietz 1999; Dietz and Mulder 2020a, b) is a domain ontology whose domain is an intersection of an enterprise and requirements acquisition (for software systems development). The authors favor Habermas's theory of communicative action. The UMF allows for modeling these principles and concepts and various other human properties, such as deception or irrationality.

9.6   How EnA Aligns with Other Social Sciences?

The UMF originated as a systems science concept. The authors wanted to explain the differences between Object-Oriented models and mental models created by the modelers. The authors were aware of the modelers' cognitive processes (e.g., thinking, reasoning) and worldview in general (Polovina 1999; Polovina and Wojtkowsk 1999). The UMF is primarily a meta-paradigm that may be used to model various social theories and situations, but the UMF itself stays rooted in systems science.

We aim to support modelers' creativity regardless of their positions and beliefs. For example, a modeler may be an objectivist and believe that the world exists fully independent of them. Or, a modeler may be a subjectivist, who believes there is no reality outside of them, who is the subject. A modeler constructivist may believe that there is some rather semi-objective reality. We aim to support all three approaches by providing a modeling meta-paradigm (i.e., UMF) that may serve all of them.

9.7   What Literature Has Been Used?

The literature informed us from multiple domains, including systems science, enterprise architecture, systems development, future studies, philosophy, anthropology, and management science. We found that knowledge about human adaptation is scattered over multiple faculties of science. Our contribution would be to collate this scattered knowledge as pertinent for the architecture or architecting, or in discovering the architecture of complex societal endeavors in one place.

Notably, we tried to present this knowledge and principles so that heterogeneous scientists and practitioners could work together and concentrate on resolving the problem at hand. The modeling at the principle UMF levels should be intuitive. In contrast, the modeling at the conceptual UMF level may be dominated by the logic of the scientific field. We assume that, at that point, collaboration among scientists and practitioners from different research fields will be more difficult.

As Habermas pointed out (2003): "…most fields of practice were impregnated and restructured by the "logic" of the application of scientific technologies". Habermas also raised the question: "Will common sense, in the end, consent to being not only instructed but completely absorbed by counterintuitive scientific knowledge?".

10   Concluding Remarks

ICT communities have used EA as an organizational concept to advance ICT and communications across an enterprise and, to a lesser extent, to facilitate ecological adaptation. However, the rise of urban areas (and the rise of their citizens), rapid and widespread societal changes (e.g., pandemics, economic crises), and interruptive AI technologies call for the undertaking of new endeavors to adapt to these changes. It has been anticipated that new agencies (i.e., governments, enterprises, communities, individuals) will emerge. We noticed that a new type of architecture is required, i.e., Endeavor Architecture (EnA). We identified ten principles of DIKW dynamics relevant for creating new epistemic relations among agencies that support societal endeavors: top-down, bottom-up, inclusion, individualization, openness, integration, collaboration, opportunism, adaptiveness, and emergence. We propose to apply these principles in setting the directions and requirements for the evolution of EnA to support ecological adaptation, research, learning, and creation of new knowledge leading to the acceptance of Endeavour Architecture (EnA) beyond Enterprise Architecture (EA).

References

Andersen J.T., Sax J., Giannozzi A.: Conjoint effects of interacting strategy-making processes and lines of defense practices in strategic Risk Management: an empirical study. Long Range Plann. (2021) 102164. https://doi.org/10.1016/j.lrp.2021.102164.

Batty, M., et al.: Smart cities of the future. The Eur. Phys. J. Spec. Top. **214**(1), 481–518 (2012). https://doi.org/10.1140/epjst/e2012-01703-3

Baxter, H.: Habermas: The Discourse Theory of Law and Democracy. Stanford University Press (2011). https://doi.org/10.11126/stanford/9780804769129.001.0001

Baxter, M., Polovina, S., Kemp, N., Laurier, W.: Underpinning layered enterprise architecture development with formal concept analysis. In: Polovina, R., Polovina, S., Kemp, N. (eds.) Aligning Computing Productivity with Human Creativity for Societal Adaptation. The 1st Measuring Ontologies for Value Enhancement (MOVE) Workshop at the 23rd ACM CSCW2020, revised selected papers. CCIS 1694. Springer Nature Switzerland. https://www.springer.com/series/7899/books (2022)

Blakemore, E.: This is What Happened When an Australian City Gave Trees Email Addresses. Smithsonian Magazine. https://www.smithsonianmag.com/smart-news/what-happened-when-australian-city-gave-trees-email-addresses-180955851/ (2015)

Bohman, J., Rehg, W.: Jürgen Habermas. In: Zalta, E.N. (ed.) The Stanford Encyclopedia of Philosophy (Fall 2017 ed.). https://plato.stanford.edu/archives/fall2017/entries/habermas/. Accessed 21 Sep 2022 (2017)

Boyd, R., Richerson, P.J., Henrich, J.: The cultural niche: why social learning is essential for human adaptation. Proc. Natl. Acad. Sci. **108**(supplement_2), 10918–10925 (2011). https://doi.org/10.1073/pnas.1100290108

Caine, J.: Advancing strategy ontology. In: Polovina, R., Polovina, S., Kemp, N. (eds.) Aligning Computing Productivity with Human Creativity for Societal Adaptation. The 1st Measuring Ontologies for Value Enhancement (MOVE) Workshop at the 23rd ACM CSCW2020, revised selected papers. CCIS 1694. Springer Nature Switzerland. https://www.springer.com/series/7899/books (2022)

Callaghan, C.: Disaster management, crowdsourced R&D and probabilistic innovation theory: Toward real-time disaster response capability. Int. J. Disaster Risk Reduction **17**, 238–250 (2016). https://doi.org/10.1016/j.ijdrr.2016.05.004

Callaghan, C.: The physics of a coronavirus pandemic: how to avoid impending apocalyptic or dystopian economic scenarios (3 April 2020). https://ssrn.com/abstract=3567585. https://doi.org/10.2139/ssrn.3567585

Cavoukian, A.: Privacy by Design. https://iapp.org/media/pdf/resource_center/pbd_implement_7found_principles.pdf (2011). Accessed 15 Sep 2022

Cecez-Kecmanovic, D., Marjanovic, O.: Ethical Implications of IT-enabled Information Flows Conceived as Intermediaries or Mediators, Australasian Conference on Information Systems, Adelaide (2015)

Chikersal, P., Tomprou, M., Kim, Y., Wooley, W.A., Dabbish, L.: Deep structures of collaboration: physiological correlates of collective intelligence and group satisfaction. In: CSCW '17: Proceedings of the 2017 ACM Conference on Computer Supported Cooperative Work and Social Computing, pp 873–888 (2017). https://doi.org/10.1145/2998181.2998250

Chourabi, H., et al.: Understanding Smart Cities: An Integrative Framework. Computer Society, IEEE (2012)

Colfer, J.L., Baldwin, Y.C.: The Mirroring Hypothesis: Theory, Evidence and Exceptions, Working Paper, Harvard Business School Working Papers Series (2016)

Continuity Central. Academic study provides insights into effective enterprise risk management. The latest enterprise risk management news from around the world (January 2022). https://www.continuitycentral.com/index.php/news/erm-news/6974-academic-study-provides-insights-into-effective-enterprise-risk-management

Conroy, N.K., Rubin, V.L., Chen, Y.: Automatic deception detection: methods for finding fake news. Proc. Assoc. Info. Sci. Technol. **52**(1), 1–4 (2015). https://doi.org/10.1002/pra2.2015.145052010082

Dawes, S.S., Bloniarz, A.P., Kelly, L.K., Fletcher, D.P.: Some Assembly Required: Building a Digital Government for the 21st Century. Center for Technology in Government, University of Albany, State University of New York. https://www.ctg.albany.edu/publications/reports/some_assembly/some_assembly.pdf (1999)

Dietz, J.L.G.: Understanding and modelling business processes with DEMO. In: Akoka, J., Bouzeghoub, M., Comyn-Wattiau, I., Métais, E. (eds.) ER 1999. LNCS, vol. 1728, pp. 188–202. Springer, Heidelberg (1999). https://doi.org/10.1007/3-540-47866-3_13

Dietz, J.L.G., Mulder, J.B.H.: The Evolution of DEMO (2020a) http://ceur-ws.org/Vol-2825/pap er6.pdf

Dietz, J.L.G., Mulder, H.B.F.: Enterprise Ontology: A Human-Centric Approach to Understanding the Essence of Organisation. Springer International Publishing, Cham (2020)

Dignum, V.: Responsible artificial intelligence: designing AI for human values. ITU J. ICT Discoveries 1(1), 1–8 (2018). https://www.itu.int/dms_pub/itu-s/opb/journal/S-JOURNAL-ICTF. VOL1-2018-1-PDF-E.pdf

Enterprise Architecture Solutions: Essential Project (2022). https://enterprise-architecture.org/. Accessed 21 Sep 2022

Few, R., Morchain, D., Spear, D., et al.: Transformation, adaptation, and development: relating concepts to practice. Palgrave Commun. 3, 17092 (2017). https://doi.org/10.1057/palcomms. 2017.92

Finkelstein, C.: Enterprise Architecture for Integration: Rapid Delivery Methods and Technologies. Artech House, Boston (2006)

Frosch-Wilke, D., Tuchtenhagen, S.: Using business intelligence systems for enterprise architecture. IADIS Int. J. 14(1), 57–69 (2016)

Gaß, O., Ortbach, K., Kretzer, M., Maedche, A., Niehaves, B.: Conceptualizing individualization in information systems – a literature review. Commun. Assoc. Inform. Syst. 37, 64–88 (2015). http://aisel.aisnet.org/cais/vol37/iss1/3

Gell-Man, M.: What is complexity? Complexity 1(1), 16–19 (1995). https://doi.org/10.1002/cplx. 6130010105

Gell-Man, M.: Interview with Murray Gell-Mann, Nobel Laureate in Physics 1969 by Joanna Rose (2001). https://www.youtube.com/watch?v=NBmUmLTGj1Q

Gell-Mann, M.: A Crude Look at the Whole. Talk given at Nanyang Technological University, Singapore (2013) https://www.paralimes.org/tag/murray-gell-mann/

Gharajedaghi, J.: Systems Thinking: Managing Chaos and Complexity: A Platform for Designing Business Architecture. Butterworth-Heinemann (2006)

Global Forest Watch: Global Forest Watch, Washington, DC. https://www.globalforestwatch.org (20002). Accessed 26 Sep 2022

Giachetti, R.E.: Design of Enterprise Systems: Theory, Architecture, and Methods. Taylor & Francis Group, CRC Press, Boca Raton, FL (2010)

Zachman, J.P.: The Zachman Framework Evolution by: John P. Zachman. Zachman International. https://www.zachman.com/ea-articles-reference/54-the-zachman-framework-evolution (2011)

Zachman, A.J.: Enterprise Architecture Defined: Primitives and Composites. https://www.zac hman.com/resources/zblog/item/enterprise-architecture-defined-primitives-and-composites (2019)

Gidley, J.: Global knowledge futures: articulating the emergence of a new meta-level field. Integr. Rev. 9(2), (2013)

Giffinger, R., Fertner, C, Kramar, H., Kalasek, R., Pichler-Milanovic, N., Meijers, E.: Smart Cities – Ranking of European medium-sized cities. Vienna University of Technology. http:// curis.ku.dk/ws/files/37640170/smart_cities_final_report.pdf (2007). Accessed 26 Sep 2022

Goertzel, B.: Artificial general intelligence: concept, state of the art, and future prospects. J. Artif. Gen. Intell. 5(1), 1–46 (2014). https://doi.org/10.2478/jagi-2014-0001

Gong, Y., Janssen, M.: The value of and myths about enterprise architecture. Int. J. Inf. Manage. 46, 1–9 (2019). https://doi.org/10.1016/j.ijinfomgt.2018.11.006

Groza, A.: Towards detecting fake news using natural language understanding and reasoning in Description Logics. In: Polovina, R., Polovina, S., Kemp, N. (eds.) Aligning Computing Productivity with Human Creativity for Societal Adaptation. The 1st Measuring Ontologies for Value Enhancement (MOVE) Workshop at the 23rd ACM CSCW2020, revised selected papers. CCIS 1694. Springer Nature Switzerland. https://www.springer.com/series/7899/books (2022)

Groza, A., Pomarlan, M.: Towards an ontology of explanations. In: Polovina, R., Polovina, S., Kemp, N. (eds.) Aligning Computing Productivity with Human Creativity for Societal Adaptation. The 1st Measuring Ontologies for Value Enhancement (MOVE) Workshop at the 23rd ACM CSCW2020, revised selected papers. CCIS 1694. Springer Nature Switzerland. https://www.springer.com/series/7899/books (2022)

Groza, A., Pop, A.: Fake news detector in the medical domain by reasoning with description logics. In: 2020 IEEE 16th International Conference on Intelligent Computer Communication and Processing (ICCP), Cluj-Napoca, Romania, pp. 145–152 (2020). https://doi.org/10.1109/ICCP51029.2020.9266270

GUA: Enterprise Ontology. The Global University Alliance. https://www.globaluniversityalliance.org/research/enterprise-ontology/. Accessed 21 Sep 2022

Hall, R., Bowerman, B, Braverman, J., Taylor, J., Todosow, H., von Wimmersperg, U.: The vision of a smart city. In: 2nd International Life Extension Technology Workshop. Paris, France (2000). https://www.osti.gov/servlets/purl/773961

Habermas, J.: The Structural Transformation of the Public Sphere: An Inquiry into a Category of Bourgeois Society. The MIT Press (1991)

Habermas, J.: The Future of Human Nature. Polity Press (2003)

Hanschke, I.: Strategic IT Management: A Toolkit for Enterprise Architecture Management. Springer, London, NY (2010)

Hammer & Company: PRISM: Dispersion and Interconnection: Approaches to Distributed Systems Architecture, Final Report. Technical report, CSC Index, Inc., Cambridge, Massachusetts (1986)

Harrison, C., Donnelly, I.A.: A theory of smart cities. In: Proceedings of the 55th Annual Meeting of the ISSS, vol. 55, issue 1. Hull, UK (2011) https://journals.isss.org/index.php/proceedings55th/article/view/1703

Harrison, C., et al.: Foundations for smarter cities. IBM J. Res. Dev. **54**(4), 1–16 (2010)

Heintz, E., et al.: Framework for systematic identification of ethical aspects of healthcare technologies: the SBU approach. Int. J. Technol. Assess. Health Care **31**(3), 124–130 (2015). https://doi.org/10.1017/S0266462315000264

Heng, M.S.H., De Moor, A.: From Habermas's communicative theory to practice on the internet. Info. Syst. J. **13**, 331–352 (2003)

Hoogervorst, J.A.P.: Enterprise Governance and Enterprise Engineering. Springer, Berlin, Heidelberg (2009). https://doi.org/10.1007/978-3-540-92671-9

Hong, A., et al.: Reconciling big data and thick data to advance the new urban science and smart city governance, J. Urban Aff. (2022). https://doi.org/10.1080/07352166.2021.2021085

Jakobsen, D., Graf (2022). Formal, measurable ontologies for worldviews. In: Polovina, R., Polovina, S., Kemp, N. (eds.) Aligning Computing Productivity with Human Creativity for Societal Adaptation. The 1st Measuring Ontologies for Value Enhancement (MOVE) Workshop at the 23rd ACM CSCW2020, revised selected papers. CCIS 1694. Springer Nature Switzerland. https://www.springer.com/series/7899/books (2022)

Jani, A., et al.: A novel ontological approach to estimate inequalities and underuse of social prescriptions for mental health in primary care in England. In: Polovina, R., Polovina, S., Kemp, N. (eds.) Aligning Computing Productivity with Human Creativity for Societal Adaptation. The 1st Measuring Ontologies for Value Enhancement (MOVE) Workshop at the 23rd ACM CSCW2020, revised selected papers. CCIS 1694. Springer Nature Switzerland. https://www.springer.com/series/7899/books (2022)

Kaisler, S., Armour, F.: Enterprise architecting: critical problems. In: 38th Hawaii International Conference on System Sciences, HICSS-38 (2005). https://doi.org/10.1109/HICSS.2005.241

Kakarontzas, G., Anthopoulos, G.L., Chatzakou, D., Vakali, A.: A conceptual enterprise architecture framework for smart cities - a survey based approach. In: 11th Int. Conf. on E-Business (ICE-B), pp. 47–54 (2014)

Kappelman, L., Zachman, J.: The enterprise and its architecture: ontology & challenges. J. Comput. Inform. Syst. **53**(4), 87–95 (2013)

Kelly, Y., Zilanawala, A., Booker, C., Sacker, A.: Social media use and adolescent mental health: findings from the UK millennium cohort study. eClinical Med., part of The Lancet Discovery Sci. **6**, 59–68 (2018). https://doi.org/10.1016/j.eclinm.2018.12.005

Kendal, E.: Ethical, legal and social implications of emerging technology (ELSIET) symposium. Bioethical Inquiry **19**, 363–370 (2022). https://doi.org/10.1007/s11673-022-10197-5

Knauss, A., Borici, A., Knauss E., Damian, D.: Towards understanding requirements engineering in IT ecosystems. In: Second IEEE International Workshop on Empirical Requirements Engineering (EmpiRE), pp. 33–36. Chicago, IL (2012). https://doi.org/10.1109/EmpiRE.2012.6347679

Lacey, J., Howden, M., Cvitanovic, C., Dowd, A.: Informed adaptation: ethical considerations for adaptation researchers and decision-makers. Glob. Environ. Chang. **32**, 200–220 (2015). https://doi.org/10.1016/j.gloenvcha.2015.03.011

Lan, M., Liu, L., Burmeister, J., Zhu, W., Zhou, H., Gu, X.: Are crime and collective emotion interrelated? a "broken emotion". conjecture from community twitter posts. Soc. Sci. Comput. Rev. (2022). https://doi.org/10.1177/08944393221113210

Lapalme, J.: Three schools of thought on enterprise architecture. IT Prof. **14**(6), 37–43 (2012). https://doi.org/10.1109/MITP.2011.109

Lapalme, J., Gerber, A., Van der Merwe, A., Zachman, J., De Vries, M., Hinkelmann, K.: Exploring the future of enterprise architecture: a Zachman perspective. Comput. Ind. **79**, 103–113 (2016). https://doi.org/10.1016/j.compind.2015.06.010

Lapouchnian, A.: Goal-Oriented Requirements Engineering: An Overview of the Current Research. Department of Computer Science, University of Toronto. http://www.cs.utoronto.ca/~alexei/pub/Lapouchnian-Depth.pdf (2005). Accessed 23 Sep 2022

Latapie, H., et al.: A Metamodel and Framework for Artificial General Intelligence from Theory to Practice. J. AI. Consci. **08**(02), 205–227 (2021)

Lom, M., Prybil, O.: Smart city model based on systems theory. Int. J. Inform. Manage. **56**, 102092 (2021). https://doi.org/10.1016/j.ijinfomgt.2020.102092

Martin, J.: The Great Transition. Using the Seven Disciplines of Enterprise Engineering to Align People, Technology and Strategy. Amacon, New York, NY (1995)

McGagh, D., et al.: A novel ontological approach to track social determinants of health in primary care. In: Polovina, R., Polovina, S., Kemp, N. (eds.) Aligning Computing Productivity with Human Creativity for Societal Adaptation. The 1st Measuring Ontologies for Value Enhancement (MOVE) Workshop at the 23rd ACM CSCW2020, revised selected papers. CCIS 1694. Springer Nature Switzerland. https://www.springer.com/series/7899/books (2022)

McMaham, P., Evans, J.: Ambiguity and Engagement. Am. J. Sociol. **124**(3), (2018). https://doi.org/10.1086/701298

Mircea, E., Toma, L., Sanduleac, M.: The smart city concept of 21st century. Procedia Eng. **181**, 12–19 (2017). https://doi.org/10.1016/j.proeng.2017.02.357

Moir, E., Moonen, T., Clark, G.: What are future cities? Government Office for Science, UK (2014)

Mohanty, S.P., Choppali, U., Kougianos, E.: Everything you wanted to know about smart cities: the Internet of things is the backbone. IEEE Consum. Electron. Mag. **5**(3), 60–70 (2016). https://doi.org/10.1109/MCE.2016.2556879

de Moor, A., et al.: Participatory collaboration mapping of design-enabled urban innovations: the MappingDESIGNSCAPES case. In: Polovina, R., Polovina, S., Kemp, N. (eds.) Aligning Computing Productivity with Human Creativity for Societal Adaptation. The 1st Measuring Ontologies for Value Enhancement (MOVE) Workshop at the 23rd ACM CSCW2020, revised selected papers. CCIS 1694. Springer Nature Switzerland. https://www.springer.com/series/7899/books (2022a)

de Moor, A., et al.: Collaborative sensemaking of design-enabled urban innovations: the MappingDESIGNSCAPES case. In: Polovina, R., Polovina, S., Kemp, N. (eds.) Aligning Computing Productivity with Human Creativity for Societal Adaptation. The 1st Measuring Ontologies for Value Enhancement (MOVE) Workshop at the 23rd ACM CSCW2020, revised selected papers. CCIS 1694. Springer Nature Switzerland. https://www.springer.com/series/7899/books (2022b)

Mora, L., et al.: Assembling sustainable smart city transitions: an interdisciplinary theoretical perspective. J. Urban Technol. **28**(1–2), 1–27 (2020). https://doi.org/10.1080/10630732.2020.1834831

Mowles, C.: Complex, but not quite complex enough: the turn to the complexity sciences in evaluation scholarship. Evaluation **20**(2), 160–175 (2014)

Munafò, M., Nosek, B., Bishop, D., et al.: A manifesto for reproducible science. Nat. Hum. Behav. **1**, 0021 (2017). https://doi.org/10.1038/s41562-016-0021

Nam, T., Pardo, T.A.: Smart City as Urban Innovation: Focusing on Management, Policy and Context. International Conference on Theory and Practice of Electronic Governance (ICEGOV), Tallinn, Estonia, 26–28 Sep. 2011

Olan, F., Arakpogun, E.O., Suklan, J., Nakpodia, F., Damij, N., Jayawickrama, U.: Artificial intelligence and knowledge sharing: contributing factors to organizational performance. J. Bus. Res. **145**, 605–615 (2022)

Op't Land, M., Proper, E., Waage, M., Cloo, J., Steghuis, C.: Enterprise Architecture: Creating Value by Informed Governance. Springer Berlin Heidelberg, Berlin, Heidelberg (2009). https://doi.org/10.1007/978-3-540-85232-2

Orr, H.A.: The generic theory of adaptation: a brief history. Nat. Rev. Genet. **6**, 119–127 (2005). https://doi.org/10.1038/nrg1523

Perks, C., Beveridge, T. (eds.): Guide to Enterprise IT Architecture. Springer New York, New York, NY (2004). https://doi.org/10.1007/b98880

Phuong, T., Biesbroek, R.G., Wals, A.E.J.: The interplay between social learning and adaptive capacity in climate change adaptation: a systematic review. NJAS: Wageningen J. Life Sci. **82**(1), 1–9 (2017). https://doi.org/10.1016/j.njas.2017.05.001

Polovina, R.: On understanding and modelling complex systems, through a pandemic. In: Polovina, R., Polovina, S., Kemp, N. (eds.) Aligning Computing Productivity with Human Creativity for Societal Adaptation. The 1st Measuring Ontologies for Value Enhancement (MOVE) Workshop at the 23rd ACM CSCW2020, revised selected papers. CCIS 1694. Springer Nature Switzerland. https://www.springer.com/series/7899/books (2022)

Polovina, R.: Formal Object Specification in Object-Oriented Modeling and their Consequences: Integration of Static and Dynamic Aspects–Data, Functions and Events. Ph.D. Thesis, Czech Technical University in Prague (1999)

Polovina, R., Wojtkowski, W.: On the nature of modeling and object orientation. In: 4th Systems Science European Congress, pp 679–688. Valencia, Spain (1999)

Polovina, R., Wojtkowski, W.: Leveraging formal specifications: integration of formal paradigms in multidimensional modeling space. In: Harindranath, G., et al. (eds.) New Perspectives on Information Systems Development, pp. 161–175. Springer US, Boston, MA (2002). https://doi.org/10.1007/978-1-4615-0595-2_13

Polovina, S., Polovina, R., Kemp, N., Pu, K.: MOVE: measuring ontologies in value-seeking environments: CSCW for human adaptation. In: CSCW'20 Companion: Conference Companion Publication of the 2020a on Computer Supported Cooperative Work and Social Computing October, pp 475–482 (2020a). https://doi.org/10.1145/3406865.3418595

Polovina, S., von Rosing, M., Etzel, G.: Leading the practice in layered enterprise architecture. In: CEUR Workshop Proceedings, pp. 62–69. http://ceur-ws.org/Vol-2574/ (2020b)

Quick, S.K., Feldman, S.M.: Distinguishing participation and inclusion. J. Plann. Educ. Res. **31**(3), 272–290 (2011)

Raphael, K., Poslad, S.: The thing with e.coli: highlighting opportunities and challenges of integrating bacteria in IoT and HCI. In: 'CHI'19 Extended Abstracts, Glasgow, Scotland, UK, 4–9 May 2019. https://doi.org/10.1145/3290607

Reader, M.S., Hager, Y., Laland, N.K.: The evolution of primate general and cultural intelligence. Phil. Trans. B **366**(1567), 1017–1027 (2011). https://doi.org/10.1098/rstb.2010.0342

Richerson, P.J., Boyd, R.: The human life history is adapted to exploit the adaptive advantages of culture. Phil. Trans. R. Soc. B **375**(1803), 20190498 (2020). https://doi.org/10.1098/rstb.2019.0498

Ross, J., Weill, P., Robertson, D.: Enterprise Architecture as Strategy: Creating a Foundation for Business Execution. Harvard Business School Press (2006)

Sarta, A., Durand, R., Vergne, J.: Organizational adaptation. J. Manag. **47**(1), 43–75 (2020). https://doi.org/10.1177/0149206320929088

Shahidi, F.F., Parnia, A., Sidiqqi, A.: Trends in socioeconomic inequalities in premature and avoidable mortality in Canada, 1991–2016. CMAJ **192**(39), E1114–E1128 (2020). https://doi.org/10.1503/cmaj.191723

Singer-Velush, N., Sherman, K., Anderson, E.: Microsoft Analyzed Data on Its Newly Remote Workforce. Harvard Business Review, 15 Jul 2020

Simonet, G., Duchemin, E.: The concept of adaptation: Interdisciplinary scope and involvement in climate change. Sapiens **3**(1) (2010). https://journals.openedition.org/sapiens/997#tocto2n1

Smit, B., Pilifosova, O., Huq, S., Challenger, B., Burton, I.: Adaptation to Climate Change in the Context of Sustainable Development and Equity. IPCC Reports. https://www.ipcc.ch/report/ar3/wg2/chapter-18-adaptation-to-climate-change-in-the-context-of-sustainable-development-and-equity/ (2001). Accessed 21 Sep 2022

Søilen, K.S.: Making sense of the collective intelligence field: a review. J/ Intell. Stud. Bus. **9**(2), 6–18 (2019). https://ojs.hh.se/index.php/JISIB/article/view/405

Sowa, F.J., Zachman, A.J.: Extending and formalizing the framework for information systems architecture. IBM Syst. J. **31**(3), 590 (1992)

Sparx Services: https://sparxsystems.us/. Accessed 14 Sep 2022

Stojakovic-Celustka, S.: FinTech and its implementation. In: Polovina, R., Polovina, S., Kemp, N. (eds.) Aligning Computing Productivity with Human Creativity for Societal Adaptation. The 1st Measuring Ontologies for Value Enhance-ment (MOVE) Workshop at the 23rd ACM CSCW2020, revised selected papers. CCIS 1694. Springer Nature Switzerland. https://www.springer.com/series/7899/books (2022)

van Steenbergen, M., van den Berg, M., Brinkkemper, S.: A balanced approach to developing the enterprise architecture practice. In: Filipe, J., Cordeiro, J., Cardoso, J. (eds.) ICEIS 2007. LNBIP, vol. 12, pp. 240–253. Springer, Heidelberg (2008). https://doi.org/10.1007/978-3-540-88710-2_19

Sternberg, R.J.: Intelligence. Dialogues Clin. Neurosci. **14**(1), 19–27 (2012). https://doi.org/10.31887/DCNS.2012.14.1/rsternberg

Stewart, D., Whalen, M.W., Cofer, D., Heimdahl, M.P.E.: Architectural modeling and analysis for safety engineering. In: Bozzano, M., Papadopoulos, Y. (eds.) IMBSA 2017. LNCS, vol. 10437, pp. 97–111. Springer, Cham (2017). https://doi.org/10.1007/978-3-319-64119-5_7

Tapscott, D., Caston, A.: Paradigm Shift – The New Promise of Information Technology. McGraw-Hill, New York, New York (1993). 0-07-062857-2

The Open Group: The Open Group Architecture Framework (TOGAF) Standard, 10th edn. https://www.opengroup.org/togaf(2022)

The Open Group: ArchiMate 3.1 Specification. https://publications.opengroup.org/downloadable/download/link/id/MC4xODA3OTQwMCAxNjYyOTIxMjQ2MTYyNDA2NDE2NjE2NjE2NDE2N0E2NjE6zAxMTIy/ (2019)

The World Bank: Urban Development Overview. https://www.worldbank.org/en/topic/urbandevelopment/overview#1 (2020)

Toppeta, D.: The Smart City vision: How innovation and ICT can build smart, "livable", sustainable cities" "The Innovation Knowledge Foundation. https://inta-aivn.org/images/cc/Urbanism/background%20documents/Toppeta_Report_005_2010.pdf (2010)

Tran., T., Cimiano, P., Ankolekar, A.: Rules for an ontology-based approach to adaptation. In: SMAP'06. IEEE (2006). https://doi.org/10.1109/SMAP.2006.31

Vinuesa, R., et al.: The role of artificial intelligence in achieving the sustainable development goals. Nat. Commun. 11, 233 (2018). https://doi.org/10.1038/s41467-019-14108-y

Washburn, D., Sindhu, U., Balaouras, S., Dines, A.R, Hayes, M.N., Nelson, E.L.: Helping CIOs Understand Smart Cities' Initiatives. Forrester. https://s3-us-west-2.amazonaws.com/itworldcanada/archive/Themes/Hubs/Brainstorm/forrester_help_cios_smart_city.pdf (2010)

Williams, K.Y., O'Reilly, C.A.: Demography and diversity in organizations: a review of 40 years of research. Res. Organ. Behav. 20, 77–140 (1998). https://ils.unc.edu/courses/2013_spring/inls285_001/materials/WIlliams.OReilly.1996.Diversity&demography.pdf

Woolley, A.W., Aggarwal, I., Malone, T.W.: Collective intelligence and group performance. Curr. Dir. Psychol. Sci. 24(6), 420–424 (2015)

Xiong, F., Pan, S., Zhu, X.: Collective behavior analysis and graph mining in social networks. Complexity 2022, 9873569 (2022). https://doi.org/10.1155/2022/9873569

Yaworsky, P.: A Model for General Intelligence. Air Force Research Laboratory, Rome, NY 13441 (2018). https://arxiv.org/ftp/arxiv/papers/1811/1811.02546.pdf

Vacha, T., Pribyl, O., Lom, M., Bacurova, M.: Involving citizens in smart city projects: systems engineering meets participation. In: Smart City Symposium Prague (SCSP) (2016)

Zachman, A.J.: Yes, "Enterprise Architecture is Relative", but it is not Arbitrary. Zachman International. https://www.zachman.com/ea-articles-reference/57-eanotarbitrary (n.d.)

Zachman, A.J.: A framework for information systems architecture. IBM Syst. J. 26(3), 276–292 (1987). https://www.zachman.com/images/ZI_PIcs/ibmsj2603e.pdf

Zachman, A.J.: John Zachman's Concise Definition of the Zachman Framework™, Zachman International. https://www.zachman.com/about-the-zachman-framework (2008)

Zachman, A.J.: Zachman Framework Rows. What are they? Zachman International. https://www.zachman.com/resources/zblog/item/zachman-framework-rows-what-are-they (2015)

Ontology Modeling

Towards Detecting Fake News Using Natural Language Understanding and Reasoning in Description Logics

Adrian Groza(✉)

Technical University of Cluj-Napoca, Cluj-Napoca, Romania
Adrian.Groza@cs.utcluj.ro
http://users.utcluj.ro/~agroza

Abstract. Fighting against misinformation and computational propaganda requires integrated efforts from various domains like law or education, but there is also a need for computational tools. I investigate here how reasoning in Description Logics (DLs) can detect inconsistencies between trusted knowledge and not trusted sources. The proposed method is exemplified on fake news for the new coronavirus. Indeed, in the context of the Covid-19 pandemic, many were quick to spread deceptive information. Since, the not-trusted information comes in natural language (e.g. "Covid-19 affects only the elderly"), the natural language text is automatically converted into DLs using the FRED tool. The resulted knowledge graph formalised in Description Logics is merged with the trusted ontologies on Covid-10. Reasoning in Description Logics is then performed with the Racer reasoner, which is responsable to detect inconsistencies within the ontology. When detecting inconsistencies, a "red flag" is raised to signal possible fake news. The reasoner can provide justifications for the detected inconsistency. This availability of justifications is the main advantage compared to approaches based on machine learning, since the system is able to explain its reasoning steps to a human agent. Hence, the approach is a step towards human-centric AI systems. The main challenge remains to improve the technology which automatically translates text into some formal representation.

Keywords: Fake news · Covid-19 · Description logics · Ontologies · Natural language understanding

1 Introduction

In the context of Covid-19 pandemic, many were quick to spread deceptive information [7]. Fighting against misinformation or computational propaganda requires actions from various domains like law or education, but also tools from the information technology domain [16,21]. We aim at proposing such tool able to signal a red flag in case of possbile fake news.

The task here is to detect inconsistencies between a trusted source and not trusted ones. One challenge is that the not-trusted information comes in natural language, e.g."Covid-19 affects only elderly". Our apporach is to automatically convert text into

© Springer Nature Switzerland AG 2022
R. Polovina et al. (Eds.): MOVE 2020, CCIS 1694, pp. 57–72, 2022.
https://doi.org/10.1007/978-3-031-22228-3_3

Description Logic (DL). For this task a machine reader is employed, namely the FRED converter [11]. Having a formal representation of the text, an inference-based tool can detect logical inconsistencies among axioms in DL. Reasoning in Description Logics is then performed with the Racer reasoner [15] [1] Since the most available ontologies in the Semantic Web are from the medical domain, the proposed approach is exemplified with a scenario from the Covid-19 pandemic.

We start by succinctly introducing the syntax of description logic and the reasoning patterns used to detect logical inconsistencies. Section 4 analyses the challenges encountered by FRED when translating various myths related to COVID-19. Section 5 illustrates the developed algorithm for automatic conflict detection. Section 6 browses related work, while Sect. 7 concludes the paper.

2   Finding Inconsistencies Using Description Logics

2.1   Description Logics

In the Description Logics, concepts are built using the set of constructors formed by negation, conjunction, disjunction, value restriction, and existential restriction [4] (Table 1). Here, C and D represent concept descriptions, while r is a role name. The semantics is defined based on an interpretation $I = (\Delta^I, \cdot^I)$, where the domain Δ^I of I contains a non-empty set of individuals, and the interpretation function $\cdot^I$ maps each concept name C to a set of individuals $C^I \in \Delta^I$ and each role r to a binary relation $r^I \in \Delta^I \times \Delta^I$. The last column of Table 1 shows the extension of $\cdot^I$ for non-atomic concepts. A terminology *TBox* is a finite set of terminological axioms of the forms $C \equiv D$ or $C \sqsubseteq D$.

Table 1. Syntax and semantics of DL

Constructor	Syntax	semantics
Conjunction	$C \sqcap D$	$C^I \cap D^I$
Disjunction	$C \sqcup D$	$C^I \cup D^I$
Existential restriction	$\exists r.C$	$\{x \in \Delta^I \mid \exists y : (x,y) \in r^I \wedge y \in C^I\}$
Value restriction	$\forall r.C$	$\{x \in \Delta^I \mid \forall y : (x,y) \in r^I \rightarrow y \in C^I\}$
Individual assertion	$a : C$	$\{a\} \in C^I$
Role assertion	$r(a,b)$	$(a,b) \in r^I$

Example 1 (Terminological box). "Coronavirus disease (Covid-19) is an infectious disease caused by a newly discovered coronavirus" can be formalised as:

$$Covid\text{-}19 \equiv CoronavirusDisease \qquad (1)$$

$$InfectiousDisease \sqsubseteq Disease \qquad (2)$$

$$CoronavirusDisease \sqsubseteq InfectiosDisease \sqcap \forall causedBy.NewCoronavirus \qquad (3)$$

---

[1] A preliminary version of this paper is [13]. The Python sources and the formalisation in Description Logics (KRSS syntax) are available at https://github.com/APGroza/ontologies.

In axiom (1) the concept *Covid-19* is the same as the concept *CoronavirusDisease*. We know from axiom (2) that an infectious disease is a disease (i.e. the concept *InfectiousDisease* is included in the more general concept *Disease*). We also learn from axiom (3) that the coronovirus disease is included in the intersection of two sets: the set *InfectionDisease* and the set of individuals for which all the roles *causedBy* point towards instances from the concept *NewCoronavirus*.

An assertional box *ABox* is a finite set of concept assertions $i : C$ or role assertions $r(i,j)$, where C designates a concept, r a role, and i and j are two individuals.

Example 2 (Assertional Box). $SARS\text{-}CoV\text{-}2 : Virus$ says that the individual *SARS-CoV-2* is an instance of the concept *Virus*. The information that SARS-Cov-2 comes from the bats is formalised with *hasSource(SARS-CoV-2, bat)*. The role *hasSource* relates two individuals *SARS-CoV-2* and *bat*, that is an instance of mammals: $bat : Mammal$.

A concept C is satisfied if there exists an interpretation I such that $C^I \neq \emptyset$. The concept D subsumes the concept C ($C \sqsubseteq D$) if $C^I \subseteq D^I$ for all interpretations I. Constraints on concepts (e.g. *disjoint*) or on roles (*domain*, *range*, *inverse* role, or *transitive* properties) can be specified in more expressive DLs. This sections provides only some basic terminologies of DLs. For a detailed explanation about families of DLs, the reader is referred to [4]. By reasoning on this mathematical constraints, one can detect inconsistencies among different pieces of knowledge, as illustrated in the following inconsistency patterns.

2.2 Inconsistency Patterns

An ontology $\mathcal{O}$ is incoherent iff there exists an unsatisfiable concept in $\mathcal{O}$.

Example 3 (Incoherent ontology). The ontology containing two axioms

$$Covid\text{-}19 \sqsubseteq InfectionDisease$$
$$Covid\text{-}19 \sqsubseteq \neg InfectionDisease$$

is incoherent because *Covid-19* is unsatisfiable, since it is included in two disjoint sets.

In most cases this patterns is hidden in more complex axioms, and therefore reasoning is required to infer that a concept is included in two disjoint concepts.

Example 4 (Reasoning to detect incoherence).

$$Covid\text{-}19 \sqsubseteq InfectionDisease \qquad (4)$$
$$InfectiousDisease \sqsubseteq Disease \sqcap \qquad (5)$$
$$\exists causedBy.(Bacteria \sqcup Virus \sqcup Fungi \sqcup Parasites)$$
$$Covid\text{-}19 \sqsubseteq \neg Disease \qquad (6)$$

From axioms (4) and (6), one can deduce that *Covid-19* is included in the concept *Disease*. From axiom (6), one learns the opposite: *Covid-19* is outside the same set *Disease*. A reasoner on Description Logics will signal an incoherence.

An ontology is inconsistent if an unsatisfiable concept is instantiated. For instance, inconsistency occurs when the same individual is an instance of two disjoint sets.

Example 5 (Inconsistent ontology).

$$SARS\text{-}CoV\text{-}2 : Virus$$
$$SARS\text{-}CoV\text{-}2 : Bacteria$$
$$Virus \sqsubseteq \neg Bacteria$$

We learn that *SARS-CoV-2* is an instance of both *Virus* and *Bacteria* concepts. Then, the axiom (6) states the viruses are disjoint of bacteria. A reasoner on Description Logics will signal an inconsistency.

There are more such antipatterns [18] that trigger both incoherence and inconsistency. Two more examples are:

Antipattern 1 (Onlyness Is Loneliness - OIL)

$$OIL_1 : A \sqsubseteq \forall r.B$$
$$OIL_2 : A \sqsubseteq \forall r.C$$
$$OIL_3 : B \sqsubseteq \neg C$$

Here, concept A can only be linked with role r to B (OIL_1). Next, A can only be linked with role r to C (OIL_2). The set C disjoint with B (OIL_3).

Example 6 (OIL antipattern).

$$OIL_1 : Antibiotics \sqsubseteq \forall kills.Virus$$
$$OIL_2 : Antibiotics \sqsubseteq \forall kills.Bacteria$$
$$OIL_3 : Virus \sqsubseteq \neg Bacteria$$

Antipattern 2 (Universal Existence - UE)

$$UE_1 : A \sqsubseteq \forall r.C$$
$$UE_2 : A \sqsubseteq \exists r.B$$
$$UE_3 : B \sqsubseteq \neg C$$

Axiom UE_2 adds an existential restriction for the concept A conflicting with the existence of an universal restriction for the same concept A in UE_1.

Example 7 (UE antipattern).

$$UE_1 : \quad Antibiotics \sqsubseteq \forall kills.Virus$$
$$UE_2 : Antibiotics \sqsubseteq \exists kills.Bacteria$$
$$UE_3 : \quad\quad Virus \sqsubseteq \neg Bacteria$$

Assume that axioms UE_2 and UE_3 come from a trusted source, while axiom UE_1 from the social web, considered untrusted. By merging three axioms, a reasoner will signal the incoherence. The technical difficulty is that information from social web comes in natural language. The natural language text nedds to be translated into axioms in DL.

3   Analysing Medical Misconceptions on Covid-19 Ontology

Sample medical misconceptions on Covid-19 are collected in Table 2. Organisations such as World Health Organisation provides fact for some myths (denoted f_i in the table). Let for instance the myth m_1 with the formalisation:

$$5G : MobileNetwork \tag{7}$$

$$covid19 : Virus \tag{8}$$

$$spread(5G, covid19) \tag{9}$$

Assume the following formalisation for the corresponding fact f_1:

$$Virus \sqsubseteq \neg(\exists travel.(RadioWaves \sqcup MobileNetworks))$$

The following line of reasoning signals that the ontology is inconsistent:

$$Virus \sqsubseteq \neg(\exists travel.MobileNetworks) \tag{10}$$

$$Virus \sqsubseteq \forall travel.\neg MobileNetworks \tag{11}$$

$$Virus \sqsubseteq \forall spread.\neg MobileNetworks \tag{12}$$

Here we additionally need the subsumption relation between roles: $travel \sqsubseteq spread$. The reasoner finds that the individual $5G$ (which is a mobile network by axiom (7)) that spreads $covid19$ (which is a virus by axiom (8)) is in conflict with the axiom (12).

As a second example, let the myth m_{33} in Table 2: $Covid\text{-}19 \sqsubseteq \forall affects.Elderly$. The corresponding fact f_{33} states: $Covid\text{-}19 \sqsubseteq \forall affects.Person$. The inconsistency is detected because the ABox contains the individual jon affected by Covid-19 and who is not elderly: $affectedBy(jon, Covid\text{-}19)$, respectively $hasAge(jon, 40)$.

We need also some background knowledge:

$$Elderly \sqsubseteq Person \sqcap (> hasAge\ 65) \tag{13}$$

$$affects^- \equiv affectedBy \tag{14}$$

$$Covid\text{-}19 \equiv one\text{-}of(Covid\text{-}19) \tag{15}$$

Based on the definition of *Elderly* and on jon's age, the reasoner learns that *jon* does not belong to that concept ($jon : \neg Elderly$). From the inverse roles $affects^- \equiv affectedBy$, one learns that the virus Covid-19 affects *jon*. Since the set Covid-19 includes only the individual with the same name Covid-19 (defined with the constructor *one-of* for nominals), the reasoner will be able to detect inconsistency. Note that the reasoner used background knowledge (like definition of *Elderly*) to signal conflict. Note also the need of a trusted Covid-19 ontology.

There is ongoing work on formalising knowledge about Covid-19. First, there is the *Coronavirus Infectious Disease Ontology* (CIDO)[2]. Second, the Semantics for Covid-19 Discovery[3] adds semantic annotations to the CORD-19 dataset. The CORD-19 dataset was obtained by automatically analysing publications on Covid-19.

---

[2] http://bioportal.bioontology.org/ontologies/CIDO.
[3] https://github.com/fhircat/CORD-19-on-FHIR.

Table 2. Sample of myths versus facts on Covid-19

	Myth		Fact (according to World Health Organisation)
m_1	5G mobile networks spread Covid-19	f_1	Viruses can not travel on radio waves/mobile networks
m_2	Exposing yourself to the sun or to temperatures higher than 25C degrees prevents the coronavirus disease	f_2	You can catch Covid-19 , no matter how sunny or hot the weather is
m_3	You can not recover from the coronavirus infection	f_3	Most of the people who catch Covid-19 can recover and eliminate the virus from their bodies
m_4	Covid-19 can not be transmitted in areas with hot and humid climates	f_4	Covid-19 can be transmitted in all areas
m_5	Drinking excessive amounts of water can flush out the virus	f_5	Drinking excessive amounts of water can not flush out the virus
m_6	Regularly rinsing your nose with saline help prevent infection with Covid-19	f_6	There is no evidence that regularly rinsing the nose with saline has protected people from infection with Covid-19
m_7	Eating raw ginger counters the coronavirus	f_7	There is no evidence that eating garlic has protected people from the new coronavirus
m_9	The new coronavirus can be spread by Chinese food	f_9	The new coronavirus can not be transmitted through food
m_{10}	Hand dryers are effective in killing the new coronavirus	f_{10}	Hand dryers are not effective in killing the 2019-nCoV
m_{11}	Cold weather and snow can kill the new coronavirus	f_{11}	Cold weather and snow can not kill the new coronavirus
m_{12}	Taking a hot bath prevents the new coronavirus disease	f_{12}	Taking a hot bath will not prevent from catching Covid-19
m_{13}	Ultraviolet disinfection lamp kills the new coronavirus	f_{13}	UV lamps should not be used to sterilize hands or other areas of skin as UV radiation can cause skin irritation
m_{14}	Spraying alcohol or chlorine all over your body kills the new coronavirus	f_{14}	Spraying alcohol or chlorine all over your body will not kill viruses that have already entered your body
m_{15}	Vaccines against pneumonia protect against the new coronavirus	f_{15}	Vaccines against pneumonia, such as pneumococcal vaccine and Haemophilus influenza type B vaccine, do not provide protection against the new coronavirus
m_{16}	Antibiotics are effective in preventing and treating the new coronavirus	f_{16}	Antibiotics do not work against viruses, only bacteria
m_{17}	High dose of Vitamin C heals Covid-19	f_{17}	No supplement cures or prevents disease
m_{19}	The pets transmit the Coronavirus to humans	f_{19}	There are currently no reported cases of people catching the coronavirus from animals
m_{22}	If you can't hold your breath for 10 s, you have a coronavirus disease	f_{22}	You can not confirm coranovirus disease with breathing exercise
m_{24}	Drinking alcohol prevents Covid-19	f_{24}	Drinking alcohol does not protect against Covid-19 and can be dangerous
m_{27}	Eating raw lemon counters coronavirus	f_{27}	No food cures or prevents disease
m_{29}	Zinc supplements lower the risk of contracting Covid	f_{29}	No supplement cures or prevents disease
m_{31}	Vaccines against flu protect against the new coronavirus	f_{31}	Vaccines against flu do not protect against Covid-19
m_{32}	Covid-19 can be transmitted through mosquito	f_{32}	Covid-19 can not be transmitted through mosquito
m_{33}	Covid-19 can affect elderly only	f_{33}	Covid-19 can affect anyone

Using such trusted knowledge sources, the reasoner can detect inconsistencies. Note that the previoulsy exemplified myths were manually translated into DL. Yet, in most of the cases we need automatic translation from natural language to description logic. This task is addressed in the following section.

4 Automatic Conversion of the Covid-19 Myths into Description Logic with FRED

Transforming unstructured text into a formal representation is an important task for the Semantic Web. Several tools are contributing towards this aim: FRED [11], OpenEI [17], controlled languages based approach (e.g. ACE), Framester [10], or KNEWS [2]. For the current task FRED is used, that takes a text an natural language and outputs a formalisation in DL.

FRED is a machine reader for the Semantic Web that relies on Discourse Representation Theory, Frame semantics and Ontology Design Patterns [8,11]. FRED leverages multiple natural language processing (NLP) components by integrating their outputs into a unified result, which is formalised as an RDF/OWL graph. FRED relies on several NLP knowledge resources (see Table 3). VerbNet [19] contains semantic roles and patterns that are structure into a taxonomy. FrameNet [5] introduces frames to describe a situation, state or action. The elements of a frame include: agent, patient, time, location. A frame is usually expressed by verbs or other linguistic constructions, hence all occurrences of frames are formalised in DL n-ary relations, all being instances of some type of event or situation.

We exemplify next, how FRED handles some technicalities like linked data, compositional semantics, plurals, modality and negations with examples related to Covid-19.

4.1 Linked Data and Compositional Semantics

Table 3. FRED's knowledge resources and their prefixes used for the Covid-19 myts ontology

Ontology	Prefix	Name Space
Covid-19 myths	covid19.m:	http://users/utcluj.ro/~groza/Covid-19/covid-19-myths.owl
VerbNet roles	vn.role:	http://www.ontologydesignpatterns.org/ont/vn/abox/role/
VerbNet concepts	vn.data:	http://www.ontologydesignpatterns.org/ont/vn/data/
FrameNet frame	ff:	http://www.ontologydesignpatterns.org/ont/framenet/abox/frame/
FrameNet element	fe:	http://www.ontologydesignpatterns.org/ont/framenet/abox/fe/
Dolce	dul:	http://www.ontologydesignpatterns.org/ont/dul/DUL.owl
WordNet	wn30:	http://www.w3.org/2006/03/wn/wn30/instances/
Boxer	boxer:	http://ontologydesignpatterns.org/ont/boxer/boxer.owl
Boxing	boxing:	http://ontologydesignpatterns.org/ont/boxer/boxing.owl
DBpedia	dbpedia:	http://dbpedia.org/resource/
schema.org	schemaorg:	http://schema.org/

Let the myth "Hand dryers are effective in killing the new coronavirus", whose automatic translation in DL appears in Fig. 1. FRED creates the individual $situation_1$: $Situation$. The role $involves$ from the boxing ontology is used to relate $situation_1$ with the instance $hand\_dryers$:

$$boxing : involves(situation_1, hand\_dryers_1)$$

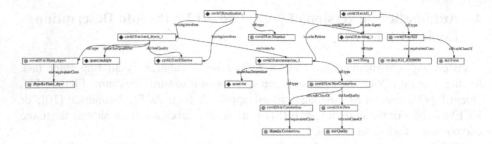

Fig. 1. Translating the myth: "Hand dryers are effective in killing the new coronavirus" in DL

Note that $hand\_dryers_1$ is an instance of the concept $Hand\_dryer$ from the DBpedia. The plural is formalised by the role $hasQuantifier$ from the $Quant$ ontology:

$$q : hasQuantifier(hand\_dryers_1, q : multiple)$$

The information that hand dryers are effective is modeled with the role $hasQuality$ from the $Dolce$ ontology: $dul : hasQuality(hand\_dryers_1, effective)$.

The instance $effective$ is related to the instance $situation_1$ with the role $involves$:

$$boxing : involves(situation_1, effective)$$

The instance $kill_1$ is identified as an instance of the $Kill_{42030000}$ verb from the VerbNet and also as an instance of the $Event$ concept from the $Dolce$ ontology:

$$kill_1 : Kill$$
$$Kill \equiv vn.data : Kill_{42030000}$$
$$Kill \sqsubseteq dul : Event$$

FREDcreates the new complex concept $NewCoronavirus$ that is a subclass of the $Coronavirus$ concept from DBpedia and has quality New:

$$NewCoronavirus \sqsubseteq dbpedia : Coronavirus \sqcap dul : hasQuality.(New)$$
$$New \sqsubseteq dul : Quality$$

Here the concept New is identified as a subclass of the $Quality$ concept from Dolce.

FRED has successfully linked the information from the myth with relevant concepts from DBpedia, Verbnet, or Dolce ontologies. FRED also nicely formalises the plural of "dryers", or uses compositional semantics for "hand dryers" and "new coronavirus".

The instance $kill_1$ has the object $coronavirus_1$ as patient. Note that the $Patient$ role has the semantics from the VerbNet ontology and there is no connection with the term patient as a person suffering from the disease. Also, the instance $kill_1$ has Agent something (i.e. $thing_1$) to which the $situation_1$ is in:

$$in(situation_1, thing_1)$$
$$vn.role : Agent(kill_1, thing_1)$$
$$vn.role : Patient(kill_1, coronavirus_1)$$

The translating meaning would be: "The situation involving hand dryers is in something that kills the new coronavirus".

One possible flaw in the automatic translation from Fig. 1 is that hand dryers are identified as the same individual as coronavirus: $sameAs(hand\_dryers_1, coronavirus_1)$. This might be because the term "are" from the myth ("Hand dryers are ....") which signals a possible definition or equivalence. This flaw requires post-processing. For instance, we can automatically remove all the relations $sameAs$ from the generated Abox.

Actually, the information encapsulated in the given sentence is: "Hand dryers kill coronavirus". Given this simplified version of the myth, FRED outputs the translation in Fig. 2. Here the individual $kill_1$ is correctly linked with the corresponding verb from VerbNet and also identified as an event in Dolce. The instance $kill_1$ has the agent $dryer_1$ and the patient $coronavirus_1$. This corresponds to the intended semantics: hand dryers kill coronavirus.

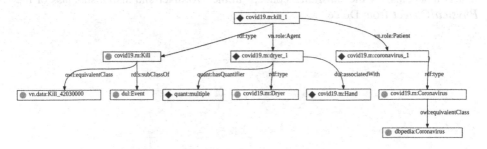

Fig. 2. Translating the simplified sentence: "Hand dryers kill coronavirus"

4.2 Modalities and Disambiguation

Deceptive information makes extensively use of modalities. Since OWL lacks formal constructs to express modality, FRED uses the Modality class from the Boxing ontology: (i) *boxing:Necessary*: e.g., will, must, should; (ii) *boxing:Possible*: e.g. may, might, where *Necessary ⊑ Modality* and *Possible ⊑ Modality*.

Let the following myth related to Covid-19 "You should take vitamin C" (Fig. 3). The frame is formalised around the instance $take_1$. The instance is related to the corresponding verb from the VerbNet and also as an event from the Dolce ontology. The agent of the verb "take" is a person and has the modality *necessary*. The individual C is an instance of concept *Vitamin*.

Although the above formalisation is correct, the following axioms are wrong. First, FRED wrongly links the concept Vitamin from the Covid-19 ontology with the singer Vitamin C from DBpedia. Disambiguation is needed to correctly identify Vitamin C as a subclass of the concept Vitamins from DBpedia. Second, the concept Person from the Covid-19 ontology is linked with Hybrid theory album from the DBpedia, instead of the Person from schema.org. By performing word sense disambiguation (see Fig. 4),

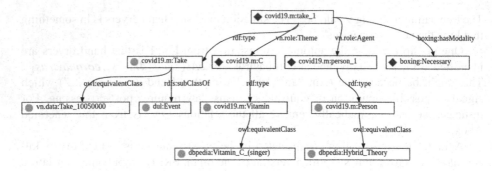

Fig. 3. Translating myths with modalities: "You should take vitamin C"

FRED correctly links the vitamin C concept with the noun *vitamin* from WordNet, that is a subclass of the *substance* concept in the WordNet and also a subclass of the *PhysicalObject* from Dolce.

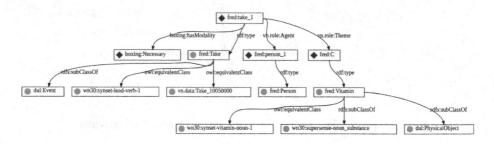

Fig. 4. Word sense disambiguation for: "You should take vitamin C"

4.3 Handling Negation

Most of the myths are in positive form. For instance, in Table 2 only myths m_3 and m_{22} include negation. Let the translation of myth m_3 in Fig. 5. The frame is built around the *recover₁* event (*recover₁* is an instance of *dul : event* concept). Indeed, FRED signals that the event *recover₁*: (i) has truth value false (axiom 16); (ii) has modality "possible" (axiom 17); (iii) has agent a person (axiom 18); (iv) has source an infection of type coronavirus (axiom 19).

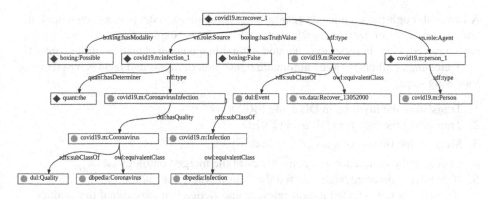

Fig. 5. Formalising negations: "You can not recover from the coronavirus infection"

$$boxing : hasTruthValue(recover_1, boxing : False) \qquad (16)$$
$$boxing : hasModality(recover_1, boxing : Possible) \qquad (17)$$
$$vn.role : Agent(recover_1, person_1) \qquad (18)$$
$$vn.role : Source(recover_1, infection_1) \qquad (19)$$
$$infection_1 : CoronavirusInfection \qquad (20)$$
$$CoronavirusInfection \sqsubseteq dbpedia : Infection \qquad (21)$$
$$\sqcap \exists hasQuality.(dbpedia : Coronavirus)$$

However, FRED does not make any assumption on the impact of negation over logical quantification and scope. The $boxing : false$ is the only element that one can use to signal conflict between positive and negated information.

Aware of these technical challenges (compositional semantics, modalities, disambiguation, negation), our algorithm detecting fake news is built on top of state of the art machine readers.

5   Detecting Fake News by Reasoning in Description Logics

Given a possible myth m_i automatically translated by FRED into a DL ontology $\mathcal{M}_i^{Fred}$, we tackle to fake detection task with two approaches: (1) signal conflict between $\mathcal{M}_i^{Fred}$ and scientific facts f_j also automatically translated by FRED $\mathcal{F}_i^{Fred}$; or (2) signal conflict between $\mathcal{M}_i$ and the Covid-19 ontology engineered by the human agent.

The system architecture appears in Fig. 8. We start with a core ontology for Covid-19. This ontology is enriched with trusted facts on COVID using the FRED converter. Information from untrusted sources is also formalised in DL using FRED. The merged axioms are given to Racer that is able to signal conflicts.

To support the user understanding which knowledge from the ontology is causing incoherences, we use the Racer's explanation capabilities. RacerPro provides explanations for unsatisfiable concepts, for subsumption relationships, and for unsatisfiable

A-boxes through the commands *(check-abox-coherence)*, *(check-tbox-coherence)* and *(check-ontology)* or *(retrieve-with-explanation)*. These explanations are given to an ontology verbalizer in order to generated natural language explanation of the conflict.

Detecting conflicts between automatic translation of myths and facts is based on the following steps:

1. Translating the myth m_i in DL using FRED: $\mathcal{M}_i^{Fred}$
2. Translating the fact f_i in DL using FRED $\mathcal{F}_j^{Fred}$
3. Merging the two ontologies $\mathcal{M}_i^{Fred}$ and $\mathcal{F}_j^{Fred}$
4. Checking the coherence and consistency of the merged ontology $\mathcal{M}\mathcal{F}_{ij}^{Fred}$
5. If conflict is detected, signal a "red flag" for possible fake news
6. If conflict is not detected import relevant knowledge that may signal the conflict
7. Verbalise explanations for the inconsistency

The steps are exemplified on the pair: the myth m_{33}: "Covid-19 can affect elderly only" and the fact f_{33}: "Covid-19 can affect anyone" (Figs. 6 and 7).

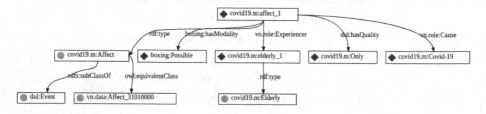

Fig. 6. Step 1: $\mathcal{M}_{33}^{Fred}$ Automatically translating the myth: "Covid-19 can affect elderly only"

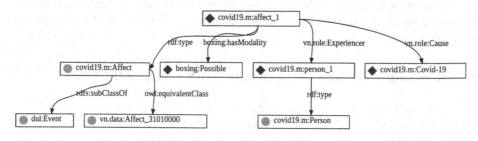

Fig. 7. Step 2: $\mathcal{F}_{33}^{Fred}$ Automatically translating the fact into DL: "Covid-19 can affect anyone".

Figure 9 shows the relevant knowledge used to detect conflict (Note that the prefix for the Covid-19-Myths ontology has been removed). The FRED tool has detected the modality *possible* for the individual $affect_1$. The same instance $affect_1$ has quality *Only*. However, the role *experiencer* relates the instance $affect_1$ with two individuals: $elderly_1$ and $person_1$.

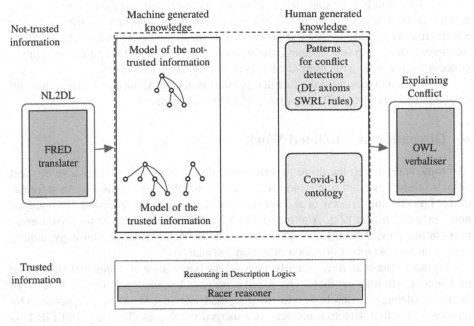

Fig. 8. A Covid-19 ontology is enriched using FRED with trusted facts and medical myths. Racer reasoner is used to detect inconsitencies in the enriched ontology, based on some patterns manually formalised in Description Logics or SWRL

$$Affect \sqsubseteq dul : Event$$
$$affect_1 : Affect$$
$$elderly_1 : Elderly$$
$$person_1 : Person$$
$$boxing : hasModality(affect_1, boxing : Possible)$$
$$dul : hasQuality(affect_1, only)$$
$$vn.role : Cause(affect_1, covid - 19)$$
$$vn.role : Experiencer(affect_1, elderly_1)$$
$$vn.role : Experiencer(affect_1, person_1)$$

Fig. 9. Step 3: Sample of knowledge from the merged ontology $\mathcal{MF}^{Fred}_{(33)(33)}$

$$Elderly \sqsubseteq Person, person_1 : \neg Elderly \qquad (22)$$
$$(?x \; Only \; hasQuality) \wedge (?x \; ?y \; Experiencer) \wedge (?x \; ?z \; Experiencer) \wedge (?y \; Elderly)$$
$$\rightarrow (?z \; Elderly) \qquad (23)$$

Fig. 10. Step 4: Conflict detection based on the pattern $\exists dul : hasQuality.Only$

The axioms in Fig. 10 state that an elderly is a person and that the instance *person*$_1$ is not elderly. The conflict detection pattern is defined as: $\exists dul : hasQuality.Only$ The SWRL rule states that for each individual ?x with the quality *only* that is related via the role *experiencer* with two distinct individuals ?y and ?z (where ?y is an instance of the concept *Elderly*), then the individual ?z is also an instance of *Elderly*.

The conflict comes from the fact that *person*$_1$ is not an instance of *Elderly*, but still he/she is affected by COVID: $experiencer(affect_1, person_1)$.

6 Discussion and Related Work

Our topic is related to the more general issue of fake news [9]. Particular to medical domain, there has been a continuous concern of reliability of online heath information [1]. In this line, Waszak et al. have recently investigated the spread of fake medical news in social media [22]. Amith and Tao have formalised the Vaccine Misinformation Ontology (VAXMO) [3]. VAXMO extends the Misinformation Ontology, aiming to support vaccine misinformation detection and analysis[4].

Teymourlouie et al. have recently analysed the importance of contextual knowledge in detecting ontology conflicts. The added contextual knowledge is applied in [20][5] to the task fo debugging ontologies. In our case, the contextual ontology is represented by patterns of conflict detection between two merged ontologies. The output of FRED is given to the Racer reasoner that detects conflict based on trusted medical source and conflict detection patterns.

FiB system [9] labels news as verified or non-verified. It crawls the Web for similar news to the current one. The retrieved news with high confidence are summarized and shown to the user. The user reads the summaries and figures out which information from the initial new might be fake. I aim a step forwards, that is to automatically identify possible inconsistencies between a given news and the verified medical content.

MERGILO tool reconciles knowledge graphs extracted from text, using graph alignment and word similarity [2]. One application area is to detect knowledge evolution across document versions. To obtain the formalisation of events, MERGILO used both FRED and Framester. Instead of using metrics for compute graph similarity, I used here knowledge patterns to detect conflict.

Enriching ontologies with complex axioms has been given some consideration in literature [12, 14]. The aim would be to bridge the gap between a document-centric and a model-centric view of information [14]. Gyawali et al. have translated text from the SIDP format (i.e. System Installation Design Principle) to axioms in description logic. The proposed system combines an automatically derived lexicon with a hand-written grammar to automatically generated axioms. The core Covid-19 ontology is enriched with axioms generated by FRED fed with facts in natural language. Instead of grammar, I formalised knowledge patterns (e.g. axioms in DL or SWRL rules) to detect conflicts.

Conflict detection depends heavily on the performance of the FRED translator. One can replace FRED by related machine readers tools such as Framester [10] or KNEWS [6]. Framester is a large RDF knowledge graph (about 30 million RDF triples)

---

[4] http://www.violinet.org/vaccineontology/.
[5] https://github.com/teymourlouie/ontodebugger.

acting as a umbrella for FrameNet, WordNet, VerbNet, BabelNet, Predicate Matrix. In contrast to FRED, KNEWS (Knowledge Extraction With Semantics) can be configured to use different external modules as input, but also different output modes (i.e. frame instances, word aligned semantics or first order logic[6]). Frame representation outputs RDF tuples in line with the FrameBase[7] model. First-order logic formulae appear in syntax similar to TPTP (Thousands of Problems for Theorem Provers) and they include WordNet synsets and DBpedia ids as symbols [6].

7 Conclusion

Even if fake news in the health domain is old hat, many technical challenges remain to effective fight against medical myths. This is preliminary work on combining two heavy machineries: natural language understanding and ontology reasoning, aiming to signal fake information related to Covid-19.

References

1. Adams, S.A.: Revisiting the online health information reliability debate in the wake of web 2.0: an inter-disciplinary literature and website review. Int. J. Med. Inf. **79**(6), 391–400 (2010). Special Issue: Information Technology in Health Care: Socio-technical Approaches
2. Alam, M., Recupero, D.R., Mongiovi, M., Gangemi, A., Ristoski, P.: Event-based knowledge reconciliation using frame embeddings and frame similarity. Knowl.-Based Syst. **135**, 192–203 (2017)
3. Amith, M., Tao, C.: Representing vaccine misinformation using ontologies. J. Biomed. Semant. **9**(1), 22 (2018)
4. Baader, F., Calvanese, D., McGuinness, D., Patel-Schneider, P., Nardi, D., et al.: The Description Logic Handbook: Theory Implementation and Applications. Cambridge University Press, Cambridge (2003)
5. Baker, C.F., Fillmore, C.J., Lowe, J.B.: The Berkeley FrameNet project. In: Proceedings of the 17th International Conference on Computational Linguistics-Volume 1, pp. 86–90. Association for Computational Linguistics (1998)
6. Basile, V., Cabrio, E., Schon, C.: KNEWS: using logical and lexical semantics to extract knowledge from natural language (2016)
7. Cinelli, M., et al.: The COVID-19 social media infodemic. arXiv preprint arXiv:2003.05004 (2020)
8. Draicchio, F., Gangemi, A., Presutti, V., Nuzzolese, A.G.: FRED: from natural language text to RDF and OWL in one click. In: Cimiano, P., Fernández, M., Lopez, V., Schlobach, S., Völker, J. (eds.) ESWC 2013. LNCS, vol. 7955, pp. 263–267. Springer, Heidelberg (2013). https://doi.org/10.1007/978-3-642-41242-4_36
9. Figueira, A., Oliveira, L.: The current state of fake news: challenges and opportunities. Procedia Comput. Sci. **121**, 817–825 (2017)
10. Gangemi, A., Alam, M., Asprino, L., Presutti, V., Recupero, D.R.: Framester: a wide coverage linguistic linked data hub. In: Blomqvist, E., Ciancarini, P., Poggi, F., Vitali, F. (eds.) EKAW 2016. LNCS (LNAI), vol. 10024, pp. 239–254. Springer, Cham (2016). https://doi.org/10.1007/978-3-319-49004-5_16

---

[6] https://github.com/valeriobasile/learningbyreading.
[7] http://www.framebase.org/.

11. Gangemi, A., Presutti, V., Reforgiato Recupero, D., Nuzzolese, A.G., Draicchio, F., Mongiovì, M.: Semantic web machine reading with FRED. Semant. Web **8**(6), 873–893 (2017)
12. Georgiu, M., Groza, A.: Ontology enrichment using semantic wikis and design patterns. Studia Universitatis Babes-Bolyai, Informatica **56**(2), 31 (2011)
13. Groza, A.: Detecting fake news for the new coronavirus by reasoning on the COVID-19 ontology. CoRR abs/2004.12330 (2020). https://arxiv.org/abs/2004.12330
14. Gyawali, B., Shimorina, A., Gardent, C., Cruz-Lara, S., Mahfoudh, M.: Mapping natural language to description logic. In: Blomqvist, E., Maynard, D., Gangemi, A., Hoekstra, R., Hitzler, P., Hartig, O. (eds.) ESWC 2017. LNCS, vol. 10249, pp. 273–288. Springer, Cham (2017). https://doi.org/10.1007/978-3-319-58068-5_17
15. Haarslev, V., Hidde, K., Möller, R., Wessel, M.: The RacerPro knowledge representation and reasoning system. Semant. Web **3**(3), 267–277 (2012)
16. Lazer, D.M., et al.: The science of fake news. Science **359**(6380), 1094–1096 (2018)
17. Martinez-Rodriguez, J.L., Lopez-Arevalo, I., Rios-Alvarado, A.B.: OpenIE-based approach for knowledge graph construction from text. Expert Syst. Appl. **113**, 339–355 (2018)
18. Roussey, C., Zamazal, A.: Antipattern detection: how to debug an ontology without a reasoner (2013)
19. Schuler, K.K.: VerbNet: A Broad-Coverage, Comprehensive Verb Lexicon (2005)
20. Teymourlouie, M., Zaeri, A., Nematbakhsh, M., Thimm, M., Staab, S.: Detecting hidden errors in an ontology using contextual knowledge. Expert Syst. Appl. **95**, 312–323 (2018)
21. Vosoughi, S., Roy, D., Aral, S.: The spread of true and false news online. Science **359**(6380), 1146–1151 (2018)
22. Waszak, P.M., Kasprzycka-Waszak, W., Kubanek, A.: The spread of medical fake news in social media-the pilot quantitative study. Health Policy Technol. **7**, 115–118 (2018)

Towards an Ontology of Explanations

Adrian Groza[1]([⊠])(iD) and Mihai Pomarlan[2]

[1] Computer Science Department, Technical University of Cluj-Napoca,
Cluj-Napoca, Romania
adrian.groza@cs.utcluj.ro
[2] Department of Linguistics, University of Bremen, 28359 Bremen, Germany
pomarlan@uni-bremen.de

Abstract. The ability of an agent to explain how it arrived at a decision is important for garnering trust in the agent, understanding its operation, and possibly gaining new and more generalizable knowledge. With AI agents becoming more complex and widespread, there is growing interest in providing them with the ability to explain themselves. Explanations, however, are more than a matter of integrating techniques to approximate machine learning models with more straightforward techniques; explanations are interactive communication acts which must be tailored to the interests of the person seeking explanations. To better represent the communication goals behind an explanation, we propose the "Explanation Interchange Format" ontology, which has several aims. First, it formally describes the communication act of Explanation and its structure based on existing theoretical work on scientific explanations. Second, the ontology enables reasoning to construct explanations, e.g. selecting explanatory structures appropriate to a questioner's interests. We illustrate reasoning on our ontology with some examples.

Keywords: Explanation · Cooperative communication · Epistemic interest of agents

1 Introduction

Natural conversations contain a mix of explanations and arguments, considered distinct [1] and complementary to each other [2,3]. The role of explanation is to increase understanding, while the role of arguments is to establish knowledge. Thus, non-understanding triggers explanatory dialogues, while conflict triggers argumentative dialogues. During natural dialogues, human agents are shifting between cooperative (i.e. explanations) and persuasive dialogues (i.e. arguments) [4].

We are interested in formalizing explanations; speech acts driven by different epistemic interests used to convey or ask for reasons and explanation schemes. The epistemic interest of each answer should match (be the same or subsume) the epistemic interest in the explanation-seeking question.

© Springer Nature Switzerland AG 2022
R. Polovina et al. (Eds.): MOVE 2020, CCIS 1694, pp. 73–85, 2022.
https://doi.org/10.1007/978-3-031-22228-3_4

In line with Vrees et al. [5], we argue the more explicit the question, the more important for explanatory success. We formalise in Description Logics (DLs) several questions and explanation formats. The type of question is used to infer the epistemic interest of the questioner by DL reasoning. Epistemic interests include therapeutic and remedial motivations, prediction, curiosity, and explanations for the unexpected. Once known, a questioner's epistemic interest guides, again via DL reasoning, a selection of an explanation format from several options such as causal or contrastive, and a selection of relevant facts and laws from those known to the explained are to be used in the explanation.

To illustrate our approach, we have considered the following scenario: a questioner wishes to understand why certain assertions may be true (facts) or false (myths) about COVID-19 and its outbreak. An explainer agent, armed with accurate facts, answers the questioner by providing appropriate explanations tailored to the questioner's epistemic interests. The explainer agent uses our ontology to construct and organize its response.

2   Formalizing Explanation

2.1   Explanation as a Cooperative, Interactive Act

Before we proceed to the formal modelling, we would like to delineate the domain we wish to capture briefly. In particular, we need to clarify tour assumptions about the nature of the scenarios we consider.

ExplanatiThe explanation, interactive act happens between two agents, one ding, or at least receiving an explanation, and the other providing this explanation. The nature of social interactions can be very complex; e.g., the agents may not trust each other or even, without one of them knowing, may have adversarial goals.

In this work, we have decided to treat only the simplest case of an explanatory interaction that is fully cooperative and, further, concerns merely the explanation of some fact. Let the two agents be hereafter referred to as Q (the questioner) and E (the explainer). We then make the following assumptions:

- Q trusts E's statements. If E asserts something is a fact, Q will henceforth also believe it is a fact; if E asserts some law, Q will also believe this law actually holds
- E is honest. Given its state of knowledge about the world and its knowledge of Q's knowledge about the world, E will construct, to the best of its ability, accurate explanations that are appropriate for Q's interests.

In subsequent sections, we will use the ontology to set up reasoning queries which, given the state of knowledge of E about the world and Q's knowledge about the world, select what explanatory structures are appropriate and what facts and laws should be marshalled for the explanation. The attitudes that E may have towards a statement or law is simply knowledge of it being true or knowledge of it being false. We will assume, as a simplification, that E has accurate knowledge.

The case of Q is more complicated, in that agent Q may:

- believe in a statement or law; Q may have inaccurate beliefs, and also we will take disbelief (belief in the negation) to be different from lack of belief (no strong commitment either way)
- does not know whether a statement is true or a law holds
- expected a statement to have been true
- desire for a statement to eventually be true.

We will assume that agent E has accurate knowledge about the attitudes of Q to various statements or laws. The kinds of laws we include in our model are:

- causal-deductive: if a set of antecedent statements describe facts that occurred, then the consequent statement describes a fact that occurred as an effect of them
- positive causal factor: if one antecedent fact occurs, usually a consequent fact occurs
- negative causal factor: if one antecedent fact occurs, a consequent statement will usually not become a fact.

Finally, we would like to distinguish between argumentation and explanation. Argumentation would be convincing agent Q to change its belief about some statement. Explanation, meanwhile, is about clarifying a statement Q already and correctly believes in, but which may be connected to other statements to which Q has different attitudes such as expectation or desire.

2.2 Explanation Ontology (EIF)

As described above, the entities that our ontology must characterize are *Statements* and *Laws*, in terms of how individual laws/statements relate to each other and how they are regarded by the agents participating in an explanatory act.

Definition 1. *A* Statement *represents an assertion about the state of the world in which the agents exist and has a truth value. A statement which is true is a* Fact.

As noted previously in Sect. 2.1, we "take the perspective" of the explainer agent E, in that *Facts* are statements that agent E believes to be true (and also, we make a simplifying assumption and presume E has accurate knowledge).

Depending on how agent Q regards it, a statement can be, e.g., *DisputedFact* when Q disbelieves it, *AgreedFact* when Q believes it, *UnknownFact* when Q has no belief either way.

Similarly, other subconcepts of *Statement* cover the other attitudes Q may have such as expectation or desire; respectively, the relevant concepts are *ExpectedStatement, UnexpectedStatement, DesiredStatement, UndesiredStatement,* and

Factual versions, e.g. *UnexpectedFact*, when the statements actually apply to the state of the world. In particular, undesired facts are, at least implicitly, incompatible with some desired state of affairs, and a similar axiom holds for unexpected facts:

$$UndesiredFact \sqsubseteq \exists incompatible.DesiredStatement$$
$$UnexpectedFact \sqsubseteq \exists incompatible.ExpectedStatement$$

Statements may be incompatible if one is true only when the negation of the other is true.

Definition 2. *A* Law *is a pattern of reasoning which offers support for some conclusion based on a set of premises. A* LawInvocation *is an instance of applying a Law to a set of statements used as premises to gather support for a particular statement, the conclusion.*

$$LawInvocation \sqsubseteq Statement \exists hasPremise.Statement$$
$$LawInvocation \sqsubseteq (=1)hasConclusion.Statement(=1)invokes.Law$$

A general syllogistic premise such as "all men are mortal" would be a *Law*. In contrast, the observation that the particular individual Socrates is a man, therefore he should be mortal as per that *Law*, would be a *LawInvocation*.

Definition 3. *An* Explanation *is a LawInvocation in which the conclusion is an AgreedFact, i.e. one known to both agents participating in an explanatory act.*

$$Explanation \equiv LawInvocation \sqcap \forall hasConclusion.AgreedFact$$

Example 1. Let the following example be purely for illustrative purposes. Suppose we have a fact that both Q and E agree on, "shops are required to enforce a 2m distance between customers". Q wants to know why this is so. A possible explanation might invoke the Law that when something is terrible, and doing an action may prevent it; one should do it. In this case, the *LawInvocation* would use the statements "spreading COVID is bad" and "separating people by at least 2m may prevent transmission of COVID between them".

Taxonomies of explanations have been proposed before, though without a formalization in DL. A taxonomy we chose to implement in our ontology is due to Kass and Leakes [6], shown in Fig. 1. However, a deeper axiomatization, beyond mere taxonomy, is ongoing work. What our ontological modelling has prioritized so far has been accounting for the epistemic interests of agent Q– the questioner demanding an explanation – and the explanation's structure.

Definition 4. *By* EpistemicInterest *we mean a description of the interest that the questioner, agent Q, has in a statement.*

$$EpistemicInterest \sqsubseteq (=1)about.Statement$$

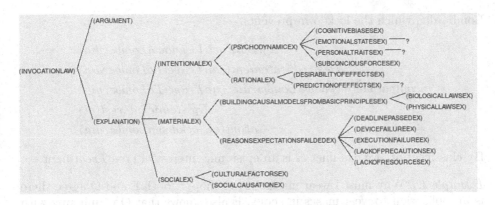

Fig. 1. Kass and Leakes's generic taxonomy of explanations [6] formalised in DL

In particular, we use *EpistemicInterests* to specify the knowledge that agent Q requires from an *Explanation*, and which is captured by the relationship between the fact to be explained, other statements, and the epistemic attitudes that agent Q has towards these other statements.

The default *EpistemicInterest* is mere curiosity; agent Q just wishes to know why a fact is true. However, other possibilities exist.

$$Curiosity \equiv EpistemicInterest \sqcap \forall about.AgreedFact$$
$$Prevention \equiv Curiosity \sqcap \forall about.(\exists incompatible.UndesiredStatement)$$
$$Treatment \equiv Curiosity \sqcap \forall about.(\exists incompatible.DesiredStatement)$$
$$Surprise \equiv Curiosity \sqcap \forall about.UnexpectedStatement$$

We will now give some examples of how to set up an A-box to represent the state of knowledge of agent E, the explainer, about the world and about agent Q's knowledge and epistemic attitudes, and discuss what one might infer about Q's epistemic interests.

Example 2. "Why did the COVID-19 pandemic start in Wuhan?": both agents Q and E about the start of the pandemic, and some epistemic interest exists on the part of Q about this fact.

$$AgreedFact(startedInWuhan)$$
$$EpistemicInterest(ei)$$
$$about(ei, startedInWuhan)$$

Via classification, we can infer that *ei* is an epistemic interest of type *Curiosity*.

Example 3. "Why is Lombardia under lockdown?": both agents Q and E agree that Lombardia is under lockdown. E knows Q would like to be able to travel to

Lombardia, which the lockdown prevents.

$$AgreedFact(lockdownLombardia)$$
$$DesiredStatement(canTravelToLombardia)$$
$$incompatible(lockdownLombardia, canTravelToLombardia)$$
$$EpistemicInterest(ei)$$
$$about(ei, lockdownLombardia)$$

By classification, we can infer ei is an epistemic interest of type $Treatment$.

Example 4. "Why must I wear masks in the shop?": both E and Q agree there is an obligation to wear masks in shops. E also knows that Q is unhappy with this, though not why.

$$AgreedFact(masksCompulsory)$$
$$UndesiredStatement(masksCompulsory)$$
$$EpistemicInterest(ei)$$
$$about(ei, masksCompulsory)$$

By classification, we can infer ei is an epistemic interest of type $Treatment$ even though, unlike the previous example, E doesn't know which statement Q would prefer to be true about the world.

Explanatory pluralism argues that the best form of explanation depends on the kind of question one seeks to answer by the explanation [5], therefore the classification of Q's epistemic interest will allow selecting an appropriate explanation structure. However, before we can illustrate how that is done, we need to formalize what explanation structures there are.

3 Explanatory Structures

3.1 Explanation Formats

Weber et al. [7] present several formats of answers to "why" questions about facts. We formalise some of these formats as concepts in DL and add a few of our own to account for the epistemic interests we have identified.

Definition 5. Causal-deductive nomological (CDN) explanations *invoke a causal law that guarantees the conclusion. All premises must be Facts.*

$$CDN \equiv Explanation \sqcap \forall invokes.CausalLaw \sqcap \forall hasPremise.Fact$$

Definition 6. PositiveCausalFactor explanations *invoke a causal law that usually supports the conclusion. All premises must be Facts.*

$$PCF \equiv Explanation \sqcap \forall hasPremise.Fact \sqcap \forall invokes.(DefaultLaw)$$

Definition 7. CausalFactor explanations *invoke a causal law that usually supports the conclusion. Some premises must be positive causal factors for the conclusion, and all these must be Facts. Some premises may be "negative" causal factors, which may prevent the conclusion in other circumstances.*

$$hasSupportingPremise \sqsubseteq hasPremise$$
$$hasDenyingPremise \sqsubseteq hasPremise$$
$$CF \equiv Explanation \sqcap \forall hasSupportingPremise.Fact \sqcap$$
$$\forall invokes.(ExceptionLaw)$$

The definitions above might suggest that the structure of an explanation is a simple application of a deductive rule where all premises are, in some sense, "atomic" statements about the state of the world. However, it is often helpful to consider more complex structures.

Definition 8. ContrastiveExplanations *are law invocations where some premises are themselves law invocations which have as conclusions the negation of a particular statement. This denied statement is often referred to as the "foil" instead of the Fact that needs explaining.*

$$Contrastive \equiv Explanation \sqcap \exists hasPremise.(LawInvocation \sqcap$$
$$\forall hasConclusion.(\exists negates.Statement))$$

Definition 9. CounterfactualExplanations *are law invocations where some premises are themselves law invocations which have some counterfactuals, i.e. non-Fact statements.*

$$CounterfactualExplanation \equiv Explanation \sqcap$$
$$\exists hasPremise.(\exists incompatible.Fact)$$

3.2 Matching Explanation Format to Epistemic Interest

We follow the erotetic explanation model, which regards explanations as answers to why-questions [8]. On the one hand, we have various explanation types with associated epistemic interests. On the other hand, there are different explanatory-seeking questions with associated epistemic interests. Our task is to match the explanation format (type + interest) to the why-question format (type + epistemic interest).

Supposing agent E has understood the question from agent Q, its task now is to select whatever might address Q's interest from its knowledge. In principle, E might know of many *LawInvocations* to support the *AcceptedFact* in need of an explanation. Still, not necessarily all of them would be appropriate answers for what Q wants to know.

We will define, therefore, a subconcept of *Explanation*, called *AppropriateExplanation*, to capture a few principles we found intuitive about what an explanation should or must contain.

An explanation must address an epistemic interest.

$$AppropriateExplanation \sqsubseteq Explanation \sqcap$$
$$\forall hasConclusion.(\exists about^-.EpistemicInterest)$$

Because of open-world DL semantics, it may be useful to define auxiliary concepts when reasoning about a particular case. E.g., when wanting to explain a fact with epistemic interest ei (an individual), one would be interested in:

$$AppropriateExplanation\_ei \sqsubseteq AppropriateExplanation \sqcap$$
$$\forall hasConclusion.(\exists about^-.\{ei\})$$

Second, suppose the fact to be explained conflicts with expectations or desires. In that case, the explanation should include as a premise a law invocation that, were all of its premises true (and, in case the invoked law admits exceptions, none of these is in effect), then it would support some unfulfilled expectation or desire of agent Q. We will show how to capture part of this requirement for epistemic interest Surprise; the situation is similar for Treatment.

$$hasConclusion \circ about^- \sqsubseteq callsFor \tag{1}$$
$$hasConclusion \circ incompatible \circ about^- \sqsubseteq addresses \tag{2}$$
$$AppropriateExplanation \sqcap \exists callsFor.Surprise \sqsubseteq \tag{3}$$
$$\exists hasPremise.(LawInvocation \sqcap$$
$$\exists hasConclusion.ExpectedStatement \sqcap$$
$$\exists addresses.Surprise)$$

Because of global restrictions on OWL-DL to maintain decidability, the axiom above does not guarantee that the two Surprise individuals will be the same. This can be addressed when setting up a particular reasoning problem, for example, by requiring that there exists a unique *EpistemicInterest* individual (i.e., subsuming the *EpistemicInterest* class to the class containing a single individual ei).

Next, suppose an appropriate explanation hasa, as a premise, a law invocation that would support a desired but untrue statement. In that case, this law invocation must either not make use of undesired statements as premises or have as premise another law invocation proving two desired statements of agent Q as inconsistent.

$$InconsistentPair \equiv Statement \sqcap (= 2)hasMember.Statement$$
$$IncDesProof \equiv LawInvocation \sqcap$$
$$\exists hasConclusion.(InconsistentPair \sqcap$$
$$\forall hasMember.DesiredStatement)$$
$$ConvenientProof \equiv LawInvocation \sqcap \forall hasPremise.DesiredStatement$$
$$DesirableProof \equiv LawInvocation \sqcap \exists hasConclusion.DesiredStatement$$

$$ConflictProof \equiv DesirableProof \sqcap (\neg ConsDesProof)$$
$$ConsDesProof \equiv ConvenientProof \sqcup$$
$$(DesirableProof \sqcap \exists hasPremise.IncDesProof)$$
$$AgreeableExplanation \sqsubseteq \neg\exists hasPremise.ConflictProof$$

The case of an appropriate explanation that either explains an undesired fact, or has as a premise a law invocation supporting an undesired statement, is similar. Law invocations that help undesired information by using desired statements without proving agent Q's desires to be inconsistent are not allowed inappropriate explanations. These final two principles help maintain an explanation that either conforms to Q's desires or communicates to Q that some of its desires are inconsistent.

4 Putting it All Together: Selecting an Explanation

We consider a couple of complete examples of an explanation request scenario from some agent Q, answered based on available knowledge by an agent E.[1]

Suppose an agent, the questioner Q, wishes to know *"why is hydroxychloroquine not officially endorsed as a COVID-19 cure"*. This suggests there are two statements agent Q is pondering: a Fact that hydroxychloroquine is not recognized as a cure and an expectation that it should be.

$$AgreedFact(hoclNotRecognized)$$
$$ExpectedStatement(hoclRecognized)$$
$$incompatible(hoclRecognized, hoclNotRecognized)$$
$$EpistemicInterest(ei)$$
$$about(ei, hoclNotRecognized)$$

This would allow agent E to use DL classification reasoning on the individual *ei*, thus recognising Q's epistemic interest as *Surprise*. Suppose then that, either from some knowledge base or other modules, E knows several facts about the world that it might communicate to Q.

These facts would boil down to "no tests show the efficacy of hydroxychloroquine against COVID-19, and a drug needs to be tested well before it is approved" However, how these facts are represented matters when, e.g., E wants to express an explanation.

$$EpistemicInterest \sqsubseteq \{ei\}$$
$$AgreedFact(noClinicalTrials)$$
$$Statement(clinicalTrials)$$
$$incompatible(clinicalTrials, noClinicalTrials)$$
$$LawInvocation(simpleAssertion)$$

---

[1] The ontology is available at http://users.utcluj.ro/~agroza/projects/eif/eif.owl.

$$LawInvocation(referToProcess)$$
$$LawInvocation(vettingProcess)$$
$$hasPremise(simpleAssertion, noClinicalTrials)$$
$$hasConclusion(simpleAssertion, hoclNotRecognized)$$
$$hasPremise(referToProcess, noClinicalTrials)$$
$$hasPremise(referToProcess, vettingProcess)$$
$$hasConclusion(referToProcess, hoclNotRecognized)$$
$$hasPremise(vettingProcess, clinicalTrials)$$
$$hasConclusion(vettingProcess, hoclRecognized)$$

(Not represented: some closure axioms on the number of *hasPremise* properties for the individual law invocations, ensuring that the invocations will use only the explicitly stated premises).

DL reasoning can then be used to select which of the statements of law invocations E knows are also appropriate explanations that it can communicate to Q. Note that we added an additional hypothesis of the uniqueness of epistemic interest.

In this case, an appropriate explanation is *referToProcess* because it also explains when the expected statement would be true. Arguably, this information is not always necessary because humans can fill in the gaps based on their knowledge and ***gricean**** conversational assumptions. Still, we would argue that it is good if agent E has an automated way of detecting which information would be relevant for Q, who may not have all the knowledge needed to fill in the gaps.

This situation is made more evident by the following example. Suppose agent Q wants there to be a vaccine for COVID-19 available when in fact, this is not so. Suppose that Q is disappointed by the lengthy vaccine development process and that Q would like the vaccine to be safe. We assume E has this information about Q. In this case, agent E could point out a vaccine would become available once we followed the lengthy vaccine development process. This explanation, however, will likely not satisfy Q, who finds a long process undesirable anyway, and would be flagged as inappropriate by our axiomatization. In contrast, an explanation in which E asserts both that a lengthy process will lead to a vaccine, that the long process is needed for safety, and that, therefore, Q's desires are inconsistent would at least be considered by our axiomatization as more appropriate. It might still not satisfy Q, but it will give them a better picture of the more relevant problem for Q's attitudes.

5   Discussion and Related Work

Classifying explanations has been given some consideration in literature, by restricting to particular explanations for a specific task: ontology mapping [9], black-box machine learning algorithms [10], medical decisions [11], or even deceptive or rebellious explanations [12] within a disaster scenario.

The explanation ontology developed by Su et al. has been integrated into the agent platform Agora [9]. Explanations strategies are also introduced to refer to the source of explanations (e.g. WordNet) or explanation ranking. Explanations are used in the context of ontology mapping and classified into four types: similar concept, narrow, broader, and related concept. Since the four types of explanations are task-oriented (i.e. ontology mapping), they are included in our general approach to explaining AI.

Taxonomies of explainability techniques for machine learning (ML) has recently been proposed [10,13]. Arrieta et al. have identified the following eight explanations used by ML practitioners: simplification, local, text, visual feature relevance, architecture modification, explanation by example, and transparent models. Bouter has proposed a taxonomy of four types of explanation: (i) explanation by explainable proxy; (ii) outcome explanation; (iii) model inspection; or (iv) a transparent box [10]. For instance, the following techniques in ML are included in the *OutcomeExplanation* concept: feature importance, prototype selection, salience map or local explanation. Here, decision trees or classification rules are included in the concept of *LocalExplanation*.

Sassoon et al. [11] has proposed four explanation templates in the medical domain: (i) treatment T should be considered as it promotes goal G, given patient facts F; (ii) treatment T should not be considered as it was not effective for this patient in the past; (iii) treatment T should not be considered as it caused side effects for this patient in the past; (iv) treatment T should not be considered as patient fact $f_i \in F$ is a counter-indication to its use. Our more generic epistemic interest *Treatment* could be used to formalise these particular explanations.

Wright et al. have investigated which reasoning models are required to generate explanations of a deceptive or rebellious nature [12]. In the context of an ecological disaster scenario, Person and Person consider explanations such as explanation with lying, explanation that withholds information, half-truth explanation, cynical explanation, or explanation with disobedience, protest-based explanation [12]. For our scenario, a protest-based explanation could refer to a healthcare worker encountering a hazardous situation and explaining their stopping action to the coordinator agent: "I will not enter into the hospital until Personal Protective Equipment is provided".

The taxonomy of explanations proposed by Kass and Leake [6] contains intentional, material, and social descriptions at the top level. Intentional explanations show 1) why an agent chose to act in a way different from what the explainer expected (in the case of rational decision-making) or 2) signals the unconscious psychodynamic factors that influence the behavior of a human agent. Material explanations refer to material properties of the world, and they are built up from causal chains based on physical laws for instance. Social explanations refer to stereotyped group behavior.

Explanations [14] have not been formalized to the same abstract level as argumentation [8]. For instance, the World Wide Argumentative Web (WWAW) aims to link and structure arguments posted on the web and relies on the Argument Interchange Format (AIF) ontology [15] that provides a generic mechanism for exchanging argument resources using description logics. However, with the recent development of explainable artificial intelligence (XAI) [16], computational models of explanation can bridge the gap between the available models of arguments.

6   Conclusion

We view the ontology of explanations as a necessary first step toward better descriptions of a software agent to a human agent. This ontology gives agents the reasoning tools they need to: i) infer the epistemic interests of the other party; ii) match the preferred structure of explanation to the given why-question.

The ontology aims to map out the territory of the explanation so that we (and other researchers) can explore it more deeply in the future. One can employ hybrid reasoning instead of description logic to operationalise explanation strategies through preference modelling and contextualisation.

Acknowledgment. A. Groza is partially supported by the grant PN-III-P2-2.1-PED-2021-2709, 2022-2024, UEFSCDI.

References

1. Mayes, G.R.: Resisting explanation. Argumentation **14**, 361–380 (2000). https://doi.org/10.1023/A:1007897325732
2. Arioua, A., Buche, P., Croitoru, M.: Explanatory dialogues with argumentative faculties over inconsistent knowledge bases. Expert Syst. Appl. **80**, 244–262 (2017)
3. Bex, F., Walton, D.: Combining explanation and argumentation in dialogue. Argument Comput. **7**(1), 55–68 (2016)
4. Groza, A.: Interleaved argumentation and explanation in dialog. In: Urbański, M., Tomasz Skura, P., (ed.) Reasoning: Logic, Cognition, Games. College Publications (2020)
5. De Vreese, L., Weber, E., Van Bouwel, J.: Explanatory pluralism in the medical sciences: theory and practice. Theor. Med. Bioeth. **31**(5), 371–390 (2010). https://doi.org/10.1007/s11017-010-9156-7
6. Kass, A., Leake, D.: Types of explanations. Technical report, Yale Univ New Haven CT Dept of Computer Science (1987)
7. Weber, E., Van Bouwel, J., De Vreese, L.: Scientific Explanation. Springer, Heidelberg (2013). https://doi.org/10.1007/978-94-007-6446-0.pdf
8. Pearl, J., Mackenzie, D.: The Book of Why: The New Science of Cause and Effect. Basic Books, New York (2018)
9. Su, X., Matskin, M., Rao, J.: Implementing explanation ontology for agent system. In: Proceedings IEEE/WIC International Conference on Web Intelligence (WI 2003), pp. 330–336. IEEE (2003)
10. Bouter, C.: Constructing an explanation ontology for the communication and combination of partial explanations in a federated knowledge environment. Master's thesis, Utrecht University (2019)

11. Sassoon, I., Kökciyan, N., Sklar, E., Parsons, S.: Explainable argumentation for wellness consultation. In: Calvaresi, D., Najjar, A., Schumacher, M., Främling, K. (eds.) EXTRAAMAS 2019. LNCS (LNAI), vol. 11763, pp. 186–202. Springer, Cham (2019). https://doi.org/10.1007/978-3-030-30391-4_11
12. Wright, B., Roberts, M.T., Aha, D.W., Brumback, B.: When agents talk back: rebellious explanations. Technical report, Navy Center for Applied Research and Artificial Intelligence (2019)
13. Arrieta, A.B., et al.: Explainable artificial intelligence (XAI): concepts, taxonomies, opportunities and challenges toward responsible AI. Inf. Fusion **58**, 82–115 (2020)
14. Miller, T.: Explanation in artificial intelligence: insights from the social sciences. Artif. Intell. **267**, 1–38 (2018)
15. Rahwan, I.: Mass argumentation and the semantic web. J. Web Semant. **6**(1), 29–37 (2008)
16. Gunning, D.: Explainable artificial intelligence (XAI). Defense Advanced Research Projects Agency (DARPA), nd Web **2** (2017)

Formal, Measurable Ontologies for Worldviews

David Jakobsen[1]($\boxtimes$) (iD) and Simon Graf[2]

[1] Aalborg University, Aalborg, Denmark
davker@hum.aau.dk
[2] Tallin, Estonia

Abstract. Formal ontology has been used in a variety of projects in the humanities. Most interesting from our perspective is the work carried out to develop an ontology of Wittgenstein's *Nachlass* since we want to take the first steps toward an ontology for the work of Arthur Norman Prior. We go through some of Prior's early attempts to describe the logic involved in reformed theology. In *The Analogy of Faith* (1940), we suggest that Prior developed a knowledge graph of what he called "the logic of the bible." We call this the Interpretative Community Graph and suggest that it can be adapted to a Prior Community Graph and used to develop a formal ontology of A.N. Prior's Nachlass. We argue that this graph suggests a deeper conceptual structure concerning object properties for the ontology than the one provided by the Wittgenstein ontology. Based on this, we demonstrate how this deeper conceptual structure can be used to derive conclusions concerning philosophical views affirmed by Prior and the philosophers relevant to his work. Finally, we suggest that the project of providing a formal ontology for A.N. Prior could be used to develop formal ontologies for theology and systems of beliefs.

Keywords: A.N. Prior · Formal ontology · Interpretative community graph

1 Introduction

The success of formal ontologies is not limited to biomedicine; they have also found their way into social media (Gonçalves et al. 2019 [3]), the digital humanities (Farrar et al. 2002 [2]), and philosophical projects like The Wittgenstein Ontology (Pichler and Zöllner-Weber 2013 [1]) and The Internet Philosophy Ontology Project (InPho).[1] Notable successes have come from these efforts, such as the Wittgenstein Source[2] and the Wittgenstein Explorer,[3] which have made it possible to carry out advanced searches in Wittgenstein's *Nachlass*. Work has also begun on gaining a deeper understanding of the internet resources for Arthur Norman Prior's Nachlass. Engerer and Albretsen (2017 [4]) have provided a formal description of the entities involved in the Prior Internet Resources, constituting an essential first step toward a Prior ontology. Somewhat surprisingly, Prior's early work points toward the possibility of a Prior knowledge graph as part of a formal

---

[1] https://www.inphoproject.org/.
[2] http://www.wittgensteinsource.org/.
[3] http://wab.uib.no/sfb/.

© Springer Nature Switzerland AG 2022
R. Polovina et al. (Eds.): MOVE 2020, CCIS 1694, pp. 86–97, 2022.
https://doi.org/10.1007/978-3-031-22228-3_5

ontology for Prior's Nachlass. It turns out that Prior in the early 1940s, worked on describing what he termed "the logic of the Bible" (Prior 1940 [5]) and "the logic of Calvinism" (Prior 2014 [6]). Prior's work in these two areas should not be understood as a claim that Calvinism constitutes an a priori given and necessarily true system; instead, it is a formalization of the reformed worldview. Prior's analysis suggests that the reformed worldview constitutes an Interpretative Community Graph and can easily be adapted to a knowledge graph of Prior's Nachlass.

Furthermore, the theological backdrop to such an ontology follows the tenets of A.N Prior's work. It also points to what could constitute a natural development of the recent community of analytic philosophers who work with analytic theology. We sketch here such a proposal based on a deeper understanding of Prior's early work on the logic of the Bible and the logic of Calvinism. This is, to some, a highly peculiar combination of study: theology on the one hand, ripe with controversy and often appearing to depend on a subjective stance, and formal ontology on the other, with its rigid logical definitions. However, as we seek to demonstrate, developments in twentieth-century analytic philosophy have given rise to branches of theology with logical, analytic investigations at the center.

Furthermore, as we demonstrate, A.N. Prior's early work on the logic of the Bible reveals a way in which the subjective aspects of theology do not prohibit a logical or formal treatment of theology. Hence, we can look at formal ontologies when rightly construed to handle and measure worldviews. We seek to demonstrate the relevance of this view by applying what we call the Interpretative Community Graph to the development of an ontology for Prior studies.

1.1 Analytic Theology

It is a peculiar fact that from 1970 onward, analytic philosophy has seen a renaissance of analytic theology comparable only to the attention theology received from logic by medieval scholars such as Ockham and Aquinas (Wolterstorff 2009 [7]). This is a surprising development considering the anti-metaphysical tenets that dominated analytic philosophy between 1930 and 1950. Indeed, one of the primary axioms of analytic philosophy was a paradigmatic adherence to what Bertrand Russell called a "fundamental principle in the analysis of propositions,"; namely, that understandable propositions "must be composed wholly of constituents with which we are acquainted" (Russell 1912 [8]). The logical positivism that dominated analytic philosophy before 1950 was deeply inspired by this view, with detrimental effects on the place given to philosophy and metaphysics. A.N. Prior was, however, convinced that this narrow understanding of analysis was not a good thing for analytic philosophy and, with his discovery of the logic of tenses, he demonstrated that philosophy did not have to leave the metaphysics of time to philosophers who, like Bergson did not model philosophy on formal logic. For Prior, logic and philosophy did not have to be kept in separate compartments but could enrich one another. This conviction led to the discovery of tense logic, which in 1954 was considered an impossibility. In *Past, Present and Future* (1967 [10]), his major work on tense logic, Prior spells out a vision for how logic and metaphysics can work together:

The logician must be somewhat like a lawyer—not in Toulmin's sense, that of reasoning less rigorously than a mathematician—but in the sense that he is there to give the metaphysician, perhaps even the physicist, the tense logic that he wants, provided that it be consistent. He must tell his client what the consequences of a given a choice will be … and what alternatives are open to him, but I doubt whether he can, qua logician, do more. (Prior A. N., 1967, p. 59 [10])

Prior's development of tense logic forced logicians to come clean with the metaphysical decisions that inform the decision to use a tenseless or tensed logic. To Prior, it is evident that what ultimately decides one's position on such ontological matters involves subjectivity. For the believer, it is a choice of the soul, but the one who disagrees will see it as mere prejudice. Prior demonstrated that logical analysis could be carried out on tenses and theological problems such as God's foreknowledge and human freedom (Prior 1962). The work begun by Prior and other philosophers like Plantinga and Adams on the analysis of theological issues within analytic philosophy served as the starting points of what is now known as analytic theology. The emergence of analytic theology should encourage those who think formal ontology should not be restricted to biomedicine but also apply to worldview analysis in the humanities. When Russell described the tradition of analytic philosophy in 1945, he had given up all hope that logical investigations and discussions could be made in theology because it had been radically changed through the influence of continental philosophers such as Jean-Jacques Rousseau. Reflection on that influence, however, made him romanticize how much better it would have been to discuss theology with medieval theologians rather than their modern counterparts. He would "prefer the ontological argument … and the rest of the old stock-in-trade, to the sentimental illogicality that has sprung from Rousseau because" contrary to modern theology, it was possible to demonstrate whether the medieval philosophy of Thomas Aquinas was valid (Russell 1945, 694 [9]). It is indeed a peculiar turn of events, which Russell would never have anticipated that barely 25 years later, theology came rushing into the analytic philosophy that Russell himself had founded. Why should we not anticipate the same about formal ontology? The first step in that direction could be a study of Prior's early considerations on what he termed the logic of the Bible and the logic of Calvinism, a study in which the present article takes the first steps.

1.2 The Logic of Reformed Theology

In *The Analogy of Faith* (1940 [5]), Prior investigates a doctrine that the reformers argued was essential to interpreting Scripture correctly. The doctrine is best described as an exegetical principle concerned with how essential reformers' doctrines depend upon a proper reformed reading of the Bible. As such, it can be labeled a meta-doctrine, motivated by the idea of *sola scriptura*. The reformers differed fundamentally from the Catholic Church in their understanding of the unique authority of Scripture. The analogy of faith is a principle claimed to flow from Scripture and from which the particular reformed doctrines could be shown to follow. It claimed that "the only authoritative interpreter of the Scripture was the same Spirit by whose inspiration they were written' (Prior 1940 [5]). The question, of course, is how to settle on the Spirit's interpretation of Scripture. Since all individuals can claim that they interpret Scripture following the analogy of faith by the Spirit, interpretation collapses into subjectivism. This is fundamentally a charge still leveled at the principle; it is ultimately surrendered to subjectivity. Prior was aware that the reformers denied this and quoted several reformers to that effect. He was furthermore convinced that by turning to the theology of the Swiss theologian Karl Barth (1886–1968), one could refute the allegation of subjectivism. What is required, Prior argues, is to give up the idea that the individual believer is the proper reader of Scripture and that "[...] the subject of the act of faith expressed in the Apostle's Creed 'is the *Church*, and therefore not the individual as such'" (Prior 1940 [5]). Subjectivity is thus made relative to the right community, namely the Church to which the author of Scripture gives the proper interpretation of Scripture. Prior also pointed out, however, that in addition to the relative-subjective element, the analogy of the faith also has an objective sense; namely the idea, also central to the reformers, that "what God says to us in one part of the Bible is to be interpreted by what He says in another, and cannot ultimately stand in contradiction to itself" (Prior 1940 [5]). Here Prior (1940 [5]) quotes a reply by John Knox to Queen Mary:

> "The Word of God is plain, and if any obscurity appears in a place the Holy Spirit, who is never contrary to Himself, explains the same more clearly in other places," and this "[...] comparison of Scripture with Scripture was what the Reformers understood by the 'analogy of the faith'" (Prior 1940 [5]).

This idea of an interplay between subjective and objective elements in communities' interpretation of a canonical text about canonical beliefs is summarized by Prior as follows:

> There is surely no higher test than this submission to "the logic of the Word of God" of whether a man's thought has really grown out of the Bible, and is not merely "dragging it in" to support ideas that come from a different source. Knox says in effect, "It was not from my own speculations, but from the Bible—and above all from the story of the Crucifixion—that I learned of God's power to bring good out of evil, and where should I learn how to draw out the practical bearings of this truth—where should I learn to 'interpret' *this* 'Biblical' truth, and not some quite different speculative one—if not from the Bible too?" (Prior 1940, Section III [5])

The analogy of faith is thus about "catching the drift" or general strain of Scripture rather than that of particular passages. The Bible should not be viewed as a collection of tenets and precepts based on which any deduction whatever may be made: "We must learn how the Bible itself makes its deductions and see that our own argumentation moves in the same way." (Prior 1940, Section II [5]). It is possible to generalize Prior's thoughts about what we call the interpretative community, which we will focus on in the following through the notion of 'Canon.' Doing this will help us develop a formal ontology for the Prior community.

2   The Interpretative Community Graph

Prior's work on the reformed community's "logic," which Prior termed "the logic of the word of God," is really a knowledge graph about how a particular community holds views (beliefs) about an objective canon that affirms various beliefs. For the reformed, this disclosure is all one can have, given their belief in *sola scriptura* taken in the extreme sense. No higher or lower or more foundational logic can be said to give logic as proof, so logic is about how Scripture, Community, and Confession form a tripartite structure: Interpreter, Canon, and Canon of Belief (Fig. 1).

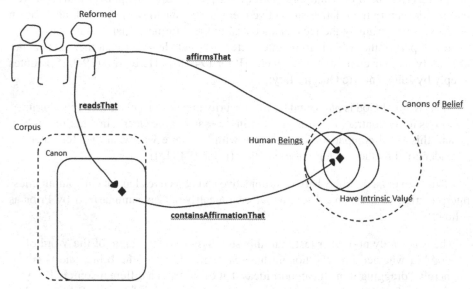

Fig. 1. The Interpretative Community Graph, where communities of believers, in this case, reformed, affirm Canons of Belief, based on the **containsAffirmationThat** relations between Canon and various propositions.

It is essential to point out that such an ontology of the reformed view does not tell us how the reformed *interpret* a given Canon in a Corpus of text. It tells us *what they read* and what the Canon confirms. It is a meta-consideration outside the ontology that this is how a Reformed believer interprets matters. The Interpreter, in Prior's Reformed Knowledgebase, **believesThat** some particular belief *p*, say, "Paula is a human being," and therefore believes that human beings have intrinsic values. Here it is suggested that moral values are part of a taxonomy of beliefs in some Canon of Belief. She does not, however, find this out of thin air in a subjective sense. She has come to believe such things in various ways. Still, as a Reformed adherent, she will likely connect the idea of having an intrinsic value with the idea in Christianity that human beings are created in the image of God. This she has found in the Canon. Thus the subjective—the belief element—is connected to a Canon where she **readsThat** human beings have intrinsic value as being created in the image of God; she thus takes it that Canon **affirmsThat** human beings have intrinsic value. In that sense, we need to establish a logical connection between the relations of **believesThat**, **readsThat**, and **affirmsThat**, which we do below when we turn to the Prior Community Graph. However, we need a taxonomy of Canons of Belief and Interpreters and Canons. In addition, we need to be able to represent naturalists like Michael Ruse, who denies the existence of objective moral values:

> Morality is a biological adaptation no less than are hands and feet, and teeth. Considered as a rationally justifiable set of claims about an objective something, ethics is illusory. I appreciate that when somebody says, "Love thy neighbor as thyself," they think they are referring above and beyond themselves. Nevertheless, such reference is truly without foundation. Morality is just an aid to survival and reproduction ... and any deeper meaning is illusory. (Ruse 1989, 262 [12])

Ruse appears to **believeThat** particular human beings like Paula. At the same time, they are human beings and do not have intrinsic value since evolution only provides aid to survival or reproduction value. In other words, how Ruse reads nature does not affirm such a thing as intrinsic value but only of instrumental value (aids to survival and reproduction). Debating Ruse, the Reformed would have to debate how to read nature and whether there is anything but nature that is a relevant source of knowledge for settling whether or not there are objective moral values (Fig. 2).

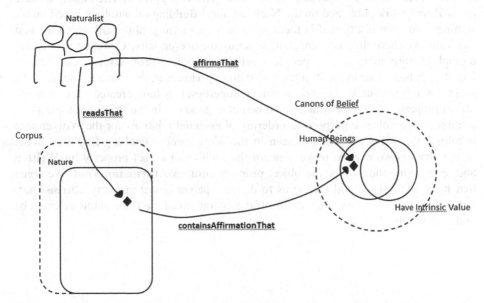

Fig. 2. The Interpretative Community graph, where communities of believers, in this case, naturalists, affirm Canons of Belief based on the **containsAffirmationThat** relations between nature and various propositions.

Perhaps some would object here that an atheist does not **readsThat** some proposition is the case in nature but **observesThat** some fact is the case. To this, there are two things to say. First, it is a minor problem that we have not examined. Second, an argument could be given for the view that even our observations of facts in nature need some idea of transparent representation of those facts in our minds. Even theories of direct awareness cannot deny the role of the mind in mediating the external world to our consciousness of it. Such philosophical discussion lies beyond the scope of this article, so it has been kept simple in the graph. Here we focus more narrowly on the community of researchers of A.N. Prior's authorship and adjust the graph with an eye on the Wittgenstein ontology to set up a deep conceptual structure that allows for deductions as to what Prior and contemporary philosophers affirmed through their authorship.

3   Prior Community Ontology

In our research on Prior, we have also considered making a formal ontology that focuses on his Nachlass, letters, unpublished papers, and notes. Some of that material is at the Bodleian Library and some at Aalborg University. A password-protected website called the Virtual Lab[4] provides researchers with access to digital scans of the various archives at Oxford and Aalborg to participate in the transcription process. The goal is to have all of Prior's work published on the Nachlass site.[5] Building an ontology based on his writings and what is affirmed in them remains a long-term goal toward which the first steps are taken here. To reach that goal, we adjust the Interpretative Community Graph to a graph of affirmations on how people in articles or books affirm various views.[6] Much has already been done in the Wittgenstein ontology. However, they have not suggested a graph for how to connect the various object properties; they have created a taxonomy of object properties, many of which could be put to good use in the Prior ontology. Their arrangement involves a purposeful ordering of essential relations for the Wittgenstein ontology, the utility of which is seen in the Wittgenstein Ontology Explorer. Some of the changes we wish to make concern the addition of object property **hasWritten** and, concerning the corpus, the object property **containsAffirmationThat**. We argue that these additions would enable us to define a parent object property **affirmsThat,** with which we believe exciting and fruitful explorations of the Prior ontology could be undertaken (Fig. 3).

---

[4] Research.prior.aau.dk.

[5] Nachlass.prior.aau.dk.

[6] We focus on affirmations but would ultimately also be interested in deducing or adding logical relations to the ontology which would make queries into disagreements possible. We are grateful to the helpful comment by one of the reviewers for pointing this importance out.

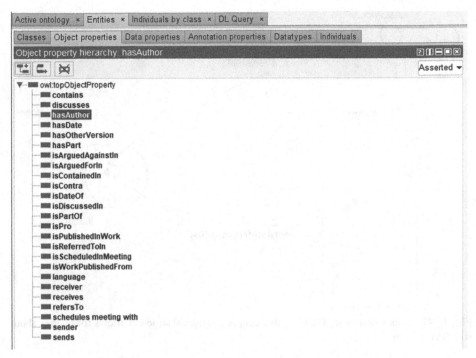

Fig. 3. The ontology of object properties used in the Wittgenstein ontology.

To achieve the possibility of carrying out a deeper conceptual exploration in line with the last community graph, we suggest an ordering of the object properties with greater conceptual depth. We suggest the Class of Persons, where we find authors such as Prior, Strawson, and Quine. These authors are chosen not only because they are some of the many philosophers with whom Prior engaged but also because their mutual engagement on whether formal logic must be tenseless is pivotal to Prior's work. Between the class of authors and particular books, letters, or articles, we have employed a **hasWritten** object property. For instance, we have:

ArthurNormanPrior **hasWritten** some SyntaxOfTimeDistinction.

"The Syntax of Time Distinctions," written by Prior in 1958, discusses Quine's and Strawson's views on whether formal logic can be tensed. Quine (1953 [13]) and Strawson (1952 [14]) agreed that it could not, but whereas Strawson perceived that as a limitation to the scope of formal logic, Quine saw it as a virtue. Thus, we have:
SyntaxOfTimeDistinction **containAffirmationThat** some FormalLogicCanBe Tensed.

We want a conceptual ordering of the object properties that allow for the conclusion:
ArthurNormanPrior **affirmsThat** some FormalLogicCanBeTensed.

The Prior Community Graph shown in Fig. 4 demonstrates how these relations are connected logically.

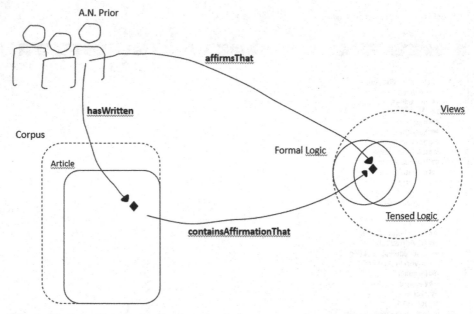

Fig. 4. The Prior Community Graph with a deeper conceptual structure allows for queries about what Prior affirms.

To achieve a deeper conceptual structure in which we can deduce what Prior affirms, we must make **hasWritten** and **containsAffirmationThat** subordinate relations under **affirmsThat. In contrast, affirmsThat** must be conceived of as a transitive relation (see Fig. 5). An author in the ontology affirms a proposition of which his writing contains affirmation.

Fig. 5. The object properties of the Prior Community Graph with a deep conceptual structure allow for conclusions on what authors affirm based on their writings and what affirmations these contain.

These transitive relations enable logical inferences between authors, texts, and views in the Prior Ontology. In formal ontology, computerized reasoners provide these inferences and the justifications for those inferences. This is demonstrated in the figures below by using the query function in Protégé, the ontology editor software (Fig. 6).

DL query:

Query (class expression)

affirmsThat some 'Formal logic can be tensed'

Execute   Add to ontology

Query results

Subclasses (3 of 3)

● Arthur Norman Prior

● Syntax of Time Distinctions

Fig. 6. Example of a query within the Prior Ontology in Protégé, the ontology editor software.

The explanation tool in Protégé explains why Arthur Norman Prior in "The Syntax of Time Distinctions" affirms that formal logic can be tensed, as Fig. 7 shows. It is, of course, a slight natural language weakness that the syntax of time distinctions is among the entities that affirm something, but it is not far away from natural language to say some book that argues that so and so is the case.

◀️ Explanation for 'Arthur Norman Prior' SubClassOf affirmsThat some 'Formal logic can be tensed'   ✕

● Show regular justifications   ● All justifications
○ Show laconic justifications   ○ Limit justifications to

Explanation 1 ☐ Display laconic explanation

Explanation for: 'Arthur Norman Prior' SubClassOf affirmsThat some 'Formal logic can be tensed'

'Arthur Norman Prior' SubClassOf hasWritten some 'Syntax of Time Distinctions'

hasWritten SubPropertyOf: affirmsThat

Transitive: affirmsThat

'Syntax of Time Distinctions' SubClassOf containsAffirmationThat some 'Formal logic can be tensed'

containsAffirmationThat SubPropertyOf: affirmsThat

OK

Fig. 7. Explanation of the Protégé query result.

4 Formal Theology

We have argued that the Interpretative Community Graph is relevant as a graph for how philosophical questions of worldviews can be engaged in an ontology for Prior's Nachlass. There is, however, no reason why such a graph should not be applied to the formalization of theology. A formal ontology of theology must consider the various communities of interpreters and canons. Here, however, one is not standing on a different ground than in a formal ontology for philosophy. A few steps have been taken toward a formal ontology of theology by mapping Biblical entities with classes such as persons, events, places, and things.[7] At first glance, one might perceive theology as too

---

[7] For more on this point, see S. Boisen (2011 [16]), SharingAndContributing_SBoisen.pdf (w3.org) and S. Graf (2018, pp. 21–25 [18]).

subjective a subject for formalization. Still, we have seen in this paper that Prior's logic of belief, recent developments in analytic theology, and the Prior Community Ontology encourage us to consider how atheology can be represented with formal ontology. Prior's formalization of Calvinism arguably constitutes a preliminary form of a measurable formal ontology for Calvinism. Prior's paper "The Logic of Calvinism" analyses the Westminster Confession of Faith, which Prior believed needed revision. Prior discerned in Calvinist theology what he called "a definite inward order and pattern" (2014 [6]). This inward order is a Ramist dichotomist structure categorizing articles of belief in topics and subtopics all transitively derived from "the Contents of the Word of God." Each topic of the confession is thus a subtopic of the content of the Bible.

Moreover, every topic of the confession is related to a series of scriptures that are thought to justify the confession's statements of belief as contents of the Bible. Prior's ordering of the logic of Calvinism suggests a formal representation of the relationship between theological topics and associated scriptures in line with the Interpretative Community Graph such that the transitive object property 'concerns' relates to topics based upon a **relatesTo** object property.[8] The ontology can classify articles of belief derived from an interpreted canon. Such an ontology could be further developed by representing relationships as objects that can themselves be categorized.[9] In this manner, it is possible to assert that any relationship between a given topic and an associated scripture arises from the interpretation of a given community, as affirmed in the Interpretative Community Graph. Theology does not arise *ex nihilo* but is rooted in an interpreted canon.

5   Conclusion

We have attempted in this paper to take the first steps to create a Prior ontology based on Prior's early work on the logic of the Bible and Calvinism. This approach may initially seem surprising but seen in the light of Prior's importance for analytic philosophy and the surprising development in analytic theology to apply logical analysis to theology, this approach is hardly farfetched. On the contrary, we find in Prior's early work a model for how to address and work around subjectivity, which we have here called the Interpretative Community Graph. It is an admission that the affirmations of various communities involve readings (or writings) of various views that are either expressed or readable in some part of a corpus. Thus, an ontology of worldviews can be made in which we can distinguish between how a reformed person, contrary to an atheist, will affirm different views on ethics. We have demonstrated that by adding the necessary object properties to an ontology, we can use this Interpretative Community Graph in the Prior ontology and make sense of discussions between him, Quine, and Strawson on whether formal logic can be tensed.

---

[8] Based on these categorizations, a formal ontology for Calvinism using Prior's analysis of the Westminster Confession was developed and displayed in S. Graf (2018, pp. 47–58). Alternatively, one might prefer an object property 'justifies' as providing the scriptural basis for the topics of the confession rather than the **relatesTo** property.

[9] The reification of relations in ontology is similarly suggested by S. Boisen in his 2007 SemTech Conference presentation (Boisen, 2011 slides 17–20 [16]).

References

1. Pichler, A., Zöllner-Weber, A.: Sharing and debating Wittgenstein by using an ontology. Lit. Linguist. Comput. **28**(4), 700–707 (2013). https://doi.org/10.1093/llc/fqt049
2. Farrar, S., Lewis, W.D., Langendoen, D.T.: An ontology for linguistic annotation. In: Semantic Web Meets Language Resources: Papers from the AAAI Workshop, Technical Report WS-02-16, Menlo Park, CA, pp. 11–19. AAAI Press, Palo Alto. https://www.aaai.org/Papers/Wor kshops/2002/WS-02-16/WS02-16-002.pdf (2002)
3. Gonçalves, R.S., et al.: Use of OWL and semantic web technologies at Pinterest. In: Ghidini, C., et al. (eds.) The Semantic Web – ISWC 2019: 18th International Semantic Web Conference, Auckland, New Zealand, October 26–30, 2019, Proceedings, Part II, pp. 418–435. Springer International Publishing, Cham (2019). https://doi.org/10.1007/978-3-030-30796-7_26
4. Engerer, V.K., Albretsen, J.: The prior internet resources 2017: information systems and development perspectives. In: Hasle, P., Blackburn, P.R., Øhrstrøm, P. (eds.) Logic and Philosophy of Time: Themes from Prior, vol. 1, pp. 223–249. Aalborg Universitetsforlag, Aalborg (2017). https://vbn.aau.dk/ws/portalfiles/portal/428420582/Logic_and_Philos ophy_of_Themes_from_Prior_ONLINE_2udg.pdf#page=228
5. Prior, A.N.: The Analogy of Faith. The Congregational Quarterly (1940)
6. Prior, A.N.: The Logic of Calvinism. The Nachlass of A.N. Prior (2014). https://nachlass. prior.aau.dk/paper/the-logic-of-calvinism
7. Wolterstorff, N.: How philosophical theology became possible within the analytic tradition of philosophy. In: Crisp, O.D., Rae, M.C. (eds.) Analytic Theology: New Essays in the Philosophy of Theology, pp. 155–168. Oxford University Press, Oxford (2009). https://doi. org/10.1093/acprof:oso/9780199203567.001.0001
8. Russell, B.: Problems of Philosophy. Henry Holt and Company, New York (1912)
9. Russell, B.: A History of Western Philosophy. Routledge, London (1945)
10. Prior, A.N.: Past, Present and Future. Clarendon Press, Oxford (1967)
11. Prior, A.N.: The formalities of omniscience. Philosophy **37**, 114–129 (1962). https://www. jstor.org/stable/3748369
12. Ruse, M.: The Darwinian Paradigm. Routledge, London (1989)
13. Quine, W.V.: Mr. Strawson on logical theory. Mind **62**(248), 433–451 (1953). https://www. jstor.org/stable/2251091
14. Strawson, P.F.: Introduction to Logical Theory. Routledge, New York (1952)
15. Prior, A.N.: The syntax of time distinctions. Franciscan Stud. **18**(2), 105–120 (1958)
16. Boisen, S.: Deploying Semantic Technologies for Digital Publishing: A Case Study from Logos Bible Software. http://semanticbible.com/other/presentations/2007-semtech/ main.html (2011)
17. Boisen, S.: Sharing and Contributing Annotations. https://www.w3.org/2014/04/annotation/ slides/SharingAndContributing_SBoisen.pdf (2014)
18. Graf, S.: Building Formal Ontologies for Theology and Systems of Belief. https://projekter. aau.dk/projekter/files/281070062/Master_Thesis_of_Simon_Josias_Graf.pdf (2018)

Enterprise Ontologies

Underpinning Layered Enterprise Architecture Development with Formal Concept Analysis

Matt Baxter[1], Simon Polovina[1], Neil Kemp[2(✉)], and Wim Laurier[3]

[1] Conceptual Structures Research Group, Sheffield Hallam University, Sheffield, UK
a7033771@my.shu.ac.uk, S.Polovina@shu.ac.uk
[2] Kemp & Associates Inc., Ottawa, ON, Canada
neil@nka-ltd.com
[3] Université Saint-Louis, Brussels, Belgium
wim.laurier@usaintlouis.be

Abstract. Organisations are fraught with myriad forms of disruption. Discrepancies in organisational language hinder response to change, giving rise to multiple inefficiencies and misunderstandings. Along with the added complexities arising from aligning technology with business needs, these issues undermine the organisation's purpose. Layered Enterprise Architecture Development (LEAD) includes a periodic table of 91 meta-objects, semantic relations, and the resulting metamodel. LEAD thus provides an enterprise ontology for overcoming the issues and moves forward with the a) standardisation of language, and b) alignment of business and technology. Mathematical validity is added to the LEAD metamodel, as demonstrated by a novel algorithm applied to a case study. The algorithm leverages CG-FCA (Conceptual Graphs and Formal Concept Analysis), which can be brought to bear on any triple structure. LEAD's characteristic layering is fully retained, with its lucid identification of organisational change levers.

Keywords: Business problem solving · Enterprise ontology · Formal concept analysis · Layered enterprise architecture development

1 Introduction

1.1 Enterprise Architecture

A modern organisation's environment is a fraught place, filled with many sources of disruption; acute disruptions (1973 Oil Crisis, Covid 19, 9/11 attacks), and chronic disruption (the pervasive change from digital technology, the rise of China) [8]. Understanding, responding to, and exploiting change requires a deep and holistic understanding of the environment and all the structural and behavioural parts of an enterprise and its relationships. This understanding must be shared and based on standardised insight into the enterprise's aspects to ensure that it is aligned, responsive, and has a solid grasp of business needs and

© Springer Nature Switzerland AG 2022
R. Polovina et al. (Eds.): MOVE 2020, CCIS 1694, pp. 101–113, 2022.
https://doi.org/10.1007/978-3-031-22228-3_6

priorities. A well-formulated Enterprise Architecture (EA) program supports these aims by upfronting the organisation's business operations. EA provides timely, repeatable advice on aligning an organisation's ecosystem of stakeholders that make up its enterprise strategy in meeting the challenges of its environment.

1.2   Challenge and Examples

Organisations often have their own language; worse, the functions and teams within an organisation can also have their own language. This can be in the shape of colloquialisms used to describe their business (e.g., 'shorts', 'incompletes', or 'balances' to describe partially fulfilled sales orders) Worse, the same term can be used to hide a multitude of meaning; 'backlog' for 'sales backlog', the time between receipt of a purchase order and delivery of the product, 'manufacturing backlog' (the time between when a product is scheduled to be built and when manufacturing starts), and so on. In each case this dissonance may be formalised with prescriptive standards that support how the organisation wants to work. In the modern setting, this is again made worse as the enabling IT applications 'bake' this language into their design, reinforcing the pre-existing stovepipes. These semantic issues exist not just within organisations but within the education system (training in marketing, does not align with finance, which is inconsistent with operations, and so on) as well as with and within the standards bodies. A very small subset of these standards would include:

- ITIL - a framework designed to standardise the selection, planning, delivery, maintenance, and overall lifecycle of IT (information technology) services within a business.
- COBIT - framework created for information technology (IT) management and IT governance.
- TOGAF - a framework that attempts to define business goals and align them with architecture objectives around then enterprise.
- Open Fair - a model and taxonomy for understanding, analysing, and measuring information risk.
- ISO 35000: Risk Management - Guidelines, provides principles, a framework, and a process for managing risk.
- NIST Enterprise Architecture Model - providing guidance for organising, planning, and building an integrated set of information and information technology architectures.

Each of these standards touches on some aspect of the enterprise, and, while each is potentially valuable, none are comprehensive and there are gaps, overlaps and issues of vocabulary alignment among them all. Generally, adopting the principles and practices described in any one can lead to an improvement in an organisation. Unfortunately, adopting two or more of them will tend to lead to an increase in the inconsistencies of the organisation and a subsequent likely decrease in performance. It stands to reason that having one unified standard throughout the organisation means everyone is 'speaking the same language',

ideas can be shared back and forth, while minimising the chance of potentially costly misunderstandings. Conversely, the lack of an agreed standard, or
implicit acceptance of multiple standards, opens the door for these kinds of misunderstandings. In a best-case scenario, this can mean spending more time (and
therefore money) on clarifying what is meant, or worst-case scenario, expensive
mistakes if intent is not fully understood and completely communicated [10].
When software is developed to enable an individual or to improve the productivity of a small team it is easy to encode the business directly into software
[7]. Issues of vocabulary are easily hidden by humans that are generally able
to map language, more or less accurately, while hiding the resulting "friction"
of miscommunication and the extra effort "as part of the job", i.e. Nonaka's
'socialisation' of tacit knowledge [9]. In these situations, the experienced business analyst becomes adept at juggling a few different languages as part of their
job. The conversation between IT and business is a difficult one. Documentation
of the issues abound [12]:

- While IT projects may vary in their approach to addressing requirements e.g.,
  waterfall versus agile, they all implicitly assume that the problem is exposing
  the requirements so they can become embedded in code [7,13], when the
  reality is that the first requirement of any business is that the requirements
  will change.
- IT continues to focus on the user, asking for user stories, user experience,
  and user requirements; an approach that is sound when building individual
  and team-centric tools, but not applicable when the "user" is the enterprise.
  Because of this, designs exclude the executive perspective and are entirely
  operations-centric and use the local dialect of the users, all while executives
  refuse to engage [4].
- While lacking any real understanding of the nature of business, IT expects
  the business to describe itself in a way that can be converted to software [13],
  while business has no understanding either of IT or how to describe itself.
  [12], and for that matter each actor in the business looks at the entirety of
  the enterprise akin to those chained to the cave's wall in Plato's Allegory of
  the Cave [11].

As compared to the automation of the tasks of an individual or small team,
automation of an enterprise end-to-end and from the executive suite to all aspects
of operations is a challenge of a different order of magnitude. The net result is
significant friction, in both the sense of conflict or animosity and in terms of the
resistance between the two perspectives [5,12].

1.3   Resolution

Resolution requires a language agnostic facility to align an organisation's languages, in all their forms, in a way that connects concepts based on their essential
characteristics in the business setting. One solution is applied by the LEADing
Practice standard framework for enterprise architecture. The framework provides

a single set of concepts and categories within the enterprise and the properties and relations between them. It provides the single, unified structure with which to standardise an organisation's language, while also aligning the business with its information technology. In its periodic table of 91 meta objects, every element of an organisation can be categorised, decomposed into component elements, and highlighting the links between those elements exposes the relationships between the concerns of each of the business, information, and technology perspectives. Figure 1 shows the LEAD periodic table, which viewed hierarchically, is comprised of three layers - Business, Information, and Technology, eight sub-layers, and ultimately the meta objects.

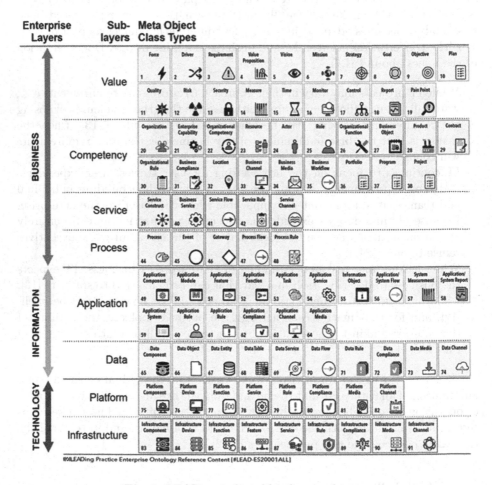

Fig. 1. LEAD periodic table of meta objects

Broadly, the content in the business, information, and technology layers is organised into a number of sublayers within each of the primary layers. These sublayers are each specific spheres of activity within the layer domains. The concepts relevant to the sublayers are then expressed as the meta objects of the ontology. We previously mentioned the links between LEAD's meta objects; those links are called semantic relations. Semantic relations are how a meta object sees itself in relation to other meta objects. Each semantic relationship exists in a form that is comprised of three parts - meta object, semantic relation, meta object. We call this a triple, with the first meta object known as the source, and the second as target. Wherever a semantic relation exists between two meta objects, the corresponding relation will exist in reverse, that is, the meta object relationships are two-way in all cases. To facilitate the making and recording of the connections between an enterprise's vocabulary, in all its variation and dialects the analytic process requires automated support. Enterprise Plus, or E+, is software that houses the LEAD reference content. Figure 2 shows a semantic relation selection tool, which allows the user to select a layer and sub-layer of the source meta object(s), before then selecting the layer, sub-layer, and meta object of the target meta object. The example selected shows the semantic relation of 'Data Object enables creation of Report'. While in this context that is an abstract concept, it is not difficult to relate to the real world - data is the foundation of many business reports.

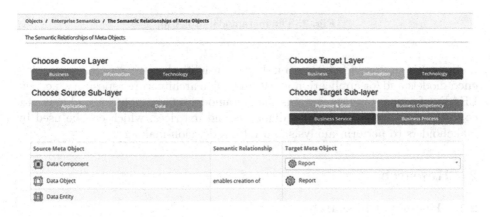

Fig. 2. E+ semantic relationship selection tool

Meta objects and semantic relations are considered the foundation of LEAD, and consequently act as the 'building blocks' of its metamodels. A metamodel involves the selection, connection, and organisation of meta objects and semantic relations to create a visual representation of an organisation or part of an organisation.

Figure 3 from the Open Group's TOGAF standard for EA identifies how the metamodel fits into the wider organisational landscape [6]. Metamodels reflect the real-world enterprise, while also possessing a reciprocal relationship with any reference models or application platforms (because changes to reference models or application platforms must be reflected in the relevant metamodels, and

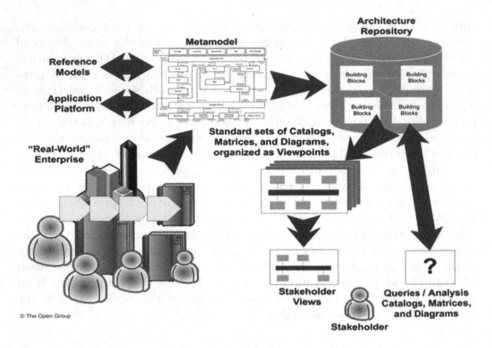

Fig. 3. The metamodel in EA [6]

metamodels can provide hitherto unknown insights that trigger change in reference models and/or application platforms). The architecture repository, i.e., the LEAD reference content, contains the metamodel building blocks, and may also contain other artefacts, such as diagrams and matrices, which can be used by stakeholders to perform analysis and inform decision-making.

2 Research

2.1 History of Research

Prior research used a metamodel as a case study and elicited its active semantic relations using a novel algorithm [2]. By active, we mean those semantic relations where one meta object directs another, or it could be said that one meta object is the driving force of the relationship. For example, in semantic relations where the verbs in the two relations are 'uses' and 'used by', 'uses' would be active, and 'used by' would be passive. After identifying the active relations in the metamodel, an application named CG-FCA (conceptual graph and formal concept analysis) was used, firstly to convert the ternary LEAD semantic relations into the binary relations required for processing by the FCA part of the software. A formal concept lattice of the active metamodel was then created. In the process of creating this lattice, the layering of LEAD's was lost, which hindered the readability of the lattice.

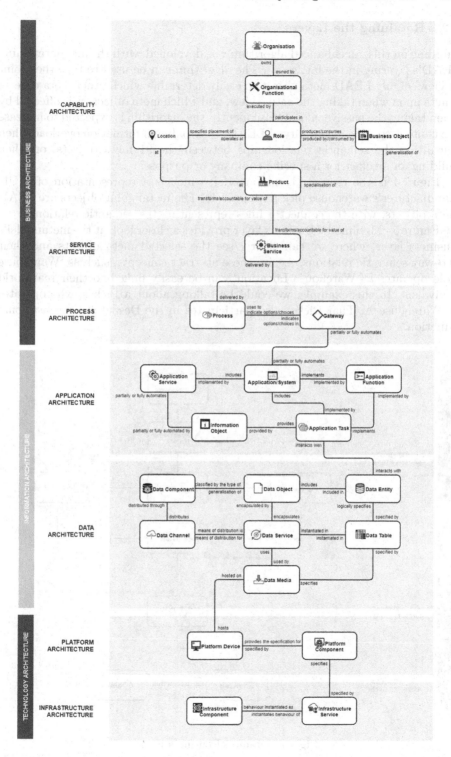

Fig. 4. Warehouse pick pack metamodel (based on LEADing practice meta model)

2.2   Retaining the Layers

Building on this, an enhanced algorithm was developed, with the aim of retaining LEAD's layering in the lattice [3]. The algorithm can be used to take the 'point of view' of any LEAD meta object to easily determine which other meta objects it acts upon when taking the active view, and which meta objects it is affected by when taking the passive view. Consequently, the algorithm is expected to increase the context-specific readability of LEAD, by avoiding information overload when consulting the semantic relationships between the 91 meta objects, or when building an artefact for a specific company or purpose.

Figure 4 is the case study metamodel, which is a representation of a UK manufacturer's warehouse pick pack process. The rectangular objects are LEAD meta objects, with the connector lines representing the semantic relations.

Figure 5 - Metamodel Business layer provides a closer look at the metamodel's Business layer, where we can clearly see the selected meta objects and their two-way semantic relations. Again, these abstract concepts, such as 'Warehouse Role operates at Warehouse Location' can be easily linked to their real-world equivalent. In this example, we could be talking about a Picker, who operates at Warehouse A. That Picker also participates in the Despatch Organisational Function.

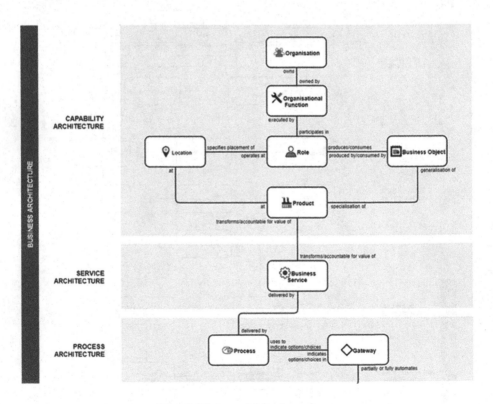

Fig. 5. Metamodel business layer

The Information layer, shown as Fig. 6 indicates that a Warehouse Application includes a Warehouse application task. In this scenario, a Warehouse Management System or ERP system includes Application Tasks, such as Pick Reporting, which confirms a successful product pick by the Picker, and triggers the relevant stock transaction.

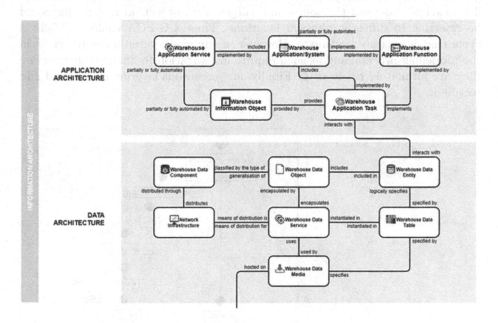

Fig. 6. Metamodel information layer

Figure 7 is the 'before' lattice. Immediately, we can see deviation from LEAD's layering, with Platform Component sitting in the top-most concept (the supremum), instead of near the bottom of the lattice in the Technology layer. A similar, but less extreme example, is Platform Device's position on the far left of lattice, in the Information layer instead of the Technology layer. Of further note are the Location and Business Service concepts on the right-hand side of the lattice. Initially, it may be that no issue is identified, as the concepts sit in the Business Layer, which is where they belong. However, this positioning is only to the human eye, and as a result of how the lattice was organised by the modeller. The two concepts are actually directly linked to the bottom-most empty concept, the infimum, and so mathematically sit at the bottom of the lattice, breaking from LEAD's layering. This speaks to the gap between how humans and computers process information.

The enhanced algorithm, viewable as Fig. 8, shows the steps taken to produce the 'after' lattice with retained LEAD layering. Firstly, the metamodel's active relations are identified and processed by the CG-FCA application. Part of the application's output is the highlighting of any semantic cycles, that is, pathways where the source and target meta object are identical. Cycles can be intended, whereby multiple instances of the same meta object are present. E.g., if 'Location' was both the source and target meta object, in reality this could be referring to different physical locations. Thus, CG-FCA could highlight a cycle that is entirely legitimate. However, many cycles often indicate errors in the modelling process, and as such require investigation by the modeller, before they are ultimately resolved [1]. Finally, any erroneous layering is reviewed and rectified.

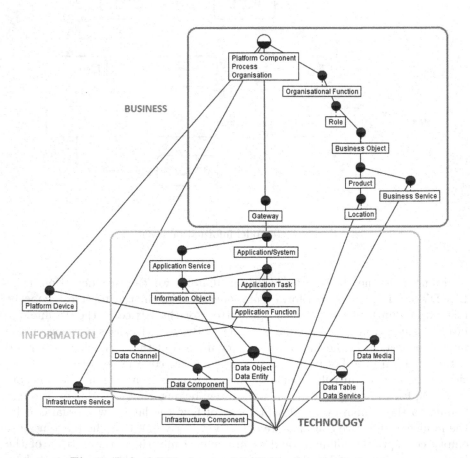

Fig. 7. 'Before' FCL showing LEAD layers to the human eye

Figure 9 is the 'after' lattice. Strikingly, the concepts are now showing LEAD layering mathematically, rather than purely visually due to how the lattice was arranged. This narrows the gap between human and computer interpretation of the case study metamodel and improves the readability of the lattice. By improving the readability, value for business decision-makers is improved when aiming to identify the levers required to effect a desired organisational change.

```
 1  begin
 2  │   A = ∅
 3  │   foreach ((o, v, s), (s, v', o)) ∈ B do
 4  │   │   if isPassive(v) then
 5  │   │   └   A = A ∪ (s, v', o)|((o, v, s), (s, v', o)) ∈ B
 6  │   │   else
 7  │   │   └   A = A ∪ (o, v, s)|((o, v, s), (s, v', o)) ∈ B
 8  │   C = TriplesInCycles(A)
 9  │   foreach (o, v, s) ∈ C do
10  │   │   if inMultipleCycles(o, v, s)) or isImplicityPassive(v)) then
11  │   │   │   A = A\(o, v, s)
12  │   │   └   A = A ∪ (s, v', o)|((o, v, s), (s, v', o)) ∈ B
13  │   │   if isTransitive((o, v, s)) then
14  │   │   └   A = A\(o, v, s)
15  │   S = ConceptsInSupremum(A)
16  │   foreach (o, v, s) ∈ A|o ∈ S and Count((o, α, β) ∈ A) > 1 do
17  │   │   A = A\(o, v, s)
18  │   └   A = A ∪ (s, v', o)|((o, v, s), (s, v', o)) ∈ B
19  │   I = ConceptsInInfimum(A)
20  │   foreach (o, v, s) ∈ A|s ∈ I and Count((α, β, s) ∈ A) > 1 do
21  │   │   A = A\(o, v, s)
22  │   └   A = A ∪ (s, v', o)|((o, v, s), (s, v', o)) ∈ B
23  end
```

Fig. 8. Layered active semantic relations algorithm

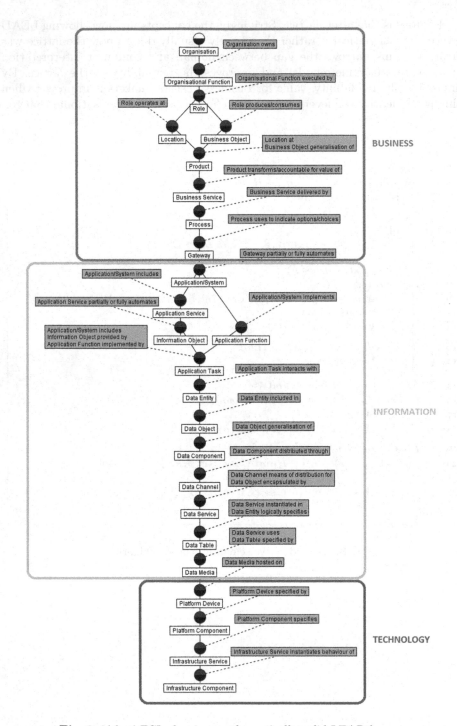

Fig. 9. 'After' FCL showing mathematically valid LEAD layers

3   Conclusion

In summary, we have proposed a common and costly industry challenge and offered LEAD as a resolution, before drilling down to a metamodel case study comprised of LEAD's meta objects and semantic relations. We then used the CG-FCA application and an enhanced algorithm to convert the metamodel into an active lattice that retained LEAD's layering. This promotes a deeper understanding of LEAD by introducing mathematical validity to its metamodels, while also improving its value proposition for industry through a more lucid identification of change levers.

References

1. Andrews, S., Polovina, S.: Exploring, reasoning with and validating directed graphs by applying formal concept analysis to conceptual graphs. In: Croitoru, M., Marquis, P., Rudolph, S., Stapleton, G. (eds.) GKR 2017. LNCS (LNAI), vol. 10775, pp. 3–28. Springer, Cham (2018). https://doi.org/10.1007/978-3-319-78102-0_1
2. Baxter, M., Polovina, S., Laurier, W., Rosing, M.: Active semantic relations in layered enterprise architecture development. In: Cochez, M., Croitoru, M., Marquis, P., Rudolph, S. (eds.) GKR 2020. LNCS (LNAI), vol. 12640, pp. 3–16. Springer, Cham (2021). https://doi.org/10.1007/978-3-030-72308-8_1
3. Baxter, M., Polovina, S., Laurier, W., von Rosing, M.: Generating layered enterprise architectures with conceptual structures. In: Braun, T., Gehrke, M., Hanika, T., Hernandez, N. (eds.) ICCS 2021. LNCS (LNAI), vol. 12879, pp. 34–47. Springer, Cham (2021). https://doi.org/10.1007/978-3-030-86982-3_3
4. Carr, N.G.: It doesn't matter, May 2013
5. Desguin, S., Laurier, W.: Acquiring and sharing the monopoly of legitimate naming in organizations, an application in conceptual modeling. In: ER 2020. LNCS, vol. 12584, pp. 200–209. Springer, Cham (2020). https://doi.org/10.1007/978-3-030-65847-2_18
6. The Open Group. 30. Content Metamodel (2018)
7. Hay, D.C.: Requirements Analysis: From Business Views to Architecture. Prentice Hall, Hoboken (2003)
8. Kane, G.C., Nanda, R., Phillips, A.N., Copulsky, J.: The digital superpowers you need to thrive: digital leaders are best positioned to meet disruptive challenges with innovation (2021)
9. Nonaka, I., Umemoto, K., Senoo, D.: From information processing to knowledge creation: a paradigm shift in business management. Technol. Soc. **18**(2), 203–218 (1996)
10. Oberg, J.: Why the mars probe went off course (1999)
11. Plato. The Republic. HarperCollins, New York, 16 September 2021
12. Redman, T.C., Sweeney, B.: Bridging the gap between it and your business, May 2013
13. Wiegers, K.E.: Software Requirements. Microsoft Press, Redmond (1999)

Advancing Strategy Ontology

Jamie Caine(✉) (iD)

Sheffield Hallam University, Sheffield, UK
j.caine@shu.ac.uk

Abstract. An ontology seeks to formalise a language and definitions for domain-related communications, thus enhancing the sharing of meaning across relevant stakeholders. A strategy ontology for enterprises should be no exception. Identifying patterns in business-level typologies advance the ontology by informing strategy direction within competitive environments. The array of strategy models that facilitate the formalisation of strategy concepts is investigated. The pathways from strategy through to competency and capability are established. This activity culminates in an extended meta-model that yields the formal concepts (meta-objects) and relations pertinent to strategy. The model's interoperability underpins the strategy ontology's value by a matrix tool that accelerates and selects the appropriate models to facilitate productive work through the strategy lifecycle.

Keywords: Strategy · Ontology · Corporate strategy · Business level strategy · Functional level strategy · Meta model

1 Introduction

The need and requirements for a Strategy Ontology are critically discussed by Caine and von Rosing (2020), highlighting the need to facilitate and enable an effective sharing of meaning across concepts that touch strategy. This need has been exuberated with increasing emphasis on the imperative link between strategy, capability and performance (Warner and Wäger 2019; Feiler and Teece 2014; O'Regan and Ghobadian 2004).

Strategy practitioners remained challenged and responsible for deriving strategic pathways that facilitate competitive advantage. With a complex landscape of strategy models, the difficulty remains in the ability to delineate alignment across strategy and capability to drive organisation performance (Teece 2007; O'Regan and Ghobadian 2004). No works exist that directly relate existing strategy models to competencies and capabilities. Moreover, how organisations compete within their respective environments also deserves attention as this drives the allocation and deployment of resources (Feiler and Teece 2014). These matters contribute to the motivation for this research which is routed upon advancing the Strategy Ontology notion. Specifically, (1) supporting practitioners in their ability to formalise and accommodate strategy concepts across the existing array of strategy models. (2) Delineating relations between concepts, models, capabilities and competencies. (3) Confirming the generic strategic types of competing within competitive environments and (4) establishing a connection back to the strategy lifecycle phases (Caine and von Rosing 2018).

© Springer Nature Switzerland AG 2022
R. Polovina et al. (Eds.): MOVE 2020, CCIS 1694, pp. 114–167, 2022.
https://doi.org/10.1007/978-3-031-22228-3_7

The notion of capability in the context of strategy is discussed and positioned upon Tecce's (2007; 2014) dynamic capabilities as a basis for establishing imperative relations back to strategy.

The author builds upon the requirements for a strategy ontology outlined by Caine and von Rosing (2020), namely, Strategy Semantics, Strategy Taxonomy and Strategy Engineering. The Strategy Semantics are visualised in an extended Strategy Meta Model that delineates relationships between meta objects as a result of analysing strategy models through a predefined lens that ensures a strict focus on models with strategic significance. The Strategy Taxonomy is represented by establishing generic strategies (typologies) based on the analysis of patterns associated with business level strategy.

Strategy Engineering is represented through the capability to instantiate different instances of strategy relevant objects, enabling and facilitating the re-use of strategy concepts across different artefacts.

The LEAD Enterprise Ontology (LEO) (von Rosing and Laurier 2015; Caine and von Rosing 2018; Caine et al. 2021) has been the basis for LEADing Practice to develop standards and reference content that spread across six high level categories, each containing several subject domains. This has resulted in artefacts that represent user informed practices structuring frameworks, taxonomies, populated maps, matrices and models (von Rosing et al. 2017; von Scheel et al. 2017; von Rosing et al. 2016). This article examines two examples of reference content that fall within the Enterprise Management standard, Strategy Taxonomy and Organisation Tier Competencies (LEADing Practice 2022). The development of this reference content has been informed by cross industry representation across different strategic contexts.

The Strategy Taxonomy content represents the analysis of patterns associated with the development of business level strategies. This has resulted in a list of commonly utilised strategy typologies, (1) Strengthen Growth, (2) Cost Efficiency, (3) Improve Competitiveness, (4) Lower Risk and (5) Improvement Operational Excellence. Each of the strategies has associated Critical Success Factors (CSFs). The CSFs are not explicitly listed in this article, however, some of them are referred to when contrasting the LEAD typologies against academically derived typologies. The reference content is cross examined and contrasted with an academic analysis of strategy typologies. The results demonstrate a correlation between the academic analysis of strategic typologies and LEAD reference content.

The Organisation Tier competency reference content groups competencies across the strategic, tactical and operational organisation tiers. This categorisation results from the analysis of patterns associating competencies with a specific organisation tier. This article cross examines these competencies with strategy models in the aim of identifying a relationship between strategy and competency. An extension of this relation results in a taxonomy that groups models according to their strategic nature and relationship to associated competencies. This provides pathways from strategy to competency and vice versa.

2 Literature Review

The review of literature expands across ontology and its connection to strategy, capabilities and competencies, strategy models and business level strategy. The discussion on ontology and its connection to strategy reveals key themes that inform the basis of advancing strategy ontology. The capabilities and competencies review support the identification of imperative links that should align back to strategy. The existing array of strategy models are reviewed as a basis to propose ontological definitions for their individual components. Finally, literature is surveyed on generic business level strategic types in aid of identifying patterns to support the acceleration of strategy development.

2.1 Ontology and Strategy

Whilst Gruber (1995) is known to have established ontology within the informatics and computing domain, the routes of ontology lay firmly within social science, based on a philosophical premise; 'the nature of being or reality' (Denzin and Lincoln 2011). Ontology allows us to share and reuse meaning through a formal specification built upon a shared conceptualisation (Gruber 1995; Borst et al. 1997).

It was Powell (2003) who initially discussed the need for a strategy ontology, highlighting this as a significant issue prohibiting the advancement of the strategic management field. Whilst there is a plethora of strategic models and concepts, there lacks a formal description that defines and removes any confusion in the definition of objects relating to strategy (Powell 2003).

Nelson and Nelson (2003) echo Powell's concern highlighting the importance of developing a structured strategy language that can lead to the development of strategic patterns. They also emphasise how technical requirements should be informed by the strategic thread, thus creating alignment and facilitating the integration of business and technology (Nelson and Nelson 2003).

Whilst there are attempts at creating ontologies that relate to strategy, there lacks a comprehensive delineation of concepts and extended relationships. Dalmau Espert et al. (2015) introduced an ontology for a strategic planning process. It is fundamentally based upon Hill and Jones's (2012) strategic planning process which can be summarised as; (1) mission and corporate goals, (2) Strengths, Weaknesses, Opportunities and Threats (SWOT) (3) Strategy and (4) Implementation of Strategy (Dalmau Espert et al. 2015). Whilst the foundations are broadly linked to the necessary concepts that relate to strategy, there are some limitations with their resulting ontology model. Firstly, it doesn't capture the ability to handle the complexity associated with the different levels of strategy. It is well documented that strategic planning has a hierarchal perspective whereby the uppermost strategy informs the lower-level strategies (Prescott 1983; Chafee 1985; De Wit 2017). There is no consideration for this which limits its practical use when orchestrating strategy across different business units. Secondly, there is no attempt to specify how strategy execution connects to technology. Failure rates with strategy execution and digital transformation have historically been overwhelmingly high (Bridges 2016) (McKinsey 2015). Developing an ontology that overlooks the connection to technology creates a blind spot that will surface alignment and integration issues when working through the lifecycle of strategy (Caine and von Rosing 2018).

Dalmau Espert et al. (2015) specify ontology as an 'Action' object that represents initiatives that address the fulfilment of the key performance indicators. As an ontology, this lacks rigour because 'Actions' could relate to a form of service, process, capability or competency. Each of these has a different nature and thus requires specific relations with other concepts that can support the engineering of strategy. Moreover, without this level of rigour issues will surface when attempting to programme manage strategy execution as services and processes will require owners. They will need to work across different departments engaging with various stakeholders. This will dictate different workflows for processes and service flows for service. Therefore, without them being defined in the ontology this will create difficulty when orchestrating services and managing business processes (Von Rosing et al. 2014).

Finally, Dalmau Espert et al. (2015) ontology hinge on SWOT which encompasses essential concepts that relate to strategy. However, SWOT is not the only model that encompasses concepts that relate to strategic planning. Kaplan and Norton's (1996) balance scorecard, Porter's (2001) value chain and Osterwalder, Piegneur, Clark and Pijl (2010) business model canvas could, amongst other models be justified for the same purpose.

Yakan and Rashid's (2016) Strategic Business Ontology builds upon Osterwalder et al. (2010) Business Model Canvas by adding key performance indicators to measure essential elements of the business model. Whilst essential components that relate to strategy are present there are some fundamental issues that surface with this ontology. The business model canvas is built upon an ontology that intends to serve as a means between the business level strategy and organisation processes (Osterwalder et al., 2010). Its foundation purpose is not to act as a 'strategy' ontology. Furthermore, it takes from the structure of Kaplan and Norton's (1996) Balance Scorecard aligning Product, Customer Interface, Infrastructure Management, and Financial Aspects to the related scorecard areas. This is a similar limitation trait to Dalmau-Espert et al. (2015) who take from SWOT. The nine building blocks of the business model canvas (value proposition, customer segment, channels, customer relationship, revenue streams, key resources, key activities, key partnerships and cost structure) (Osterwalder et al. 2010) are the core of Yakan and Rashid's (2016) strategy ontology. It does not intend to capture essential concepts such as environmental factors that motivate or push an organisation towards a certain direction i.e., drivers and forces. Although it adds the key performance indicator, the ability to connect this to information and technology layer components is missing. Therefore, failing to address the essential alignment between strategy and technology (Nelson and Nelson 2003; Ross 2006).

Kemp (2021) progressed development towards a strategy ontology. Informed by a fundamental premise that strategy is assembled through 'Ends, Means and Ways', his ontology provides insight into some of the essential elements that compose a strategy. A portion of the elements i.e. (strategy, force, driver, value, risk, end, vision, performance, culture) are directly named in the compilation of Caine and von Rosing (2018)'s strategy lifecycle, founded upon the LEAD Enterprise Ontology (von Rosing and Laurier 2015) and orchestrated through a lifecycle phases model which is underpinned by a 'first cut' strategy ontology meta model. The remaining elements provide detail on a selection of scopes including value and differentiation, along with time and resources. These are considered through the lifecycle phase steps which denote specific actions through the use of artefacts that relate to domain model practices (value model, revenue model, service model, performance model, operating model and cost model) (Caine and von Rosing 2018; von Rosing and von Scheel 2016).

Kemp's (2021) noteworthy critique of the levels of military decision making and its relationship to strategy levels, affirms corporate, business and functional level strategies (Prescott 1986; Chafee 1985; De Wit 2017). Distinctively, it further delineates operational planning, tactics and technology as decompositions following on from levels of strategy (Kemp 2021). This article extends Kemp's work by expanding on the nature of competencies required at the business level of strategy, this also further develops the 'means', as resources and capabilities are needed to create a competency (Madhok 1997). Furthermore, analysis of the generic types of strategy applied at the business level and an extended delineation of concepts associated with strategy, courtesy of an extended strategy models review; provide advancement to the strategy ontology notion.

Principles of Ontology Application.   Several articles discuss how an ontology should be used (Guarino 1997; Falbo et al. 2002; Roussey et al., 2011) which all encompass the three principles discussed by Uschold and Grunniger (1996). From a systems and organisation perspective, they are categorised into three principles **Communication**, **Interoperability** and **Systems Engineering.**

The **Communication** category seeks to *"...reduce conceptual and terminological confusion by providing a unifying framework within an organisation"* (Uschold and Grunniger 1996, p. 98). This supports a shared understanding across all stakeholders within an organisation who have their individual viewpoints and organisational context. For a strategy to be effective, it must be understood and relate to different viewpoints where the communication used does not become an additional task for deciphering and relating to a specific context. A Strategy Ontology should facilitate effective communication and enable a shared meaning, addressing Powell's (2003) 'game of language' concern that highlights the issues of having multiple meanings attached to the same strategy concept. The Strategy Ontology should enable a shared meaning across the main layers of an organisation, namely business, information and technology.

Interoperability foscusses on addressing the integration needs of *"...users that need to exchange data or who are using different software tools"* (Uschold and Grunniger 1996, p. 98). This requires the application of enterprise modelling to support the integration of tools that users need to perform their job (Uschold and Grunniger 1996). The Strategy Ontology will need to demonstrate how it supports the interoperability of tools used by stakeholders of different viewpoints. From an enterprise modelling perspective, tools (which are also referred to as artefacts) entail **Maps**, **Matrices** and **Models** (von Rosing and von Scheel 2016). Maps detail a list of composed or decomposed concepts, from a strategy context this could be a list of Strategy Objectives for a given organisational area. Matrices fundamentally consist of rows and columns that delineate where concepts are related to each other. The concepts may already be in the form of a Map but will be enhanced by a Matrix view displaying where concepts relate. Models are developed from concepts taken from the Map or Matrix. The Strategy Ontology will integrate the practice of enterprise modelling to produce tools that support stakeholders from specific viewpoints.

Systems Engineering focuses on the role ontologies play in supporting the design and development of software systems. Whilst the focal point of the Strategy Ontology does not focus on designing and developing software systems, it will apply some of the traits associated with systems engineering. One of those traits is reusability.

The ontology should facilitate which concepts are "...reusable between different domains and tasks." Uschold and Grunniger 1996, p. 98). It should also "...provide an "easy to re-use" library of class objects for modelling problems and domains" (Uschold and Grunniger 1996, p. 98).

Reusability also aligns with the Liskov and Wing (1994) substitution principle which supports the validation of decomposition where stereotypes, types and subtypes all adhere to their class type meta object (where the 'is a' relationship exists). Instances of a class type can be reused across different domains and applied to different maps, matrices and models.

The strategy ontology will involve engineering concepts that relate to strategy. Once engineered, this will support the ability to reuse them across different artefacts i.e. maps matrices and models.

Ontology provides us with the ability to enhance the way in which we work with strategy. This review delineated key themes that inform the scope, applicability and fundamental principles that will underpin the development of an enhanced strategy ontology.

2.2 Competencies, Capabilities and Competitive Advantage

Competitive advantage is commonly associated with competencies and capabilities as they are deemed to enable an organisation to differentiate its position in the competing market (Teece et al. 1997; O'Regan and Ghobadian 2004). Achieving competitive advantage through leveraging competencies and capabilities requires effective strategic planning, thus alignment of strategy, competency and capability are essential (Teece et al. 1994). These two terms are sometimes loosely interchanged (Marino, 1996). It is, therefore, necessary to understand why so confusion can be limited when working with the two concepts.

Cambridge dictionary definitions make clear distinctions between the two, competency is defined as an essential skill to perform a specific job. Whereby a capability is the ability to perform something (Cambridge University Press 2022). Henderson and Cockburn (1994) define competencies as local abilities combined with the knowledge required to perform day to day tasks. Madhok (1997) makes a clear connection between resources, capabilities and competencies by defining competencies as a result of combing capability (ability to do something) with the necessary resources required. Marino's (1996) definition relates to these highlighting competencies that have knowledgebase or technology components that result in a skill. He also effectively distinguishes between the two highlighting that capabilities are '...rooted more in processes and business routines' (Marino 1996, p. 41). Meaning they are of a complex nature and often involve interaction with people, organisation structures and technology (Marino 1996) (Teece et al. 1997). The distinction between the two can be blurred, especially when the competency assessment developed by pioneers on the notion of 'Core Competencies' Prahalad and Hamel (1990), can be applied to capabilities and competencies (Marino 1996). Their assessment places three tests on a competency, namely: (1) does it enable an organisation to compete in more than one market, (2) will it provide value to the end product/service and (3) is it difficult for competitors to imitate (Prahalad and Hamel 1990). To date, there is still ambiguity surrounding the distinction between the two terms in practice. When applying the distinction criteria discussed above this results in an argument for both capability and competency. Nevertheless, they both hold significance when working through the lifecycle of strategy.

Scholarly work on the connection between competency and strategy grew exponentially following the 'Core Competency' notion. This resulted in greater emphasis on capabilities, particularly dynamic capabilities and how they support a competitive strategic endeavour. Tecce and Pisano (1994) introduced the notion of dynamic capabilities which expanded the competitive advantage paradigm. The term is rooted in two perspectives, (a) recognising that the business environment has a continuous character shift and this requires a dynamic strategic response to support time to market and innovation. (B), emphasis on adapting, integrating and aligning internal and external skills, resources and functional competences in building capability towards a changing environment (Teece and Pisano 1994). Progression of this notion resulted in the frequently cited 'Sensing, Seizing and Transforming/Reconfiguring' framework (Teece et al. 1997) which has been often utilised as a vehicle for scholarly research on dynamic capabilities and more recently, its connection to digital transformation and strategy (Vanpoucke et al. 2014; Breznik et al. 2018; Matysiak et al. 2017; Enkel and Sagmeister, 2020; Ince and Hahn 2020; Warner and Wäger 2019; Bojesson and Fundin 2021). Research output derived from empirical industrial analysis and orchestration of fundamental concepts have delineated several frameworks that identify essential activities for developing dynamic capabilities.

'Ultimately, good performance requires strong dynamic capabilities to sense, seize, and transform in conjunction with a good strategy' (Teece 2014).

Identifying and developing dynamic capabilities is essential for creating and maintaining a sustainable competitive advantage. Implementing them entails doing the right thing, at the right time, supported with the management and orchestration of new processes that lead to the development of an adaptive culture (Teece 2014). Alongside dynamic capabilities, it is also essential to attain technical efficiency in the operations, administration and governance of core business functions. Moving the emphasis away from doing the right things, this focuses on 'doing the things right' (Teece 2014). Numerous terms are used to describe 'doing the things right' capabilities, 'static' (Collis 1994), 'first order' (Danneels 2002) and 'substantive' (Sharker et al. 2006). Teece (2014) uses the term 'ordinary capabilities' and effectively distinguishes the differences when contrasted with dynamic capabilities (Table 1).

Building on the endeavour to delineate relations between concepts, models, capabilities and competencies, this article will contrast frameworks and essential activities from (Day and Schoemaker 2016; Breznik et al. 2018; Bojesson and Fundin 2021; Warner and Wäger 2019) all of which take from Tecce's (2007) Sensing, Seizing and Reconfigure/Transform structure. Consideration will be given to ordinary capabilities and their nature, thus also aligning them back to strategic models where applicable (Tables 2, 3 and 4).

Contrasts will be drawn from the LEAD Organisation Tier Competency reference content and where possible aligned back to strategic models. Competencies across the strategic, tactical and operational tiers are listed in Table 5 (LEADing Practice 2022). A

Table 1. Tecce's (2014) comparison of ordinary and dynamic capabilities

	Ordinary capabilities	Dynamic capabilities
Purpose	Technical efficiency in business functions	Achieving congruence with customer needs and with technological and business opportunities
Mode of attainability	Buy or build (learning)	Build (learning)
Tripartite schema	Operate, administrate, and govern	Sense, seize, and transform
Key routines	Best practices	Signature processes
Managerial emphasis	Cost control	Entrepreneurial asset orchestration and leadership
Priority	Doing things right	Doing the right things
Imitability	Relatively imitable	Inimitable
Result	Technical fitness (efficiency)	Evolutionary fitness (innovation)

Table 2. Attributed capabilities for sensing dynamic capability

Dynamic capabilities (sensing)	
Author	Attributed capabilities
(Day and Schoemaker 2016; Breznik et al. 2018; Bojesson and Fundin 2021)	Peripheral Vision – Involves scoping which determines how wide to scan and the nature of the issues scanned. The scope is informed by past analysis, present issues, trends and forces
(Day and Schoemaker 2016)	Vigilant Learning – Outside of orientation for products and services, ensuring employees are empowered to share their voice on important matters that impact the business, suppressing biases, and triangulating perspectives for complex issues
(Warner and Wäger 2019)	Digital Scouting – Scanning for tech trends, screening for competitors and sensing customer-centric trends
(Warner and Wäger 2019)	Digital Scenario Planning – Analysing scouted signals, interpreting digital future scenarios, Formulating digital strategies

(continued)

'culture' related competency has been added to each tier in respect of the significance it holds in connection to the development of strategy (Tallman et al. 2021).

Table 2. (*continued*)

Dynamic capabilities (sensing)

Author	Attributed capabilities
(Bojesson and Fundin 2021; Warner and Wäger 2019)	Establishing a long-term digital vision, enabling an entrepreneurial mindset, promoting a digital mindset
(Tecce 2007)	Research & Development selection of New Tech
(Tecce 2007)	Supplier, Complementor, and technology Innovation Tapping – building off the developments of others to create something purpose fit for the new business model

Table 3. Attributed capabilities for seizing dynamic capability

Dynamic capabilities (seizing)

Author	Attributed capabilities
(Tecce 2007; Day and Schoemaker 2016 Breznik et al. 2018; Warner and Wäger 2019)	Delineating the Customer Solution and Business Model – Recognising and designing mechanisms to capture value. Probe-and-Learn Experimentation, developing real options for management to consider
(Tecce 2007; Warner and Wäger 2019; Bojesson and Fundin 2021)	Selecting Decision-Making Protocols & Strategic Agility – including financial model to govern decision making, agile resource allocation, agile strategic response
(Tecce 2007; Breznik et al. 2018)	Building Loyalty and Commitment – Managers form special networking teams for straightforward and focused networking activities
(Tecce 2007)	Establishing Boundaries for Compliment Controls and Platforms
(Breznik et al. 2018; Day and Schoemaker 2016)	Developing Strategic Partnerships – Firms must look beyond their own organisational and market boundaries, probing for insights from a wide array of peer companies, pre-cursors, and network partners
(Warner and Wäger 2019)	Balancing Digital Portfolio – portfolio management

The intention behind aligning capability and competency back to strategic models will facilitate the identification of appropriate tools to strengthen the coordination

Table 4. Attributed capabilities for transforming dynamic capability

Dynamic capabilities (transforming)	
Author	Attributed capabilities
(Breznik et al. 2018; Tecce 2007)	Governance – control mechanisms, appropriate management structure i.e., Chief Digital Officer
(Day and Schoemaker 2016; Breznik et al. 2018; Tecce 2007)	Redesign, Decentralisation and Flat Structures – Modularise/Decomposability
(Warner and Wäger 2019; Tecce 2007)	Continuous Improvement – Digital maturity workforce and readiness, digital knowledge management, digital ecosystems

Table 5. LEAD organisation tier competencies LEAD-ES0000BC

Organisation tier	Competency
Strategic tier	Mission development
	Vision development
	Strategy development
	Business planning
	Forecasting
	Budgeting
	Value management
	Culture assessment and design
Tactical tier	Strategic advice
	Strategic guidance & compliance
	Monitoring
	Reporting
	Evaluation and/or audit
	Policies, rules & guidelines
	Procedures
	Measurements

(continued)

between strategy, capability and competency. It will also provide 'upstream' and 'downstream' pathways from strategic models through to capabilities and competencies. This extends the work of Feiler and Teece (2014) who did not delineate where strategic models support the development of dynamic and ordinary capabilities. Furthermore, the tool will provide a practical application of devising dynamic capabilities from strategy which

Table 5. (*continued*)

Organisation tier	Competency
	Administration
	Communication
	Performance management
	Risk management
	Culture development and monitoring
Operational tier	Operational administration
	Issue management
	Operational planning
	Process management
	Operational oversight and monitoring
	Operational reporting
	Evaluation and/or audit
	Operational measurements
	Operational advice and/or guidance
	Processing
	Culture realisation

can support the development of business models (Warner and Wäger 2019). Affirming the relationship between dynamic capabilities, strategy, and business models thus facilitating the ability to create competitive advantage (Achtenhagen et al. 2013; DaSilva and Trkman 2014; Teece, 2018; Velu 2017; Warner and Wäger 2019).

2.3 Strategy Models Review

Academia has produced an extensive amount of strategy tools that facilitate the opportunity for strategy practitioners to create strategic models for a specific focus. Previous works exist on collating these tools into a form of grouping to help decipher the appropriate model for a given situation. However, there is no formal ontological work performed on the extensive array of models to inform a taxonomy that groups strategic models by their ontological nature. Moreover, the significance between strategy and its relationship to capability, competency, business model and implementation calls for further inquiry (Hoverstadt et al. 2020). An ontology related to the array of strategic models in connection to the pertinent strategy concepts will advance strategic literature.

In their twelfth edition of 'Exploring Strategy' (Johnson et al. 2020) group associated strategic tools through 'Strategic Position', 'Strategic Choices' and 'Strategy in Action'. Their text provides a comprehensive narrative on strategy, detailing critical perspectives on renown models and frameworks. The intention behind the book is to support academic studies and strategic management curriculum delivery. The three broad categories are not designed to capture and group the pure ontological nature of strategic model concepts, however, it serves the purpose well of providing a critical perspective on the notion of strategy. Mintzberg et al. (2020) formed the ten schools of strategy, which provide a useful lens on working with strategy concepts. However, it does not intend, nor does it provide a discussion on the array of tools produced in the strategic management discipline. Other strategic management texts provide a narrative on the notion of strategy critically discussing approaches to strategic development and their individual perspectives on strategy (Johnson et al. 2020; Mintzberg et al. 2020; Baylis et al. 2018). Whilst there is a shortage of literature that attempts to provide a contemporary grouping on strategy models in relation to pertinent concepts, the work of Berg and Pietersma (2015) provide the most recent attempt. This alongside (Have, Stevens, Elst, Pol-Coyn and Walsh 2007) work has been used as a basis to examine the array of strategy models. Berg and Pietersma (2015) group 75 models across eight functional categories: models within the leadership, human resource, operations supply chain management procurement, finance, marketing and sales are disregarded as the models within do not focus on fundamental strategic concepts. Pertinent strategic concepts are considered as; (a) concepts that inform the positioning of an organisation within an industry, (b) concepts that inform how to compete within a competitive environment, (c) concepts that inform that functional deployment of resources with a link back to strategic concepts that drive how the organisation competes and (d); concepts that inform the overall future direction of an organisation (Prescott 1986; Chafee 1985; De Wit 2017). In addition to Berg and Pietersma (2015), and Have et al. (2007) also produced works on grouping strategy tools. This entails 70 models across strategy, organisation, functional process, people and behaviour and primary process. In alignment with the pertinent strategy concepts, models considered for this review are taken from the strategy and organisation groups. Models outside of these categories do not meet the criteria defined above.

In an attempt to build and extend the previous work, an ontological nature of the selected models will be determined. The 91 meta objects from the Business Ontology have been used as a basis to map the concepts contained in each of the models (Polovina et al. 2020). These objects have been formally described and placed within sublayers of the Business, Information and Technology layers. Semantic relationships between the objects have been described which facilitate the ability to relate concepts within and across the layers of the organisation (Polovina et al. 2020). In addition, a link back to competency and capability will be established to help strengthen the ability to exercise the usefulness in relating strategy to competency and capability since these drive effective business models and execution of strategy (Teece 2018).

Each selected model has been analysed according to three principles: (1) identify and map the nature of the objects back to the LEAD Business Ontology, (2) identify and map the relevant competencies from the LEAD reference content and (3) identify and map the connection to Tecce's (2014) dynamic and ordinary capabilities in accordance with the discussed attributes. The first principle facilitates the ability to delineate a link from each object back to Caine and von Rosing's (2018) strategy lifecycle phases. This provides an opportunity to integrate lifecycle phases into an extended strategy meta model, this is elaborated on in the results section.

In total, thirty-three models have been reviewed in alignment with the three principles. Due to constraints on the length of the article, two examples are provided in detail
demonstrating the application of the principles. Table 6 lists the total models that have
been analysed. In the results, additional models will be presented demonstrating the
application of the three discussed principles (Fig. 1).

Table 6. Models selected for strategy analysis

Selected strategy models for analysis
5 Ps model of strategy implementation (Pryor et al. 2007)
7-S framework (Waterman et al. 1980)
Activity-based costing (Cooper and Kaplan 1988)
Agile strategy management process cycle (Lyngso 2017)
Ashridge mission model (Campbell and Yeung 1991)
Balanced scorecard (BSC) (Kaplan and Norton 2005)
Benchmarking (Watson 1994)
Big hairy audacious goal (BHAG) (Collis 1994)
Boston consulting group (BCG) Matrix (Boston Consulting Group 1970)
Business definition model (Abell 1980)
Blue ocean strategy – strategy canvas (Kim and Mauborgne 2014)
Business model canvas (Osterwalder et al. 2010)
Core competencies (Prahalad and Hamel 1990)
Formal strategic planning process (Armstrong 1982)
Greiner's Growth Model (Greiner 1998)
House of purchasing and supply (Kearney 2002)
European foundation for quality management (EFQM 1992)
Offshoring/Outsourcing (Aron and Singh 2005)
Organisational configurations (Mintzberg 1983)
Overhead value analysis (Berg and Pietersma 2015)
Porter's generic strategies (Porter 2004)

(continued)

2.4 Blue Ocean Strategy Canvas Example

See Tables 7, 8 and 9.

Porter's Value Chain Example

See Fig. 2 and Tables 10 and 11.

The Value Chain of Porter (2001) does not have a link to the Dynamic Capabilities
mapping.

Table 6. (*continued*)

Selected strategy models for analysis
Porter's value chain (Porter 2001)
Porter's five forces (Porter 1997)
Scenario planning (Heijden 2006)
SWOT analysis (Andrews and Andrews 1980)
Strategy map (Kaplan and Norton 2004)
Value disciplines (Treacy and Wiersema 1995)
Internationalisation strategy framework (Lem et al. 2013)
Road-mapping (Farrukh et al. 2003)
Ansoff's product/market grid and geographic vector (Ansoff 1987)
Competing values of organizational effectiveness (Quinn and Rohrbaugh 1983)
Levels of control (Simons 1995)
Market attractiveness business activity (MABA) (Have et al. 2007)

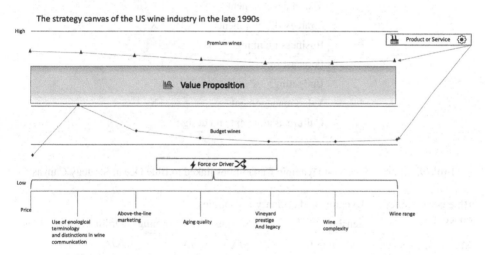

Fig. 1. Blue ocean strategy with concept to object visual layer (Kim and Mauborgne 2014)

Table 7. Matrix of LEAD Meta Objects to Blue Ocean Strategy Canvas Concepts

LEAD meta objects	Blue ocean strategy canvas concepts		
	Market space state	Product/service	Market offerings
Driver	X		
Forces	X		
Value proposition			X
Product		X	
Service		X	

Table 8. Summary of relevant LEAD competencies linked to Blue Ocean Strategy Canvas (only applicable in the Strategic Competency Tier)

Organisation tier	Tier competency	Blue ocean strategy canvas relevance
Strategic tier competencies	Mission development	
	Vision development	
	Strategy development	X
	Business planning	
	Forecasting	
	Budgeting	
	Value management	X
	Culture assessment and design	

Table 9. Matrix of relevant Dynamic Capabilities linked to Blue Ocean Strategy Canvas

Blue ocean strategy concept	Dynamic and ordinary capabilities			
	Sensing	Seizing	Transforming	Ordinary capabilities
Market space state	Screening for competitors (Warner and Wäger 2019)	N/A	N/A	N/A
Product/Service	Screening for competitors (Warner and Wäger 2019)	N/A	N/A	N/A

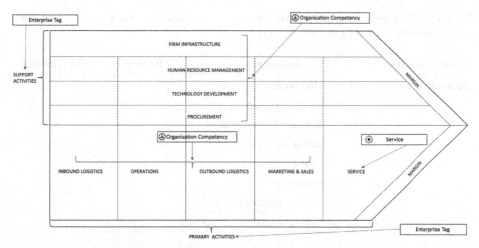

Fig. 2. Porter's Value Chain (2001) with concept to object visual layer and enterprise tag indication

Table 10. Matrix of LEAD Meta Objects to Porter's (2001) Value Chain Concepts

		Porters Value Chain Concepts								
		Firm Infrastructure	Human Resource Management	Technology Development	Procurement	Inbound Logistics	Operations	Outbound Logistics	M&S	Service
LEAD Meta Objects	Compe-tency	X	X	X	X					
	Organisa-tion				X					
	Service									X
Enter-prise Tags	Primary Activities					X	X	X	X	X
	Supporting Activities	X	X	X	X					

2.5   Business Level Strategy – a Review of Industry Strategic Typologies

Academia has firmly established the strategy management discipline which now boasts an extensive amount of frameworks, concepts and models. Whilst, in contrast, the practice of strategy in industry uses far less frameworks; academia has played a role in informing and undertaking several modes of analysis on applied strategies.

To focus on the practice of strategy in industry, it is necessary to confirm the level of strategy concerned. Levels of strategy have been discussed by numerous scholars to help establish a premise in which a strategy seeks to make an impact. Determining the environment domain, how an organisation interacts within the domain and the internal adjustments made to remain competitive have been classified across three strategic levels. Namely corporate level strategy, business level strategy and functional level strategy

Table 11. Summary of relevant LEAD competencies linked to Porter's Value Chain (only applicable in the Strategic Competency Tier)

Organisation tier	Tier competency	Porter's value chain relevance
Strategic tier competencies	Mission development	
	Vision development	
	Strategy development	X
	Business planning	
	Forecasting	
	Budgeting	
	Value management	X
	Culture assessment and design	

(Mintzberg et al. 2005; Ohmae 1988; Prescott 1983; Chafee 1985; De Wit 2017). Corporate level strategy concerns itself with 'what business should we operate in? Whereas business or organisation level strategy is focused on 'how you compete in a given environment'. Functional level of strategy focuses on how resources are allocated to areas of the business. The focus of analysis for this article is primarily on business level strategy, as the majority of models analysed fit this profile.

During the late'70s and'80s, there was a significant academic surge in the analysis of identifying generic business strategy types applied in industry (Miles and Snow 1978; Porter 1979; Douglas and Rhee 1989; Prescott 1986; Treacy and Wiersema 1995). This analysis was mainly spearheaded through an empirical lens to support an understanding of the types of business level strategies used in practice. As a result of this endeavour, patterns have been identified in the way strategies are applied to compete in a competitive environment. These patterns are commonly referred to as 'strategic typologies' (Treacy and Wiersema 1995; Miles and Snow 1978; Douglas and Rhee 1989; Anwar and Hasnu 2016). A Typology represents a categorisation of general types associated with a specific domain. In the context of strategy, this enables the grouping of different strategy types to support the ability to compete within a given industry (Anwar and Hasnu 2017). Strategic typologies were first introduced following the work of Miles and Snow (1978), who produced business level strategic typologies based on their study of strategy across four industries. Subsequent literature discussing strategic typology often cite Miles and Snow (1978) using their research as a basis to further investigate the types of strategies used at a business level (Tavakolian 1989; Douglas and Rhee 1989; Slater and Narver 1993; Moore 2005; Blumentritt and Danis 2006; Anwar and Hasnu 2017). Regarded as the most validated classification of strategy (Anwar and Hasnu 2016), the Miles & Snow framework has been debated and interrogated in various business domains. They introduced four strategic typologies Defender, Prospector, Analyzer, and Reactor that represent strategic orientation for business level strategies (Miles and Snow 1978).

The Defender typology adopts an approach that focusses on enhancing efficiency with a heavy investment towards improving the production and distribution of products and services. There is an emphasis on current products and services in its attempt to seal of the market. Whilst this can create a position difficult to dislodge in the market, significant changes in the market can cause disruption to this approach (Miles and Snow 1978).

With a somewhat opposite stance, the Prospector typology represents an approach that focuses on research and development, new product development and opportunities to penetrate new markets. Resources are heavily deployed to increase growth and revenue through product and service innovation (Miles and Snow 1978).

Residing between Defender and Prospector, the Analyzer typology is a combination of both with an emphasis on minimising risk and maximising profit. New markets are penetrated only when they are analysed and proven to demonstrate viability. In most cases, this would follow the entrance of a Prospector into a given market. Alongside this, a stable core maintaining current products and services ensures operating efficiency in stable market areas (Miles and Snow 1978).

The Reactor typology, unlike the other three, is reactive by nature and lacks consistency and stability in its strategic approach towards the environment of operation. It is described as a 'residual' strategy when neither of the other typologies are followed. The Reactor typology is commonly disregarded as a valid typology (Anwar and Hasnu 2016).

The typologies of Miles and Snow have permeated throughout the work of several strategy scholars. Notably, a significant amount of academic research has used their typologies as a vehicle to assess relationships between strategy and performance through analysing empirical data from the Profit Impact Market Survey (PIMS).

Initiating in 1970, the Profit Impact Market Survey (PIMS) was focused on quantifying the associated factors that differentiate business performance (Buzzell 2004). These factors included market condition, the current competitiveness of a business unit and adopted strategies that drive performance (Buzzell 2004). With foundational routes in Cambridge, Massachusetts and affiliations to the Harvard Business School, PIMS initiated its empirical analysis with General Motors (GE) in the 1960s. A large corporation with several business units, GE provided PIMS with access to data which enabled the analysis of corporate data that provided the platform to extend PIMS to other businesses across different industries. Indeed, PIMS extended to over five hundred companies, differing in size and industry including, samples from the Fortune 500 helping to establish PIMS as a dominant empirical source for strategy up to 1990 (Buzzel 2004). The evolution of PIMS enabled deeper analysis into "market share, relative product quality, capital intensity, capacity utilization, labour productivity and the growth rate of a business unit's served market." (Buzzell 2004). It also established 'PIMS Principles' that represent general relationships between strategic variables that contribute towards profitability and overall success for organisations (Buzzell and Gale 1987; Kotabe et al. 1991). The 'Principles' do not provide solution foundations for successfully operating a business; however, they do support a situational analysis that informs effective decision making (Jaworski and Varadarajan 1989).

Academic analysis of the results of PIMS provides insights into the nature and form of strategy within organisations. Ramanujam and Venkatraman's 1984 research laid a foundation for subsequent research streams that were performed on PIMS (Ramanujam and Venkatraman 1984). This article builds upon their defined 'Empirical Derivation of

Strategic Typologies' research stream. Whilst Ramanujam and Venkatraman's (1984) did not capture some of the later research surrounding strategic typologies, this stream of research is still relevant for the purpose of identifying the different types of generic strategies. This empirical lens approach extends to the work of Anwar and Hasnu (2017), who analysed patterns in strategic typologies across 307 joint stock organisations spreading over twelve industries in Pakistan. This represents a data sample outside the scope of PIMS, providing an opportunity to detect different generic typologies that may differentiate from the research performed on PIMS. The other research streams discussed by Ramanujam and Venkatraman (1984), focus on factors relating to marketing, performance and environmental drivers that influence strategy. However, the outputs associated with these streams do not delineate typologies, therefore they are disregarded in this article.

This article contrasts analysis from Galbraith and Schendel (1983), Prescott (1983), Douglas and Rhee (1989), Luoma (2015) and Anwar and Hasnu (2017) in the attempt to identify commonalities associated with strategy typologies. Each author's work aligns with the 'Empirical Derivation of Strategic Typologies' and therefore provides a basis to identify common patterns in strategic typologies. Discarded from the analysis is research that focuses on typologies around exit and sustainability strategies. Exit strategies detract from a strategic focus that attempts to sustain, compete or outperform within a competitive business environment. Sustainability strategy typologies warrant an independent focus building on the previous research that has identified typologies of this nature (Azzone and Bertelè 1994; Hart 1995; Nidumolu et al. 2009; Orsato 2006; Roome 1992; Gauthier 2017).

Galbraith and Schendel's Typologies. In Galbraith and Schendel's (1983) study into the patterns of strategy associated with the PIMS database, 1200 organisations were included in their analysis. They categorised the types of strategy according to a **consumer product focus** and **industry product focus**. The types of strategy associated with consumer products consisted of: (1) Harvest, (2) Builder, (3) Cashout, (4) Niche or Specialization, (5) Climber and (6) Continuity. Each of these strategies has distinct characteristics and associated patterns (Galbraith and Schendel 1983).

The Harvest strategy type emphasises 'disinvestment' and seeks effective means to apply cost efficiencies in the provision of consumer products. Driving the cost down on product distribution can influence cost savings with administration supporting a reduction in sales fulfilment. In some cases, this can facilitate discounted products for end consumers (Galbraith and Schendel 1983). Driving costs down through a strategic focus strikes similar contrast with Miles and Snow (1978) Defender typology and Prescott's (1983) Low-Cost strategy type. There is a strategic focus on reducing expenses incurred through operating processes to maximise profitability and return on investment (ROI). This aligns with the LEAD 'Cost Efficiency' typology. The Harvest typology represented 6% of the sample taken within the consumer product focused strategy typologies (Galbraith and Schendel 1983).

The Builder strategy type presents, somewhat, an opposite approach to Harvest through strategic intent towards investment into promotion and research and development. Strengthening organisation growth to increase market share is a strong intention with this typology. It shares characteristics with "...Hofer and Schendel's (1978) 'share-increasing strategies', Buzzell et al.'s (1975) 'building strategy, Utterback and Abernathy's (1975) sales maximization strategies and Vesper's (1979) multiplication strategy' (Galbraith and Schendel P13., 1983). All of this represents a notion of the 'Strengthening Growth' typology from the LEAD reference content which 'Refers to a positive change in market share and/or revenue, often over a period of time' (LEADing Practice 2022). The Builder typology accounted for 11% of the strategic typologies within the consumer product focus.

The Cashout strategy is focussed on maximising profit from an existing product range and strengthening an organisation's competitiveness during this process. The reason for the term 'cashout' is because patterns associated with this typology evidence low investment into research and development which leads to a limited emphasis on product improvement. However, it shares characteristics with the 'Generic Profit Strategy' (Hofer and Schendel 1978) and 'Profit Maximizing' strategies (Kotler 1965) that emphasise generating the most profit from sales distribution activities. This again reflects the 'Strengthening Growth' typology which includes success factors that seek to optimise revenue and services (LEADing Practice 2022). It is important to note that different success factors are associated with the Cashout and Builder, although they share the same 'Strengthen Growth' typology. The Cashout typology represented for 17% of the strategic typologies within consumer product focus.

The Niche typology represents a focus on quality and innovation, taking similar Contrasts with 'performance maximizing' from Utterback and Abernathy (1975) as well as 'specialization' from Vesper (1979). There is an emphasis on enhancing excellence associated with product and service delivery alongside research and development to facilitate innovation and transformation. This typology matches the rationale behind two typologies from LEAD, 'Increase Operational Excellence' and 'Improve Competitiveness' (LEADing Practice 2022). Operational excellence focuses on the continuous improvement of processes to support efficiency and standardisation where applicable (Ross 2006). Improving competitiveness focuses strategic direction towards gaining an advantage within the market through enhancing product and service provision (Luoma 2015). The Niche typology accounts for 9% of the strategic typologies within consumer product focus.

The Climber typology typifies a strategic focus that emphasises cost efficiency. Whilst steady profitability is observed in organisations that adopt this typology, this is pursued through the guise of cost consciousness. Comprising on high quality and product prices is evident with the negative values associated Cost Posture and Quality (Galbraith and Schendel 1983). The strategic focus that seeks to minimise expenses relating to resources and time to support enhanced ROI represents a 'Cost Efficiency' typology within the LEAD reference content. The Climber success factors relate to a reduction of costs across administration and sales informing the positive output associated with Climber's Cost Structure output. This typology accounts for 9% of the strategic typologies within consumer product focus.

Representing 47% of the strategic typology within the consumer product focus is the Continuity typology. Here there is little evidence of organisations displaying a proactive strategic direction, rather a focus is emphasised on business continuity and the ability to react to competitors or market conditions (Galbraith and Schendel 1983). This typifies a 'Lower Risk' typology from the LEAD reference content which seeks to reduce the possibility of low performance and loss of profits (LEADing Practice 2022). Success factors also relate to enhancing insight into competitor activity which is integral to the Continuity typology.

The strategic typologies associated with industrial products consist of (1) Low commitment, (2) Growth, (3) Maintenance and (4) Niche or Specialization. The low commitment typology represents low and negative output towards strategic posture and strategic direction. This signifies minimum low risk and emphasis on cost efficiencies. Drawing some comparison with the Harvest and Climber typologies. Therefore, sharing characteristics from the Lower Risk and Cost Efficiencies strategic typologies from the LEAD reference content (LEADing Practice 2022). The Low commitment typology accounts for 17% of the strategic typologies within industrial product focus.

The Growth typology represents a strong commitment towards expanding market position with notable investment. Measures against promotion and strategic postures are high and there are similarities with the 'Builder' typology for consumer products. Characteristics from the Strengthen Growth LEAD typology are evident with traits common to increasing revenue and market share over a period of time (LEADing Practice 2022). The Growth typology accounts for 25% of the strategic typologies within industrial product focus.

The Maintenance typology shares characteristics with the Continuity and Cost Reduction typologies. There is a focus on cost efficiencies as well as maintaining market position. Additional contrasts can be drawn from Utterback and Abernathy's (1975) 'cost minimizing' strategy that applies the same emphasis. This typology represents 49% of the strategic typologies within the industrial product focus and takes characteristics from the Lower Risk and Cost Efficiencies strategic typologies from the LEAD reference content (LEADing Practice 2022).

The Niche or also referred to as the Specialisation typology focuses on superior quality and high pricing posture. There is a narrow product line as the emphasis is on quality rather than quantity. This has similar traits to the 'Increase Operational Excellence' and 'Improve Competitiveness' LEAD typologies (LEADing Practice 2022). It also resembles its equivalent typology in the consumer product focus and accounts for 9% of the typologies.

Galbraith and Schendel's typologies cover all five LEAD typologies. There is no evidence to suggest an additional typology beyond that which has been aligned.

Prescott Typologies. Prescott (1983) critiqued typologies in connection with how organisations strategically deploy resources to compete within a competitive environment. He confirms the typology studies of Miles and Snow (1978), Miller and Friessen (1977) and Porter (1979) confirming patterns of strategy application that imply how resources are deployed. Porter (1979) refers to the patterns as strategic groups that divide the differences amongst firms competing in a competitive environment. 'At the business level, decisions must be made concerning both the thrust (such as marketing or production or R&D) and level (how much to each area) of resource deployments (Prescott P205, 1983). The level refers to the relative amount in relation to measures such as financial investment, assets and employees. The combination of 'thrust' and 'level' is termed a strategic profile (Prescott 1983). This essentially builds on the previous typology study and provides another analytical lens to the study of strategic types.

Prescott's (1983) study confirms 5 strategic typologies: (1) Differentiation: Market Share Domination, (2) Differentiation: Follow the Leaders, (3) Focus: Low Costs, (4) Prestige Market and (5) Differentiation: Low Quality Product.

Typology (1) represents a strategic focus that reflects growth and a dominant market share within a competitive environment. Typical characteristics display commitment towards high quality and significant breadth of product and service lines (Prescott 1983). This typology shares characteristics with Galbraith and Schendel (1983) Builder typology which also aligns with patterns confirmed by Hofer and Schendel (1978), Buzzell et al. (1975), Utterback and Abernathy (1975) and Vesper (1979). With clear evidence of optimising products and services through a high-quality endeavour and increasing growth through penetrating new segments of the market, the Differentiation Market Share Domination shares attributes of the 'Strengthen growth' typology from the LEAD reference content.

The Follow the Leaders typology shares similarities with Market Share Domination, however, there is a distinction between the two as there is less emphasis on the product breadth, product quality and relative market share (Prescott 1983). This typology boasts low direct costs indicating an emphasis on process improvement. Therefore in relation to the LEAD typologies, there appears to be a dual nature in the organisational strategic 'thrust'. Process improvement includes increasing efficiency in the execution of processes that support product and service delivery (Von Rosing et al. 2014). Whilst enhancing processes, the opportunity to reduce operating costs through efficiency savings is present. The 'Operational Excellence' typology has characteristics that emphasise process improvement (LEADing Practice 2021). Due to the traits associated with Market Share Domination, there is reason to also assign the 'Strengthen Growth' Typology.

The Focus: Low-Cost typology typically has a narrow product and service line along with traits of low manufacturing expenses to revenue, receivables to revenue and marketing expenses to revenue. This typology draws a contrast with Porter's Cost Leadership which also focusses on exploiting sources of cost advantage (Porter 1997). There is a salient theme that also suggests the Low-Cost typology exercises characteristics to defend its position within a niche market, something that Miles and Snow (1978) also group under their Defender Typology Strategy. The LEAD 'Cost Efficiency' typology has attributes that align with the Low-Cost typology, this includes exploring the reduction of all costs associated with the cost of products and services sold, administration and taxation.

The Prestige Market typology is focused on high product quality, demanding a relatively high price. It draws on some similarities with Porter's (2001) Differentiation typology, where attention to a premium price is underpinned by an organisation positioning itself around a select number of attributes that a customer segment deems important (Porter 2001). The quality and uniqueness justify the premium price. Like the Niche typology from Prescott (1983), this aligns with the 'Increase Operational Excellence' LEAD typology, however, there isn't a high emphasis on innovation through research and development. Therefore, it doesn't align with the 'Improve Competitiveness' like the Niche typology.

The Differentiation: Low Quality Product represents the majority of organisation samples from Prescot's research. It is difficult to assign this to a LEAD typology as the only distinct characteristic is associated with the low quality variable. However, what is clear from the research is that there is an associated low market share with this characteristic. This indicates that there isn't a strategic thrust to penetrate new markets or increase revenue to support growth. If there is little emphasis on product quality, then an organisation does not compete on the prestige of its product. There is a slightly above average indicator for the investment intensity, this is not towards the quality of the product which then leaves options for service and product fulfilment which is a characteristic of the LEAD Operational Excellence typology. This is the closest alignment although there are attributes from this typology that do not represent the Low Quality product focus such as strengthening development.

In summary of the five generic strategy typologies, Prescott (1983) indicates that the patterns associated with strategic types serve as a basis for examining performance in different environments. Within the typologies, the variables enable further insight into the factors that impact performance across metrics such as market share and ROI.

Chafee Typologies. Chafee'S (1985) three models of strategy are built upon the empirical and theoretical discourse on strategy between 70s and mid 80s. She grouped together specific variables that exhibit attributes and behaviours associated with strategy, integrating scholarly perspectives on strategic types (Chafee 1985). This resulted in (1) Linear Strategy, (2) Adaptive Strategy and (3) Interpretive Strategy.

The Linear Strategy model contains attributes that emphasise penetrating markets with new or enhanced products and services. The associated measures such as product diversity and market share are also found with 'Builder' and 'Growth' (Galbraith and Schendel 1983), 'Differentiation Dominant Market Share' (Prescott 1983), 'Innovator' (Douglas and Rhee 1989) and 'Strengthen Presence' (Luoma 2015). All instances mentioned aligning with the LEAD Strengthen Growth typology that has distinct characteristics relating to the above-mentioned.

Striking an effective balance between the opportunities and the risks present within the environment, the Adaptive Strategy model exhibits attributes that seek to enhance competitiveness. This entails product quality, positioning and differentiation within a strategic thrust that is commonly found within niche business environments (Chafee 1985). These attributes are also found in 'Customer Value through Competence' and 'Structural Renewal' (Luoma 2015), 'Nicher' from both Douglas and Rhee (1989) and Galbraith and Schendel (1983). The LEAD Improve Competitiveness typology is accordingly aligned with the Adaptive Strategy model.

The final model Chaffe (1985) examines strategy from a participant perspective, meaning there is more emphasis on evaluating perspectives from those involved in developing and influencing strategy. There is a focus on harnessing relationships, attitudes and the culture of the organisation. This approach moves away from the traditional measures of strategy and has relations with (Hoverstadt et al. 2020) 'strategy manoeuvres' which pays attention to the key interactions between organisations and actors to inform the success of strategy formulation and execution. However, Chaffe's (1985) interpretative model is vague in terms of a strategic thrust and is more centred on qualitative analysis of participants to examine and inform culture development. The results of such analysis could inform the progression of an 'Operational Excellence' typology because once a co-created culture is identified then the integration and standardisation of this can be progressed. However, this work isn't evident and there is a lack of a direct strategic thrust therefore no LEAD typology is aligned.

Douglass and Ree Typologies. Douglas and Rhee (1989) examined 437 organisations across different industry settings from the PIMS database. At the time of their research, there had been little attention to the strategic typology patterns outside of U.S. Their study extended the analysis of patterns within Europe alongside U.S. They identified six strategic typologies: (1) Quality Broadliner, (2) The Innovator, (3) Integrated Marketer, (4) Low Quality, (5) Nicher and (6) Synergist.

The Quality Broadliner had strategic thrusts in its broad market scope and high product quality. Distinct characteristics demonstrated emphasis on increasing market share and enhancing their competitiveness through their product quality. High revenue and ROI are evident within this typology which represented 15% of the sampled businesses (Douglass and Ree 1989). This typology shares characteristics from Builder (Galbraith and Schendel 1983) Growth and Market Share Domination (Prescott 1983) typologies. All of which align with the Strengthen Growth LEAD typology. In addition, it is necessary to align Quality Broadliner with the Improve Competitiveness typology due to its significance with maintain high quality.

The Innovator typology shares characteristics with the Market Share Domination from (Prescott 1983), they both emphasise breadth in the product and service line. This is the smallest represented organisation sample. It has a focus on the introduction of new products which aligns to the LEAD Strengthen Growth typology, boasting characteristics of supporting growth through the introduction of new products and services.

The Integrated Marketer is described as very similar to the Quality Broadliner, evidencing broad market scope and high product quality. The difference being high levels of vertical integration enhancing the customer centric processes. This, therefore, shares characteristics from two LEAD typologies Strengthen Growth and Improve Operational Excellence.

The Low Quality typology has low performance across the key variables. It has low product quality, market share and ROI. There is some resemblance to Prescott's (1983) Differentiation: Low Quality of Product, however, there is no evidence of intensity in the investment of customer centric processes so there is no justification to align with the Operational Excellence typology from LEAD. As there are no distinct features that suggest a new strategic typology nor, alignment to an existing one, it is not assigned.

The smallest organisation sample was made up of the Nicher typology. Focussing on a low breadth product line with high quality, this typology facilitates an above average financial performance. Market share is low due to the niche of the product. However, there is an emphasis on maintaining competitiveness through continuous improvement of product quality. This has similarities to the Niche/Specialization typology of Galbraith and Schendel (1983) from a perspective of increasing quality through research and development. The LEAD Improve Competitiveness typology fits the Nicher profile through the strong characteristic of meeting or exceeding customer expectations through product quality.

The largest representation from the sample size is the Synergist typology representing 30%. This typology displays a distinct focus on shared marketing expenditure evidencing the endeavour to create effective partnerships and synergies. This is a characteristic of the Strengthen Growth typology from LEAD which places emphasis on seeking growth through partnering. Whilst operating in a narrow market, this endeavour supports growth within the competitive environment.

Although the work of Douglas and Rhee (1989) took samples from outside the U.S, there is no identification of additional typologies.

Luoma Typologies. Luoma'S (2015) study on the relationship between strategy and performance deviated away from the previous study on strategic typologies that assumed established frameworks such as Porter's (1979) Generic Strategies and Miles and Snow (1978) typologies. His research design employed an endogenous approach to deriving typologies rather than underpinning the development of strategic types with predefined strategic groups. The organic framing of typologies included (1) Effective and improving operations, (2) Structural renewal, (3) Dynamic networks, (4) Strengthening presence, (5) Social and ecological awareness and (6) Customer value through competence.

The Effective and improving operations typology relates to business process improvement and its connection to financial performance. Driving efficiency is essentially transforming the existing into a better state that should drive costs down (Ross et al. 2006). This trait is evident in 'performance maximizing' from Utterback and Abernathy (1975). The vertical integration indicated by Douglas and Rhee (1989) highlights the importance of process integration for customers, this is accommodated by business process improvement. These similarities are all aligned with the Improve Operational Excellence typology from LEAD.

Luoma's (2015) Structural renewal has an organic mix of different strategic focus points. On one hand, there is brand and reputation management, and market positioning related to the Improve Competitiveness LEAD typology. In addition, there is a focus on structural changes and change management which aligns with some of the characteristics of the Improve Operational Excellence LEAD typology, specifically improving resource management. Therefore, it is fitting to align the Structural Renewal strategy type with both LEAD typologies.

The Dynamic Networks, again, represent an organic mix of aligned typologies. With an emerging theme connected to wider impact through connected networks, this instantiates the Strengthen Growth typology which contains a characteristic that increases growth through partnering. Besides this, there is also an emphasis on digital security which is aligned with the Lower Risk typology.

A clear alignment to the LEAD Strengthen Growth typology is evident with the Strengthening presence type of Luoma (2015). Penetrating new markets for growth and developing an international presence is radiant with this strategy type.

Luoma's (2015) Social and Ecological Awareness strategy type is themed around sustainability. The strategy reference content of LEAD does not have a specific adherence to corporate sustainability. Whilst there isn't a specific fit for this typology it is certainly an instantiation of strategic typology that must be considered. Corporate sustainability is a force for large organisations across sectors and industries (Gauthier 2017). There have been considerable developments towards how organisations tackle sustainability and these warrant independent research focused on sustainability strategic types due to the complexities and advancements in corporate sustainability (Gauthier 2017).

Customer Value through Competence has a dual focus. Firstly, an endeavour to enhance customer experience and quality of service and product that all represent customer value. Secondly, the continuous development of competencies across the workforce feed into the creation of customer value. This dual focus aligns with two of the LEAD typologies, Improve Competitiveness which has characteristics of enhancing customer satisfaction and loyalty alongside improving service and product quality. The Improve Operational Excellence typology is also aligned due to the development of the workforce which can link to competencies that contribute towards creating customer value.

Anwar and Hasnu Typologies. Anwar and Hasnu (2017) used the Miles and Snow (1978) typologies as a vehicle to assess the different strategic patterns in 307 joint stock firms across twelve industries in Pakistan. Building on their study in 2016, they contributed a classification of hybrid strategies to Miles and Snow typologies building upon the pure typologies i.e. Defender, Prospector, Analyser and Reactor. Firms lying between 'Defender' and 'Analyzer' are classified as 'Defenders-Analyzers-Like'. Whilst organisations lying between 'Prospector' and 'Analyzer' are classified as 'Prospector-Analyzer-Like'. Hybrid strategies represent a combination of strategic orientations that enable effective adaptation to unpredictable environmental change. In contrast, pure strategic typologies are generally better suited to more stable market conditions (Anwar and Hasnu 2016). The underlying nature of typologies still takes from Miles and Snow (1978), albeit having a blend between two typologies. This implies alignment to the following LEAD typologies; Cost Efficiency, Improve Competitiveness, Improve Operational Excellence and Strengthen Growth which all have traits linking back to the Miles and Snow (1978) typologies.

2.6 Summary of Academic Strategy Typologies

Evidently, typologies of strategy have provided a means for organisations to focus resources in a strategic manner within a competitive environment. Empirical research on organisation performance related to strategic typologies, reveals patterns in the way organisations strategically deploy their resources. The reference content from LEAD appears to align with the majority of typologies critiqued above. However, there are some limitations that need to be considered in its application.

Firstly, Prescott's (1983) notion of 'Strategic Profiles' indicate the importance of distinguishing between the strategic **thrust** and **level** of investment. Level of investment enables the ability to embed essential measures and capabilities into business level strategy such as the amount of investment, leveraging of existing assets and human resource management. The LEAD typologies focus on the 'thrust', i.e., where do we increase our strategic focus for competing? Undertaking business level strategic planning without considering Prescotts's 'level', may prove ineffective and force changes to be made after exerting time in pursuing typology paths.

Secondly, none of the authors in their critique of typologies discussed generic strategies in the context of government local authorities. The empirical research covered organisations across various sectors and industries that warrant the need to gain a competitive advantage. Government local authorities do not compete in most services they provide as in many cases there are no paying customers (Cohen 2001). This presents an opportunity to develop additional typologies befitting for governments and local authorities that encompass a more civic societal premise.

Finally, sustainability strategic typologies are also absent in empirical research. Therefore, the patterns discussed do not resonate with an organisation's sustainability agenda. Previous studies exist on sustainability typologies (Azzone and Bertelè 1994; Hart 1995; Nidumolu et al. 2009; Orsato 2006; Roome 1992; Gauthier 2017) and the critical review offered in this article does not contribute to that body of knowledge. Any application of the LEAD typologies will need to consider the above limitations. Whilst they may accelerate the pace in which an organisation progresses in business level strategy work, there will be additional work required outside the typologies when strategising for sustainability and government local authorities.

3 Methodology

An inductive approach to the theory development has been employed across the thirty-three strategy related models and the academic derived strategy typologies. A deductive approach was applied to analysing the generic typologies using the LEAD strategy typologies as a basis to contrast the academically derived strategy typologies from industrial research. Secondary research on dynamic capabilities was used as a basis to group attributes connected to Sensing, Seizing and Transforming.

The development of a map (listing of concepts), matrix (intersecting concepts where they relate) and model (producing a view from the matrix contained) led to the creation of the extended Strategy Meta model. The matrix was engineered in a spreadsheet that facilitated the ability to apply filters, facilitating several options for shortlisting models to support a specific contextual outcome.

4 Results

The results have been structured according to the intended outcomes derived through the applied inquiry methods. Alongside this is the addition of a tool that has been generated from the results, accelerating the ability to analyse and select relevant models that support the strategic endeavour. Furthermore, insights and connections to Caine and von Rosing's (2018) Strategy Lifecycle is also presented.

4.1 Strategy Models – Ontological Concept Confirmation

The analysis of thirty-three models informed the mapping of specific objects that spread across the business and information layers of the organisation. In total thirty-nine objects have been mapped to represent the nature of the models. The size of the artefact that contains the mapping is too large to display as a single view, therefore a selected sample of models will be used throughout this section to demonstrate mapping across all three principles.

Figures 3 and 4 are views that display (1), the examples of models mapped against objects and (2), the representation of objects spread across the two of the core reference layers and their respective sub-layers i.e., Business and Information (core layer), Value, Capability, Service, Process and Application (sub-layer).

Strategy Ontology Models Matrix — BUSINESS LAYER — VALUE LAYER

Strategy Ontology Models Matrix	1. Force (external/ internal)	2. Driver	3. Vision	4. Mission	5. Requirement	6. Value Proposition	7. Strategy (Strategic Objective)	8. Goal (e.g. business, application, …	9. Objective (Critical Success Fact…	10. Plan	11. Quality	12. Security	13. Risk	14. Measure	15. Report	16. Time	17. Monitor	18. Control	19. Pain Point
Business Definition Model (Abell, 1980)						x													
Blue Ocean Strategy – Strategy Canvas (Kim & Mauborgne 2014)	x	x				x													
Business Model Canvas (Osterwalder & Pigneur 2010)						x													
Core Competencies (Prahalad & Hamel 1990)																			
Formal Strategic Planning Process (Armstrong, 1982)							x		x								x	x	
Greiner's Growth Model (Greiner, 1998)						x			x						x				
House of Purchasing and Supply (Kearney's Framework, 2002)							x							x					
European Foundation for Quality Management (EFQM, 1992)			x	x			x							x					
Offshoring / Outsourcing (Aron & Singh 2005)	x	x					x						x	x	x				
Organisational Configurations (Mintzberg, 1992)																			
Overhead Value Analysis (Mowen & Hansen 2006)														x	x				
Porter's Generic Strategies (Porter 2004)							x												
Porter's Value Chain (Porter, 1985)																			
Porter's Five Forces (Porter, 1980)	x	x																	

Strategy Ontology Models Matrix — BUSINESS LAYER — CAPABILITY LAYER

Strategy Ontology Models Matrix	20. Organisation	21. Enterprise Capability	22. Organisational Competency	23. Resource	24. Actor	25. Role	26. Organisational Function	27. Business Object	28. Product	29. Contract	30. Organisation Role	31. Business Compliance	32. Location	33. Business Channel
Business Definition Model (Abell, 1980)		x	x			x								
Blue Ocean Strategy – Strategy Canvas (Kim & Mauborgne 2014)									x					
Business Model Canvas (Osterwalder & Pigneur 2010)			x	x		x								x
Core Competencies (Prahalad & Hamel 1990)	x		x						x					
Formal Strategic Planning Process (Armstrong, 1982)														
Greiner's Growth Model (Greiner, 1998)			x			x						x		x
House of Purchasing and Supply (Kearney's Framework, 2002)			x											
European Foundation for Quality Management (EFQM, 1992)			x	x	x	x					x			
Offshoring / Outsourcing (Aron & Singh 2005)			x			x				x		x	x	x
Organisational Configurations (Mintzberg, 1992)						x	x							
Overhead Value Analysis (Mowen & Hansen 2006)					x	x	x		x					x
Porter's Generic Strategies (Porter 2004)														
Porter's Value Chain (Porter, 1985)	x		x											
Porter's Five Forces (Porter, 1980)				x	x				x		x			x

Fig. 3. Models mapped to LEAD objects, core business and domain reference layers

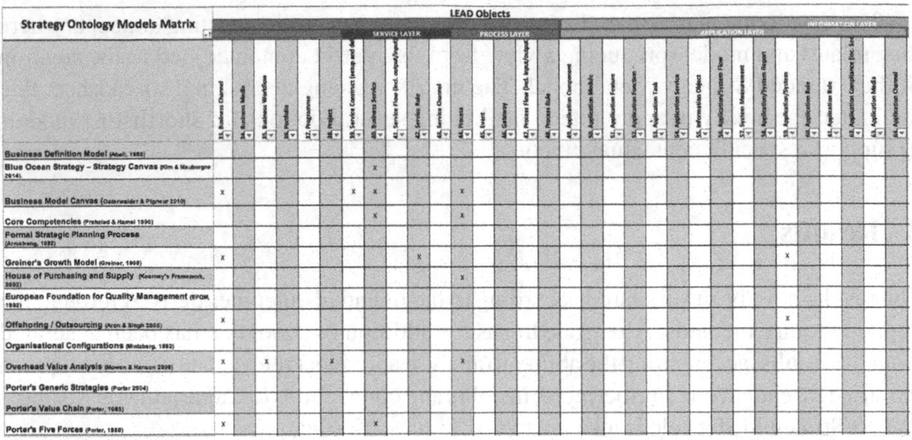

Fig. 4. Models mapped to LEAD objects, core business, information and domain reference layers

Not all models contained the 'Strategy' object, however, all models had objects within the Business Layer of the LEAD Enterprise Ontology. Five of the models have an object in the Information Layer providing an ontological link from strategy to digital applications. One of the models had a broad concept of technology so in practical application, it may entail connecting to the Technology layer, however for this example it has been mapped to an object within the Information layer.

The mapping of model concepts to objects disambiguates interpretations and definitions of the concepts that are present in all the models documented. This provides the basis to establish the relations (semantics) between each of the objects, thus enabling a deeper understanding of how pertinent objects connected to strategy relate to each other. The construct of the semantics has been informed through semantics in Caine and von Rosing (2018) and OMG's Business Model Motivation. These semantics are visible in the Extended Strategy Meta Model in Sect. 4.6.

It was necessary to utilise 'Enterprise Tagging' in addition to the concept of Object mapping as nine of the models had pertinent concepts within them that required documentation. These concepts (Table 12) were not part of the 91 objects from the LEAD ontology, however, they still needed to be captured. Nine of the models mapped to selected concepts from the Enterprise Tagging list (Fig. 5).

Table 12. Sample models mapped against enterprise tags

Model and author	Enterprise tagging list
Activity-based costing (Cooper and Kaplan 1998)	Cost categorisation
Business definition model (Abell 1980)	Customer segmentation

(*continued*)

Table 12. (*continued*)

Model and author	Enterprise tagging list
Greiner's growth model (Greiner 1998)	Cost categorisation, performance model practices, operating model practices
Porter's value chain (Porter 2001)	Supporting activities and primary activities
Scenario planning (Heijden 2006)	Critical forces & drivers, scenario uncertainty (low/high)
SWOT analysis (Hill and Westbrook 1997)	Revenue opportunity, value opportunity, critical forces & drivers
Value disciplines (Treacy and Wiersema 1995)	Outperforming practices, best practices
Internationalisation strategy framework (Lem et al. 2013)	Integration, Coordination
Road-mapping (Farrukh et al. 2003)	New customers, supporting activities
Market attractiveness business activity (MABA) (Have et al. 2007)	Customer segmentation

Strategy Ontology Models Matrix	Enterprise Tagging													
	ROI Opportunity	Revenue Opportunity	Value Opportunity	Customer Segments	Performance	Operating	Critical Forces & Drivers	Scenario Uncertainty (Low/High)	Outperforming Practice	Best Practice	Integration	Coordination	New Customers	Supporting Activities	Primary Activities
Business Definition Model (Abell, 1980)				X											
Blue Ocean Strategy – Strategy Canvas (Kim & Mauborgne 2014).															
Business Model Canvas (Osterwalder & Pigneur 2010)															
Core Competencies (Prahalad & Hamel 1990)															
Formal Strategic Planning Process (Armstrong, 1982)															
Greiner's Growth Model (Greiner, 1998)					X	X									
House of Purchasing and Supply (Kearney's Framework, 2002)															
European Foundation for Quality Management (EFQM, 1992)															
Offshoring / Outsourcing (Aron & Singh 2005)															
Organisational Configurations (Mintzberg, 1992)															
Overhead Value Analysis (Mowen & Hanson 2006)															
Porter's Generic Strategies (Porter 2004)															
Porter's Value Chain (Porter, 1985)														X	X
Porter's Five Forces (Porter, 1980)															

Fig. 5. Models mapped to enterprise tags

4.2 Correlation with Strategy, Competencies and Capabilities

The mapping of concept to object in addition to the LEAD competency mapping provided insight into a categorisation of the model type. Sixteen out of the thirty-three models that contained the 'Strategy' object were found to either inform the positioning of an organisation within an industry or, insinuate how it should compete within a given environment, thus supporting the development of the future direction. Each of these models had links back to competencies in the strategic tier. These were grouped under a 'Strategy Model' category (Table 13).

Table 13. Caine strategy model categorisation

Model category group	Model and author
Strategy model	5 Ps Model of Strategy Implementation (Pryor and Anderson 2007; Toombs and Humphreys 2007)
Strategy model	7-S Framework (Waterman et al. 1980)
Strategy model	Agile strategy management process cycle (Lyngso 2017)
Strategy model	Ashridge mission model (Campbell and Yeung 1991)
Strategy model	Balanced Scorecard (BSC) (Kaplan and Norton 2005)
Strategy model	Formal strategic planning process (Armstrong 1982)
Strategy model	House of purchasing and supply (Kearney's Framework 2002)
Strategy model	European foundation for quality management (EFQM 1992)
Strategy model	Offshoring/outsourcing (Aron and Singh 2005)
Strategy model	Porter's generic strategies (Porter 2004)
Strategy model	Scenario planning (Heijden 2006)
Strategy model	Strategy map (Kaplan and Norton 2004)
Strategy model	Value disciplines (Treacy and Wiersema 1995)
Strategy model	Internationalisation strategy framework (Lem et al. 2013)
Strategy model	Ansoff's product/market grid and geographic vector (Ansoff 1987)
Strategy model	Levels of control (Simons 1995)

Fifteen out of the thirty-three models that did not contain the 'Strategy' object still had the same nature of the Strategy Models. They each had links back to the Strategic Tier competencies. The main difference between them and the Strategy Models was that they did not contain the 'strategy object' and therefore a practitioner would not be able to create instances of strategy objectives when working with these models. A Strategic Model category was given to these fifteen models (Table 14).

Table 14. Caine strategic model categorisation

Model category group	Model and author
Strategic model	Activity-based costing (Kaplan and Cooper 1998)
Strategic model	Big Hairy Audacious Goal (BHAG) (Collin and Porras 1994)
Strategic model	Boston Consulting Group (BCG) Matrix
Strategic model	(Boston Consulting Group 1970)
Strategic model	Business definition model (Abell 1980)
Strategic model	Blue ocean strategy – strategy canvas (Kim and Mauborgne 2014)
Strategic model	Business model canvas (Osterwalder et al. 2010)
Strategic model	Core competencies (Prahalad and Hamel 1990)
Strategic model	Organisational configurations (Mintzberg 1993)
Strategic model	Overhead value analysis (Mowen and Hanson 2006)
Strategic model	Porter's Value Chain (Porter 2001)
Strategic model	Porter's Five Forces (Porter 1979)
Strategic model	SWOT Analysis (Hill and Westbrook 1997)
Strategic model	Road-mapping (Farrukh et al. 2003)
Strategic model	Competing values of organizational effectiveness (Quinn and Rohrbaugh 1983)
Strategic model	Market Attractiveness Business Activity (MABA) (Have et al. 2007)

Two out of the thirty-three models informed the functional deployment of resources with a link back to strategic concepts that drive how an organisation competes. These models had a majority of LEAD competencies residing in the tactical tier as opposed to the strategic tier as with the case for the Strategy and Strategic Models. A 'Strategic Tactical Model' category was given to these models (Table 15 and Figs. 6 and 7).

Table 15. Caine strategic tactical model categorisation

Model category group	Model and author
Strategic tactical model	Benchmarking (Watson 1994)
Strategic tactical model	Greiner's growth model (Greiner 1998)

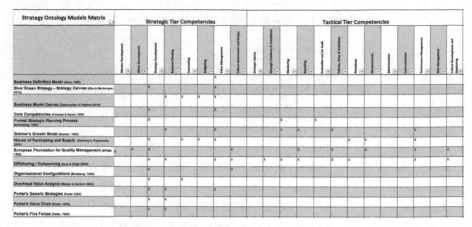

Fig. 6. Sample models mapped against strategic and tactical competencies

Strategy Ontology Models Matrix	Issue Management	Operational Planning	Process Management	Operational Oversight and Monitoring	Operational Reporting	Evaluation and/or Audit	Operational Measurements	Procedures2	Operational Advice and/or Guidance	Processing	Culture Realisation	Strategy Tool	Strategic Tool	Strategic Tactical Tool	Strategic Operational Tool
Business Definition Model (Abell, 1980)												X			
Blue Ocean Strategy – Strategy Canvas (Kim & Mauborgne 2014).												X			
Business Model Canvas (Osterwalder & Pigneur 2010)		X	X									X			
Core Competencies (Prahalad & Hamel 1990)												X			
Formal Strategic Planning Process (Armstrong, 1982)													X		
Greiner's Growth Model (Greiner, 1998)				X										X	
House of Purchasing and Supply (Kearney's Framework, 2002)		X											X		
European Foundation for Quality Management (EFQM, 1992)		X								X	X				
Offshoring / Outsourcing (Aron & Singh 2005)													X		
Organisational Configurations (Mintzberg, 1992)												X			
Overhead Value Analysis (Nowan & Hanson 2006)													X		
Porter's Generic Strategies (Porter 2004)												X			
Porter's Value Chain (Porter, 1985)												X			
Porter's Five Forces (Porter, 1980)												X			

Fig. 7. Sample models mapped against operational competencies

Each of the thirty-three models was mapped against LEAD tier competencies and dynamic capability traits where applicable. All models that mapped to the 'Sensing' dynamic capability trait were grouped as Strategy or Strategic models. Further analysis is required to discover potential pathways or patterns that relate to the competencies, capabilities and resulting models. The tool (further discussed in 4.6) has limitations in pattern discovery subject to the filtering capability (Figs. 8 and 9).

All models had links back to the competencies whereas six out of the thirty-three models had no link back to dynamic capabilities. Seven of the models had links back to 'Ordinary Capabilities' emphasising operational excellence through best practices and

Fig. 8. Sample models mapped against sensing dynamic capability attributes

Strategy Ontology Models Matrix	Sensing						
	Peripheral Vision (Day and Schoemaker 2016; Breznik et al, 2018; Bojesson & Fundin, 2021) - Involves scoping which determines how wide you scan and the nature of the issues you scan for. Scope is informed by past analysis, present issues and trends and f	Vigilant Learning (Day and Schoemaker 2016; Tecce, 2007) - Outside in orientation for products and services, ensuring employees are empowered to share voice on important matters that impact the business, surprising biases, triangulating perspectives / Outside In Orientation	Digital Scouting (Warner & Wilger, 2019) - Scanning for tech trends, screening for competitors, sensing customer-centric trends	Digital Scenario Planning (Warner & Wilger, 2019) - Anaylsing scouted signals, interpretating digital future scenarios, Formualating digital strategies	Digital Mindset Crafting (Warner & Wilger, 2019; Bojesson & Fundin, 2021) - Establishing a long-term digital vision, enable entrepreunrial mindset, promoting a digital mindset	R&D and selection of New Tech (Tecce, 2007)	Supplier, Complimentor, and technology Innovation Tapping(Tecce, 2007) - building off the developments of others to create something purpose fit for the new business model
Business Definition Model (Abell, 1980)							
Blue Ocean Strategy – Strategy Canvas (Kim & Mauborgne 2014)			Screening for Competitors				
Business Model Canvas (Osterwalder & Pigneur 2010)		Outside In Orientation					
Core Competencies (Prahalad & Hamel 1990)							
Formal Strategic Planning Process (Armstrong, 1982)							
Greiner's Growth Model (Greiner, 1998)							
House of Purchasing and Supply (Kearney's Framework, 2002)		Outside In Orientation					
European Foundation for Quality Management (EFQM, 1992)						Research and Development	
Offshoring / Outsourcing (Aron & Singh 2005)			Screening for Competitors				
Organisational Configurations (Mintzberg, 1992)							
Overhead Value Analysis (Nowen & Hanson 2006)							
Porter's Generic Strategies (Porter 2004)							
Porter's Value Chain (Porter, 1985)							
Porter's Five Forces (Porter, 1980)			Screening for Competitors				

Fig. 9. Sample models mapped against seizing and transforming dynamic capability attributes

Strategy Ontology Models Matrix	Seizing						Transforming			
	Delineating the Customer Solution and Business Model (Tecce, 2007; Day and Warner & Wilger, 2019) - Recognising and designing mechanisms to capture value. Probe-and-Learn Experimentation, developing real options for ma / Delineate Customer Solution	Selecting Decision-Making Protocols & Strategic Agility (Tecce, 2007; Warner & Wilger, 2019; Bojesson & Fundin, 2021) - including financial model to govern decision making, agile resource allocation.	Building Loyalty and Commitment (Tecce, 2007; Breznik et al, 2018) - Managers form special networking teams for straightforward and focused	Establishing Boundaries for Compliment Controls and Platforms (Tecce, 2007)	Developing Strategic Partnerships (Breznik et al, 2018; Day and Schoemaker 2016) - Third, firms must look beyond their own organizational and market boundaries, probing for insights from a wide array of peer	Balancing digital portfolio (Warner & Wilger, 2019) - portfolio management	Governance (Breznik et al, 2018; Tecce, 2007) - control mechanisms, appropriate management structure i.e. Chief Digital	Redesign, Decentralisatio n and Flat Structures (Day 2018; Tecce, 2007) and Schoemaker 2016; Breznik 2018; Modularise/	Continuous Improvement (Warner & Wilger, 2019; Tecce 2007) - Digital maturity readiness, digital knowledge management, digital ecosystem	Reward Systems (Warner & Wilger, 2019)
Business Definition Model (Abell, 1980)	Delineate Customer Solution									
Blue Ocean Strategy – Strategy Canvas (Kim & Mauborgne 2014)										
Business Model Canvas (Osterwalder & Pigneur 2010)					Strategic Partnerships					
Core Competencies (Prahalad & Hamel 1990)										
Formal Strategic Planning Process (Armstrong, 1982)										Culture (seek commitment)
Greiner's Growth Model (Greiner, 1998)							Management Structure	Decentralise		
House of Purchasing and Supply (Kearney's Framework, 2002)										
European Foundation for Quality Management (EFQM, 1992)			Building loyalty and Commitment							
Offshoring / Outsourcing (Aron & Singh 2005)										
Organisational Configurations (Mintzberg, 1992)										
Overhead Value Analysis (Nowen & Hanson 2006)									Decentralise	
Porter's Generic Strategies (Porter 2004)										
Porter's Value Chain (Porter, 1985)										
Porter's Five Forces (Porter, 1980)										

process management. As the majority of models are linked to both competencies and capabilities, a strong correlation back to strategy is confirmed (Fig. 10).

4.3 Relationship with the Strategy Lifecycle

The strategy lifecycle developed by Caine and von Rosing (2018) outlined six high level phases that frame typical strategy development work. These phases, namely (1) Analyse & Understand, (2) Options and Design, (3) Develop, (4) Execute, (5) Govern and (6) Continuous Improvement; contain steps that orientate action necessary within a specific phase. These steps call upon specific objects and it is through this that further

Strategy Ontology Models Matrix	Ordinary Capabilities	No Link to Capabilities
Business Definition Model (Abell, 1980)		
Blue Ocean Strategy – Strategy Canvas (Kim & Mauborgne 2014).		
Business Model Canvas (Osterwalder & Pigneur 2010)		
Core Competencies (Prahalad & Hamel 1990)		Missing
Formal Strategic Planning Process (Armstrong, 1982)		
Greiner's Growth Model (Greiner, 1998)		
House of Purchasing and Supply (Kearney's Framework, 2002)		
European Foundation for Quality Management (EFQM, 1992)	Operating excellence and best practice for process	
Offshoring / Outsourcing (Aron & Singh 2005)		
Organisational Configurations (Mintzberg, 1992)		Missing
Overhead Value Analysis (Mowen & Hanson 2006)		
Porter's Generic Strategies (Porter 2004)		Missing
Porter's Value Chain (Porter, 1985)		Missing
Porter's Five Forces (Porter, 1980)		

Fig. 10. Sample models mapped against ordinary capability attributes

insight can be drawn. The thirty-nine objects identified from the strategy models review provide the opportunity to delineate a link back to the Strategy Lifecycle. The steps identified by Caine and von Rosing (2018) have been contrasted with the thirty-nine objects, resulting in labelling of strategy phases for each object. This is visible in the Extended Strategy Meta Model, Sect. 4.4.

4.4 Extended Strategy Meta Model

A total of thirty-nine objects were mapped from the concepts that consisted of the thirty-three models. These objects informed the development of an Extended Strategy

Meta Model, building on the meta model presented in Caine and von Rosing (2018). The semantic relations between the thirty-nine objects are derived from Caine and von Rosing (2018) and the Business Model Motivation (OMG 2015). The objects are placed across the core reference and domain ontologies. They are labelled by their architecture layer disposition. Each architecture layer is referenced back to either Corporate, Business and Functional level strategy. This provides useful insight into how the architecture layers relate to the different levels of strategy. Execution is assigned to the service and process domain ontologies as the nature of this relates to the implementation of intended services derived from strategic development. Information and Technology enablement is assigned to the Application domain and Technology core reference layer as they essentially enable the services and processes from an information, application and technology perspective. This satisfies the importance of ensuring that strategy informs technical requirements and alignment between business and technology (Nelson and Nelson 2003).

The legend denotes the type of models that integrate the objects, Strategy Model (S), Strategic Model (SM) and Strategic Tactical Model (STM). In addition, integration of the competencies associated across the Strategic Tier (C1), Tactical Tier (C2) and Operational (C3) are identified with each object. Furthermore, insight into creating a strategic path towards developing dynamic capabilities is noted through Seizing (D1), Sensing (D2) and Transforming (D3). Figure 11 displays a visual interpretation of the legend which explains the modelling notation applied (Fig. 12).

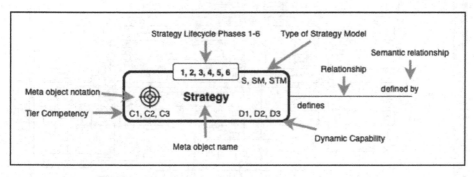

Fig. 11. Model notation for extended strategy meta model

Strategy Lifecyle Phases

| 1 | Analyse & understand | 2 | Options and Design | 3 | Develop | 4 | Execute | 5 | Govern | 6 | Continuous Improvement |

Tier Competency

C1 = Strategic Tier Competency, C2 = Tactical Tier Competency, C3 = Operational Tier Competency

Dynamic Capability

D1 = Sensing, D2 = Seizing, D3 = Transforming

Strategy Model Type

S = Strategy Model, SM = Strategic Model, STM = Strategic Tactical Model

Fig. 12. Legend for extended strategy meta model

Due to the size of the Extended Strategy Meta Model, it has been divided into three figures (Figs. 13, 14 and 15).

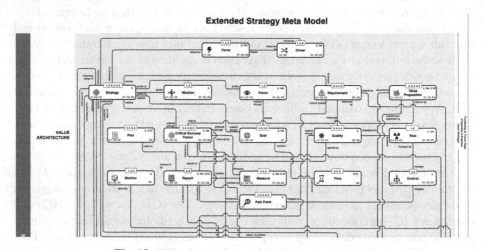

Fig. 13. Value layer of extended strategy meta model

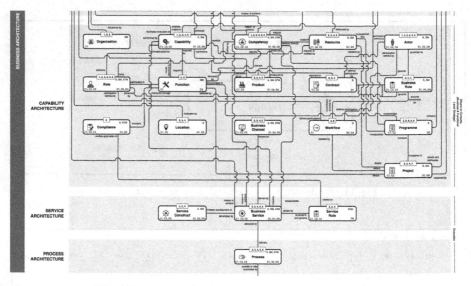

Fig. 14. Capability layer of extended strategy meta model

4.5 Patterns with Strategy Typologies

A summary of the analysis with strategic typologies (Table 15) confirms that generic business level strategies have a strong correlation with the LEAD Strategy Taxonomy

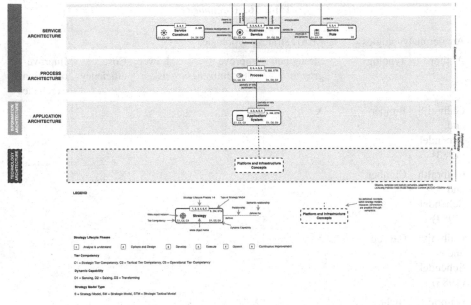

Fig. 15. Service, process and application layer of extended strategy meta model

reference content. Since each of the generic typologies represents an instance of the 'Strategy' object, it provides a useful basis to help direct strategic intent at the business strategy level. Models that incorporate typologies will form a type of Strategy Model as it contains the strategy object.

Table 16 displays a summary view of the academic typologies and their link back to LEAD typologies.

Table 16. Academic derived typologies mapped to LEAD typologies

Academic typologies		LEAD strategy typologies				
Author	Typology	Strengthen growth	Improve competitiveness	Lower risk	Cost efficiency	Improve operational excellence
Galbraith and Schendel (1983)	Harvest				X	

(continued)

Table 16. (*continued*)

Academic typologies		LEAD strategy typologies				
Author	Typology	Strengthen growth	Improve competitiveness	Lower risk	Cost efficiency	Improve operational excellence
Galbraith and Schendel (1983)	Builder	X				
Galbraith and Schendel (1983)	Climber				X	
Galbraith and Schendel (1983)	Cashout	X				
Galbraith and Schendel (1983)	Niche		X			
Galbraith and Schendel (1983)	Continuity			X		
Galbraith and Schendel (1983)	Growth	X				
Galbraith and Schendel (1983)	Maintenance			X		
Galbraith and Schendel (1983)	Low commitment			X	X	
Prescott (1983)	Differentiation dominant market share					X
Prescott (1983)	Low cost				X	

(*continued*)

Table 16. (*continued*)

Academic typologies		LEAD strategy typologies				
Author	Typology	Strengthen growth	Improve competitiveness	Lower risk	Cost efficiency	Improve operational excellence
Prescott (1983)	Prestige					X
Prescott (1983)	Low quality					X
Douglas and Rhee (1989)	Quality broadliner	X	X			
Douglas and Rhee (1989)	Innovator	X				
Douglas and Rhee (1989)	Integrated marketer	X				X
Douglas and Rhee (1989)	Low quality	No assigned typology				
Douglas and Rhee (1989)	Nicher		X			
Douglas and Rhee (1989)	Synergist	X				
Luoma (2015)	Effective and improving operations					X
Luoma (2015)	Structural renewal		X			
Luoma (2015)	Dynamic networks	X		X		
Luoma (2015)	Strengthen presence	X				
Luoma (2015)	Social and ecological awareness	Nothing present in the LEAD strategy taxonomy that relates to sustainability typologies				
Luoma (2015)	Customer value through competence		X			

(*continued*)

Table 16. (*continued*)

Academic typologies		LEAD strategy typologies				
Author	Typology	Strengthen growth	Improve competitiveness	Lower risk	Cost efficiency	Improve operational excellence
Chafee (1986)	Linear strategy	X				
Chafee (1986)	Adaptive strategy		X			
Chafee (1986)	Interpretive strategy	Model is vague and more centred on qualitative analysis from participants to examine and inform culture development				
Miles and Snow (1978)	Defender				X	X
Miles and Snow (1978)	Prospector	X				
Miles and Snow (1978)	Analyzer		X			
Miles and Snow (1978)	Reactor	No assigned typology				
Anwar and Hasnu (2017)	Defender				X	X
Anwar and Hasnu (2017)	Prospector	X				
Anwar and Hasnu (2017)	Analyzer		X			
Anwar and Hasnu (2017)	Defender & Analyzer		X		X	X
Anwar and Hasnu (2017)	Prospector & Analyzer	X	X			

4.6 A Tool for Grouping Models Related to Strategy Development

The ontological work carried out on the strategy models has been engineered in a spreadsheet. The structure of the information takes the form of a matrix (rows and columns) listing the models for each row and the concepts they relate to across each column. Each concept can be filtered which lists the models relating to a specific concept.

Based on the contextual setting, the strategy practitioner can accelerate their ability towards selecting the most appropriate model to work with dependent upon strategic nature, organisation tier competencies, dynamic capabilities or specific meta objects (Figs. 16, 17, 18 and 19).

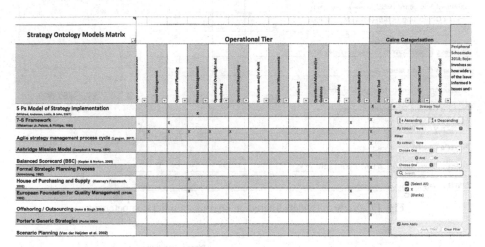

Fig. 16. Caine categorisation filtered on strategy tools

5 Discussion

5.1 Strategy Models – Ontological Concept Confirmation

The results from reviewing the thirty-three models formalise concepts associated with strategy models. The formalisation links back to the LEAD Enterprise Ontology, attributing defined objects to each of the concepts. This removes ambiguity when interpreting any of the concepts, as a formal definition is presented for each object. With a formal description in place, it is possible to communicate meaning that is consistent across different stakeholders who have a common interest in the objects concerned (Borst et al. 1997). The ontological mapping was essential as this provided the basis to orchestrate relations (semantics) between the concepts supporting the ability to develop an extended meta model. Another derivative of the mapping was the ability to understand which objects contribute towards the development of competencies and dynamic capabilities. Furthermore, the confirmation of objects enabled a connection back to the strategy lifecycle (Caine and von Rosing 2018), extending insights into the objects that play a role through the lifecycle of strategy development.

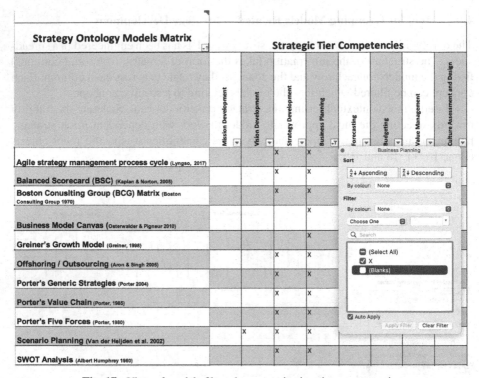

Fig. 17. View of models filtered on organisation tier competencies

Fig. 18. View of models filtered on seizing dynamic capability attributes

5.2 Correlation Between Strategy, Competency and Capability

The analysis of the reviewed models affirmed a correlation between organisation tier competencies, dynamic capabilities and strategy. More specifically, a delineation of models that support the development of competencies and dynamic capabilities enables

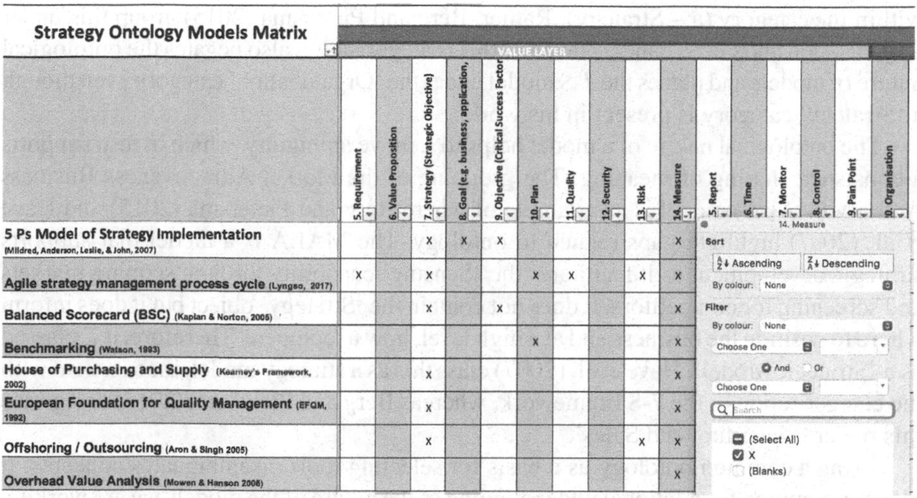

Strategy Ontology Models Matrix

Model	5. Requirement	6. Value Proposition	7. Strategy (Strategic Objective)	8. Goal (e.g. business, application)	9. Objective (Critical Success Factor)	10. Plan	11. Quality	12. Security	13. Risk	14. Measure
5 Ps Model of Strategy Implementation (Mildred, Anderson, Leslie, & John, 2007)			x	x	x					X
Agile strategy management process cycle (Lyngso, 2017)	X		x		x	x			x	X
Balanced Scorecard (BSC) (Kaplan & Norton, 2005)			x		x					X
Benchmarking (Watson, 1993)					x					X
House of Purchasing and Supply (Kearney's Framework, 2002)			x							X
European Foundation for Quality Management (EFQM, 1992)			x							X
Offshoring / Outsourcing (Aron & Singh 2005)			x						x	X
Overhead Value Analysis (Mowen & Hanson 2008)										X

(Filter panel overlay on columns 15–20: Sort — Ascending / Descending — By colour: None; Filter — By colour: None — Choose One — And / Or — Choose One — Search — (Select All) / X / (Blanks))

Fig. 19. View of models filtered on the 'measure' LEAD object

the ability to strategically align organisations to increase performance and enhance competitiveness.

The analysis revealed that each of the thirty-three models had links back to organisation tier competencies, however, six of the models had no link back to dynamic capabilities. Practitioners need to consider this when undertaking strategic development as failure to strategically align dynamic capabilities can result in the inability to 'do the right things' that enable a response to volatile markets (Warner and Wäger 2019). Furthermore, within the context of industry 4.0 and the additional emphasis on the significance of dynamic capabilities, ensuring strategic alignment is imperative to avoid execution failure (Warner and Wäger 2019).

The grouping of model types derived from the analysis supports the ability to accelerate the selection of models that inform (a) the positioning of an organisation within an industry, (b) insinuate how it should compete within a given environment or (c) the deployment of functional resources. These categories align with corporate, business and functional level strategies. Whilst the majority of the models fell under categories (a) and (b), it was necessary to differentiate these from the basis of whether they contained the 'Strategy' object. Throughout the lifecycle of working with strategy it is imperative that we create instances of strategic objectives, models without the 'Strategy' object don't allow this to happen.

Models under category (a – Strategy) and (b – Strategic) support the development of either corporate or business level strategy. Whereas category (c – Strategic Tactical) supports the development of resource allocation and business operations. In contrast to the categorisation of Berg and Pietersma (2015), the grouping applied highlights where their work has not considered the nature of the 'Strategy' object within models. This can cause confusion as their grouping of models under 'Corporate and Business Level Strategy' disregards models such as 7-S Framework (Waterman and Phillips, 1980) which contains the 'Strategy' object and has enough competency traits to sit within the category (a – Strategy). Rather, Berg and Pietersma (2015) group this under Organisation and Governance. Have's (2007) categorisation also negates the ontological nature of models and places the 7-S model under the 'Organization' category even though a 'Strategy' category is present in his work.

The ontological nature of a model helps to remove ambiguity, which in turn supports a consistent sharing of meaning. The grouping of the Market Attractiveness Business Activity (MABA) model is an example of where Berg and Pietersma (2015) and Have et al. (2007) highlight gaps related to ontology. The MABA is a model that supports strategic development as it facilitates the 'Sensing' capability through scoping markets and screening for competitors. It does not contain the 'Strategy' object but it does inform where to position the business and at a high level, how to compete. Therefore, it is classed as a 'Strategic Model'. Have et al. (2007) class this as a strategy model, inconsistent with the categorisation of the 7-S Framework, whereas Berg and Pietersma (2015) categorise this under 'Marketing and Sales'.

Using a common ontology as a basis for selecting tools disambiguates concepts. It places a common foundational understanding of the nature of the models we are working with as it formalises the strategy concepts within the models.

5.3 Relationship with the Strategy Lifecycle

The Strategy Lifecycle (Caine and von Rosing 2018) positions a framework that facilitates the ability to work through the lifecycle of strategy. The steps and artefacts identified in each of the phases were generated from patterns and practices gained from practitioner industry experience. The integration presented in this article provides a more rigorous academic approach building on the analysis of thirty-three models associated with strategy, a critical review of Tecce's (2007) dynamic capabilities, LEAD Organisation Tier Competencies and an ontological grouping of models linking back to objects. Whilst this article does not present a lifecycle view, the extended meta model provides the basis to extend and enhance Caine and von Rosing's (2018) work virtue of the rigour that underpins the extended strategy meta model.

5.4 Extended Strategy Meta Model

The extended Strategy Meta model formalises the concepts (objects) taken from the models and establishes relations between them. It produces an overview of objects and relations pertinent to the strategic management field. It provides insight into how the objects support strategic positioning (Corporate Level Strategy), how to compete in a given business environment (Business Level Strategy) and deployment of strategically aligned resources (Functional Level Strategy). The model encompasses the notion of competencies and capabilities with reference to the patterns associated with LEAD Competency reference content and Tecce's (2007) Dynamic Capabilities. This provides a strategic insight into the models and objects associated with translating strategy into capabilities and competencies supporting the development of competitive advantage (Warner and Wäger, 2019). By virtue of the ontological mapping to the thirty-three objects, it extends the strategy metal model produced by Caine and von Rosing (2018).

There is now a clear link across the three core layers (Business, Information and Technology), whereas the model produced by Caine and Von Rosing (2018) only covered the business layer. Having an ontological view across the three layers is imperative with the increasing emphasis on aligning business with IT (Ilmudeen et al. 2019).

The extended Strategy Meta model satisfies the basis of ontology application. It removes ambiguity and supports a shared meaning when communicating strategy concepts. Each of the objects has formal descriptions and relations that link back to different models. The integration of models within the extended Strategy Meta model supports enterprise modelling through an object-orientated approach. Models can be engineered (decomposed) by selected objects which can then be used across maps, matrices and models. The ability to reuse objects in different artefacts enables the ability to develop an integrated enterprise modelling environment where different stakeholders can effectively share meaning across integrated artefacts.

The semantic relations depicted in the extended Strategy Meta model afford the opportunity to apply formal concept analysis to validate the relationship through dependency pathways. This will provide a logical assessment of the constructed semantics outside of this article.

5.5 Patterns with Strategy Typology

The contrast of typologies analysed from industry through academic research draws on similar patterns identified through the analysis of patterns by LEAD. With few exceptions, the typologies of LEAD correlate with those discovered from academic research. Strategy typologies accelerate the ability to set strategic direction. The typologies fit within the 'business level' strategy and therefore inform the allocation of resources that filter through to functional level strategies. This supports the integration of strategy and aligns resources with strategic intention, reducing the probability of strategy execution failure (Caine and von Rosing 2018). Each of the typologies instantiates an instance of the strategy object, therefore the engineering and reuse of strategy can be facilitated across different artefacts. To this end, strategy effectively works across the different layers of the organisation (Polovina et al. 2020).

5.6 Tool for Grouping Strategy

The complexity of concepts suffices the need to have the ability to quickly shortlist models based on a defined criterion. Whilst working through the lifecycle of strategy practitioners need to consider several factors that influence their development. Models and frameworks are there to help accelerate the ability to develop views that inform the execution of strategy across corporate, business and functional levels. The ontological mapping and matrixing to competencies and capabilities provided the ability to apply filtering that groups the different types of strategy models. The developed tool facilitates an efficient shortlisting of specific strategy related tools that support a given agenda. For example, if the strategy context requires practitioners to develop artefacts that can support business planning, then filtering on the 'business planning' competency will list all relevant models that support this agenda (Fig. 20).

Strategy Ontology Models Matrix		Coordination	New Customers	Supporting Activities	Primary Activities	Column1	Mission Development	Vision Development	Strategy Development	Business Planning
Agile strategy management process cycle (Lyngso, 2017)									X	X
Balanced Scorecard (BSC) (Kaplan & Norton, 2005)									X	X
Boston Consulting Group (BCG) Matrix (Boston Consulting Group 1970)									X	X
Business Model Canvas (Osterwalder & Pigneur 2010)										X
Greiner's Growth Model (Greiner, 1998)										X
Offshoring / Outsourcing (Aron & Singh 2005)									X	X
Porter's Generic Strategies (Porter 2004)									X	X
Porter's Value Chain (Porter, 1985)				X	X				X	X
Porter's Five Forces (Porter, 1980)									X	X
Scenario Planning (Van der Heijden et al. 2002)								X	X	X
SWOT Analysis (Albert Humphrey 1960)									X	X
Strategy Map (Kaplan & Norton, 2004)									X	X
Internationalisation Strategy Framework (Lem, Tulder & Geleynse, 2013)	X	X							X	X
Road-Mapping (EIRMA, 1997; Farrukh, Phaal & Probert, 2003)			X	X					X	X
Ansoff's Product / Market Grid and Geographic Vector (Ansoff 1987)									X	X

Fig. 20. Business planning strategy related models

The flexibility to determine the criterion for filtering for specific objects or competencies is extensive. Moreover, the need to strategically inform the development of dynamic capabilities is supported by the ability to filter upon designated attributes connected to sensing, seizing and transforming (Tecce 2007). As digital transformation is supported by the ability to enact dynamic capabilities (Warner and Wäger 2019), the tool acts as a facilitator in aiding the selection strategy models that support a strategic digital agenda (Fig. 21).

Strategy Ontology Models Matrix		Sensing	
	Vigilant Learning (Day and Schoemaker 2016; Tecce, 2007) - Outside in orientation for products and services, ensuring employees are empowered to share voice on important matters that impact the business, surpressing biases, triangulating perspectives	Digital Scouting (Warner & Wäger, 2019) - Scanning for tech trends, screening for competitors, sensing customer-centric trends	Digital Scenario Planning (Warner & Wäger, 2019) - Anaylzing scouted signals, interpretating digital future scenarios, Formaulating digital strategies
House of Purchasing and Supply (Kearney's Framework, 2002)	Outside in Orientation		
Strategy Map (Kaplan & Norton, 2004)	Outside in Orientation		
Value Disciplines (Treacy & Wiersema, 1995)	Outside in Orientation		
Ansoff's Product / Market Grid and Geographic Vector (Ansoff 1987)	Outside in Orientation	Scanning for tech trends	

Fig. 21. Sensing (vigilant learning) dynamic capability attributed related strategy models

6 Conclusion

The objective of this article was to advance strategy ontology by analysing strategy models that inform the development of strategy across corporate, business and functional levels of strategy. This analysis facilitated the confirmation of strategy concepts (objects) and their relations that semantically connect them across the layers of the enterprise. The critique of competencies and capabilities and their connection back to strategy, enabled the matrixing of their attributes back to specific strategy models thus, providing strategic insight into the relevant models that support competency and capability development.

Moving beyond corporate strategy requires an emphasis on strategically informing how the organisation will compete within a given market. Strategy typologies help to accelerate strategic direction and associated resources (Anwar and Hasnu 2017). This article confirmed the patterns associated with LEAD strategy typologies and the academic analysis of strategic typologies. The five confirmed typologies provide a basis to accelerate business level strategy and can be used within strategy development scenarios when there is a requirement to establish a strategic thrust that informs the functional deployment of resources.

The resulting extended Strategy Meta model capitulates the objects, semantics and their link to the development of competencies and dynamic capabilities. The patterns identified across the thirty-three analysed models informed an effective grouping across three categories (Strategy, Strategic and Strategic Tactical). This was indicated on each of the objects, further informing the nature of models that fall under these categories. Due to the ontological mapping of concepts to objects, a link back to Caine and von Rosing's (2018) Strategy Lifecycle is included in the extended Strategy Meta model, further informing which objects are triggered across the six lifecycle phases (Understand, Design, Develop, Execute, Govern and Continuous Improve). The principles of ontology application, namely Communication, Interoperability and Systems Engineering are satisfied and summarised through the extended Strategy Meta model. Communication is enhanced through a foundational shared meaning, objects are defined along with semantics providing the basis to share consistent meaning across strategy concepts. Interoperability is evidenced through the integration of categorised models that facilitate the reuse of objects across different artefacts. The ability to engineer concepts related to strategy can be gained through each object within the extended Strategy Meta model. An example of this is through the five confirmed strategy typologies which create instances from the strategy object.

The developed tool accelerates the ability to work with strategy concepts that can adapt to different strategic contexts. Strategy practitioners need to be agile and flexible when undertaking strategic development work. The tool is efficient and can be a basis for providing value for stakeholders who require insight into models that can assist their strategic endeavour.

Further research will be undertaken to test the application of the advanced strategy ontology presented in this article. Validation of the dependencies with the semantic relations will be undertaken through formal concept analysis. The nature of the ontology work presents several opportunities to further examine pattern dependency. Examples may include example, object relationship dependency in connection to the categorised models, competencies in relation to mapped objects and dynamic capabilities in connection to mapped objects.

A case study drawing upon the need to engineer strategy and relate pertinent strategy concepts will facilitate a test of the advanced strategy ontology. Further research is required to examine whether the objects and relations can facilitate practical strategic work throughout the lifecycle of strategy.

To this end, an assessment of whether the advanced strategy ontology can inform the development of effective views that enhance the ability of stakeholders to drive their strategy development will be carried out. This will extend evidence on the potential value that can be attained through the use of an advanced strategy ontology.

References

Abell, D.: Defining the business of a company. Explanation Three Dimensional Bus. Definition Model **12**, 20–30 (1980)

Achtenhagen, L., Melin, L., Naldi, L.: Dynamics of business models–strategizing, critical capabilities and activities for sustained value creation. Long Range Plan. **46**(6), 427–442 (2013)

Andrews, K.R.: The Concept of Corporate Strategy (1980)

Ansoff, H.I.: Corporate Strategy, revised Penguin Books, London (1987)

Anwar, J., Hasnu, S.A.F.: Strategy-performance linkage: methodological refinements and empirical analysis. J. Asia Business Studies **10**(3), 303–317 (2016)

Anwar, J., Hasnu, S.: Strategic patterns and firm performance: comparing consistent, flexible and reactor strategies. J. Organ. Chang. Manag. **30**(7), 1015–1029 (2017). https://doi.org/10.1108/JOCM-03-2016-0053

Aron, R., Singh, J.V.: Getting offshoring right. Harv. Bus. Rev. **83**(12), 135–143 (2005)

Azzone, G., Bertelè, U.: Exploiting green strategies for competitive advantage. Long Range Plann. **27**, 69–81 (1994)

Baylis, J., Wirtz, J., Gray, C.: Strategy in the Contemporary World. Oxford University Press, USA (2018)

Berg, G.V.D., Pietersma, P.: Key Management Models: The 75+ Models Every Manager Needs to Know. Pearson, Harlow, England (2015)

Blumentritt, T., Danis, W.M.: Business strategy types and innovative practices. J. Manag. Issues, 274–291 (2006)

Bojesson, C., Fundin, A.: Exploring microfoundations of dynamic capabilities – challenges, barriers and enablers of organizational change. J. Organizational Change Manage. 34(1), 206–222 (2021). https://doi.org/10.1108/JOCM-02-2020-0060

Borst, W.N., Borst, W.N., Akkermans, J.M.: Construction of engineering ontologies for knowledge sharing and reuse. Fac. Electr. Eng., Math., Comput. Sci., 1–243 (1997)

Breznik, L., Lahovnik, M., Dimovski, V.: Exploiting firm capabilities by sensing, seizing and reconfiguring capabilities: an empirical investigation. Econ. Bus. Rev. 21(1), 5–36 (2018)

Bridges: Strategy implementation Survey Results 2016. http://www.implementation-hub.com/res ources/implementation-surveys (2016)

Buzzell, R.D., Gale, B.T., Sultan, R.G.M.: Market share-a key to profitability. Harv. Bus. Rev. 53(1), 97–106 (1975)

Buzzell, R.D., Gale, B.T.: The PIMS Principles: Linking Strategy to Performance, p. 322. The Free Press, New York (1987)

Buzzell, R.D.: The PIMS program of strategy research: a retrospective appraisal. J. Bus. Res. 57(5), 478–483 (2004)

Caine, J., Rosing, M.: Introducing the strategy lifecycle: Using ontology and semiotics to interlink strategy design to strategy execution. In: Liu, K., Nakata, K., Li, W., Baranauskas, C. (eds.) ICISO 2018. IAICT, vol. 527, pp. 136–144. Springer, Cham (2018). https://doi.org/10.1007/978-3-319-94541-5_14

Caine, J., Rosing, M.: The need and requirements to a strategy ontology. In: CEUR Workshop Proceedings, pp. 70–77 (2020). http://ceur-ws.org/Vol-2574/short7.pdf

Caine, J., Gilroy, J., Greaves, M., Madriaga, M.: Principles of success: facilitating sustainable transformation through a progressive relational pedagogy. Soc. Policy Soc. 21(1), 106–122 (2022). https://doi.org/10.1017/S1474746421000658. Cambridge University Press, Competency meaning. https://dictionary.cambridge.org/dictionary/english/competency

Campbell, A., Yeung, S.: Creating a sense of mission. Long Range Plan. 24(4), 10–20 (1991)

Chaffee, E.E.: Three models of strategy. Acad. Manag. Rev. 10(1), 89–98 (1985). https://doi.org/10.2307/258215

Cohen, S.: A strategic framework for devolving responsibility and functions from government to the private sector. Public Adm. Rev. 61(4), 432–440 (2001)

Collis, D.J.: Research note: How valuable are organizational capabilities? Strateg. Manag. J. 15, 143–152 (1994). https://doi.org/10.1002/smj.4250150910

Cooper, R., Kaplan, R.S.: Measure costs right: Make the right decisions. Harv. Bus. Rev. 66(5), 96–103 (1988)

Dalmau Espert, J.L., Llorens Largo, F., Molina-Carmona, R.: An ontology for formalizing and automating the strategic planning process. In: eKNOW 2015, The Seventh International Conference on Information, Process, and Knowledge Management. Lisbon, Portugal 22–27 Feb 2015

Danneels, E.: The dynamics of product innovation and firm competences. Strateg. Manag. J. 23(12), 1095–1121 (2002). https://doi.org/10.1002/smj.275

Day, G.S., Schoemaker, P.J.: Adapting to fast-changing markets and technologies. Calif. Manage. Rev. 58(4), 59–77 (2016)

DaSilva, C.M., Trkman, P.: Business model: What it is and what it is not. Long Range Plan. 47(6), 379–389 (2014)

De Wit, B.: Strategy Synthesis For Leaders, 5th edn. Cengage Learning (2017)

Denzin, Lincoln, Y.S.: The SAGE handbook of qualitative research, 4th edn. Sage (2011)

Douglas, S.P., Rhee, D.K.: Examining generic competitive strategy types in U.S. and European markets. J. Int. Bus. Stud. 20(3), 437–463 (1989). https://doi.org/10.1057/palgrave.jibs.849 0855

EFQM: In European Foundation for Quality Management (Ed.), Total quality management: The European model for self-appraisal (1992)

Enkel, E., Sagmeister, V.: External corporate venturing modes as new way to develop dynamic capabilities. Technovation **96–97**, 102128 (2020). https://doi.org/10.1016/j.technovation.2020.102128

Falbo, R.d.A., Guizzardi, G., Duarte, K.C.: An ontological approach to domain engineering. In: Proceedings of the 14th International Conference on Software Engineering and Knowledge Engineering, pp. 351–358 (2002)

Farrukh, C., Phaal, R., Probert, D.: Technology roadmapping: linking technology resources into business planning. Int. J. Technol. Manage. **26**(1), 2–19 (2003)

Feiler, P., Teece, D.: Case study, dynamic capabilities and upstream strategy: Supermajor EXP. Energ. Strat. Rev. **3**, 14–20 (2014)

Galbraith, C., Schendel, D.: An empirical analysis of strategy types. Strateg. Manage. J. **4**(2), 153–173 (1983)

Gauthier, J.: Sustainable business strategies: typologies and future directions. Soc. Bus. Rev. **12**(1), 77–93 (2017). https://doi.org/10.1108/SBR-01-2016-0005

Greiner, L.E.: Evolution and revolution as organizations grow. Harv. Bus. Rev. **76**(3), 55–64 (1998)

Gruber, T.R.: Toward principles for the design of ontologies used for knowledge sharing? Int. J. Hum. – Comput. Stud. **43**(5–6), 907–928 (1995). https://doi.org/10.1006/ijhc.1995.1081

Guarino, N.: Understanding, building and using ontologies. Int. J. Hum Comput Stud. **46**(2–3), 293–310 (1997)

Hart, O.: Corporate governance: some theory and implications. Econ. J. **105**(430), 678–689 (1995)

Have, S.T., Have, W.T., Stevens, F., Elst, M.V., Pol-Coyne, F., Walsh, C.: Key Management Models the Management Tools and Practices that will Improve your Business. Financial Times Prentice Hall, Harlow (2007)

van der Heijden, K.: The Sixth Sense: Accelerating Organizational Learning with Scenarios. Wiley (2006)

Henderson, R., Cockburn, I.: Measuring competence? exploring firm effects in pharmaceutical research. Strat. Manage. J. **15**(S1), 63–84 (1994). https://doi.org/10.1002/smj.4250150906

Hill, T., Westbrook, R.: SWOT analysis: it's time for a product recall. Long Range Plan. **30**(1), 46–52 (1997)

Hofer, C.W., Schendel, D.: Strategy Formulation: Analytical Concepts. West Publ. (1978)

Hoverstadt, P., Loh, L., Marguet, N.: Measuring the performance of strategy. Measuring Bus. Excellence (2020)

Ilmudeen, A., Bao, Y., Alharbi, I.M.: How does business-IT strategic alignment dimension impact on organizational performance measures: conjecture and empirical analysis. J. Enterp. Inf. Manag. **32**(3), 457–476 (2019)

Ince, I., Hahn, R.: How dynamic capabilities facilitate the survivability of social enterprises: a qualitative analysis of sensing and seizing capacities. J. Small Bus. Manage. **58**(6), 1256–1290 (2020). https://doi.org/10.1111/jsbm.12487

Jaworski, B.J., Rajan Varadarajan, P.: Book review: the PIMS principles: linking strategy to performance. J. Mark. **53**(2), 126–129 (1989). https://doi.org/10.1177/002224298905300210

Johnson, G., Whittington, R., Regnér, P., Angwin, D., Scholes, K.: Exploring Strategy. Pearson, UK (2020)

Kaplan, R.S., Norton, D.P.: The Balanced Scorecard: Translating Strategy into Action. Harvard Business Press (1996)

Kaplan, R.S., Norton, D.P.: The strategy map: guide to aligning intangible assets. Strategy Leadersh. **32**(5), 10–17 (2004)

Kaplan, R.S., Norton, D.P.: The balanced scorecard: measures that drive performance. Harv. Bus. Rev. **83**(7), 172 (2005)

Kearney, A.T.: The new procurement mandate: Growing within tomorrow's supply websites. www. atkearneypas.com/knowledge/publications/2000/mandate.pdf (2002)

Kemp, N.: Toward an ontology of strategy in an enterprise context. Int. J. Bus. Strategy Autom. 2(4), 1–23 (2021). https://doi.org/10.4018/IJBSA.288040

Kim, W.C., Mauborgne, R.: Blue Ocean Strategy, Expanded Edition: How to Create Uncontested Market Space and Make the Competition Irrelevant. Harvard Business Review Press (2014)

Kotabe, M., Duhan, D., Smith, D., Wilson, R.: The perceived veracity of PIMS strategy principles in Japan: an empirical inquiry. J. Mark. 55(1), 26 (1991). https://doi.org/10.2307/1252201

LEADing Practice: Enterprise management. https://www.leadingpractice.com/enterprise-standa rds/enterprise-management/ (2022)

Lem, M., van Tulder, R., Geleynse, K.: Doing Business in Africa: A Strategic Guide for Entrepreneurs. Berenschot (2013)

Liskov, B., Wing, J.: A behavioral notion of subtyping. ACM Trans. Program. Lang. Syst. 16(6), 1811–1841 (1994). https://doi.org/10.1145/197320.197383

Luoma, M.A.: Revisiting the strategy-performance linkage: an application of an empirically derived typology of strategy content areas. Manag. Decis. (2015)

Lyngso, S.: Agile Strategy Management: Techniques for Continuous Alignment and Improvement. CRC Press (2017)

Madhok, A.: Cost, value and foreign market entry mode: the transaction and the firm. Strateg. Manag. J. 18(1), 39–61 (1997)

Marino, K.E.: Developing consensus on firm competencies and capabilities. Acad. Manag. Perspect. 10(3), 40–51 (1996)

Matysiak, L., Rugman, A.M., Bausch, A.: Dynamic capabilities of multinational enterprises: the dominant logics behind sensing, seizing, and transforming matter! Manag. Int. Rev. 58(2), 225–250 (2017). https://doi.org/10.1007/s11575-017-0337-8

McKinsey: Changing change management. https://www.mckinsey.com/featured-insights/leader ship/changing-change-management (2015)

Miles, R.E., Snow, C.: Organizational Strategy, Structure and Process. McGraw-Hill (1978)

Mintzberg, H.: Structure in Fives: Designing Effective Organisations. Prentice-Hall (1983)

Mintzberg, H.: Structure in Fives: Designing Effective Organizations. Prentice-Hall, Inc. (1993)

Mintzberg, H., Ahlstrand, B.W., Lampel, J.: Strategy Bites Back it is a Lot More, and Less, than you Ever Imagined. Prentice Hall/Financial Times, Harlow, England (2005)

Mintzberg, H., Ahlstrand, B.W., Lampel, J.: Strategy Safari: The Complete Guide Through the Wilds of Strategic Management. Financial Times Prentice Hall, Harlow, England (2020)

Moore, M.: Towards a confirmatory model of retail strategy types: an empirical test of Miles and Snow. J. Bus. Res. 58(5), 696–704 (2005)

Mowen, M.M., Hansen D.R.: Management accounting: the cornerstone for business decisions. Thomson/South-Western (2006)

Nelson, K., Nelson, H.: The need for a strategic ontology. In: Proceedings of the MIS (Management Information Systems) Quarterly Special Issue Workshop on Standard Making: A Critical Research Frontier for Information Systems, pp. 12–14 (2003)

Nidumolu, R., Prahalad, C.K., Rangaswami, M.R.: Why sustainability is now the key driver of innovation. Harv. Bus. Rev. 87(9), 56–64 (2009)

O'Regan, N., Ghobadian, A.: The Importance of Capabilities for Strategic Direction and Performance. MCB University Press, Bradford, England (2004). https://doi.org/10.1108/002517404 10518525

Ohmae, K.: Getting back to strategy. Harv. Bus. Rev. 66(6), 149 (1988)

OMG: Business motivation model. https://www.omg.org/spec/BMM/1.3/PDF (2015)

Orsato, R.J.: Competitive environmental strategies: when does it pay to be green? Calif. Manage. Rev. 48(2), 127–143 (2006)

Osterwalder, A., Pigneur, Y., Clark, T., Pijl, P.v.d.: Business Model Generation a Handbook for Visionaries, Game Changers, and Challengers. Wiley, Hoboken, N.J (2010)

Polovina, S., von Rosing, M., Etzel, G.: Leading the practice in layered enterprise architecture. CEUR Workshop Proc. **2574**, 62–69 (2020)

Porter, M.E.: How Competitive Forces shape strategy. Harv. Bus. Rev. **57**(2), 137–145 (1979)

Porter, M.E.: Competitive strategy. Measuring Bus. Excellence **1**(2), 12–17 (1997). https://doi.org/10.1108/eb025476

Porter, M.E.: The value chain and competitive advantage. Underst. Bus.: Processes 50–66 (2001)

Porter, M.E.: Competitive Advantage: Creating and Sustaining Superior Performance. Free, New York (2004)

Powell, T.C.: Strategy without ontology. Strateg. Manag. J. **24**(3), 285–291 (2003). https://doi.org/10.1002/smj.284

Prahalad, C.K., Hamel, G.: The core competence of the corporation. Harv. Bus. Rev. **68**(3), 79 (1990)

Prescott, J.E.: Competitive Environments, Strategic Types, and Business Performance: An Empirical Analysis. The Pennsylvania State University ProQuest Dissertations Publishing (1983)

Prescott, J.E.: Environments as moderators of the relationship between strategy and performance. Acad. Manag. J. **29**(2), 329–346 (1986)

Pryor, M.G., Anderson, D., Leslie, A.T., John, H.H.: Strategic implementation as a core competency: the 5P's model. J. Manag. Res. **7**(1), 3 (2007)

Quinn, R.E., Rohrbaugh, J.: A spatial model of effectiveness criteria: towards a competing values approach to organizational analysis. Manage. Sci. **29**(3), 363–377 (1983). https://doi.org/10.1287/mnsc.29.3.363

Ramanujam, V., Venkatraman, N.: An inventory and critique of strategy research using the PIMS database. Acad. Manag. Rev. **9**(1), 138–151 (1984). https://doi.org/10.5465/amr.1984.4278111

Roome, N.: Developing environmental management strategies. Bus. Strateg. Environ. **1**(1), 11–24 (1992)

Ross, J.W.: In: Weill P., Robertson D. (Eds.), Enterprise Architecture as Strategy: Creating a Foundation for Business Execution. Harvard Business School Press, Boston (2006)

Ross, J.W., Weill, P., Robertson, D.: Enterprise Architecture as Strategy: Creating a Foundation for Business Execution. Harvard Business School Press, Boston (2006)

Roussey, C., Pinet, F., Kang, M.A., Corcho, O.: An introduction to ontologies and ontology engineering. In: Ontologies in Urban Development Projects. Advanced Information and Knowledge Processing, vol. 1. Springer, London (2011)

Armstrong, J.: The value of formal planning for strategic decisions: review of empirical research. Strateg. Manag. J. **3**(3), 197–211 (1982). https://doi.org/10.1002/smj.4250030303

Sharker, A.Z., Harry, J.S., Davidson, P.: Entrepreneurship and dynamic capabilties: a review, model and research agenda. J. Manage. Stud. **43**(4), 917 (2006)

Slater, S.F., Narver, J.C.: Product-market strategy and performance: an analysis of the Miles and Snow strategy types. Eur. J. Mark. **27**(10), 33–51 (1993)

Simons, R.: Levers of Control: How Managers use Innovative Control Systems to Drive Strategic Renewal. Harvard Business School Press (1995)

Tallman, S.B., Shenkar, O., Wu, J.: 'Culture eats strategy for breakfast': Use and abuse of culture in international strategy research. Strategic Manage. Rev. (2021)

Tavakolian, H.: Linking the information technology structure with organizational competitive strategy: a survey. MIS Q., 309–317 (1989)

Teece: Explicating dynamic capabilities: the nature and microfoundations of (sustainable) enterprise performance. Strat. Manag. J. **28**(13), 1319–1350 (2007). https://doi.org/10.1002/smj.640

Teece, D.J.: The foundations of enterprise performance: dynamic and ordinary capabilities in an (economic) theory of firms. Acad. Manag. Perspect. **28**(4), 328–352 (2014). https://doi.org/10.5465/amp.2013.0116

Teece, D.J.: Business models and dynamic capabilities. Long Range Plan. **51**(1), 40–49 (2018). https://doi.org/10.1016/j.lrp.2017.06.007

Teece, D.J., Pisano, G., Shuen, A.: Dynamic capabilities and strategic management. Strateg. Manage. J. **18**(7), 509–533 (1997). https://doi.org/10.1002/(SICI)1097-0266(199708)18:73.0.CO;2-Z

Teece, D., Pisano, G.: The dynamic capabilities of firms: an introduction. Ind. Corp. Chang. **3**(3), 537–556 (1994)

Treacy, M., Wiersema, F.: The Discipline of Market Leaders: Choose your Customers, Narrow your Focus, Dominate your Market. Collins (1995)

Uschold, M., Gruninger, M.: Ontologies: principles, methods and applications. The Knowle. Eng. Rev. **11**(2), 93–136 (1996). https://doi.org/10.1017/S0269888900007797

Utterback, J.M., Abernathy, W.J.: A dynamic model of process and product innovation. Omega **3**(6), 639–656 (1975)

Vanpoucke, E., Vereecke, A., Wetzels, M.: Developing supplier integration capabilities for sustainable competitive advantage: a dynamic capabilities approach. J. Oper. Manag. **32**(7–8), 446–461 (2014). https://doi.org/10.1016/j.jom.2014.09.004

Velu, C.: A systems perspective on business model evolution: the case of an agricultural information service provider in India. Long Range Plan. **50**(5), 603–620 (2017)

von Rosing, M., Fullington, N., Walker, J.: Using the business ontology and enterprise standards to transform three leading organizations. Int. J. Conceptual Struct. Smart Appl. **4**(1), 71–99 (2016). https://doi.org/10.4018/IJCSSA.2016010104

von Rosing, M., Laurier, W.: An introduction to the business ontology. Int. J. Conceptual Struct. Smart Appl. **3**(1), 20–41 (2015). https://doi.org/10.4018/IJCSSA.2015010102

von Rosing, M., Okpurughre, P., Grube, D.: Using ontology and modelling concepts for enterprise innovation and transformation: Example SAL heavylift. Int. J. Conceptual Struct. Smart Appl. **5**(1), 70–104 (2017). https://doi.org/10.4018/IJCSSA.2017010104

von Rosing, M., von Scheel, H.: Using the business ontology to develop enterprise standards. Int. J. Conceptual Struct. Smart Appl. **4**(1), 48–70 (2016)

Von Rosing, M., Von Scheel, H., Scheer, A.: The Complete Business Process Handbook: Body of Knowledge from Process Modeling to BPM. Morgan Kaufmann (2014)

von Scheel, H., von Rosing, M., Bach, B.: Using ontology and modelling concepts to develop smart applications: example Dutch railway. Int. J. Conceptual Struct. Smart Appl. **5**(1), 48–69 (2017). https://doi.org/10.4018/IJCSSA.2017010103

Warner, K.S.R., Wäger, M.: Building dynamic capabilities for digital transformation: an ongoing process of strategic renewal. Long Range Plan. **52**(3), 326–349 (2019). https://doi.org/10.1016/j.lrp.2018.12.001

Waterman, R.H., Jr., Peters, T.J., Phillips, J.R.: Structure is not organization. Bus. Horiz. **23**(3), 14–26 (1980)

Watson, G.: A perspective on benchmarking. Organization **1**, 1 (1994)

de Wit, B., Meyer, R.: Strategy an International Perspective. Cengage Learning, Australia (2014)

Yakan, A., Rashid, A.: Strategic business ontology model. Kurdistan Acad. J. **12**, 19 (2016)

Knowledge Discovery and Innovations

Participatory Collaboration Mapping of Design-Enabled Urban Innovations: The MappingDESIGNSCAPES Case

Aldo de Moor[1]([⊠]), Evi Papalioura[2], Evi Taka[3], Dora Rapti[4], Annika Wolff[5], Antti Knutas[5], and Tomas te Velde[6]

[1] CommunitySense, Tilburg, The Netherlands
ademoor@communitysense.nl
[2] Ministry of Environment and Energy, Thessaloniki, Greece
e.papalioura@prv.ypeka.gr
[3] Municipality of Neapolis-Sikeon, Thessaloniki, Greece
taka.eugenia@n3.syzefxis.gov.gr
[4] Thessaloniki, Greece
[5] Department of Software Engineering, LUT University, Lappeenranta, Finland
{Annika.Wolff,Antti.Knutas}@lut.fi
[6] Suit-Case, Delft, The Netherlands
tomas@suit-case.nl

Abstract. Wicked societal problems, such as environmental issues and climate change, are complex, networked problems involving many intertwined issues, no optimal solutions, and numerous stakeholders. Cities are problem owners and living labs for finding solutions through design-enabled innovation initiatives. However, to reach collective impact, it is paramount that these initiatives can learn from one another and align efforts through collaborative sensemaking. In the MappingDESIGNSCAPES project, we piloted a participatory collaboration mapping approach for cross-case sensemaking across design-enabled urban innovation initiatives. We used the CommunitySensor methodology for participatory community network mapping and the Kumu online network visualization tool to help representatives of three urban prototype cases share and collectively make sense of their design lessons. In this first of two papers, we describe how we set up the MappingDESIGNSCAPES project as part of the DESIGNSCAPES urban design innovations R&D program; how we created a conceptual model of the collaboration ecosystems around design-enabled urban innovations; and co-created a visual knowledge base centered around the case and cross-case maps grounded in this conceptual model. We end this paper with a discussion of participatory mapping lessons learned. In the accompanying paper [1], we show how we used this visual knowledge base to drive a process of collaborative sensemaking to share lessons learned across cases.

Keywords: Design-enabled urban innovation · Participatory collaboration mapping · Conceptual models · Visual knowledge bases

© Springer Nature Switzerland AG 2022
R. Polovina et al. (Eds.): MOVE 2020, CCIS 1694, pp. 171–202, 2022.
https://doi.org/10.1007/978-3-031-22228-3_8

1   Introduction

Wicked societal problems, such as climate change, are hugely complex, networked problems involving numerous intertwined issues, solution directions, and many stakeholders [2]. Cities are a significant contributor to these problems but can also be catalysts in finding ways out, acting as living labs to prototype and scale up solutions through design-enabled urban innovations [3]. Scaling up these innovations, however, requires an ongoing process of reflection: situating existing innovation projects in the overall problem space, identifying conceptual and operational connections between various initiatives, and identifying collaborative gaps and opportunities within and between new initiatives [4, 5].

DESIGNSCAPES (Building Capacity for Design-enabled Innovation in Urban Environments) is an EU H2020 program. Its aim is "to exploit the generative potential of urban environments in the highest possible number of European Cities to encourage the uptake and further enhancement and up scaling of Design-Enabled Innovations by existing enterprises, start-up companies, public authorities and agencies, and other urban stakeholders"[1]. In successive calls (*Feasibility Studies*, *Urban Prototypes*, and *Scalability Proofs*), many local design-enabled innovation initiatives of different focus and maturity have been developed.

The DESIGNSCAPES initiatives vary widely, demonstrating many scopes, interpretations, and approaches to making these design-enabled innovations work. However, the value and potential impact of DESIGNSCAPES as a consortium and program of projects go beyond the local impacts of the individual initiatives. The whole - breaking both conceptual and practical ground in approaching design-enabled innovations (DEI) - may well be much greater than the sum of its parts.

MappingDESIGNSCAPES was one of the 41 funded so-called urban prototype projects in the second call of DESIGNSCAPES. In the call, prototypes were defined as "[a]n experimental release of a new product, service, process or other innovative solution, built according to a predefined guideline (including a feasibility study) and tested in a laboratory environment and/or in real life conditions, with or without the participation of its prospective end users."[2] MappingDESIGNSCAPES could be considered a special kind of prototype, a meta-urban prototype, as it aimed to help other urban prototypes learn from one another's experiences, representatives of those prototypes being the "end users" in our case. The design-enabled innovation of the project was therefore not to be yet another local urban innovation. Instead, it aimed at developing a prototype of a systematic yet practical participatory mapping-driven collaborative sensemaking approach to catalyze the sharing of lessons learned across design-enabled urban innovation projects.

In MappingDESIGNSCAPES, we used the CommunitySensor methodology for participatory community network mapping [6] and the Kumu online network visualization tool[3] to help representatives of selected DESIGNSCAPES urban prototypes share and

---

[1] https://designscapes.eu/.

[2] http://designscapes.eu/wp-content/uploads/2018/10/Designscapes_call_announcement_final_3.pdf.

[3] http://kumu.io.

collectively make sense of their design lessons learned. This paper presents how we developed two essential knowledge resources – a conceptual framework and a visual knowledge base. The following paper presents their role in prototyping a systematic yet practical cross-case collaborative sensemaking approach. We did not aim to come up with a fully developed methodology. Instead, we wanted to show a proof of concept that it is feasible to make sense across multiple design-enabled urban innovation cases towards collective impact in addressing wicked societal problems.

The paper is structured as follows: first, we introduce the main ideas behind participatory collaboration mapping of design-enabled urban innovations. Next, we outline the MappingDESIGNSCAPES project, including the cases and the overall design approach. We then introduce the conceptual model underlying our participatory mapping and sensemaking efforts, followed by a description of the visual knowledge base used to construct and apply the conceptual model. We continue with a discussion of participatory mapping lessons learned and end with conclusions.

2 Participatory Collaboration Mapping of Design-Enabled Urban Innovations

We introduce design-enabled urban innovations and then describe participatory collaboration mapping as a process to capture and visualize the essential elements and connections of collaboration ecosystems. Next, we introduce the roles of the Kumu network visualization tool and the CommunitySensor methodology for participatory community network mapping in supporting the process.

2.1 Design-Enabled Urban Innovations

Global society is awash in wicked environmental problems, including climate change, war, migration, social exclusion, and health issues. These complex problems often seem impossible to solve, are long-standing, intractable, and come with many different opinions about possible ways to go about them [7].

A necessary condition for addressing such intricate problems is to build collaborative networks that focus on knowledge sharing and developing a common focus for interpreting and using that knowledge [8]. Social innovation, in which new ideas are put to work in meeting social goals, is a crucial process for such collaborative networks to engage in [9]. According to Smith et al., such innovation processes should be sufficiently broad in scope and ambition; adopt a multi-level perspective on socio-technical transformations; and take place via many pathways in evolving socio-technical systems of niches, regimes, and landscapes. Socio-technical regimes are the mainstream, highly institutionalized way of currently realizing societal functions, whereas, in niches, novel alternatives arise. Niches and regimes, in turn, are situated in broader (land)scapes of social and physical factors providing a macro-level context [10].

Innovation is closely interrelated with design, with design activities having user needs, aspirations, and abilities as their starting point. Involving users as core innovation process agents in co-design and co-creation is key [4, 11]. This design for innovation involves many different human and non-human design agencies, including expert and diffuse design by humans. However, the larger scapes and regimes also exert design influences, involving many meanings and functions [12].

Cities are stimulating and productive ecosystems for innovation design. They are the arenas where wicked problems materialize, provide many transition opportunities, and need innovations that align and synergize towards transition. Cities are thus crucial environments for the emergence of innovative interactions and relationships [13]. Still, how do the numerous stakeholders involved in cities work together effectively in such complex societal co-design activities, especially if they move beyond individual initiatives towards more impactful collaborations?

Reflective design communities can play an essential capacity-building role. Such communities are embedded in cultures of participation and have a clear design rationale, including the meta-design of getting the participants to act as designers and be creative [14]. Yet, how to organize and catalyze productive community reflection in a complex urban environment? One way to go about this is through a process of participatory collaboration mapping.

2.2 Participatory Collaboration Mapping

Society can be seen as a supra-community, a "community of communities" [15]. We prefer to speak of networks of communities, as not all communities need to be tightly interconnected. Urban society consists of richly overlapping, more or less interrelated, and interacting networks of communities and other stakeholders, such as neighborhoods, clubs and associations, learning communities around local schools, business communities, and, of course, the cultural sector.

To better understand what community networks are and how to strengthen them, both the network and community dimensions need to be considered. The network-aspect concerns the relationships, interactions, and connections among participants, providing affordances for learning and collaboration; the community aspect refers to developing a shared identity around a topic or set of challenges [16].

Community networks entail significant social complexity due to the number and diversity of the social players involved. Such social complexity results in the need for new understandings, processes, and tools that are attuned to the fundamentally social and conversational nature of work [17]. Communities working together means finding ways to build bridges across communal boundaries of cultures, languages, and practices. Those boundaries can be hard to cross, leading to many misunderstandings and much fragmentation. Essential here is sensemaking: turning circumstances into a situation that is comprehended explicitly in words and that serves as a springboard into action [18]. For members of community networks to learn from one another across their community boundaries, they require a well-supported process of collaborative sensemaking of the collaboration ecosystems – the organically growing systems of interconnected participants, purposes, interactions, content, and resources - that they form. This entails jointly finding out what their collaboration is about, what relationships and interactions their communities and contexts consist of, what collaboration resources are available, and what concrete opportunities exist for better working communities [6].

Still, how to make such collaborative sensemaking of collaboration ecosystems work in the case of large-scale transition innovation design? Maps may be instrumental, as they help to navigate complex territory. Visualizations, such as maps, are crucial in enabling societal transformations: they determine what we can and cannot see, what we notice, and what we ignore, and in this way, shape all that follows [19]. Yet how to create and use such maps in scalable urban innovation is still unclear. New methodologies for mapping such transitions from a multilevel perspective are therefore needed [10].

ICT - provided it is used correctly - can support the innovative design and the formation of creative clusters, which are complexes of interconnected activity, encompassing multiple domains and providing opportunities and incentives for productive cross-fertilization [20]. One ICT with powerful features for creating, analyzing, and interconnecting community network maps is the online network visualization tool Kumu.

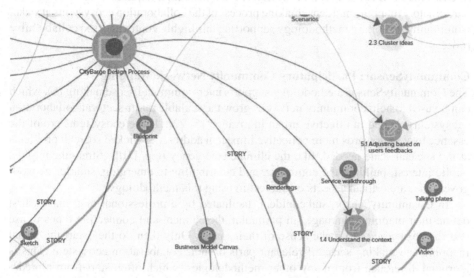

Fig. 1. An example of a Kumu map

Kumu: Online Network Visualization

Kumu[4] is a web-based tool to capture, visualize, and leverage community and network relationships. Kumu maps consist of elements and connections between those elements (Fig. 1). A core feature of Kumu is that both elements and connections can be typed, and different layouts can be applied to different types. For instance, elements of a particular type can be visualized by their colors, icons, and sizes. In contrast, connections of a particular type can be represented by lines with a specific combination of color, width, and pattern (e.g., solid or dashed). Different views can then be applied to each map, in which Kumu shows custom selections of elements and connections of interest in the layout desired. Views can be constructed by selecting subsets of the elements and connections on the map and then applying a certain focus and/or filters. Focus allows one to zoom in on and out of the context of a selection on the map. Filter is used to select which types of elements and connections should be made visible according to advanced

---

[4] http://kumu.io.

search criteria. A wide range of layout options can be applied based on the properties of the elements and connections selected. The resulting views get their own customized hyperlinks and can be easily shared.

However, mapping is not a neutral technology. What is to be mapped (but also what is NOT), who can access the maps, and how and by whom they are to be used is often very political: there tend to be many interests at stake and numerous different ways to look at these interests [21]. Providing ICT access is, therefore, insufficient in a societal context: the effective community (network) use of such powerful technologies needs to be explicitly shaped as well [22]. Creating community network maps and putting them to good use in supporting collaborative design communities for urban innovation like those in DESIGNSCAPES is therefore far from trivial. Instead, it requires a carefully tailored participatory mapping and sensemaking process of the collaboration ecosystems at stake. CommunitySensor is a methodology supporting this highly contextualized collaborative process.

CommunitySensor: Participatory Community Network Mapping

The CommunitySensor methodology supports inter-communal sensemaking [6], which can be used to help community networks grow the scalable multi-sectoral collaboration ecosystems needed in effective urban innovation [5, 22]. These ecosystems are of the essence to work towards more collective impact in addressing wicked societal problems at the societal scale needed, like the climate emergency (e.g. [10]). Strengthening the public interest, building the commons, and contributing to emerging, smarter network governance are critical aspects of interest in using this methodology.

In CommunitySensor, stakeholders, facilitated by a professional map maker, first define their mapping language (in particular, the element and connection types to use and the perspectives to make sense of their maps). Only then do they start the actual mapping and making sense of relevant parts of their collaboration ecosystem. This is a crucial difference from many other methodologies, which often start from a prede- fined set of knowledge types and modes of reflection. In CommunitySensor, participants first explore what is *essential* in their collaboration, starting from the everyday shared working language that conceptually connects them. This language is the first layer of common ground on which they build their maps. Participants then explore the maps on their own and collectively via a set of relevant perspectives in the ensuing collaborative sensemaking processes.

Participatory community network mapping is the participatory and iterative process of capturing, visualizing, and analyzing community network relationships and inter- actions and applying the resulting insights for community sensemaking, building, and evaluation purposes [6]. Applied to collaborative contexts, such as the case in design innovation communities, we also refer to this process as participatory collaboration mapping. Collaboration ecosystem maps are the core socio-technical design artifacts produced in and driving this collective mapping process forward.

In CommunitySensor, participants do not try to map their collaboration ecosystem fully, nor all at once: it is not a comprehensive information systems analysis or data modeling process. Instead, the initial "seed map" of the most important (in the eyes of the stakeholders) elements and connections only sketches the collaboration context around a common problem or question that is relevant, maybe even urgent, now.

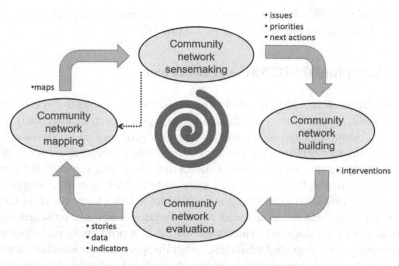

Fig. 2. The CommunitySensor methodology

In the subsequent sensemaking process, stakeholders then reflect upon the seed map using relevant map perspectives to jointly identify issues, priorities, and subsequent actions, as part of the common agenda-setting activities of the community network. These insights, grounded in an - at least partially - common conceptual reality, help inform stakeholders in designing and connecting their community network building activities. In this respect, CommunitySensor acts as a meta-methodology: it augments other community building and network development approaches but does not prescribe how this community network building will take place. Finally, relevant stories, data, and indicators can be added to the seed map in the community network evaluation stage. The process is reiterated, solidifying, and scaling up the collaborative common ground over time (Fig. 2).

In earlier work, we applied the combination of the CommunitySensor methodology and Kumu tool to many different collaborative community network settings. These include supporting the building of a local community of urban farmers; multidisciplinary agricultural field building at conferences; strengthening agricultural collaborations across local, regional, and national levels in a developing country; and identifying collaborative potentials in budding climate action coalitions [23–26]. However, the case most closely related to DESIGNSCAPES was part of another EU innovation project: BoostINNO. In that project, ten major European cities - with the Ukrainian city of Lviv as an observer - worked together on sharing knowledge about local social innovations learned in and with the public sector. Using CommunitySensor, we conducted two participatory collaboration mapping experiments: (1) finding relevant collaboration partners and (2) comparing social innovation lessons learned about urban spaces developed by each of the cities [27].

In MappingDESIGNSCAPES, we wanted to take the BoostINNO findings one step further. Whereas in BoostINNO, our primary focus was comparing the structures of the social innovation collaboration ecosystems of the participating cities (the WHAT), in MappingDESIGNSCAPES, we concentrated on the design processes in which such urban social innovations are being co-designed (the HOW).

3 The MappingDESIGNSCAPES Project

In MappingDESIGNSCAPES, our design-enabled innovation objective was to develop a proof-of-concept participatory collaboration mapping approach for effectively making sense across design-enabled urban innovations. Our goal was not to develop a fully developed methodology but to show proof of concept of the conceptual and practical steps needed. Underlying this approach was a conceptual model that provided the common meta-language on which to base mapping and sensemaking activities. Mapping and sensemaking results were to be stored in a visual knowledge base, which in turn was to be used as input for the next round of collaborative mapping, sensemaking, and conceptual model development. Thus, we engaged in a profoundly participatory co-design process of the MappingDESIGNSCAPES mapping and sensemaking approach, as well as the knowledge resources the approach produced and used. After introducing these knowledge resources, we present the cases in which we developed them and the design approach adopted in the remainder of this section. In the following sections, we will describe the conceptual model and visual knowledge base in greater detail.

3.1 The MappingDESIGNSCAPES Knowledge Resources

The MappingDESIGNSCAPES conceptual model and visual knowledge base drove the participatory mapping and sensemaking processes.

MappingDESIGNSCAPES Conceptual Model
The MappingDESIGNSCAPES conceptual model was to cover collaboration ecosystems around design-enabled innovations and to be grounded in the overall DESIGN-SCAPES approach. At its core was to be the high-level MappingDESIGNSCAPES community network ontology: the element types, connection types, and core collaboration patterns that capture combinations of element and connection types relevant to the collaborative community. These patterns were a conceptual starting point for constructing relevant perspectives to make individual and collective sense of the maps produced. The ontology was to seed, position, contextualize and conceptually interconnect the MappingDESIGNSCAPES urban prototype case maps.

MappingDESIGNSCAPES Visual Knowledge Base
A visual knowledge base was to be largely implemented in Kumu, with its knowledge architecture firmly grounded in the conceptual model. The knowledge base was to implement and illustrate the conceptual model (including case examples taken from the knowledge base to illustrate the concepts); contain the urban prototype case maps, the aggregate maps for cross-case comparison, the core collaboration patterns, the common and individual perspectives applied to the maps; as well as a set of sensemaking stories produced in making sense of the individual and cross-case maps through the various perspectives.

3.2 The MappingDESIGNSCAPES Cases

Although the base layer of the conceptual model had already been constructed in prior work and a literature review at the start of the current project, the urban prototype cases were to play an important role in iteratively further refining and validating the conceptual model and knowledge base. The urban prototypes were to provide inputs for constructing their case maps, make sense of the conceptual common ground between their maps, and provide feedback on iterations of the conceptual model, visual knowledge base and mapping/sensemaking methodology. We selected three existing DESIGNSCAPES urban prototype cases. Given the limited resources, this ensured having sufficient differences in scopes and approaches, while still having enough capacity to go into enough depth in making sense within and across the cases. One selection criterion was that the cases needed to be from different regions in the EU. They should also have at least one broad thematic interest in common, so that representatives would be sufficiently willing and able to learn from the other cases.

Out of the 40 other urban prototypes, the selected cases were The Landmarks Net (Greece), SciberCity (Finland) and CityBarge (the Netherlands). The thematic interest they had in common was environmental sustainability. Here is a synopsis of their cases in their own words:

- **The Landmarks Net (Thessaloniki, Greece):** "the design and construction of a [green spaces] landmarks' web, along in the area of the Municipality of Neapoli – Sykies (Greece) and their connection to the existing free-space urban context, parallel to the activation of a human network through educational interaction and participatory design"
- **SciberCity (Lahti, Finland):** "a participatory process to create future personas called 'SciberPunks' that could be used in more than human design scenarios for the purpose of building empathy towards the environment and its non-human inhabitants. The design process utilized real data and information as well as arts-based methods to support building empathy via data."
- **CityBarge (Delft, the Netherlands):** "contributes to the livability of cities by reviving the canals and providing a clean, easy and affordable water logistics solution. Together with its partners, Skoon Energy, KOTUG International and FYNLY, City-Barge developed a fully electric push-boat combined with a system of mini-hubs on the canals."

3.3 The MappingDESIGNSCAPES Design Approach

Our design approach involved three main stages: (1) defining (and refining) our conceptual model, which was to act as our common mapping language; (2) making the maps, including the conceptual model map and individual case seed maps, as well as the cross-case maps; (3) and individually and collectively making sense of the case and cross-case maps.

Stage 1: Initializing the Conceptual Model
We started our design process by taking the CommunitySensor community network conceptual model [23] and analyzing the visual knowledge base developed in the related URBACT BoostINNO project for element and concept types relevant to DESIGN-SCAPES [27]. Furthermore, the initial version of our conceptual model included concepts selected from the DESIGNSCAPES body of research and program resources[5].

Stage 2: Seeding the Maps
Using the conceptual framework as the foundation, we then defined the architecture of the visual knowledge base and implemented it in Kumu. Next, the knowledge base's initial version was filled with case maps. Via interviews and surveys, using the conceptual framework as a basis for the survey design, case representatives were asked to outline their seed maps. A seed map is a starting map that captures an essential part of a collaboration ecosystem of a case around a topic of common interest to its stakeholders. It does not provide a complete or utterly accurate information or knowledge model but rather sketches the most important elements and connections, as seen through the eyes of the stakeholders. Since all maps used the same underlying conceptual model, they could be aggregated into collective maps, showing how things are done across cases. This allows various sensemaking questions to be asked, such as: how do/could you do similar things in your case? Why do you do similar things differently? Do we mean the same things by things that look the same? A conceptual model can thus make sensemaking exercises more connected, focused, productive, and scalable.

Stage 3.0: Sensemaking - the Plan: Focusing on Face-To-Face Design Sessions with Local Stakeholders
By analyzing and discussing the individual/aggregate maps from various perspectives, we aimed to explain and make sense of the lessons learned and further develop and test the conceptual model and knowledge base.

In our original plan, on-site face-to-face sensemaking was to take center stage. We planned field visits for the project leader to come to each city as a participant-observer in design workshops. The seed maps prepared in advance would sketch the respective local collaboration ecosystems on which the design projects focused. These maps were to focus on the design processes and roles related to the innovation interventions in the local collaboration ecosystems. In the design workshops, they would be discussed and revised with local stakeholders. This would lead to deeper insights about design roles and concerns and allow the project leader to collect additional observations on the design practices on site. Time was a constraining factor for the cases (case representatives joined MappingDESIGNSCAPES after their projects had already started, and their participation was voluntary). During those field visits, the project leader would first engage in a preparatory meeting with each design team, followed by the actual stakeholder design meeting and an evaluation meeting with the design team afterward.

---

[5] https://designscapes.eu/resources/.

The project leader would summarize local observations and cross-case patterns in post-workshops research analysis. These findings would then be discussed in some additional joint online sensemaking sessions with all case representatives.

Stage 3.1: Sensemaking in Pandemic Times - Going Entirely Online with (Just) the Case Representatives

Due to COVID, the field visits and physical sensemaking sessions in co-creation workshops had to be canceled. Without access to local stakeholders for our initial purposes, our project now had to take place entirely online. We shifted the focus from analyzing detailed local design observations to iteratively developing the knowledge resources and collaborative sensemaking approach of the design-enabled urban innovation process in more depth. We focused on further detailing (1) the conceptual interrelationships of design concepts within and between the critical dimensions of problem domains, project scopes, and design processes; (2) the collaboration patterns, common/individual perspectives through which to view them, and (3) the individual and collaborative sensemaking processes.

As our alternative collaboration approach, we had the project leader construct draft versions of the various MappingDESIGNSCAPES knowledge resources and then validate and refine them with the case representatives in a series of online collaborative sensemaking sessions over several months. In total, 12 online individual sensemaking sessions between the project leader and representatives of the three cases separately and six plenary cross-case sensemaking sessions with representatives of all cases were held (Fig. 3). Furthermore, a closed Facebook group was used for additional informal updates and discussion in between joint sessions.

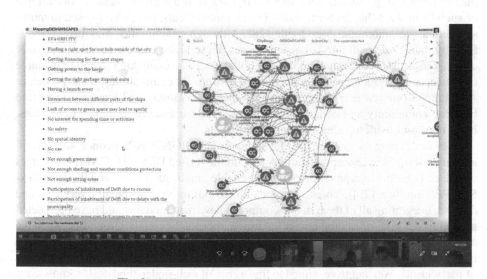

Fig. 3. Online cross-case collaborative sensemaking

In the online sensemaking sessions, we examined different kinds of maps (the conceptual framework map, case seed maps, and cross-case maps) and various perspectives.

Session outcomes included (1) identification of valuable and usable *collaboration patterns* in the various maps, (2) *common and individual perspectives* through which to examine those patterns (3) *interpretations* of the possible meaning of the content of the maps in the form of *sensemaking stories* and (4) *suggestions to change* the conceptual model, map content, perspectives, visualizations, and processes.

We present in more detail our conceptual model and visual knowledge base, which formed the mapping foundation of the cross-case collaborative sensemaking approach of MappingDESIGNSCAPES.

4   The MappingDESIGNSCAPES Conceptual Model

As significant effort was spent throughout the project on the (re)making of the conceptual model, we first summarize its development process before outlining the model itself.

4.1   Developing the Conceptual Model

The MappingDESIGNSCAPES conceptual model represents the DESIGNSCAPES take on the essence of collaboration ecosystems around design-enabled urban innovations. The foundation of this model was the existing CommunitySensor community network conceptual model. It was distilled from a range of collaborative community network projects by classifying common concepts being used in such projects in practice. It provides a set of main element and connection type categories related to the dimensions of *Purposes, Interactions, Participants, Content,* and *Resources* [23]. For example, an element type subcategory under *Purposes* is overarching *Themes*. An example of such themes are the UN Sustainable Development Goals, increasingly used in multistakeholder collaborations worldwide [28]. Although communities may use very differently named element and connection types, these broad categories help to provide crucial cross-case "conceptual hooks" for collaborative sensemaking. Another example of conceptual common ground concerns *Interactions*. In communities, these processes - including *Conversations, Discussions, Meetings, Workshops,* and *Events* - are vital to building community and collaboration: they are of the essence to make connections, build trust, and work together on common interests.

Before defining the first version of the MappingDESIGNSCAPES conceptual model, a brief review of the conceptualizations used in the related DESIGNSCAPES resources was done (e.g., the interpretation of design-enabled innovation in [3] and the DESIGNSCAPES Toolbox [29]). These resources turned out to be conceptually very rich and diverse. Integrating all of them in one comprehensive metamodel would have been detrimental to our goal of finding and comparing conceptual common ground between the cases with efficacy. Creating an overly complex conceptual model would have hampered mapping and making sense across cases in practice, given the real-world time pressures of participants. We, therefore, aimed to find a core of well-understood design knowledge constructs that could act as conceptual "boundary spanners" between cases of a very different nature [30]. Societal context dimensions we considered of particular importance, given the challenges of wicked problems. Such societal aspects are often lacking in more technically (software) engineering takes on design.

The starting point for this effort was obvious: the core conceptual structures under-lying the DESIGNSCAPES urban prototype proposal form (e.g., *Problems, Fields of Action, Project Focus, Project Orientation, Design Activities,* and *Design Tools*). Much thinking had gone into those structures by the program management framing them and the project teams interpreting and writing their proposals around them. This meant those categories were shared, "alive," and laden with potentially case-crossing meaning. On the other hand, the categories used were still abstract and likely not immediately action-able in the local contexts of the various cases. So, a further knowledge engineering task was to translate those DESIGNSCAPES categories to the "lifeworld" of participants so that these "conceptual bridges" were also rooted in very different local realities. Only after establishing this grounded conceptual foundation - a "sensemaking interlingua" - can it become helpful to start adding more specialized design concepts, such as possibly the numerous specific design tools and methods listed in the DESIGNSCAPES Toolbox [29].

Due to COVID, we could not observe local stakeholders jointly making sense of their design innovations while engaged in rich conversations. We had no access to their situated and subtle interpersonal interpretation, adoption, validation, and adaptation processes of design innovation concepts in their physical, hands-on design tasks. Instead, we concentrated on the conceptual meta-analysis of the knowledge resources and cross-case sensemaking processes. What our conceptual model now lacked in local stakeholder design diversity, it gained in methodological validation and applicability across the cases. For example, we now paid much more attention to cross-case sensemaking essentials: collaboration patterns and various types of sensemaking perspectives and practices, including cross-case storytelling.

The conceptual model evolved throughout our mapping and sensemaking journey with the case representatives. As it was so fundamental as a backbone to all our mapping and cross-case sensemaking efforts, we renamed it into the conceptual *framework*. In total, it took nine iterations to arrive at its final form (Fig. 4). Core changes in the frame-work included the classification of the elements and connections; the clustering of the elements, as well as their relative positioning on the map; differences between the con-ceptualization of local and global (= cross-case) elements; and alternative visualizations of the elements and connections.

Next, we outline the conceptual framework that resulted from those iterations.

4.2 The MappingDESIGNSCAPES Conceptual Framework

In analyzing the proposal structure, we arrived at three core dimensions to map design-enabled innovation projects: *Problem Domain, Project Scope,* and *Design.* They form the conceptual backbone for mapping and sensemaking activities and include main element types and connection types describing possible relationships between element types. Figure 5 shows the critical element types making up those dimensions.

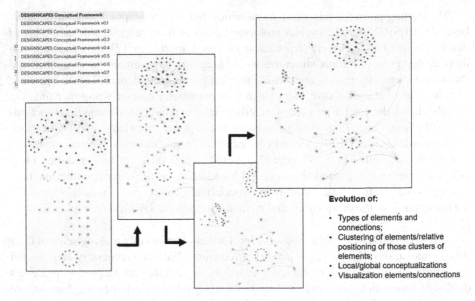

Fig. 4. The making of the MappingDESIGNSCAPES conceptual framework

- Problem Domain
  - DESIGNSCAPES Problems
  - DESIGNSCAPES Fields of Action
  - Local Problems
  - Local Solutions
- Project Scope
  - Project Focus
  - Project Orientation
  - Innovation Targets
  - Design Agency
  - Design Approaches
- Design
  - Design Projects
  - Design Process
  - Design Activities
  - Design Tools
  - Design Proposals
  - Design Context

Fig. 5. Key element types of the MappingDESIGNSCAPES conceptual framework

Problem Domain
The *Problem Domain* makes DESIGNSCAPES stand out from more technology-driven urban design innovation programs with a more limited societal scope. Design-enabled innovation from the program's perspective is about impacting the outside world, in this case contributing to the common good in the city. The core problem domain concept type categories from the application form concerned the *DESIGNSCAPES Problems* and *Fields of Action*. These are examples of "boundary objects that can be used to facilitate knowledge sharing across professional boundaries" [30], forming an interlingua between design projects regarding their WHY? and WHAT? Still, these categories are just abstract terms from the local stakeholders' perspective. Therefore, they were mapped to *Local Problems* and *Local Solutions,* representing the actionable working languages in the various cities.

Project Scope
The *Project Scope* concepts help position each design-enabled innovation project. On the one hand, they characterize the local stakeholder network in terms of its innovation aims. On the other hand, they summarize the design approach used to try and achieve the objectives.

Main proposal terms related to the project scope connect the problem domain and design dimensions and include the *Innovation Target, Project Focus, Project Orientation, Design Agency,* and *Design Approach.* As the possible value options for each of these aspects were prescribed in the proposal template, using these to find minimal common ground on which to compare the scopes of different projects was relatively straightforward. However, as those options were broad in scope (e.g., *Process Innovation* as one of the options for *Project Focus*), there were still many degrees of freedom to interpret these concepts. This ambiguity was not a barrier in our experiments but in fact helped trigger inspiring discussions.

Design (Process, Outputs, Impacts, Context)
Design has many aspects, which we could not even begin to cover in depth in our model. With the *Design Project* as the bridge between the *Project Scope* and the other *Design* dimensions, we focused on the *Design Process* adopted in the design project as the conceptual core of this dimension.

In our model, each design process includes several *Design Activities* and supporting *Design Tools.* We only included the list of design activities used in the proposal form as this was relatively comprehensive and could provide a standardized language across cases. In design process research, numerous frameworks exist for classifying design activities. Allowing each stakeholder to define their own activity classification would have created too little conceptual overlap for effective cross-case sensemaking.

In modeling the design process, we looked at the activities and tools as initially *planned,* but also at those in fact *applied.* Complex socio-technical design innovation projects are often implemented very differently from initially envisioned, as the COVID crisis has abundantly clarified. However, as our mapping and sensemaking processes proceeded, we found that several additional *local tools* were used in the various projects.

These differences turned out to be important in the cross-case conversations. We, therefore, relaxed the constraint in the conceptual model about only using the DESIGN-SCAPES list of predefined tools and also allowed local tools to be mapped on the case maps.

As to modeling the outputs of the projects, we focused on the *Design Proposals*. These were the most concrete and fully developed results that all the projects had in common. Given case time, budget, and COVID constraints, the envisioned implementations of the proposals could only be partially completed. In future work, we aim to focus more on the implementation and scalability of the prototypes. More mature outputs of the design-enabled innovation cycle, such as fully developed, tested, and adopted products and services, could then also be considered.

For a tentative analysis of (potential) *Impacts* of these proposals (and their ultimate, scaled implementations), we engaged in mapping and sensemaking exercises on how they *might* contribute to addressing the problems and solutions identified in the problem domain. Such impacts were represented as connections between the conceptual model's *Design* and *Problem Domain* dimensions. A typical connection found in the case maps would be how a particular *design proposal* could be a *design for* (addressing a) particular *local problem* or (implementing a) specific *local solution*.

We only did a very preliminary exploration of the *Design Context*. This is still a black box in the literature, involving many political, infrastructural, organizational, and societal conditions [12]. Context concepts may modify the other design concepts from the framework. Despite our limited analysis, we did find that certain contextual factors sometimes helped make better sense of the impacts of designs. An example was the *Landmarks* and *Landmark Locations* in The Landmarks Net case. These findings suggest such contextual concept types could, for instance, be included in domain mapping templates that might be used to initiate urban design innovation projects on green spaces in other cities.

5   The MappingDESIGNSCAPES Visual Knowledge Base

Having defined the initial version of the MappingDESIGNSCAPES conceptual framework, we started validating, testing, and refining it. To do so, we created an initial version of the visual knowledge base. Note that an ontology (in our case: the conceptual framework) and its associated knowledge base are entwined, with only a fine distinction between where the ontology ends and the knowledge base begins [31]. The knowledge base comprises the (implementation of the) ontology and the instances of its types (in our case, the element and connection types).

Based on the MappingDESIGNSCAPES conceptual framework, we defined the knowledge architecture - containing the map structure, element, and connection type definitions (including their field definitions and visualization conventions), and some initial perspectives such as the *bird's eye view* on the collaboration ecosystem. We further populated the knowledge base with the case seed maps. We filled the knowledge base with common and individual perspectives and sensemaking stories (stored outside the Kumu platform). As we went along, we adjusted the conceptual framework, the perspectives, and the visualizations of the maps.

We now introduce our maps: the conceptual framework map, the three case seed maps, and three cross-case maps. The following paper presents the other knowledge base components (collaboration patterns, common perspectives, and sensemaking stories) as part of the collaborative sensemaking process [1].

5.1 The Conceptual Framework Map

The most fundamental map in the knowledge base is the conceptual framework map (Fig. 6), which underlies all other maps. It is abstract in that it only shows the possible combinations of element and connection types, not their instances (represented in the case maps). The conceptual framework map shows the *element types* at the heart of the conceptual model; the *connection types* by which these elements are connected; and the *topological regions* in which these element types are positioned.

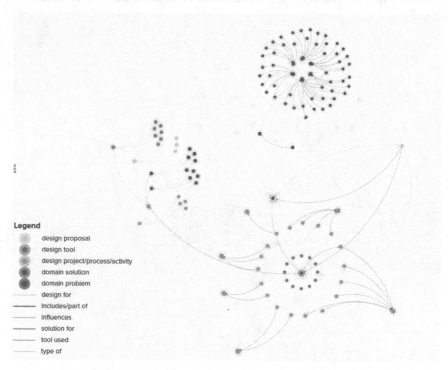

Legend
- design proposal
- design tool
- design project/process/activity
- domain solution
- domain problem
- design for
- includes/part of
- influences
- solution for
- tool used
- type of

Fig. 6. The MappingDESIGNSCAPES conceptual framework map

General Visualization Conventions

- Circular shapes stand for organic concepts (e.g., interactions and individual participants); rectangular shapes for resources, content, and institutional actors (e.g., organizations).

- Large size and bulls-eye elements indicate *concept type categories*.
- Shadows indicate common, cross-case concepts (e.g., *DESIGNSCAPES Problems*).
- Solid lines in the problem domain indicate connections between common concepts (e.g., a *DESIGNSCAPES Field of Action* being a <u>solution for</u> a *DESIGNSCAPES Problem*), dashed lines between a local and a common concept (e.g., *History and Identity Connection* being an <u>example of</u> (DESIGNSCAPES Field of Action) *Arts and Culture*).

Map Regions

- An essential finding in our sensemaking sessions was the value of using different "map regions" to quickly visually position and contrast design dimensions across case maps (Fig. 7).

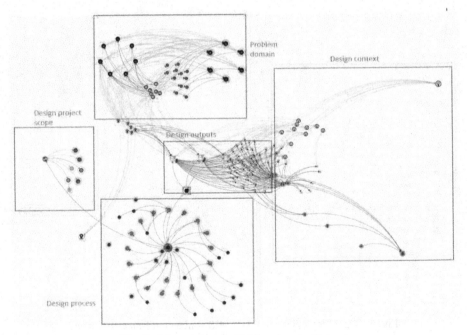

Fig. 7. Map regions in The Landmarks Net case

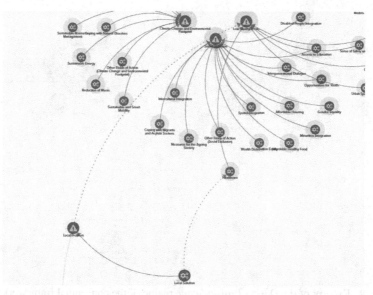

Fig. 8. Excerpt of the *Problem Domain* region of the conceptual framework map

Map Region: Problem Domain

- At the top of the conceptual framework map, the problem domain is modeled: the *DESIGNSCAPES Problems* (*Crisis of Values, Social Exclusion,* etc.), with their associated *DESIGNSCAPES Fields of Action* addressing these problems (Fig. 8). An example would be the field of action *Alternative Democratic Models* as a solution for the (DESIGNSCAPES) problem *Crisis of Democracy.*
- This map region also shows how *Local Problems* and *Local Solutions* are examples of *DESIGNSCAPES Problems* and *Fields of Action,* respectively. Note that the conceptual framework map does not provide actual examples of such local problems and solutions (that is what the (cross-)case maps are for). It does visualize which particular DESIGNSCAPES fields of action are related to what DESIGNSCAPES problems, however, as these are both cross-case common concepts, indicated by their both being shadowed.
- We use red to indicate problems and green to indicate solutions.

Map Region: Design Project Scope

- The *Design Project* is the starting point here (Fig. 9).
- The various project scope dimensions have different colors. Each project scope dimension's possible values are modeled in the same color.
- Since all project scope dimensions and their values are common concepts, they all have shadows surrounding them.

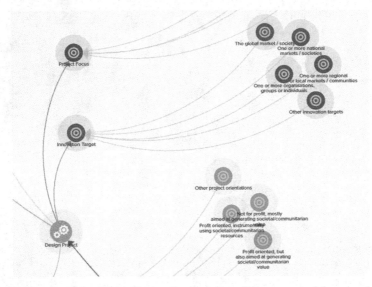

Fig. 9. Excerpt of the *Design Project Scope* region of the conceptual framework map

Map Region: Design Process

- We made the *Design Process* element big with a bull's eye in the middle (Fig. 10). This central - but abstract - "container concept" can thus act as a clear visual anchor on which to focus in sensemaking discussions easily.
- Surrounding this central element – in the inner circle, are the *Design Tools*.
- The standardized *Design Activities* have a fixed position and surround the Design Process element in an outer circle. Design activities are grouped by the *Design Process Step* they belong to in the proposal (e.g., Design activity *2.1 Draw Ideas* belongs to step *2. GENERATING IDEAS*), these steps being on the outside of the design activities ring and visualized as (slightly larger) design activities themselves and capitalized.
- A *Design Tool planned* to support a design activity is represented by a *dashed* brown line, the fact that it was in fact *used* is modeled as a *solid* brown line in the (cross)-case maps.
- Design process/activity/tool concepts are modeled in shades of yellow, orange, and brown. All are shadowed since they are cross-case concepts in the conceptual framework (apart from local tools).

Map Region: Design Outputs/Impacts

- The solid conceptual connection between the design process and its outputs (i.e., proposals) is represented by a thick yellow line (Fig. 11)

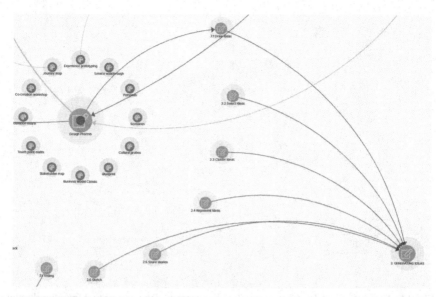

Fig. 10. Excerpt of the *Design Process* region of the conceptual framework map

- Similar to the *Design Process,* we made the *Design Proposals*-container element large with a bullseye in the middle.
- In some case maps, design proposal *categories* helped structure large amounts of design proposals and clarify their semantics (which helps better to understand their potential impacts on the problem domain). Design proposal categories are represented as larger versions of design proposal icons on the map.
- Design proposals are connected to the *Local problems* and *Local Solutions* they aim to impact in the case maps.

Map Region: Design Context
Design context elements vary widely in scope and function (e.g., acting as inputs for design processes or classifying design proposals or local problems/solutions). Their visualization was therefore not standardized. Instead, we used symbols that matched their local context of use. Future work could use more standardized visualizations representing meaningful design context concept types (e.g., *Landmarks*).

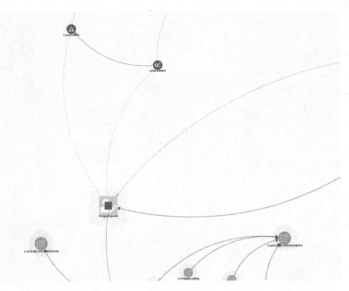

Fig. 11. Excerpt of the *Design Outputs/Impacts* region of the conceptual framework map

5.2 The Case Maps

The visual knowledge base also contains case maps. For all three cases, an initial seed map was created. To this purpose, the project leader extracted relevant elements, connections, and descriptive text using the conceptual model as a lens to analyze the urban prototype proposal form submitted for each case. Case teams also answered two surveys to elicit additional information for the seed maps. The first survey captured how they saw their problem domain. The second survey was sent after some initial sensemaking sessions to capture in more detail what their design process looked like, both as initially planned and as it had turned out in practice regarding design activities and tools actually used.

Here we briefly characterize each of the case maps in turn. Note that although the maps differ in content and structure, one can recognize in each case map the underlying conceptual framework map in the topology of the map regions, the types of elements and connections, and their visualizations. One could argue that even when just looking at an individual case map, the other maps - and the cases they represent - are mentally present in the background this way.

Seed Map: The Landmarks Net
The Landmarks Net map (Fig. 12) shows many different design proposals at its center, many more than the other cases. This is a direct effect of the COVID crisis. Initially, the plan was to have a few physical co-design workshops with selected stakeholders, including citizens and experts, to develop elaborate landmark designs. Due to COVID, all those workshops had to be canceled. Instead, citizens were invited to create digital designs from home, using a template with landmark design elements such as plants, furniture, and people. They could then submit their designs online, which were exhibited

via an online notice board. Instead of having only a few in-depth design proposals, there were now around 50 citizen submissions. Although the technical quality of the proposals was much less than the expert-assisted ones initially envisioned, the result was more participatory in terms of hearing many more citizens' voices.

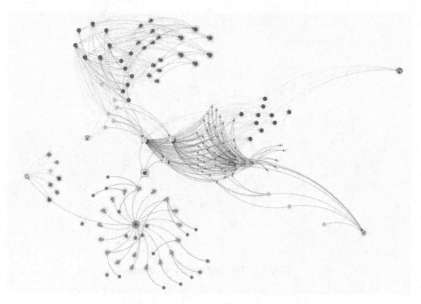

Fig. 12. The Landmarks Net seed map

Seed Map: SciberCity
In the SciberCity map (Fig. 13), the rich set of design tools and activities stands out, in contrast to its - compared to The Landmarks Net - much smaller set of problem domain concepts and design proposals. This could be explained by its focus on developing an innovative technical design format instead of exploring the problem domain in-depth. The result was a more standard software engineering design trajectory than The Landmarks Net's.

Seed Map: CityBarge
At first sight, CityBarge - like SciberCity - also seems rather traditional software design process-orientated, as many technical engineering issues need to be resolved (Fig. 14). Still, by comparing the maps, one immediately sees that the CityBarge problem domain was modeled much more extensively. Numerous (business, government, citizen...) stakeholder interests must be balanced to get an actual barge sailing and operating in a city's busy canals. So, this case is an interesting example of a combination of social (problem domain) and technical (design) complexity.

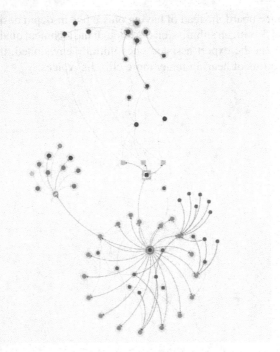

Fig. 13. The SciberCity seed map

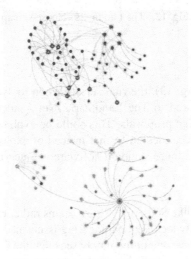

Fig. 14. The CityBarge seed map

5.3 The Cross-Case Maps

The next step was aggregating the case maps along the different *Problem Domains*, *Project Scope*, and *Design*-dimensions. For each cross-case map, we show an excerpt of a map discussed in one of the joint cross-case sensemaking sessions (more details on that collaborative sensemaking process in the accompanying paper [1]).

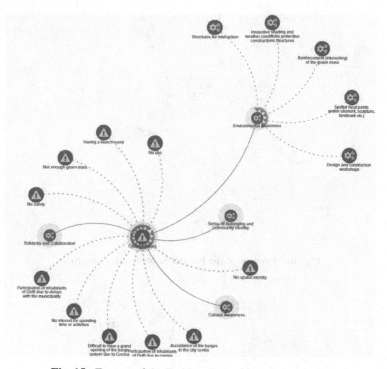

Fig. 15. Excerpt of the Problem Domains-cross case map

The Problem Domains-Cross Case Map
In the *Problem Domains*-cross case map (Fig. 15), *Crisis of Values* was a problem addressed by all cases, while two also developed *Environmental Awareness* fields of action to address them. This helped the case representatives realize they were all engaged in a form of (environmental) value driven-development.

The Project Scopes-Cross Case Map
In the *Project Scopes*-cross case map (Fig. 16), all cases turned out to be working with *Design Methods to Generate Ideas*. This was a good starting point for a rich discussion on the shared common methodological ground in the various design approaches used in the cities.

The Design-Cross Case Map
Figure 17 shows an interesting application of how all three cases (not shown in the excerpt) used either one or both of the *Personas* and *Experience Prototyping* tools to support design activities that are part of three separate design process steps (*Sketch, Listen to the feedback of users, Create insight by observation*). Such shared patterns proved to be starting points for often surprisingly rich discussions.

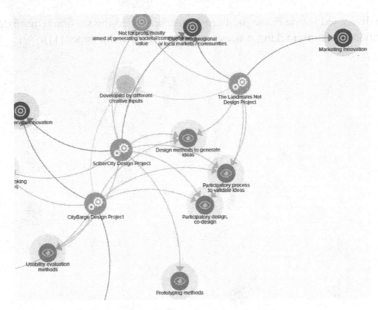

Fig. 16. Excerpt of the Project Scopes-cross case map

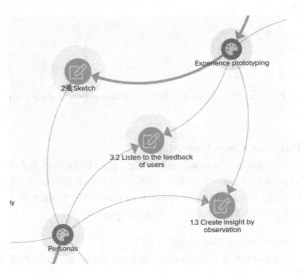

Fig. 17. Excerpt of the Design cross-case map

These "dimensional cross-case maps" reduced complexity by each showing only a subset of elements and connections from a particular angle of analysis, compared to the overall map showing the complete collaboration ecosystem. However, we found them still relatively hard to interpret without further guidance. How could we more effectively and efficiently make sense of what we see here by making and taking "the right" perspectives? We describe the participatory mapping-driven collaborative sensemaking process we prototyped to address this question in our second paper [1].

6 Discussion

In this paper, we described how we prototyped two essential knowledge resources (a conceptual model and visual knowledge base centered around various types of maps) in the process of participatory collaboration mapping. This sets the stage for a process of collaborative sensemaking to compare and discover design-enabled approaches to addressing wicked problems at the local city level and beyond [1]. Such an approach is an example of collaborative visualization: the shared use of computer-supported (interactive) visual representations of data by more than one person with the common goal of contributing to joint information processing activities. Information processing in this definition refers to those cognitive activities involved in individual or collaborative visual information processing, such as reading, understanding, applying knowledge, discussing, or interpreting [32]. The main goal of collaborative visualization systems, strategies, and techniques is to achieve common ground, of which shared mental models are the foundation [33]. Significant collaborative visualization research challenges remain around analyzing and making sense of the data, including many social, task, and cognitive aspects [32, 33]. In MappingDESIGNSCAPES, we aimed to address at least some of those issues.

In this discussion, we reflect on the lessons learned and point at directions for future research and development concerning the mapping foundation of the collaborative sensemaking approach. We do so by examining the intertwined knowledge creation processes of collaborative ontology engineering and participatory mapping.

6.1 Collaborative Ontology Engineering: Laying the Conceptual Foundation Together

Creating a shared vision, brainstorming, exchanging creative ideas, and evaluating them in diverse multi-stakeholder partnerships presupposes first devising a shared language to reach a common understanding [34]. One fundamental process of participation - often forgotten in co-design- is having case representatives co-define the visual language they use to construct their maps and make sense of them. Ideas on creating meaningful collaboration languages can be found in the field of ontology engineering.

Ontology engineering is a consensus-building process in which a community of stakeholders agrees upon a common view of a domain of interest and how their shared knowledge can be conceptually structured in an ontology. In *collaborative* ontology engineering, stakeholders jointly agree upon their requirements and priorities, then propose and discuss various alternatives to create a conceptual model complying with these requirements and reflecting both their interests and the shared goals of their community of interest [35]. In MappingDESIGNSCAPES, we created a practical collaborative ontology engineering methodology that balances representing conceptual common ground and individual interests. We created a (design-enabled urban innovation) conceptual framework that grounded individual seed maps and cross-case aggregate maps.

Ontologies define a common knowledge-sharing vocabulary in a domain [31]. Many ontologies are heavyweight, including rigorous axiomatic definitions of concepts, relations, and functions. Our MappingDESIGNSCAPES conceptual model, however, is an example of a lightweight ontology, with only loosely formalized semantics, making concepts open to multiple interpretations [36]. This is in line with standard practice in ontology engineering, to model the concepts among which domain experts commonly make a distinction without modeling the distinctions themselves [31]. This limited degree of formalization sufficed for our purpose, with our maps only providing seed content to trigger rich sensemaking conversations across cases. Through our experiments, we established and validated our conceptual foundation regarding core elements and connection types. We did not define semantic constraints on, for instance, canonical (permitted) uses of concept types in connection types or permitted attribute values within concepts and connections. This could be future work, although creating meaningful higher-order socio-technical collaboration pattern languages and processes for sparking and focusing *human* conversations rather than machine-dominated pattern generation and analysis remains our primary goal.

As to what such socio-technical pattern languages might entail, some promising, potentially more universal *domain* patterns came to the fore. For example, in the City-Barge case, many socio-technical design considerations in their local problem domain were mapped. Such proto patterns might also be helpful for sensemaking when introducing waste barges in other congested cities. Similarly, the design considerations around introducing green spaces in The Landmarks Net, including such concept types as *Landmarks* and *Landmark Locations* and knowledge categories like *Historical Identity, Sentimental Interaction*, and *Connecting with Nature*, could be instructive in similar projects in cities elsewhere. Our collaboration patterns are still rudimentary and specific, as they were created for the practical sensemaking needs experienced by just our participants. In future work, we aim to expand the reusability and interlinking of these patterns, leading to more mature collaboration pattern languages for design-enabled urban and regional innovation. Related design pattern languages to draw inspiration from can be found in the Human-Computer Interaction tradition, e.g. [37, 38]. Although helpful, these are not sufficient to capture the societal dimensions, such as problem domain and design contexts, that need to be considered when scaling up collaborations towards real collective impact. Higher-level "societal-technical" pattern languages could prove inspiring here as well. Existing urban and regional design pattern languages like [39] come to mind. Another example is the LiberatingVoices pattern language for empowering communities, which we used to design collaborative scenarios for collective climate action in related work [2].

6.2   Participatory Mapping: Applying the Concepts to the Messy Real World

In collaborative ontology engineering, community members systematically evolve their joint ontology in incremental consensus-building processes [35]. For us, our ontology/conceptual framework is not a goal, but a means for collaborative sensemaking. It provides the initial common conceptual structure(s) to create maps that provide an overview, focus, and connection. Such maps need to be meaningful within and between their communities of use. For "[Kitchin and Dodge], maps are fleeting, without any 'ontological security' [...] Maps are practices: 'they are always *mappings*': they argue that we need to shift from ontology (how things are) to ontogenesis (how things become)" [40]. Just grounded in their own isolated reality, such fleeting maps are often the output of physical brainstorming sessions. Here participants create detailed maps, often by sticking numerous post-its on empty walls. Enthusiasm is high, but the half-life of its collective meaning is often short once the participants have left and gone back to their organizations. We would argue that our maps are between the situatedness of such fleeting maps and the more or less stable representations of typical ontologies. Our conceptual framework provides just enough ontological security, helping to anchor and find meaningful connections across case maps while also allowing the maps to preserve local, situated terminologies. This way, maps can act as shared boundary objects to talk about, think with, and coordinate perspectives and actions [33]. Boundary objects inhabit several communities of practice and maintain a constant identity [41, p. 16]. They help communicate and coordinate the perspectives of various constituencies by performing a brokering role involving translation, coordination, and alignment among the perspectives of different communities of practice coming together in a community of interest [14]. Our cross-case MappingDESIGNSCAPES community is a meta-community of multiple interest spanning local communities of (design) practice. Their seed and cross-case maps, viewed from various perspectives, provide the conversation triggers and conceptual bridges for effective collaborative sensemaking processes.

One more remote yet intriguing mapping finding of our project can be described as "the overview effect." Yaden et al. describe this phenomenon as the overwhelming sense of oneness and connectedness reported by astronauts seeing Earth from space. It has been shown to help shape how individuals understand and approach new concepts, generating the motivation to make sense of such an intense experience in one's life narrative. By altering the conceptual framework through which individuals approach new information and make sense of old experiences, it prompts changes in conscious reflection [42]. Of course, our "bird's eye views" of collaboration ecosystems were only a much-watered-down version of such transcendent outer space experiences. Still, we did occasionally experience "micro-overview effects" of our own. What properties of maps might induce them more systematically could be a fascinating topic of investigation.

7 Conclusion

Wicked problems such as climate change urgently need much increased societywide collaborative capacity. Cities are a crucial enabler of this transition, with design-enabled urban innovations leading the way forward in the multiple transitions underway. This first of two papers outlined the participatory mapping foundation of an approach for collaborative sensemaking across design-enabled urban innovations: the MappingDE-SIGNSCAPES methodology. The core of the mapping foundation consists of two knowledge resources: a conceptual framework and a visual knowledge base of individual and cross-case maps. MappingDESIGNSCAPES itself is grounded in the CommunitySensor methodology for participatory community network mapping. We used the CommunitySensor community network ontology as an "upper ontology" to circumscribe the MappingDESIGNSCAPES conceptual framework tailored to the more specific needs of urban innovation design collaboratives. We found this weaving of a generic community network mapping approach with an urban design innovation-domain fruitful. It helped to efficiently map the essence of local urban design innovations into concepts and terms that were both locally meaningful and could be connected and compared across local cases. How those connections helped to make better collaborative sense of both wicked problems and design solutions within and across urban cases is what our second MOVE paper [1] is about.

Acknowledgements. The current study is part of the project DESIGNSCAPES (Building Capacity for Design enabled Innovation in Urban Environments) funded by the EU Horizon2020 call CO-CREATION-02-2016 - User-driven innovation: value creation through design-enabled innovation, under Grant Agreement No. 763784.

References

1. de Moor, A., et al.: Collaborative sensemaking of design-enabled urban innovations: the MappingDESIGNSCAPES case. In: Polovina, R., Polovina, S., Kemp, N. (eds.) Aligning Computing Productivity with Human Creativity for Societal Adaptation. The 1st Measuring Ontologies for Value Enhancement (MOVE) Workshop at the 23rd ACM CSCW2020, revised selected papers CCIS 1694. Springer Nature, Switzerland (2022)
2. Schuler, D., de Moor, A., Bryant, G.: New community research and action networks: addressing wicked problems using patterns and pattern languages. In: Proceedings of the 7th International Conference on ICT for Sustainability, New York, NY, USA, pp. 330–337 (2020). https://doi.org/10.1145/3401335.3401818
3. Concilio, G., Tosoni, I. (eds.): Innovation Capacity and the City: The Enabling Role of Design. Springer, Berlin (2019)
4. Abbasi, M., et al.: A triplet under focus: innovation, design and the city. In: Concilio, G., Tosoni, I. (eds.) Innovation Capacity and the City: The Enabling Role of Design, pp. 15–41. Springer, Cham (2019). https://doi.org/10.1007/978-3-030-00123-0_2
5. Baccarne, B., Logghe, S., Schuurman, D., Marez, L.: Governing quintuple helix innovation: urban living labs and socio-ecological entrepreneurship. Technol. Innov. Manag. Rev. **6**, 22–30 (2016). https://doi.org/10.22215/timreview/972
6. de Moor, A.: CommunitySensor: towards a participatory community network mapping methodology. J. Community Inform. **13**(2), 35–58 (2017)
7. Gwynne, K., Cairnduff, A.: Applying collective impact to wicked problems in aboriginal health. Metrop. Univ. **28**(4), 115–130 (2017)
8. Weber, E.P., Khademian, A.M.: Wicked problems, knowledge challenges, and collaborative capacity builders in network settings. Public Adm. Rev. **68**(2), 334–349 (2008)
9. Mulgan, G.: Social Innovation: What Is It, Why It Matters, How It Can Be Accelerated. The Young Foundation, London (2007)
10. Smith, A., Voß, J.-P., Grin, J.: Innovation studies and sustainability transitions: the allure of the multi-level perspective and its challenges. Res. Policy **39**(4), 435–448 (2010). https://doi.org/10.1016/j.respol.2010.01.023
11. Coulson, S., Woods, M., Scott, M., Hemment, D.: Making sense: empowering participatory sensing with transformation design. Des. J. **21**(6), 813–833 (2018). https://doi.org/10.1080/14606925.2018.1518111

12. Concilio, G., et al.: Innovation and design. In: Concilio, G., Tosoni, I. (eds.) Innovation Capacity and the City: The Enabling Role of Design, pp. 61–83. Springer, Berlin (2019). https://doi.org/10.1007/978-3-030-00123-0_4

13. Concilio, G., Li, C., Rausell, P., Tosoni, I.: Cities as enablers of innovation. In: Concilio, G., Tosoni, I. (eds.) Innovation Capacity and the City: The Enabling Role of Design, pp. 43–60. Springer, Berlin (2019). https://doi.org/10.1007/978-3-030-00123-0_3

14. Fischer, G., Shipman, F.: Collaborative design rationale and social creativity in cultures of participation. Hum. Technol. 7(2), 164–187 (2011)

15. Etzioni, A.: Creating good communities and good societies. Contemp. Sociol. 29(1), 188–195 (2000)

16. Wenger, E., Trayner, B., de Laat, M.: Promoting and Assessing Value Creation in Communities and Networks: A Conceptual Framework. Ruud de Moor Centrum, Open University, Heerlen, The Netherlands (2011)

17. Conklin, J.: Wicked problems and social complexity. In: Dialog Mapping: Building Shared Understanding of Wicked Problems, pp. 3–40. John Wiley and Sons, Hoboken, N.J (2006)

18. Weick, K.E., Sutcliffe, K.M., Obstfeld, D.: Organizing and the process of sensemaking. Organ. Sci. 16(4), 409–421 (2005). https://doi.org/10.1287/orsc.1050.0133

19. Raworth, K.: Doughnut Economics: Seven Ways to Think Like a 21st-Century Economist. Random House, London (2017)

20. Mitchell, W., Inouye, A.S., Blumenthal, M. (eds.): Beyond Productivity: Information Technology, Innovation, and Creativity. National Academies Press (2003)

21. Garfield, S.: On the Map: Why the World Looks the Way It Does. Profile Books, London (2013)

22. Gurstein, M.: Effective use: a community informatics strategy beyond the digital divide. First Monday 8(12) (2003)

23. de Moor, A.: A community network ontology for participatory collaboration mapping: towards collective impact. Information 9(7), preprint no 151 (2018)

24. de Moor, A.: Towards a participatory community mapping method: the tilburg urban farming community case. In: Proceedings of the Work-In-Progress Track of the 7th International Conference on Communities and Technologies, Limerick, Ireland, pp. 27–30 (June 2015). In: International Reports on Socio-Informatics (IRSI), vol. 12(1), pp. 73–82 (2015)

25. de Moor, A.: White, N.: Bohn, A.: Using participatory community network mapping for field building: the INGENAES conference case. In: Proc. of the 14th Prato CIRN Conference 25–27 October 2017 Monash Centre, Prato, Italy (2017)

26. de Moor, A.: Increasing the collective impact of climate action with participatory community network mapping. Livingmaps Rev. 8 (2020)

27. de Moor, A.: Co-discovering common ground in a collaborative community: The BoostINNO participatory collaboration mapping case. In: Communities &Technologies (C&T) Conference 2019, June 3–7, Vienna, Austria, pp. 255–262 (2019). https://doi.org/10.1145/3328320.3328404

28. Wu, J., Guo, S., Huang, H., Liu, W., Xiang, Y.: Information and communications technologies for sustainable development goals: State-of-the-Art, needs and perspectives. IEEE Commun. Surv. Tutor. 20(3), 2389–2406 (2018). https://doi.org/10.1109/COMST.2018.2812301

29. Morelli, N., Simeone, L., van Dam, K.: DESIGNSCAPES Toolbox: An Inventory of Design Tools and Methods to Support Urban Innovation', DESIGNSCAPES, 2nd edition, (Sep 2021). Available: https://issuu.com/designscapes/docs/designscapes_toolkit_final

30. Kimble, C., Grenier, C., Goglio-Primard, K.: Innovation and knowledge sharing across professional boundaries: political interplay between boundary objects and brokers. Int. J. Inf. Manag. 30(5), 437–444 (2010). https://doi.org/10.1016/j.ijinfomgt.2010.02.002

31. Noy, N.F., Mcguinness, D.L.: Ontology Development 101: A Guide to Creating Your First Ontology. Stanford University, Stanford, CA (2001)

32. Isenberg, P., Elmqvist, N., Scholtz, J., Cernea, D., Ma, K.-L., Hagen, H.: Collaborative visu-alization: definition, challenges, and research agenda. Inf. Vis. **10**(4), 310–326 (2011). https://doi.org/10.1177/1473871611412817
33. Yusoff, N.M., Salim, S.S.: A systematic review of shared visualisation to achieve common ground. J. Vis. Lang. Comput. **28**, 83–99 (2015). https://doi.org/10.1016/j.jvlc.2014.12.003
34. Mamykina, L., Candy, L., Edmonds, E.: Collaborative creativity. Commun. ACM **45**(10), 96–99 (2002). https://doi.org/10.1145/570907.570940
35. Simperl, E., Luczak-Rösch, M.: Collaborative ontology engineering: a survey. Knowl. Eng. Rev. **29**(01), 101–131 (2014). https://doi.org/10.1017/S0269888913000192
36. Usman, Z., Young, R.I.M., Chungoora, N., Palmer, C., Case, K., Harding, J.: A manufacturing core concepts ontology for product lifecycle interoperability. In: van Sinderen, M., Johnson, P. (eds.) IWEI 2011. LNBIP, vol. 76, pp. 5–18. Springer, Heidelberg (2011). https://doi.org/10.1007/978-3-642-19680-5_3
37. Dixon, D.: Pattern languages for CMC design. In: Whitworth, B., de Moor, A. (eds.) Hand-book of Research on Socio-Technical Design and Social Networking Systems, pp. 402–415. Information Science Reference, Hershey PA (2009)
38. Pan, Y., Stolterman, E.: Pattern language and HCI: expectations and experiences. In: CHI'13, April 27-May 2, Paris, France, pp. 1989–1998 (2013)
39. Alexander, C., Ishikawa, S., Silverstein, M.: A Pattern Language: Towns, Buildings. Oxford University Press, Construction (1977)
40. Crampton, J.: Cartography: performative, participatory, political. Prog. Hum. Geogr. **33**(6), 840–848 (2009)
41. Bowker, G.C., Star, S.: Sorting Things Out: Classification and Its Consequences. The MIT Press (2000). https://doi.org/10.7551/mitpress/6352.001.0001
42. Yaden, D.B., et al.: The overview effect: awe and self-transcendent experience in space flight. Psychol. Conscious. Theory Res. Pract. **3**(1), 1–11 (2016). https://doi.org/10.1037/cns0000086

Collaborative Sensemaking of Design-Enabled Urban Innovations: The MappingDESIGNSCAPES Case

Aldo de Moor[1]($\boxtimes$), Evi Papalioura[2], Evi Taka[3], Dora Rapti[4], Annika Wolff[5], Antti Knutas[5], Tomas te Velde[6], and Ingrid Mulder[7]

[1] CommunitySense, Tilburg, The Netherlands
ademoor@communitysense.nl
[2] Ministry of Environment and Energy, Thessaloniki, Greece
e.papalioura@prv.ypeka.gr
[3] Municipality of Neapolis-Sikeon, Thessaloniki, Greece
taka.eugenia@n3.syzefxis.gov.gr
[4] Thessaloniki, Greece
[5] Department of Software Engineering, LUT University, Lappeenranta, Finland
{Annika.Wolff,Antti.Knutas}@lut.fi
[6] Suit-Case, Delft, The Netherlands
tomas@suit-case.nl
[7] Delft University of Technology, Delft, The Netherlands
I.J.Mulder@tudelft.nl

Abstract. Wicked societal problems, such as environmental issues and climate change, are complex, networked problems involving numerous intertwined issues, no optimal solutions, and a wide range of stakeholders. Cities are problem owners and living labs for finding solutions through design-enabled innovation initiatives. However, to reach collective impact, it is paramount that these initiatives can learn from one another and align efforts through collaborative sensemaking. In the MappingDESIGNSCAPES project, we piloted a participatory collaboration mapping approach for cross-case sensemaking across design-enabled urban innovation initiatives. We used the CommunitySensor methodology for participatory community network mapping together with the Kumu online network visualization tool to help representatives of three urban prototype cases share and collectively make sense of their design lessons learnt. In this second of two papers, we build on the participatory mapping foundation introduced in [1]. We describe the collaborative sensemaking approach used, then present the core collaboration patterns and common perspectives that form the sensemaking scaffolding. We show how we collaboratively made sense by first taking individual perspectives, then making common sense together. An extended discussion puts our findings in a larger context of how an approach like MappingDESIGNSCAPES can be used to move from collaborative sensemaking to collective impact in design-driven urban innovation.

Keywords: Design-enabled urban innovation · Participatory mapping · Collaborative sensemaking · Collective impact

© Springer Nature Switzerland AG 2022
R. Polovina et al. (Eds.): MOVE 2020, CCIS 1694, pp. 203–226, 2022.
https://doi.org/10.1007/978-3-031-22228-3_9

1 Introduction

In [1], we discussed how cities are instrumental in addressing wicked societal problems, such as climate change, environmental issues, and social exclusion. Besides being the locations where these problems manifest themselves, cities can also act as living labs to develop working solutions. We introduced the EU DESIGNSCAPES[1] program which aims to foster the building of capacity for design-enabled innovation in urban environments. We introduced the MappingDESIGNSCAPES project, in which we used the CommunitySensor methodology for participatory community network mapping [2], together with the Kumu online network visualization tool[2], to help representatives of selected DESIGNSCAPES urban prototypes share and collectively make sense of their urban design innovation lessons learnt.

In the previous paper we described how we developed two key knowledge resources – a conceptual framework and a visual knowledge base. Together, they form the participatory mapping knowledge foundation of the collaborative sensemaking process for design-enabled urban innovation that we piloted in MappingDESIGNSCAPES. We outline the collaborative sensemaking approach used in Sect. 2. In Sect. 3, we introduce the knowledge layer that forms the sensemaking scaffolding: a set of core collaboration patterns and common perspectives. In Sect. 4, we show how we used these perspectives to collaboratively make sense by first taking individual perspectives, then making common sense together. An extended discussion in Sect. 5 puts our findings in a larger context of how an approach like MappingDESIGNSCAPES can be used to move from collaborative sensemaking to collective impact in design-driven urban innovation settings. Discussion topics include participation as a multi-faceted process; how collaborative sensemaking can help diverse stakeholders see the bigger picture together; how using the right tools can amplify our collaborative mapping and sensemaking capabilities; and finally, how these capabilities can empower design-enabled urban innovation processes and help them accomplish more collective impact. We end the paper with conclusions.

2 Collaborative Sensemaking of Design Enabled Urban Innovations

Collaborative sensemaking is the goal of participatory collaboration mapping. Maps can quickly become overly complex to interpret in rich domains like urban innovation. In this section, we share how we operationalized the participatory mapping-driven process to collaboratively make sense of design-enabled urban innovations. We begin with some conceptual starting points, then outline the sensemaking approach we adopted in MappingDESIGNSCAPES.

2.1 Collaborative Sensemaking: Conceptual Starting Points

Sensemaking is commonly understood as the processes through which people interpret and give meaning to their experiences. However, these interpretive processes have taken

---

[1] https://designscapes.eu/.
[2] http://kumu.io.

on many different meanings, depending on by which academic discipline the term is being used [3].

In our own take, we base ourselves on the interpretation by Weick, who introduced sensemaking in the context of organizations [4]. One quote in particular sums up the essence for us: "To focus on sensemaking is to portray organizing as the experience of being thrown into an ongoing, unknowable, unpredictable streaming of experience in search of answers to the question, 'what's the story?'" [5]. This question, however, begs another question: *whose* story? Each stakeholder looks at the same complex collaboration reality from a different perspective and may have a very different story to tell about what, at first sight, is the same phenomenon. The parable of the "Blind Men and the Elephant" comes to mind: six blind men feel different parts of the same elephant. Each person, however, thinks it to be something very different, depending on whether they touch its trunk, leg, or tail. How now to make them see the whole, starting from their limited individual perspectives? [6].

In cross-boundary knowledge sharing, the interplay between brokers and boundary objects is of the essence [7]. Stories are an important tool in making sense within and across communities. In [8], we showed how an ongoing process of storytelling can help make sense across the boundaries of social innovation cases. Along similar lines, in MappingDESIGNSCAPES, stories and storytellers were to make sense together across their design innovation cases.

Very elaborate stories can often be told about just a few elements and connections. As these stories get told, deeper meanings of the connections between the elements are being teased out: what could be the implications of particular connections, or the lack of them? Additional stories can be told to explore further, triggered by participants noticing related elements and connections of particular interest to them. In short, participatory maps are not objective representations of the world. Instead, to community members their maps can be focal points and triggers for the sharing of rich, situated knowledge through sometimes very personal stories.

By having design innovators represent *their* elements, *their* connections, and *their* stories, they become owners and ambassadors of their case. Case elements can be connected via intermediate, boundary spanning concepts like the *DESIGNSCAPES Problems, Fields of Action*, and *Design Activities*. Through these boundary-spanning elements, stories across different cases can be connected and jointly made sense of. Through better joint understanding of commonalities and differences, new designs, collaborations, and ultimately increasingly collective impacts could be catalyzed.

To illustrate how this might be done in practice, we now outline our own participatory mapping-driven collaborative sensemaking process, as it grew out of our iterative efforts.

2.2 Collaborative Sensemaking: The MappingDESIGNSCAPES Approach

Collaborative sensemaking took place in several individual and cross-case online sessions. The emerging maps offered focal points for reflection and discussion. At the same time, the sessions helped in further bootstrapping the conceptual framework underlying the mapping and sensemaking.

In six joint online plenary sensemaking sessions we discussed the individual and cross-case maps. Using a set of initial, tentative perspectives, grounded in previous related cases like BoostINNO, we started to get a sense of the "collaborative lay of the land". Rather than working on increasing the level of detail of the case maps themselves, we focused our attention on further developing the structure and role of map *perspectives* in triggering, informing, and catalyzing the sensemaking process. In summary:

- On top of the conceptual framework, we defined a set of *core collaboration patterns*:
  - meaningful combinations of element and connection types acting as sensemaking contours.
- These collaboration patterns formed a conceptual foundation for subsequently defining a set of *common perspectives*. These are selections and visual renderings of elements and connections of a map that help stakeholders to jointly look in the same relevant but general direction when making sense across cases.
- Next, case representatives defined *individual perspectives* within those common perspectives. To do so, they further selected elements and connections from these common perspectives that were meaningful to them personally in characterizing a design situation about which they could tell a local *sensemaking story*.
- Finally, in a *joint sensemaking session,* case representatives presented and discussed each other's sensemaking stories, enriching and connecting them and in this way arriving at new, collective lessons learnt.

3 Sensemaking Patterns and Perspectives

3.1 Core Collaboration Patterns

As we found out in our initial cross-case sensemaking efforts, it does not suffice to "unleash" the full complexity of the collaboration ecosystem upon the participants, for them to then somehow make sense productively. Sensemakers digesting the potential meaning of all present and possible concepts and connections at once does not work. Instead, participants need to be guided in their sensemaking conversations. What to focus on, though?

The first step toward finding a productive focus was provided by our conceptual framework's core dimensions and concepts: the *Problem Domain, Project Scope*, and *Design* dimensions. However, how to proceed from there? We did not know of a theoretical, pre-defined starting point for collaborative sensemaking that would work in (our) practice.

As an intermediate conceptual scaffolding, we defined a number of *core collaboration patterns*. Collaboration patterns are conceptual structures that model the essence of the socio-technical systems of collaborative communities and can be used to capture collaborative lessons learned in, for instance, social innovation cases [9]. In the MappingDESIGNSCAPES case, starting points for defining its collaboration patterns were the individual and cross-case problem domain, project scope, and design maps that had already been validated when discussing them through their initial, still quite generic perspectives.

An example of a collaboration pattern that we kept revisiting and which helped generate many insights about the various maps was the *Problem Domains*-collaboration pattern (Fig. 1). This collaboration pattern focuses on the relationships between the

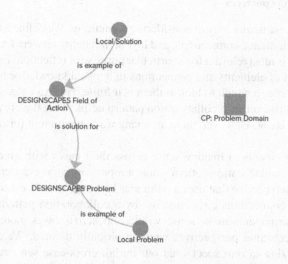

Fig. 1. The Problem *Domains* collaboration pattern

problems and solutions within and across cases. The *DESIGNSCAPES Problems* and *Fields of Action* provide the conceptual common ground, with the *Local Problems* and *Local Solutions* case examples of those concepts. This collaboration pattern is an excellent example of identifying minimal conceptual common ground between the cases. Individual cases may also have additional conceptualizations not part of the cross-case common ground. For example, some local problems and solutions were further classified by locally-defined knowledge categories, such as the design proposal categories identified in The Landmarks Net [1].

After our iterations, we identified six core collaboration patterns: *Map Signatures, Problem Domains, Design Project Scopes, Design Processes, Design Contexts,* and *Design Impacts.* Each pattern captures meaningful combinations of element types and connection types that form a relevant starting point for productive sensemaking conversations about design-enabled innovations. They were elicited in practice and are not meant to be seen as *the* patterns for all design-enabled urban innovation projects everywhere. The criterion for a collaboration pattern to be included in the set was pragmatic: it turned out to have been a focal point for productive conversations, as surfaced in our open-ended individual and joint sensemaking sessions. Still, as they turned out to help make sense across cases as diverse as in our project, we think they are interesting starting points for future conceptual framework development and case analysis.

The collaboration patterns were still only conceptual constructs. To make them work in practice, we further refined and visualized them by applying specific filters and layouts in *common perspectives.*

3.2 Common Perspectives

A perspective is a particular way of considering something. We define a map perspective as a selection of elements, connections, and layout that helps viewers focus on a part of a map in a way that is most relevant for a particular purpose of reflection. Even though there is only a finite set of elements and connections in a visual knowledge base, the number of perspectives through which to look at them is infinite. For example, a comprehensive bird's eye perspective on each collaboration pattern helps to see the big picture of where the action is – or is not. However, there are many ways to zoom in further and visualize those selections.

To guide participants in making sense across their cases with greater efficacy, we defined – for each collaboration pattern – one or more common perspectives. A common perspective is a perspective that uses a particular layout to show a meaningful selection of elements and connections circumscribed by a collaboration pattern. Common perspectives help participants make sense within and across cases more effectively and efficiently. Our common perspectives were empirically defined. We created them by informally analyzing in retrospect what our initial, cross-case sensemaking conversations tended to drift towards. In doing so, we noticed which of the selections of elements and connections, shown in what particular visualizations, triggered the most focused, rich, and energetic conversations.

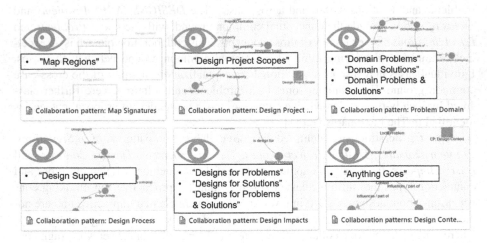

"The **common perspectives** help us to all look in the same direction, the **individual perspectives** are what each of us sees then."

Fig. 2. Common perspectives (organized by collaboration pattern)

We defined ten common perspectives on our six collaboration patterns (Fig. 2).

To show how they may be applied, we give examples of how we used the common perspectives in our case. Each perspective is applied to either an individual case seed map or a cross-case map, as a perspective is meaningless without an underlying map.

Common Perspective: Map Regions

In the previous paper, we explained how we developed the idea of map regions to provide topological cues for making sense of design-enabled innovations: at the top of each map, we positioned the *Problem Domain*, on the left-hand side the *Project* Scope, the *Design Processes* at the bottom, the *Design Outputs* in the middle, and the *Design Contexts* on the right-hand side.

This perspective helps to quickly get a broad sense of where the design focus of a particular case is. In this perspective applied to The Landmarks Net map, for instance, immediately the large number of design proposals stood out, as we saw in ([1], Fig. 7). However, we can also compare the different case maps by positioning them next to one another and comparing their topologies (Fig. 3).

This cross-case comparison confirms that *The Landmarks Net* has many more proposals than the other two cases. Similarly, *CityBarge* has a significant problem domain compared to the others, particularly *SciberCity*. Both observations indeed led to engaging discussions.

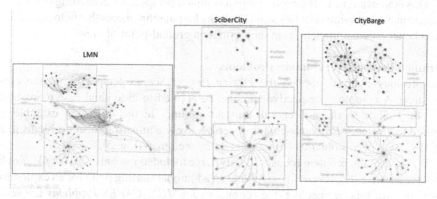

Fig. 3. Common perspective *Map Regions* applied to cross-case map

Common Perspective: Design Project Scopes

Initially, in the *Design Project Scopes*-collaboration pattern, we had just defined the overall perspective on the map showing all elements and connections related to the design project scope. In the next iteration of this perspective, we refined several things. We greyed out those elements that had only one connection. This means that one can immediately focus on those elements with two or more connections, which means that at least two cases have that element in common. We also increased the relative size of the elements depending on the number of connections that comes in (Fig. 4).

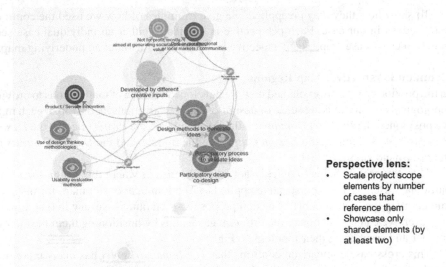

Perspective lens:
- Scale project scope elements by number of cases that reference them
- Showcase only shared elements (by at least two)

Fig. 4. Common perspective *Design Project Scopes* applied to cross-case map

This is an example of the evolution of a common perspective, consisting of changing element and connection selections and applying layout refinements that help participants focus better on what matters from their common ground-point of view.

Common Perspective: Domain Problems

The previous example applied the *Design Project Scopes*-perspective to the cross-case map. A common perspective can also be applied to individual case maps to see how they relate to the conceptual common ground. In the following example, we applied the *Domain Problems*-common perspective – comparing local problems to the DESIGNSCAPES problems – to the CityBarge seed map (Fig. 5).

We see that the problem focuses of CityBarge included not only *Crisis of Values* but also, for instance, *Economic Crisis*, giving an additional starting point for an exploratory discussion. In this perspective, the (common) *DESIGNSCAPES Problems* are scaled by the number of incoming connections. Although the perspective was applied to the CityBarge local map, we did not size the DESIGNSCAPES problems depending on how often CityBarge local problems link to them. Instead, those elements were sized by the incoming connections *for all maps,* as calculated in the *Problem Domains cross*-case map. This means that the size of those common *DESIGNSCAPES Problem*-elements is a rough visual indicator for how important *all the cases together* find this concept to be. One could say that this common perspective applied to the CityBarge map shows how much this project might contribute to what "Europe as a whole" thinks to be societally important.

Although a common perspective applied to an individual case in first instance benefits representatives of that case, its usefulness may go beyond them. In this example,

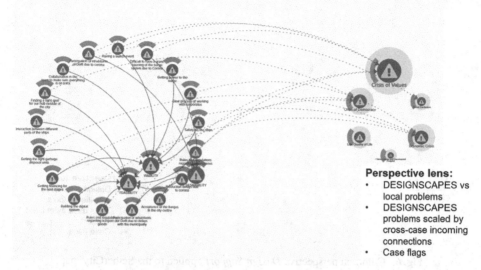

Perspective lens:
• DESIGNSCAPES vs local problems
• DESIGNSCAPES problems scaled by cross-case incoming connections
• Case flags

Fig. 5. Common perspective *Domain Problems* applied to CityBarge map

CityBarge representatives initially could have a story to tell around their local problem-category *Viability*. SciberCity looking at the CityBarge map from this common perspective, however, could say that they also recognize the local CityBarge problem of the *Slow process of working with corporates*, as they had to deal with that problem in their Finnish context.

Common Perspective: Design Support
In this perspective, we mainly look at the design activities and tools making up the design process. It only shows the tools that support at least one activity. Colored "flags" indicate the colors of the case, with brown flags indicating common concepts, such as design activities. In Fig. 6, we applied this perspective to the SciberCity case map:

One observation immediately standing out is the size (and thus of the number of incoming connections representing uses) of the *Co-Creation Workshop* tool (on the left), which is linked to many different design activities. We also see that it is connected by many *thin* brown lines, indicating that this tool was *planned* to be used but not used in reality in the design processes of the various cases. This, as discussed before, was a direct effect of the COVID crisis. It is an extreme case of what often happens in design trajectories: the discrepancy between design plans and realizations, which is a fruitful starting point for sensemaking stories and discussions.

Common Perspective: Designs for Solutions
Designs for Solutions is a common perspective that is grounded in the *Design Impacts*-collaboration pattern, which is about what these designs (may) contribute to in the real world (Fig. 7). The yellow flags stand for The Landmarks Net, which offers numerous local solution proposals, grouped into three categories. In particular, their *History and identity connection* is linked to many *DESIGNSCAPES Fields of Action*, such as *Urban*

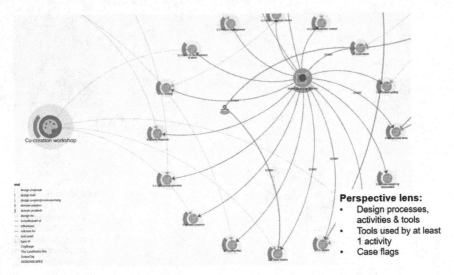

Fig. 6. Common perspective *Design Support* applied to the SciberCity map.

Space Quality, Intergenerational Dialogue, and *People's Participation*. So, in terms of design priority and focus, design proposals contributing to this local solution category may be important ones to consider, at least in the Landmarks Net case. Beyond that, the Landmarks Net case may provide other cases about regreening their cities with many concrete and inspiring ideas on addressing the linked common fields of action in their cases.

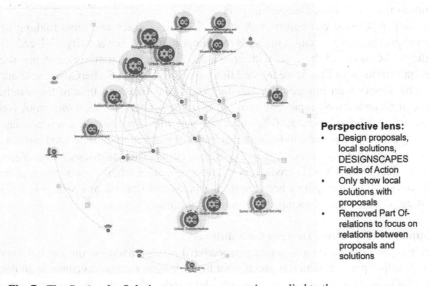

Fig. 7. The *Design for* Solutions common perspective applied to the cross-case map

4 Making Sense Together

We had thus built a knowledge base of seed and (cross) case maps and common perspectives that provide analytical lenses consisting of relevant selections of elements, connections, and visualizations. How now do you methodically use them to make sense together effectively and efficiently? In this section, we propose a general outline of such a process which we experimented with in MappingDESIGNSCAPES.

4.1 Taking Individual Perspectives

First, case representatives were free to choose a common perspective that appealed to them. They then defined an *individual* perspective by selecting particular elements and connections within that common perspective. Whereas the role of the common perspectives is to have all sensemakers look in the same general direction, the individual perspectives are what the sensemakers in fact observe in the map to which they apply it. This personalized perspective further constrains the common perspective by selecting only those elements and connections about which a participant has something interesting to say: a *sensemaking story*.

To illustrate, for the collaboration pattern *Design Impacts,* one of the common perspectives is *Designs for Problems & Solutions.* SciberCity applied this perspective to the cross-case *Problem Domains* map and created an individual perspective that they named "*Solving a crisis of values*" (Fig. 8). In essence, they concluded that values are at the heart of driving so many things, including design processes and should therefore be taken as a starting point for design project setup.

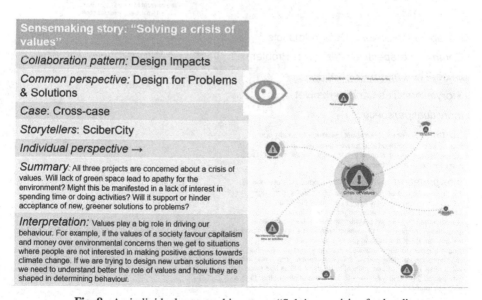

Fig. 8. An individual sensemaking story: "Solving a crisis of values"

4.2 Making Common Sense

Participants representing different cases compared and contrasted their individual perspectives in a final joint sensemaking activity. They interpreted commonalities and differences by "looking through each other's eyes." This entailed reading and discussing the individual sensemaking stories they had each contributed. In their collective discussion, they added another layer of interpretation of what the perspectives and stories may mean and imply regarding issues, priorities, and subsequent actions.

To illustrate this final common sensemaking step: another sensemaking story was told by The Landmarks Net, who applied to their case the *Designs for Problems*-common perspective of the same collaboration pattern SciberCity picked: *Design Impacts* (Fig. 9). In essence, their story "*Democratic use of space*" was that communal green spaces in the city are not just about feeling good and healthy as individual citizens, but also that they have a political dimension, including economic, environmental, and democratic empowerment aspects. Their individual perspective showed that their proposal categories of *Historical identity, Sentimental interaction,* and *Connecting with nature* (which had come out of their first round of internal sensemaking discussions) provided concrete ways to go about many of their local problems, like *Not enough green mass, No spatial identity*, etc. From their perspective, these local problems were clear examples of the *Crisis of Democracy-*DESIGNSCAPES (common ground) problem. In our final joint sensemaking session,

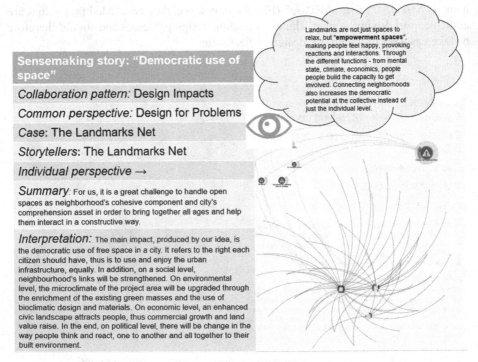

Fig. 9. Making common sense: co-imagining "empowerment spaces"

we discussed this particular sensemaking story, ultimately together coming up with the idea of "empowerment spaces."

5 From Collaborative Sensemaking to Collective Impact

In this paper, we described how we made collaborative sense across local design-enabled urban innovations using a visual knowledge base created in the process of participatory collaboration mapping, as we described in [1]. The goal of the MappingDESIGN-SCAPES "urban prototype" project was to provide a practical proof of concept of how to go about such a mapping-driven cross-case sensemaking process.

In this section, we reflect on our lessons learned and point at future research and development directions on participatory mapping-driven collaborative sensemaking in an urban design innovation context. We do this at length since our proof of concept should be firmly embedded in different strands of thinking and practice to take root and further prove its potential. We start by examining what we mean by "participation" in participatory collaboration mapping and the collaborative sensemaking guided by the maps created. We then move from conceptual foundation via sensemaking practice to – hopefully – societal impact. We do so by examining participation as a multi-faceted process, then finding out how sensemaking depends on seeing the bigger picture together, exploring the tools supporting this process, and finally moving to reflect on how to embed such processes in larger urban contexts catalyzing societal transformations.

5.1 Participation: A Multi-faceted Process

Achieving measurable outputs and outcomes of the prototyping cases is not the immediate goal of using MappingDESIGNSCAPES. The direct benefits for the participants are that they get deeper insights into their project scopes, meanings, and (potential) impacts through the cross-case, participatory mapping-based collaborative sensemaking process. This provides ideas directly usable in their own design trajectories (e.g., the citizen project proposal categories identified in the Landmark Nets case) and helps case representatives document and present their project results once their project has finished.

A general precondition for pilot/prototype participants to engage in a collaborative sensemaking process like MappingDESIGNSCAPES is that they are willing to reflect, learn, and collaborate. Such an involved process is particularly suited for collaboration ecosystems addressing wicked problems, with the problem and solution spaces and stakeholder networks being fuzzy and requiring multiple perspectives to make actionable sense of. The overall DESIGNSCAPES program had already preselected cases that met these conditions. Within that range, for MappingDESIGNSCAPES, we further selected cases on the criteria of motivation, regional EU distribution, and variety in design challenges. This helped create an interesting mix of highly motivated case representatives with enough in common yet also experiencing enriching differences to make for engaging and ongoing conversation and collaboration.

Our methodology of using participatory collaboration mapping to make sense within and across urban design innovation cases is within the tradition of participatory design between the public sector and local communities. In such design collaborations, participation is multi-faceted and far from trivial, requiring answers to thorny issues like whether to empower citizens or municipal workers; to promote participation for now or for long-term future ideas; and whether to effectively involve just the vanguards or everybody [10]. Other bottlenecks, specifically in participatory mapping processes, include participatory options not being actively propagated by the responsible authorities, there not being a specific enough interest for the public, and, especially in the early stages, there not being a legally binding obligation to include the voices of the public [11].

We far from addressed all these participation issues, but at least explicitly surfaced many in our discussions and dealt with some of them in our projects:

- The level and type of participation in the design processes differed widely in each case. For example, CityBarge and SciberCity worked with dedicated, small, semi-professional design teams involved in the full process, from ideation to prototype definition. In The Landmarks Net case, however, many citizens submitted rudimentary design visions, which were then processed by a small team of urban design professionals.
- The Landmarks Net created a role for local institutional stakeholders to *catalyze* participation of other stakeholders in the design: city hall and local newspapers were instrumental in promoting the design project, which led to a high number of green space proposals from citizens.
- As we have argued, participation is not just necessary in the design process itself but also in the reflective sensemaking *about* the design processes, in both of which processes participatory collaboration mapping can be helpful. In our case, participation of local stakeholders in design sensemaking was only partial; however, case *representatives* created and made sense across their maps *on behalf of* their stakeholders, constrained as they were by the COVID pandemic in organizing local activities. In contrast: in a case on strengthening agricultural collaborations in Malawi, we involved villagers directly in physical collaborative sensemaking by having them first map their local collaboration ecosystems, with mapping professionals only present as facilitators. They then jointly discussed the connections they observed between their different (cross-case) maps [12]. One intriguing exception to the lack of direct stakeholder collaborative sensemaking participation in our project happened in The Landmarks Net case. An online portal was used to display citizen design proposals alongside another as they were being submitted, triggering other citizens also to submit a proposal of their own. Finding effective co-design combinations of shared (material/digital) objects and processes can empower citizens and local communities [13]. In future (post-COVID) work, we would like to develop such hybrid combinations further.
- Note that creating a shared vision, brainstorming, exchanging creative ideas, and evaluating them in diverse multi-stakeholder partnerships presupposes first devising a shared language to reach a common understanding [14]. One fundamental process of participation – often forgotten in co-design- was having case representatives co-define the visual *language* they used to construct their maps and make sense of them. This is what we explored in the previous paper [1]. However, to further scale reflection within the collaboration ecosystem, co-definition of meanings through collaborative sensemaking is key to connecting the variety of collaborators in the ecosystem and

ensuring ownership not only of the visual language but also of the respective outcomes in order to scale the reflective practices with efficacy.

5.2   Collaborative Sensemaking: Seeing the Bigger Picture Together

How now to use these maps created in a participatory way? Collaborative sensemaking involves new understandings, processes, and tools in which stakeholders across the board collaborate in complex thinking and decision-making processes [15]. Selvin and Shum make a case for knowledge cartography. This is about improving our capacity to create and use human-interpreted higher-level visualizations, complementing low-level, machine-driven pattern-mining approaches like big data and simulation. Through knowledge cartography, we can "grow our collective capacity for sensemaking: to make sense of overwhelming amounts of data; to assess conflicting judgments about its trustworthiness; to resolve polarized interpretations about the implications, and to negotiate effective courses of action that all parties can commit to" [16].

Sensemaking departs from the premise that humans live in a world of gaps, which participatory mapping approaches can help span [17]. Bridging these gaps between conceptual knowledge and the lived stories within and between the cases in which these concepts are applied – is at the core of MappingDESIGNSCAPES. Such conceptual bridge-building takes place at many levels. Participants first used the various maps to make sense of their local urban design innovation cases, showing considerable socio-technical complexity. By mapping their local terminologies (e.g., their *Local Problems/Solutions*) to more generic (DESIGNSCAPES) categories, they were inspired to think more deeply about the meaning of their cases. For example, in The Landmarks Net, our collaborative sensemaking helped them to distinguish knowledge categories to classify their numerous citizen design proposals. This added a whole new layer of meaning to their project and helped them make better sense of the thrust of it. COVID prevented physical local design workshops, but in future work, the maps and sensemaking stories collected could also be inputs for follow-up local, reflective, and action-generating efforts. Second, the methodology helped make sense across the cases, identifying the deeper meanings connecting them. For example, we discussed urban design innovations' values and emancipatory potentials during our joint sensemaking sessions. This could be called a process of triple-loop social learning. Whereas second-loop learning is about exploring the context of new situations that do not fit existing patterns and schemes, third-loop learning also explores the deeper guiding norms, values, and paradigms underlying the cases [18].

Collaboration patterns and common perspectives played a fundamental role in our sensemaking approach. These intermediate conceptual structures helped to catalyze and focus the collaborative sensemaking process and to tease out the higher-order learnings from the maps. We created these patterns and perspectives inductively, co-evolving them through our initial conceptual framework, the case seed maps, the cross-case maps, the stories, and all the conversations that emerged around them. As we explored the maps and tinkered with the perspectives, we found out what concepts and connections the participants deemed essential and how to make sense of them in practice.

In other urban design-enabled innovation contexts, civic hackathons prototypes have been used as boundary objects to consolidate ideas and communicate/reflect on them [19]. It would be interesting to see how hacking prototypes and collaboration ecosystem maps agree and differ in their boundary-spanning roles for looking back versus forward in collaborative sensemaking (cf the retrospective and forward-looking action-orientated aspects of organizational sensemaking [5]). We hypothesize that hacking prototypes trigger design discussions of more immediate problem-solving concerns to stakeholders. Collaboration ecosystem maps are explicitly grounded in problem domains, thus making more significant societal concerns explicit (such as in the DESIGNSCAPES problems and fields of action). They may thus steer reflection in a longer-term, societal-orientated direction. Post-COVID, we would like to pursue experiments with hybrids of hackathon prototyping- and map-driven collaborative sensemaking activities. This could also include approaches to gamify mapping outcomes and use them to catalyze sensemapping efforts in stakeholder workshops [20].

To formalize our elaborate collaborative sensemaking process, we propose the notion of a "sensemaking ladder," which stakeholders could climb, moving from understanding the core concepts in common to achieving scalable collective impact (Fig. 10). Many different kinds of ladders have been proposed in the field of information and knowledge systems. An example is the "semiotic ladder," in which the lowest level refers to the material world of physical signs, and the highest level comprises the social world of shared understanding [21]. Another example is the "Reader-to-Leader Framework," in which social media users move from mere readers of content to becoming engaged leaders in their community [22].

- Collective impacts
- Common actions
- Common interpretations
- Individual interpretations
- Individual perspectives
- Common perspectives
- Collaboration patterns
- Cross-case maps
- Individual case maps
- Conceptual framework

Fig. 10. The sensemaking ladder

Climbing the ladder, one starts on a solid shared meaning foundation of a *conceptual framework*. Stakeholders then use local and common concepts from the conceptual framework to represent meaningful (to them) parts of their cases in *individual case maps*. These (seed) maps are aggregated in *cross-case maps*. Collaboration patterns are distilled from a growing body of cases to make sense of the maps. Based on this collaboration pattern foundation, a set of *common perspectives* is defined that help stakeholders look in the same general direction around relevant topics of interest. Within these common perspectives, stakeholders then define their *individual perspectives*, which they interpret by telling their own *sensemaking stories*. In joint discussions, *common interpretations* are co-created, enriching and interlinking the individual stories. We think this alternating between individual and collective meaning-making to be a fundamental contribution of our project. Not studied yet in this pilot, but part of future work will be to translate these insights into collective actions and impacts, in which common agenda setting plays a key role [23].

Some final words about the all-important role of storytelling in collaborative sensemaking. Storytelling has long been acknowledged as a crucial approach toward sensemaking in organizations and communities, increasingly also being supported by digital technologies [24, 25]. In MappingDESIGNSCAPES, individual and collective sensemaking stories were the main instrument for capturing and contrasting the meanings of the maps. Crucial, especially in societal application domains like social and urban innovation, is to ensure the quality of both the stories and the processes in which they are created, shared, and applied. In [8], we proposed a storytelling cycle of trust: a conceptual framework to help ensure the legitimacy and authenticity of the stories being told; the synergy in combining stories to represent multiple stakeholder perspectives; and the commons (such as online repositories) in which stories can be discovered and used to help span boundaries across cases and domains. With the expanded collaborative sensemaking framework presented in this paper, it would be of great interest to revisit that storytelling cycle.

5.3 Using the Right Tools: Amplifying Collaborative Mapping and Sensemaking

Creating and using relevant map representations was essential in participatory mapping and collaborative sensemaking. The right tools can make a difference in supporting these complex collaborative processes. A core tool for us was the online network visualization platform Kumu. This tool is particularly useful for our purposes because of its features to create elaborate and customized perspectives. The tool enables these to be automatically generated based on the types and properties of the elements and connections mapped. We already mentioned the overview effect. From what could be called a user interface point of view, one possible explanation for this effect is that Earth's holistic features against the blackness of space emphasize both the perceptual and conceptual themes and feelings of awe [26]. Discovering what perceptual and conceptual themes might strengthen overview effects in collaborative sensemaking in urban societal contexts might be a fruitful line of inquiry.

Despite its many capabilities, Kumu comes with its technical limitations. For example, if multiple participants add an element with the same type and label, the most recently added version overwrites the properties of those added earlier. Another limitation is that multiple connections of the same type between the same two elements are superimposed upon one another. This is problematic when engaging in collaborative mapping and sensemaking, as distinguishing between multiple stakeholder points of view is paramount.

Other tools might be useful as well. [27] give an overview of types of tools of particular relevance to design-enabled urban innovation, from "personas" and "Idea Evaluation Matrix" to "Value Proposition Canvas" and "design orienting scenarios". The wise use of such tools could further enrich our mapping and sensemaking processes. However, research on which (combinations of) design tools to use and how best to use them is still in its infancy, especially in complex societal design contexts. In reviewing the related class of creativity support tools, [28] conclude that it is hard to make an authoritative tool use-fulness assessment. Instead, they propose to evaluate such tools on specific dimensions, like particular types of user groups, forms of interfaces, complexity, or phases of the creative process supported. Interestingly, they do not mention the social/societal context these tools might be classified on. Our societal context-orientated approach explicitly tackles this context. By making sense of the problem domain and the (potential) impact designs might have in addressing wicked urban problems, our approach helps fill this gap.

Finally, we looked at sensemaking stories as individual and collaborative interpreta-tions of the societal context of design tools. We left the associated discussion processes themselves as black boxes. An interesting related field is contested collective intelligence. For example, the visual analytics of debates can bring more structure and sensemaking power to these discussion processes [29]. In future work, we hope to explore further how such "argumentation mapping" may augment the societal context domain mapping we have been exploring in MappingDESIGNSCAPES.

5.4 Design-Enabled Urban Innovation: Towards Collective Impact

Design-enabled urban innovation "[should] be more than the injection of design methods and tools into innovative activities. It has to be about creating a diffuse design attitude, including the capability of 'listening to the context,' the capacity to support participation, the ability to synthesize and visualize solutions, the skill to devise complex solution architectures, and the attitude to connect 'micro' initiatives with 'macro' infrastructural interventions [30, p. 8]". Our approach helps build this capability to listen to the context and synthesize and visualize solutions bridging the gap between micro-initiatives and macro-context.

The MappingDESIGNSCAPES approach is in line with the overall ambition of the DESIGNSCAPES capacity-building program. It can be seen as a complementary tool to spur the reflective practice among urban initiatives and their ecosystems [31]. The DESIGNSCAPES program identified the roles and capabilities of various stakeholders in the awarded pilots. It developed a capacity-building program through a cross-project understanding of the tools, processes, instruments, and techniques in design-enabled innovation to stimulate the full potential of design to trigger a systemic change in tack-ling societal challenges. The program showed that financial support stimulated the use of design (methods) in developing solutions and broadening design capacity. Within this context, the premise is that strengthening the collaboration and exchange among different urban innovators could facilitate the scaling of their best practices and ultimately increase the impact of these urban initiatives. In other words, for enabling urban transformations that tackle complex issues, developing more systematically collaborative learning and co-creative partnerships is critical [32]. At the same time, to facilitate the adoption of such radical social innovation at an urban scale, urban innovation processes need to consider a broad range of stakeholders: a collaboration ecosystem. Our participatory and visual methodology helps scale the reflective practice and ensure ownership within the collaboration ecosystem. As said before, it is not straightforward whom to select to ensure representative participation, as the methodology is quite time-consuming. In an ideal situation, all actors within the collaboration ecosystem are part of the collaboration mapping and sensemaking process, allowing the effective translation of interpretations into action directions. MappingDESIGNSCAPES at least has the potential to act as a bi-directional action repertoire. First, it facilitates the translation of the common interpretations into project-specific actions and helps stakeholders to transfer the lessons into their urban contexts. Second, it provides ideas for, for instance, program management for more impactful interventions at the meso ("regime") and macro ("scape") levels. More specifically, participatory mapping-driven collaborative sensemaking of experimentation within and across local pilots, through relevant perspectives and stories, could help better identify the roles and capacities of various stakeholders, including local government and EU policy-making processes.

The MappingDESIGNSCAPES methodology is in the spirit of approaches like exploratory data work, which mainly supports the problem-finding stage in the early stages of the design of urban innovations. In this process, framing what data to collect is crucial and non-trivial [33, 34]. However, instead of scraping and interpreting open data from social media, we co-defined and made sense – through storytelling and ongoing conversations – of meaningful *concepts* framing the connections between problems, solutions, and designs, guided by a solid underlying conceptual framework. It would be interesting to explore how these exploratory conceptual and data-driven approaches for urban innovation design might complement one another in future work.

A strength we observed in all the cases was the flexibility of their design processes, in quickly adapting to rapidly changing circumstances and formidable obstacles such as the COVID crisis. We think this flexibility and resilience might be a fundamental property that all design-enabled urban innovation cases (should) have. Although on the surface, the design proposals differ considerably from what was described in the original project proposals, the underlying fundamental design values and qualities are still very much present. As we demonstrated, participatory mapping and collaborative sensemaking – grounded in solid conceptual models of design-enabled innovation – could further increase the flexibility, resilience, interconnectivity, and collective impact of design projects and programs by reflecting on their "core values space."

Collective impact implies the commitment of stakeholders from different sectors to a common agenda for solving specific social problems. Realizing this impact requires a systemic approach to social impact that focuses on the relationships between organizations and the progress towards shared objectives [35]. It also means that individual initiatives need to be aligned. Such alignment requires focusing on what outcomes to achieve and drawing a big picture to see how and why efforts need to be connected [36]. In MappingDESIGNSCAPES, we inductively developed an impact-orientated conceptual framework and validated it using it in individual and cross-case design sensemaking practice. A way to scale up the use of such cross-case participatory collaboration mapping approaches towards collective impact was pioneered in the related CIDES project. This project was about strengthening the role of Czech local public libraries in developing design-enabled social innovations. In that project, we applied CommunitySensor as part of a situated Research through Design-methodology. By integrating design thinking and participatory community network mapping, we helped catalyze and connect local social innovation incubators across the Czech Republic [37]. In future work, we hope to integrate incubator-driven scaling-up processes with participatory mapping-driven collaborative sensemaking approaches, as presented in this paper. Combining the power of collaborative sensemaking with the ability to scale up and connect urban innovation initiatives should make the long and winding road towards collective impact somewhat easier to travel.

Socio-technical transitions take place in a complex, dynamic ecology of mainstream regimes, innovating niches, and a macro-level landscape context, requiring multi-level perspectives to make sense of them [38]. We have provided a conceptual lens for innovation niches to position themselves in the broader set of regimes and scapes, offering a more precise overview of and focus on relevant issues at stake. Zooming out, participatory collaboration mapping and collaborative sensemaking might also help to transform design project contexts themselves towards transition, at least at the regime level [39], but perhaps also towards design for scapes that "embraces a multi-level perspective and addresses shifts in dimension and scale and aims for an expanded long-lasting impact of the design action across wider contexts of application in response to global societal challenges" [40]. Different transition pathways have been identified to move between these levels [41], which our approach could help augment and catalyze. One example is our *Design Impacts* collaboration pattern. This pattern connects designs/proposals with the local problems and solutions, which in turn are examples of the larger societal (DESIGNSCAPES) problems and fields of action. This may support one of the main aims of urban living labs: facilitating urban transitions through an accumulation of experiments. Although they have proven successful at the meso (i.e., project) level, urban living labs still lack more formal value capture and retention processes at the macro (i.e., ecosystems and overarching organization) level [42]. Using our approach in the context of urban living labs, we can meaningfully connect many projects, making both conceptual and actionable sense across cases. Abstract capacity-building programs can thus become more alive and actionable by grounding them in relevant aspects of local cases while strengthening the participation, collaboration, and visibility of numerous local stakeholders. This combination may help locals become true co-designers: creating concrete, feasible ideas for tackling collective issues that reflect the knowledge and experience of those most impacted by the challenges at hand [43].

Finally, some thoughts on the possible contribution of our approach to research methodology. Design-enabled innovations take place in a unique context of niches, regimes, and scapes; have very flexible design trajectories; and are often complicated by unforeseen external pressures, like COVID and climate change. They are typically not replicable nor fit typical randomly controlled trial research. Our research methodology could be considered a type of mid-range theory formation. On the one hand, this acknowledges the importance of abstraction, representation, and refinement of general principles that apply across multiple situations. On the other hand, it recognizes the limitations of such abstractions in accurately representing emergent, contingent, and locally specific reality [44]. Our seed and cross-case maps help make sense by viewing them through various relevant perspectives and could be seen as collections of concrete design hypotheses and examples. For instance, they suggest what specific impacts particular (types of) design proposals may have on the types of wicked problems and solutions addressed in the regimes and scapes that more theory-orientated design-enabled innovation research is working on. Connected to the visual knowledge base are also the sensemaking stories and linkages to representatives of the local communities that theory-building researchers could engage with in follow-up conversations. As such, they could be seen as a form of grounded theory-building research capacity. In such research, emerging theory helps explain, in conceptual terms, what is going on in the substantive field of research [45]. For example, the proposal categories developed in The Landmarks Net case could be considered hypotheses about green spaces' critical roles in urban innovation contexts. Through their conceptual connections, sensemaking stories across cases can be contrasted, creating a scalable knowledge base of cross-case qualitative data and interpretations. This, in turn, could inform theory construction and testing about the societal effects of design-enabled urban innovations.

6 Conclusion

Addressing wicked problems such as climate change requires societal transitions fast. Design-enabled urban innovations help blaze the trails we urgently need to address the immense challenges we face. However, to build collective impact at the scale needed, we must go beyond promoting individual innovation initiatives, often taking place in isolation. Crucial is that we can collaboratively make sense of the multitude of initiatives, projects, and programs and find conceptual and actionable common ground toward collective societal impact. It is necessary to catalyze the sharing of lessons learned, the discovery of new collaborative connections, and forging coalitions for impact at the local, regional, and international levels. However, how to collaboratively make societal sense with efficacy across design-enabled urban innovation cases is not trivial. Practical methodologies for scalable cross-case sensemaking and coalition building are needed, yet few and far between.

In this and the accompanying paper [1], we outlined one promising approach for participatory mapping-driven collaborative sensemaking across design-enabled urban innovations: the MappingDESIGNSCAPES methodology. At its core is a participatory collaboration mapping methodology grounded in two knowledge resources: a conceptual framework and a visual knowledge base of individual and cross-case maps, common and individual perspectives, and sensemaking stories. We presented a practical collaborative sensemaking process built on these knowledge resource foundations. We described at length our considerations – from initial conceptual grounding to impactful societal application. We do not claim to have found definitive answers to the collaborative sensemaking challenges we face, although we think we showed a sound proof of concept. By sharing the details of our still tentative tale, we hope we inspire others to build or adapt related approaches.

In dealing with global challenges through local innovation, *"the need to activate values and meanings that are crucial for the transformation process* is unquestionable [46, p. 6, our emphasis]". Through MappingDESIGNSCAPES, we hope to have contributed to unlocking such values and meanings in design-enabled urban innovation in Europe and beyond.

Acknowledgments. The current study is part of the project DESIGNSCAPES (Building Capacity for Design enabled Innovation in Urban Environments) funded by the EU Horizon2020 call CO-CREATION-02–2016 – User-driven innovation: value creation through design-enabled innovation, under Grant Agreement No. 763784.

References

1. de Moor, A., et al.: Participatory collaboration mapping of design-enabled urban innovations: the MappingDESIGNSCAPES case. In: Polovina, R., Polovina, S., Kemp, N. (eds.) Aligning Computing Productivity with Human Creativity for Societal Adaptation. The 1st Measuring Ontologies for Value Enhancement (MOVE) Workshop at the 23rd ACM CSCW2020, revised selected papers. CCIS 1694. Springer Nature, Switzerland (2022)
2. de Moor, A.: CommunitySensor: towards a participatory community network mapping methodology. J. Community Inform. **13**(2), 35–58 (2017)
3. Urquhart, C., Lam, L.M.C., Cheuk, B., Dervin, B.L.: Sense-making/Sensemaking. In: Oxford Bibliographies, Oxford (2020). Accessed 1 Sep 2020
4. Weick, K.: Sensemaking in Organizations. Sage, Thousand Oaks, CA (1995)
5. Weick, K.E., Sutcliffe, K.M., Obstfeld, D.: Organizing and the process of sensemaking. Organ. Sci. **16**(4), 409–421 (2005). https://doi.org/10.1287/orsc.1050.0133
6. Venters, C., et al.: The blind men and the elephant: towards an empirical evaluation framework for software sustainability. J. Open Res. Softw. **2**(1),1 (2014). https://doi.org/10.5334/jors.ao
7. Kimble, C., Grenier, C., Goglio-Primard, K.: Innovation and knowledge sharing across professional boundaries: political interplay between boundary objects and brokers. Int. J. Inf. Manag. **30**(5), 437–444 (2010). https://doi.org/10.1016/j.ijinfomgt.2010.02.002
8. Copeland, S., de Moor, A.: Community digital storytelling for collective intelligence: towards a storytelling cycle of trust. AI Soc. **33**, 101–111 (2018)
9. de Moor, A.: Creativity meets rationale: collaboration patterns for social innovation. In: Creativity and Rationale: Enhancing Human Experience by Design, pp. 377–404. Springer (2013)
10. Bødker, S., Zander, P.-O.: Participation in design between public sector and local communities. In: Proceedings of the 7th International Conference on Communities and Technologies, pp. 49–58, New York, NY, USA, 2015. https://doi.org/10.1145/2768545.2768546
11. Müller, S., Backhaus, N., Buchecker, M.: Mapping meaningful places: a tool for participatory siting of wind turbines in Switzerland? Energy Res. Soc. Sci. **69** (2020). https://doi.org/10.1016/j.erss.2020.101573
12. de Moor, A.: A community network ontology for participatory collaboration mapping: towards collective impact. Information **9**(7), 151 (2018)
13. Zamenopoulos, T., et al.: Types, obstacles and sources of empowerment in co-design: the role of shared material objects and processes. CoDesign **17**(2), 139–158 (2021). https://doi.org/10.1080/15710882.2019.1605383
14. Mamykina, L., Candy, L., Edmonds, E.: Collaborative creativity. Commun ACM **45**(10), 96–99 (2002). https://doi.org/10.1145/570907.570940
15. Conklin, J..: Wicked problems and social complexity. In: Dialog Mapping: Building Shared Understanding of Wicked Problems, pp. 3–40. John Wiley & Sons, Hoboken, NJ (2006)
16. Selvin, A., Buckingham Shum, S.: Constructing Knowledge Art: An Experiential Perspective on Crafting Participatory Representations, vol. 7. Morgan & Claypool (2014) [Online]. Available: http://www.morganclaypool.com/doi/abs/10.2200/S00593ED1V01Y201408HCI023. Accessed 15 Feb 2015

17. van Biljon, J., Marais, M.: Social mapping for communal sensemaking: the case of development informatics researchers in South Africa. In: Choudrie, J., Islam, M.S., Wahid, F., Bass, J.M., Priyatma, J.E. (eds.) ICT4D 2017. IAICT, vol. 504, pp. 280–291. Springer, Cham (2017). https://doi.org/10.1007/978-3-319-59111-7_24

18. Johannessen, Å., et al.: Transforming urban water governance through social (triple-loop) learning. Environ. Policy Gov. **29**(2), 144–154 (2019). https://doi.org/10.1002/eet.1843

19. Jaskiewicz, T., Mulder, I., Morelli, N., Pedersen, J.S.: Hacking the Hackathon format to empower citizens in outsmarting "smart" cities. Interact. Des. Archit. S **43**, 8–29 (2019)

20. Brayshay, B., Mackie, D.: New maps: social systems mapping in the London Borough of Lambeth. Living Maps, no. 12 (2022)

21. Stamper, R.K.: Organisational semiotics: informatics without the computer? In: Liu, K., Clarke, R.J., Andersen, P.B., Stamper, R.K. (eds.) Information, Organisation and Technology: Studies in Organisational Semiotics, pp. 115–171. Springer, Boston, MA, 2001. https://doi.org/10.1007/978-1-4615-1655-2_5

22. Preece, J., Shneiderman, B.: 'The reader-to-leader framework: motivating technology-mediated social participation. AIS Trans. Hum.-Comput. Interact. **1**(1), 13–32 (2009)

23. De Moor, A.: Common agenda setting through participatory collaboration mapping: a knowledge base-driven approach. In: Proc. of the 16th CIRN Conference, Prato, Italy, 24–26 Oct 2018

24. Denning, S.: The Springboard: How Storytelling Ignites Action in Knowledge-era Organizations. Routledge, New York (2001)

25. Lambert, J.: Digital Storytelling: Capturing Lives, Creating Community. Routledge, New York (2013)

26. Yaden, D.B., et al.: The overview effect: awe and self-transcendent experience in space flight. Psychol. Conscious. Theory Res. Pract. **3**(1), 1–11 (2016). https://doi.org/10.1037/cns0000086

27. Morelli, N., Simeone, L., van Dam, K..: DESIGNSCAPES toolbox: an inventory of design tools and methods to support urban innovation. In: DESIGNSCAPES, 2nd edn, Sep 2021. [Online]. Available: https://issuu.com/designscapes/docs/designscapes_toolkit_final

28. Frich, J., Vermeulen, L.M., Remy, C., Biskjaer, M.M., Dalsgaard, P.: Mapping the landscape of creativity support tools in HCI. In: Proceedings of the 2019 CHI Conference on Human Factors in Computing Systems, New York, NY, USA, May 2019, pp. 1–18. https://doi.org/10.1145/3290605.3300619

29. Ullmann, T.D., De Liddo, A., Bachler, M.: A visualisation dashboard for contested collective intelligence. learning analytics to improve sensemaking of group discussion. RIED Rev. Iberoam. Educ. Distancia **22**(1), 41–80 (2019)

30. The Designscapes Consortium: Green Paper on Design Enabled Innovation in Urban Environments. DESIGNSCAPES.EU, 2019 [Online]. Available: http://designscapes.eu/wp-content/uploads/2019/06/Green-Paper-on-Design-Enabled-Innovation-in-Urban-Environments.pdf

31. Magni, A., González, A.C., Mulder, I.: Supporting urban innovators' reflective practice. In: Mealha, Ó., Dascalu, M., Di Mascio, T. (eds.) Ludic, Co-design and Tools Supporting Smart Learning Ecosystems and Smart Education. SIST, vol. 249, pp. 15–26. Springer, Singapore (2022). https://doi.org/10.1007/978-981-16-3930-2_2

32. Mulder, I..: Co-creative partnerships as catalysts for social change. Strateg. Des. Res. J. **11**(3), 178–185 (2018)

33. Kun, P., Mulder, I., de Götzen, A., Kortuem, G..: Creative data work in the design process. In: Proceedings of the 2019 on Creativity and Cognition, New York, NY, USA, Jun 2019, pp. 346–358. https://doi.org/10.1145/3325480.3325500

34. Mulder, I., Jaskiewicz, T., Morelli, N.: On digital citizenship and data as a new commons: Can we design a new movement? Cuaderno **73**, 97–109 (2019)

35. Kania, J., Kramer, M.: Collective impact. Stanf. Soc. Innov. Rev. **9**, 36–41 (2011)
36. Irby, M., Boyle, P.: Aligning collective impact initiatives. Stanf. Soc. Innov. Rev. **12**(4), 15–16 (2014)
37. Suchá, L.Z., et al.: Designing an incubator for social innovations in libraries: learnings from the research through design approach. Interact. Des. Archit. **47**, 215–236 (2020)
38. Smith, A., Voß, J.-P., Grin, J.: Innovation studies and sustainability transitions: the allure of the multi-level perspective and its challenges. Res. Policy **39**(4), 435–448 (2010). https://doi.org/10.1016/j.respol.2010.01.023
39. Concilio, G., Li, C., Rausell, P., Tosoni, I.: Cities as enablers of innovation. In: Concilio, G., Tosoni, I. (eds.) Innovation Capacity and the City. SAST, pp. 43–60. Springer, Cham (2019). https://doi.org/10.1007/978-3-030-00123-0_3
40. Concilio, G., et al.: Innovation and design. In: Concilio, G., Tosoni, I. (eds.) Innovation Capacity and the City. SAST, pp. 61–83. Springer, Cham (2019). https://doi.org/10.1007/978-3-030-00123-0_4
41. Abbasi, M., et al.: A triplet under focus: innovation, design and the city. In: Concilio, G., Tosoni, I. (eds.) Innovation Capacity and the City. SAST, pp. 15–41. Springer, Cham (2019). https://doi.org/10.1007/978-3-030-00123-0_2
42. Baccarne, B., Logghe, S., Schuurman, D., Marez, L.: Governing Quintuple Helix innovation: urban living labs and socio-ecological entrepreneurship. Technol. Innov. Manag. Rev. **6**, 22–30 (2016). https://doi.org/10.22215/timreview/972
43. Coulson, S., Woods, M., Scott, M., Hemment, D.: Making sense: empowering participatory sensing with transformation design. Des. J. **21**(6), 813–833 (2018). https://doi.org/10.1080/14606925.2018.1518111
44. Thompson, M.: Ontological shift, or ontological drift? Reality claims, epistemological frameworks and theory generation within organization studies. Acad. Manage. Rev. **36**(4), 754–773 (2011)
45. Fernández, W.D., Lehmann, H.: Achieving rigour and relevance in information systems studies: using grounded theory to investigate organizational cases. Grounded Theory Rev. **5**(1), 79–107 (2005)
46. Concilio, G., Tosoni, I. (eds.): Innovation Capacity and the City: The Enabling Role of Design. Springer, Berlin (2019)

A Novel Ontological Approach to Track Social Determinants of Health in Primary Care

Dylan McGagh[1] , Anant Jani[2] , John Williams[1] , Harshana Liyanage[3] ,
Uy Hoang[1] , Cecilia Okusi[1] , Julian Sherlock[1] , Filipa Ferreira[1] ,
Ivelina Yonova[4] , and Simon de Lusignan[1,4,5](✉)

[1] Department of Primary Care Radcliffe Primary Care Building, University of Oxford, Radcliffe
Observatory Quarter, Woodstock Road, Oxford OX2 6GG, Oxfordshire, UK
simon.delusignan@phc.ox.ac.uk
[2] Heidelberg Institute for Global Health, Im Neuenheimer Feld 130.3, 69120 Heidelberg,
Germany
[3] Department of Health and Social Care, UK Health Security Agency, London, UK
[4] School of Biosciences and Medicine, University of Surrey, Guildford, UK
[5] Royal College of General Practitioners, 30 Euston Square, London, UK

Abstract. The associated morbidity and mortality from COVID-19 and the public
health response to prevent the spread of the virus has repeatedly demonstrated the
significant impact of social determinants of health (SDoH) and social inequities on
health outcomes. Social prescriptions are interventions aimed at tackling SDoH.
In 2019, NHS-England committed to support the use of social prescribing across
England. NHS-England commissioned the Oxford-Royal College of General Practitioners (RCGP) Research and Surveillance Centre (RSC) sentinel network to
monitor the distribution of social prescribing services within English primary
care and, within that, monitor the impact of the COVID-19 pandemic response
on SDoH. To track incidence of people presenting to primary care with SDoH-
related issues, we implemented an ontological approach to curate SDoH indicators
in computerised medical records (CMR) using the Systematized Nomenclature of
Medicine - Clinical Terms (SNOMED CT). These indicators were then extracted
from the RCGP-RSC sentinel network database to present weekly incidence rates
per 10,000 people to assess the impact of the pandemic on these SDoH. Pre- versus
peri-pandemic, we observed an increase in the recording of several of our SDoH
indicators; namely issues related to homelessness, unemployment, mental health,
harmful substance use and financial difficulties. As far as we are aware, this is
the first time that routinely collected primary care CMR data has been utilised for
the monitoring and surveillance of SDoH and demonstrates the feasibility of this
approach for future surveillance.

Keywords: Medical record systems · Computerised · Health informatics ·
COVID-19 · Ontology · Primary care · Social determinants of health · Sentinel
surveillance · Social prescribing · Homeless persons

D. McGagh and A. Jani—These Authors contributed equally to this manuscript.

© Springer Nature Switzerland AG 2022
R. Polovina et al. (Eds.): MOVE 2020, CCIS 1694, pp. 227–240, 2022.
https://doi.org/10.1007/978-3-031-22228-3_10

1 Introduction

Social determinants of health, which account for 80–90% of health outcomes [1, 2], encompass a broad range of factors including health related behaviours (such as physical activity, diet, smoking, alcohol consumption), socioeconomic factors (such as employment, access to adequate housing, access to transport) and environmental factors (such as access to clean air, clean water).

Modern interventions aimed at addressing social determinants of health first developed at the dawn of the industrial revolution in the mid-nineteenth century through initiatives such as social medicine and community health [3]. More recently, a new initiative termed 'social prescribing' has emerged in European countries to address social determinants of health. Social prescriptions have been used for several years across European countries. The National Health Service (NHS) in England defines social prescribing as "a way of linking patients in primary care with sources of support within the community to help improve their health and well-being [4]." Social prescriptions themselves are varied and can include activities focused on physical/mental health such as physical activity programmes, dietary support, sports, leisure/arts activities as well as broader social determinants of health such as addictions support services, benefits signposting, domestic violence support, education support, skills development, employment support or parental support services.

In January 2019, NHS England published its Long Term Plan, which laid out a vision for how the English NHS would develop to ensure the health and care needs of its citizens were met [5]. A core pillar of the Long Term Plan is delivering personalised care, which is defined as care that:

"...means people have choice and control over the way their care is planned and delivered. It is based on 'what matters' to them and their individual strengths and needs [6]."

Social prescribing is one of the six components of the comprehensive model of personalised care and NHS England announced a major expansion of social prescribing in the English NHS through a standard model, the link worker model, of social care to ensure individuals have access to community support for their non-medical needs [6].

Evaluations of social prescribing to date have shown benefits for patients and healthcare systems but despite its promise, a major barrier to the evaluation of social prescribing is the lack of data on what social prescribing activity is taking place and the outcomes delivered for people taking up social prescribing. This limitation is due to the lack of information on social prescriptions prescribed as well as variation in data quality [7]. Recognising these limitations, in 2019 NHS England worked with a group of stakeholders (including social prescribing connector schemes, primary care staff, local authorities, local NHS, voluntary community and social enterprises (VCSE) organisations, academics, researchers, public health leaders and other government agencies) to create a consensus Common Outcomes Framework (COF) on the outcomes and outputs that could be measured to demonstrate the impact of social prescribing [4]. In the COF, NHS England recommended the use of three primary care codes to standardize the recording of social prescribing activity in primary care: social prescribing offered, social prescribing declined and referral to social prescribing service, which are characterised as 'finding', 'situation' and 'procedure', respectively, in the SNOMED CT Top Level concept hierarchy [4].

Standardising the recording of social prescriptions in primary care is essential to create transparency on how much social prescribing is being used as well as the impact it is delivering so the approach taken by NHS England with the COF is sound. However, the codes recommended by the COF have several limitations. The COF codes are very general in nature – if we had equivalent codes for pharmaceutical prescriptions, they would be 'pharmaceutical prescription offered', 'pharmaceutical prescription declined' and 'pharmaceutical prescription given'. The general natures of these codes means that it would be impossible to extrapolate what the presenting complaint of the individual was, the actual social prescription delivered and the outcomes that could have realistically been delivered by the social prescription. Given these limitations, it would be impossible to know for certain whether social prescriptions are delivering any benefit if we only relied on the COF [8].

One well established means through which we may be able to overcome the current limitations of the COF and create more transparency on the impact of social prescribing is to design and utilize ontologies. Ontologies are regularly used to model the semantics of medical concepts and to facilitate exchange of medical data between different health care service providers [9]. In this manuscript, we highlight the process we used to design and build a set of ontologies for social prescribing focused on identifying the presenting social need of individuals, linked to social determinants of health, as well as the non-medical social prescriptions actually delivered.

2 Methods

2.1 Data Source

The primary care data used for our analyses was derived from the Oxford-Royal College of General Practitioners (RCGP) Research and Surveillance Centre (RSC). The RSC has been the primary source for sentinel surveillance in England for over 50 years, and it has been collecting data since 1957 making it one of Europe's oldest general practice sentinel networks [10]. The RSC is one of only six Trusted Research Environments within the UK's Health Data Research Innovation Gateway [11]. There are currently over 1800 registered practices covering over 15 million registered patients across practices and being a representative network, there are only small differences with the national population (Fig. 1) [12].

The RSC uses pseudonymised information extracted from computerised medical records (CMRs) for disease surveillance and is compliant with General Data Protection Regulation (GDPR) Article 6 in the use of personal data and Article 9 in the use of sensitive data (such as health data). The RSC works within all relevant governance frameworks including NHS Digital and is compliant with all existing legislation and national guidance on the use of patient level data. Patients also have an 'opt out' option if they do not wish to share their data [3].

The RSC's pseudonymised data extracts are either daily or twice-weekly and capture information about demographics, diagnoses and symptoms, drug exposures, vaccination history, laboratory tests and referrals to hospital and specialist care [10]. Being an active

Clinical System ●EMIS ●INPS Vision ●TPP SystmOne

Fig. 1. Map showing the geographical distribution of registered practices within the RSC. Colours indicate the clinical systems (i.e. the type of electronic health record software) used by a practice. Figure adapted from reference 12.

research and surveillance unit that collects and monitors data from its practice members, the RSC supports a wide range of research and surveillance studies (qualitative; quantitative; retrospective; prospective etc.) as highlighted in the table below (Table 1):

The unique and most important aspects of the RSC include [10]:

- **Near real-time England population health data** - with twice weekly data extractions, the dataset is one of the most up to date in the UK
- **Longitudinal and representative data** - The RCGP RSC is the oldest sentinel network in Europe and is representative of the English population on a variety of domains, both demographic and clinical

Table 1. Uses of the RCGP RSC

RCGP RSC can be used for	Scope and scale of RCGP RSC data
Retrospective research using its data	> 15 million records uploaded each week
Prospective research in volunteer practices, including quality improvement interventions and pragmatic trials	< 25 million patients ever
Linkage studies – an approved pseudonymisation technique is used, and linking to hospital, death, or other data is possible	> 4.2 billion encounters
Machine learning or advanced analytics can be sited within the secure network	> 1.8 billion prescriptions
Creation of observatories or weekly reports about a particular illness or health area	> 89 million BP recordings

- **High quality-assured data** - RSC practices receive continuous support and training by a dedicated team of Practice Liaison Officers. Practice members also have access to personalised dashboards, which shows an aggregated version of their data by week and compared with the rest of the network.
- **Data linkage capability** – the RSC team have the capability to link to numerous other health datasets, via pseudonymised NHS numbers.
- **Direct link with practices** – The Practice Liaison team have direct links with RSC practices, who are willing to administer questionnaires, take biological samples, put on focus groups, and take part in trials. The network can participate in research, quality improvement and surveillance beyond providing data.

2.2 Variable Curation

Clinical coding in CMRs is standard practice in UK primary care and has been used for over three decades [13]. Practice staff, ranging from general practitioners and nurses to clinical coders and administrators, can record entries within the individual patient records. Since 2016, NHS Digital, the national information and technology partner to the English NHS, has governed the transition of English primary care coding from traditionally deployed terminologies, such as Read codes and Clinical Terms Version 3 (CTV3), to the contemporaneous Systematized Nomenclature of Medicine Clinical Terms (SNOMED CT) terminology. These now retired coding terminologies deployed a flat hierarchy representing specific conditions and clinical procedures. SNOMED CT is an international, polyhierarchical human- and machine-readable clinical terminology which contains more than 350,000 concepts permitting recording of all necessary patient-related events, from diagnoses and symptoms through to clinical measurements, procedures and medications. Previous efforts have been made to fit the SNOMED CT terminology to a standardised ontology format [14, 15]. Within the SNOMED ontology, concepts are grouped into a top-level hierarchy of concept classes or domains known as "semantic tags". These semantic tags provide information about the type of concept represented and consist of groupings such as clinical findings, procedures, observable entities and substances, amongst others. These semantic tags serve to disambiguate concepts which contain the same or similar commonly used words or phrases to create vertical division across the concept hierarchy.

Within the UK, SNOMED CT is maintained by NHS Digital, which permits local extension of the library of SNOMED CT concepts accessible within CMR systems relevant for NHS-specific service provision, as part of the overall SNOMED CT UK Edition [16]. As part of efforts by NHS England to bring social prescribing into mainstream primary care clinical workflows, local SNOMED CT extensions related to social prescribing referral, offered and declined have been developed and activated in CMR systems. Previous work by the authors has investigated patient-level factors and regional variation related to the use of these social prescribing concepts [8].

2.3 Design of the Social Need Ontology

The social prescribing ontologies are based on a taxonomy built on concepts associated with social prescribing practices and the wellbeing of social prescribing recipients. The primary purpose of the taxonomy and ontology is to harmonise data sources containing measures and indicators of social prescribing across various parts of the health system. The taxonomies we developed cover several key pillars from social determinants of health. To define core areas of exploration across social determinants of health, we first used several key principles derived from the five ways to wellbeing model proposed by the New Economics Foundation [17], as well as Wilkinson and Marmot's work on social determinants of health [2]. The measures of increased social need we aimed to represent from these background texts include concepts such as: social gradient, stress, early life, social exclusion, work/unemployment, social support, addiction, food, transport, ethnic inequalities, health inequalities at older ages, neighbourhood housing and health, sexual behaviours [3].

The ontologies describe these key concepts within social prescribing and, additionally, the social prescribing recipient will have one or more characteristics, which will be organised according to the biopsychosocial model, that would qualify them as a social prescribing recipient [18].

2.4 Ontological Approach to the Development of the Social Need Indicators

Building on previous experience developing application ontologies [19-21], we sought to create an ontology for a number of indicators of social need, for use principally in extracting primary care CMR data. These indicators can then be used against data from health systems utilising SNOMED CT or mapped to other coding terminologies such as Read V2 and CTV3. We implemented our established three-step method to develop the ontology, separating ontological concept development from mapping to SNOMED CT and data extraction and validation (Fig. 2). To develop our unique social need indicators (SNI) in SNOMED CT, we followed a similar multi-step process to variable development, as previously employed in ontology development. To achieve our objective, we integrated domain-level expertise from the fields of social determinants of health and primary care, clinical informatics and database management expertise.

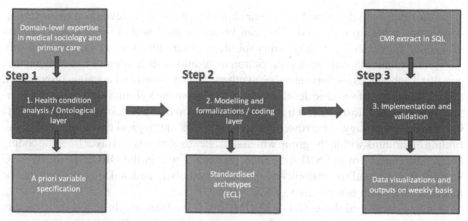

Fig. 2. Development of the social need indicators following a three-step process from ontological layer to coding layer and finally implementation and validation through a logical data extraction approach.

Following identification of these core principles of social need from background texts, we sought to establish an a priori definition for each social need indicator. Once this had been established, variables were generated comprising all SNOMED CT concepts across the top-level hierarchy which could satisfy this case definition. We incorporated concepts related to clinical findings, procedures and situations which would imply that an individual patient had an increased social need (Table 2).

Table 2. Key categories within the Marmot and Wilkinson taxonomy and their corresponding variables in SNOMED CT.

Marmot and Wilkinson categories	Variable names in ORCHID variable library
Issues related to mental health	Mental Disorder
Issues relating to managing a long-term condition	Various conditions in ORCHID-RCGP RSC database
Issues relating to substance misuse	Harmful Use of Substance
Issues relating to abuse	Victim of Abuse
Issues with employment	Finding of Unemployment
Issues relating to parenting	Finding of Parenting Problem
Issues relating to money	Finding of Financial Problem
Issues relating to housing	Finding of Homelessness

Algorithms which defined the overarching variables were developed to capture as wide a reach within each SNI. This can be represented within the variable *"Harmful Use of Substance"* which contains sub-defined variables related to individual substances, not limited to: alcohol, prescription medications such as opioids and hypnotics, and illicit substances such as cannabis, synthetic cannabinoids and cocaine. Importantly, this methodology of variable development separates out background domain-level understanding of a variable of interest from the coding system of interest, in this case SNOMED CT. This methodology is borrowed from the previous ontological development of case-finding algorithms within the group which separates the ontological layer from the coding layer. The entirety of the SNI were then catalogued within the ORCHID-RCGP RSC variable library to allow visibility to external researchers and stakeholders and can be updated along with new releases of SNOMED CT [22].

Having developed these SNI in SNOMED CT, we then sought to test their validity running data extracts of these variables against the ORCHID-RCGP RSC database as part of a wider logical data extract framework. This step in the process systematically tests the variables developed to ensure outputs are consistent with the requirements of the use case. Data extraction was undertaken in SQL server management studio. Extraction queries were developed, permitting the identification of individuals within the dataset who presented to primary care with a social need covered in our ontology. These raw extracts then permit development of data visualisations in Tableau software as part of a wider Social Needs Observatory (see Fig. 3) [23]. There is capacity within the ORCHID-RCGP RSC database to update these extracts and resulting visualisations on a weekly basis though currently it is updated monthly, permitting surveillance of these of indicators through the Covid-19 pandemic and recovery period.

3   Results

3.1   Data Visualisation with Social Needs Observatory

We developed a Social Need Observatory to visualise the recording of our unique SNI within the RSC database. The resulting observatory (Fig. 3) can be used to examine rates of recording across a range of factors including regional variation, age, gender, ethnicity and local socioeconomic status (as captured within the index of multiple deprivation (IMD)).

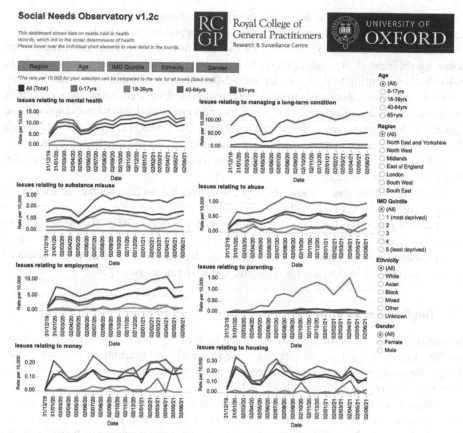

Fig. 3. Screenshot of the Social Needs Observatory, currently displaying recording of SNI by age categories [23].

4 Implications

To our knowledge, this is the first time that routinely collected primary care CMR data has been utilised to examine individuals presenting to primary care with an issue related to a social need stemming from a social determinant of health. Whilst routine primary care data is typically used to investigate trends and burdens of communicable and non-communicable diseases, our social needs observatory has demonstrated that these data can be deployed for surveillance of these wider social determinants of health. Given the impact of social determinants on health, SNOMED International is making a commitment to integrate a wider list of concepts into future updates therefore permitting more accurate and granular recording of a person's social and environmental status in their individual patient record [24]. One example of this commitment is the Gravity project, which is aimed at standardising social determinants of health data collection and storage in CMR systems ultimately providing syntactic and semantic interoperability of social determinants of health information within clinical records. Our ontological approach of creating variables in SNOMED CT which represent a specific social need demonstrates how semantic sense can be applied through domain expertise of social determinants of health and can be operationalised in primary care to deliver impact.

Through the observatory, we can track the recording of all SNI we measured broken down by different demographic characteristics (Fig. 3). The general trends we see in individuals presenting to primary care with different types of social needs can be compared to other national statistics to get a better understanding need, variation, inequalities in access to and use of primary care services and unmet need when we compare those presenting to primary care with national level data. Our findings are also consistent with the reported increases in these social need categories across the UK by other sources:

-Mental Health: Adults experiencing some form of depression doubled during the first lockdown period [25].

-Addictions/Substance Abuse: In Sept 2020, over 8.4 million people were drinking at high risk compared to 4.8 million in Feb 2020 [26].

-Employment: The UK's jobless rate rose to 5.1% in Feb 2021, the highest rate in nearly five years [27].

-Domestic Abuse: There was an increase in offences flagged as domestic abuse as well as an increase in demand for domestic abuse victim services [28].

4.1 Implications for Practice

In addition to the pressures already being felt by primary care because of the pandemic and the vaccination drive, this large increase in social need presents an important challenge that needs to be addressed. Indeed, even before the pandemic, 84% of GPs said they had an unmanageable workload [29].

Through an observatory, primary care practitioners can identify the areas that require their attention (need, variation, inequalities, unmet need) and see the impact of their initiatives on social need through a learning health system approach because of the feedback provided through the regular data updates. This approach would support them to:

– Identify variation: compare their area to others across the country with regard to different SNI

  o Tackle variation: working with and learning from other areas that are doing relatively better on different SNI

– Identify inequalities: identify the different demographics that are presenting to primary care with different types of social need

  o Tackle inequalities: design solutions that are more likely to address the specific needs of the different demographics presenting to primary care with social needs (e.g. taking into account patient preferences and cultural factors)

– Identify unmet need: compare population survey data, for example from the Office of National Statistics in the UK, to individuals presenting to primary care to determine whether there are likely individuals in the population with a social need who are not presenting to primary care

o Tackle unmet need: design solutions to ensure those with a social need are able to access primary care services to address their needs

Furthermore, with the recent commitment in England to integration across the national health service, local councils and other partners delivering health and care services, an SNI-linked observatory could support a multi-agency approach to tackle complex social determinant of health-related needs [30]. Sharing data across these agencies could also support a more holistic approach to identifying needs in the population and designing effective solutions to address them.

4.2 Further Developments and Considerations

The benefit of this ontological approach, separating ontological layer from the clinical terminology system allows resilience in the recording of SNI. Despite the promise of the ontological approach, there are some important considerations that must be taken into account – much of which is shared by most approaches utilising real world health and care data.

Firstly, there is marked heterogeneity in the quality and accuracy of coding across different clinical contexts. While computer-assisted clinical coding (CAC) is an emerging solution in this area, much coding is still done manually which results in different interpretations of clinical activity and, therefore, the codes used. This means that even though an ontological approach has advantages over using single clinical codes, it will still be limited in its ability to accurately capture clinical activity. CAC can help to resolve some of these issues but it will take time to implement this systematically across healthcare settings [31].

Secondly, while the SNIs highlighted using the ontological approach within our observatory can indicate need within the population, there is a larger question as to whether clinicians in primary care have the experience to deal with these types of social issues. NHS England has taken steps to address these concerns by creating and funding a new role within primary care: social prescribing link workers (SPLW). SPLW are trained to work with patients to understand their social needs and connect them with community groups and agencies to provide them with the support they need [4]. Furthermore, England's commitment to integrated care between the English NHS, local councils and partner organisations will also help to ensure those who need support for their social needs can receive it [30]. Though SPLW and integrated care are a step in the right direction, the substantial increase in social need stemming from the COVID-19 pandemic means that there may still be gaps in the availability of staff who have the sufficient training to effectively address SNI.

Finally, though there are exciting opportunities that arise through England's shift to integrated care, there are also some important concerns – mainly around privacy, ethics and security considerations of sharing large datasets between different health and care organisations [32, 33]. For the RSC dataset, there is an option for patients to opt-out but with the evolution of integrated care across England, there is a question as to whether patients will be aware of all of the purposes their data can be used for. Furthermore, though RSC data is pseudonymised, if integrated with datasets from other health and care organisations, there is a risk that data can be de-identified, which poses obvious risks for privacy and identification of at-risk groups that could lead to stigmatisation. There is also a concern around equity in the representation of different groups within health and care datasets, which was explicitly highlighted in a recent report on poor ethnicity recording within health datasets in England [34].

These considerations will have a significant impact on the design and use of ontological approaches but it is important to note that none of them is intractable in the health care system's commitment to respect individual autonomy, maintain equity, protect privacy and mitigate any potential adverse outcomes. In England, patients and the public must be made aware of the use of their data in integrated care systems where data can be shared between different health and care organisations and these organisations also must implement appropriate safeguards to ensure equity, privacy and security of datasets. Furthermore, with the commitment to grow the concept lists that capture social determinants of health in SNOMED CT, our ontological approach could adapt to these local SNOMED extensions to ensure that the true breadth of concepts is represented within each SNI. Furthermore, with the appropriate safeguards, our approach could be easily adapted for surveillance of social determinants of health across other CMR systems which deploy SNOMED CT or are similarly mapped to other clinical coding systems, enabling research within and between other countries and care systems.

References

1. Hood, C.M., Gennuso, K.P., Swain, G.R., Catlin, B.B.: County health rankings: relationships between determinant factors and health outcomes. Am J Prev Med (2016). https://doi.org/10.1016/j.amepre.2015.08.024
2. Wilkinson, R., Marmot, M.: Determinants of Health. The Solid Facts, 2nd Edition. World Heal Organiztaion (2003)
3. Jani, A., et al.: Use and impact of social prescribing: A mixed-methods feasibility study protocol. BMJ Open (2020). https://doi.org/10.1136/bmjopen-2020-037681
4. NHS England: Social prescribing and community-based support: Summary guide (2019). https://www.england.nhs.uk/wp-content/uploads/2019/01/social-prescribing-community-based-support-summary-guide.pdf. Accessed 2 June 2021
5. NHS England: NHS Long Term Plan (2019). https://www.longtermplan.nhs.uk/. Accessed 2 June 2021
6. NHS England: What is personalised care? (2021). https://www.england.nhs.uk/personalised care/what-is-personalised-care/. Accessed 2 June 2021
7. Bickerdike, L., Booth, A., Wilson, P.M., Farley, K., Wright, K.: Social prescribing: Less rhetoric and more reality. A systematic review of the evidence. BMJ Open (2017). https://doi.org/10.1136/bmjopen-2016-013384
8. Jani, A., et al.: Using an ontology to facilitate more accurate coding of social prescriptions addressing social determinants of health: feasibility study. J Med Internet Res (2020). https://doi.org/10.2196/23721
9. Liyanage, H., Krause, P., De Lusignan, S.: Using ontologies to improve semantic interoperability in health data. J Innov Heal Informatics (2015). https://doi.org/10.14236/jhi.v22 i2.159

10. RCGP RSC: RCGP Research and Surveillance Centre (RSC) (2021). https://www.rcgp.org.uk/clinical-and-research/our-programmes/research-and-surveillance-centre.aspx. Accessed 2 June 2021
11. HDI: ORCHID - Health Data Research Innovation Gateway (2021). https://web.www.healthdatagateway.org/collection/5626663352808625. Accessed 2 June 2021
12. Oxford-RCGP RSC: ORCHID-RCGP RSC Practice Map (2021). https://orchid.phc.ox.ac.uk/index.php/orchid-practice-map/. Accessed 2 June 2021
13. Benson, T.: Why general practitioners use computers and hospital doctors do not—Part 1: Incentives. BMJ (2002). https://doi.org/10.1136/bmj.325.7372.1086
14. El-Sappagh, S., Franda, F., Ali, F., Kwak, K.S.: SNOMED CT standard ontology based on the ontology for general medical science. BMC Med Inform Decis Mak (2018). https://doi.org/10.1186/s12911-018-0651-5
15. Unified Medical Language System: SNOMED CT BioPortal Ontology (2021). https://bioportal.bioontology.org/ontologies/SNOMEDCT. Accessed 2 June 2021
16. NHS Digital: SNOMED CT UK Edition (2021). https://isd.digital.nhs.uk/trud3/user/guest/group/0/pack/26. Accessed 2 June 2021
17. Aked, J., Marks, N., Cordon, C., Thompson, S.: Five Ways to Wellbeing: A report presented to the Foresight Project on communicating the evidence base for improving people's well-being (2009)
18. Engel, G.L.: The clinical application of the biopsychosocial model. Am J Psychiatry (1980). https://doi.org/10.1176/ajp.137.5.535
19. Liyanage, H., Williams, J., Byford, R., De Lusignan, S.: Ontology to identify pregnant women in electronic health records: Primary care sentinel network database study. BMJ Heal Care Informatics (2019). https://doi.org/10.1136/bmjhci-2019-100013
20. Cole, N.I., et al.: An ontological approach to identifying cases of chronic kidney disease from routine primary care data: A cross-sectional study. BMC Nephrol (2018). https://doi.org/10.1186/s12882-018-0882-9
21. de Lusignan, S., et al.: COVID-19 surveillance in a primary care sentinel network: In-pandemic development of an application ontology. JMIR Public Heal Surveill (2020). https://doi.org/10.2196/21434
22. Oxford-RCGP RSC: Using Oxford-RCGP RSC for observational studies (2021). https://orchid.phc.ox.ac.uk/index.php/orchid-data/
23. Oxford-RCGP RSC: Social Needs Observatory (2021). https://orchid.phc.ox.ac.uk/index.php/social-needs-observatory/ accessed 2 June 2021
24. SNOMED CT International: A commitment to grow social determinants of health content within SNOMED CT (2020). https://www.snomed.org/news-and-events/articles/social-determinants-health-care-SNOMED-CT
25. Office for National Statistics: Coronavirus and depression in adults, Great Britain - Office for National Statistics. Off Natl Stat (2020). https://www.ons.gov.uk/peoplepopulationandcommunity/wellbeing/articles/coronavirusanddepressioninadultsgreatbritain/june2020
26. Royal College of Psychiatrists: Addiction services not equipped to treat the 8 million people drinking at high risk during pandemic, warns Royal College (2020). https://www.rcpsych.ac.uk/news-and-features/latest-news/detail/2020/09/14/addiction-services-not-equipped-to-treat-the-8-million-people-drinking-at-high-risk-during-pandemic-warns-royal-college. Accessed 2 June 2021
27. ONS: Labour market overview, UK: March 2021. Stat Bull (2021). https://www.ons.gov.uk/employmentandlabourmarket/peopleinwork/employmentandemployeetypes/bulletins/uklabourmarket/march2021
28. ONS: Domestic abuse during the coronavirus (COVID-19) pandemic, England and Wales: November 2020 (2020). https://www.ons.gov.uk/peoplepopulationandcommunity/crimeandj

ustice/articles/domesticabuseduringthecoronaviruscovid19pandemicenglandandwales/nov
ember2020

29. British Medical Association: National survey of GPs: the future of general practice 2015 (2015)

30. NHS England: What are integrated care systems, UK (Jan 2022). https://www.england.nhs.uk/integratedcare/what-is-integrated-care/

31. Campbell, S., Giadresco, K.: Computer-assisted clinical coding: a narrative review of the literature on its benefits, limitations, implementation and impact on clinical coding professionals. Health Inf Manag (2020). https://doi.org/10.1177/1833358319851305

32. Howe Iii, E.G., Elenberg, F.: Ethical Challenges Posed by Big Data. Innov Clin Neurosci. 17(10–12), 24–30 (2020). Oct 1

33. Weinhardt, M.: Ethical Issues in the Use of Big Data for Social Re search. Historical Social Research / Historische Sozialforschung 45(3), 342–368 (2020)

34. Nuffield Trust: Ethnicity coding in English health service datasets, UK (June 2021). https://www.nuffieldtrust.org.uk/research/ethnicity-coding-in-english-health-service-datasets

A Novel Ontological Approach to Estimate Inequalities and Underuse of Social Prescriptions for Mental Health in Primary Care in England

Anant Jani[1] (iD), Harshana Liyanage[2] (iD), Cecilia Okusi[3] (iD), Julian Sherlock[3] (iD), Uy Hoang[3] (iD), Dylan McGagh[3] (iD), John Williams[3] (iD), Filipa Ferreira[3] (iD), Ivelina Yonova[4] (iD), and Simon de Lusignan[3,4,5](✉) (iD)

[1] Heidelberg Institute for Global Health, Im Neuenheimer Feld 130.3, 69120 Heidelberg, Germany

[2] Department of Health and Social Care, UK Health Security Agency, London, UK

[3] Department of Primary Care Radcliffe Primary Care Building, University of Oxford, Radcliffe Observatory Quarter, Woodstock Road, Oxford OX2 6GG, Oxfordshire, UK
simon.delusignan@phc.ox.ac.uk

[4] School of Biosciences and Medicine, University of Surrey, Guildford, UK

[5] Royal College of General Practitioners, 30 Euston Square, London, UK

Abstract. Mental health conditions are a significant contributor to morbidity and mortality and cost an estimated £1.6 trillion per year globally. The COVID-19 pandemic and its associated lockdowns have contributed to increases in common mental health problems (CMHP) like depression. Bodies in the UK recommend the use of non-medical interventions like social prescriptions to support individuals suffering from CMHP. In 2019, NHS-England committed to support the use of social prescribing across England. Despite this commitment, the proportion of eligible individuals with a CMHP that actually receive a social prescription remains unknown. To overcome this knowledge gap, a novel ontological approach was used to estimate the proportion of individuals with a CMHP that received a social prescription, disaggregated by different attributes (region, ethnicity, socio-economic status, sex, age) across a four-year period from 2017–2020. We discovered two general trends. First, there was a 1.4-fold increase in the presentation of individuals, across all attributes, to primary care with a CMHP across the four-year period analysed. There was also marked variation in the presentation to primary care with a CMHP based on different attributes (2020 variation figures - regions: 2.8-fold; ethnicity: 1.8-fold; socio-economic status: 1.4-fold; sex: 1.7-fold; age: 3.9-fold). Second, despite an increase in the use of social prescribing for mental health, there was still substantial underuse of it across all attributes in England (the highest percentage seen across all attributes in 2020 was 14%). The general trends revealed through our analyses provide valuable insights that can help to inform both policy and practice to address variation, health inequalities as well as to proactively design and implement appropriate services.

Keywords: Medical record systems · Computerised · Health informatics · COVID-19 · Ontology · Primary care · Social determinants of health · Health

R. Polovina et al. (Eds.): MOVE 2020, CCIS 1694, pp. 241–255, 2022.
https://doi.org/10.1007/978-3-031-22228-3_11

inequalities · Sentinel surveillance · Social prescribing · Mental health ·
Depression · Anxiety

1 Introduction

Mental health conditions are a significant contributor to morbidity and mortality and
cost an estimated £1.6 trillion per year globally [1]. Across mental health conditions,
common mental health problems (CMHP) like depression can also have significant
negative impact - depression is the leading cause of disability and premature death in
people aged 18–44 years, a trend also seen in the UK [2–5]. Worldwide, we have seen
the COVID-19 pandemic and its associated lockdown measures also having a significant
negative impact on many of the factors that can influence the incidence of CMHP. For
example, unemployment and job insecurity are linked to higher rates of mental distress,
depression, anxiety, substance misuse and suicide [6–9]. During the first lockdown in
2020, the UK saw was a two-fold increase in the incidence of depression in adults [10].

Primary prevention, early detection, and treatment of CMHP and conditions which
put individuals at increased risk of developing it, would be ideal but these remain major
challenges for population health in countries around the world (NHS-E has invested
resources into Improving Access to Psychological Therapies (IAPT) but the wait lists
for IAPT can be very long [11]). Tackling these problems requires shifting away from the
purely biomedical model of health and requires the recognition that 70–80% of health
outcomes are due to social determinants of health (e.g. access to housing, education, jobs,
transportation, nutritious food, support services for substance misuse, support services
to domestic abuse, etc.) [12–14]. Actively promoting health, preventing disease and
intervening to tackle risk factors early requires that we shift away from only focusing on
the highest risk groups in our population to shifting the entire population risk profile to
a lower risk status by addressing the factors that have the greatest impact on health – i.e.
social determinants of health (Fig. 1) [12, 13].

The National Health Service in England (NHS-E) has committed to improving population health by addressing social determinants and also addressing health inequalities
for the most deprived 20% of the population as well as population groups (such as ethnic
minorities, coastal communities, people experiencing homelessness, etc.) experiencing
poorer than average health outcomes [16, 17]. An important class of interventions NHS-
E is supporting to address social determinants of health and health inequalities is termed
'social prescribing', which is defined as "a way of linking patients in primary care with
sources of support within the community to help improve their health and well-being
[18]." For mental health-related issues, social prescribing provides alternative, non-
medical interventions to encourage individuals to gain more control over their health
and wellbeing through connections to community groups and resources [19]. NHS-E
announced a major expansion of social prescribing in 2019 as part of its Long Term Plan
[20, 21].

The use of non-medical interventions for CMHP is consistent with guidance from
the UK National Institute of Health and Care Excellence (NICE), which recommends
these types of interventions as part of the second step of stepped care models for mild-
moderate depression and generalised anxiety disorders [22, 23]. The Royal College of

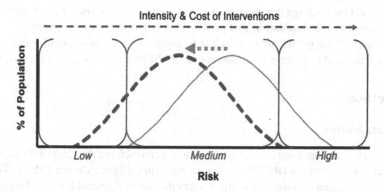

Fig. 1. *The Rose Curve: shifting risk profiles to promote health. Rose's model of improving health by shifting risk profiles. The x-axis represents different risk subgroups going from low risk at the left to high risk at the right. To improve health, transitions must be made from the yellow bell-shaped curve to the blue dashed bell-shaped curve. Overlaid onto the different risk strata are the intensity and cost of intervention needed to prevent transitions to states of ill health (red arrow above). (*Adapted, with permission, from reference [15]).

Psychiatrists and Royal College of Occupational Therapists also recently recommended "For social prescribing to be available to all mental health service users in all community and inpatient settings, including primary care" because of the recognition of the benefits social prescriptions can provide to service users throughout all stages of the journey through mental illness [19]. Furthermore, the negative impact of the COVID-19 pandemic and lockdowns reinforced the importance of social prescribing being made available as a treatment option to address wider factors affecting mental health [19].

Despite the guidance and recommendations from various bodies for the use of social prescribing for mental illness, a systematic account of their use in practice has not been carried out. To begin to address this, NHS-E worked with a multi-stakeholder group to create a consensus Common Outcomes Framework (COF) to capture the use, outcomes and outputs that could be measured to demonstrate the impact of social prescribing [18]. The COF recommends the use of two primary care codes to standardize the recording of social prescribing activity in primary care: social prescribing declined and referral to social prescribing service [18]. While the COF represents an important step, the codes recommended by the COF have several limitations. The general nature of the codes means that it would be impossible to extrapolate what the presenting complaint of the individual was, or the actual class of social prescription delivered. Given these limitations, it would be impossible to know for certain what problems people were presenting with, the type of social prescription given or the outcomes that could be reasonably attributed to the social prescription [24].

We have previously demonstrated the use of ontologies as a means of overcoming some of the limitations of the COF [24]. In this manuscript we present a more detailed account of our findings on the burden of CMHP and use of mental-health related social prescriptions in England from 2017–2020 across different attributes including region, ethnicity, Index of Multiple Deprivation (IMD – an indicator of socioeconomic status), sex and age. Our findings demonstrate a novel method for the use of ontologies to serve as a proxy baseline population that could be used to estimate inequalities and over-/under-use of social prescriptions for CMHP in primary care in England – a method that could be extended to other presentations that could benefit from social prescriptions.

2 Methods

2.1 Data Source

The primary care data used for our analyses was derived from the Oxford-Royal College of General Practitioners (RCGP) Research and Surveillance Centre (RSC). The RSC has been the primary source for sentinel surveillance in England for over 50 years, and it has been collecting data since 1957 making it one of Europe's oldest general practice sentinel networks [25]. The RSC is one of only six Trusted Research Environments within the UK's Health Data Research Innovation Gateway [26]. There are currently over 1800 registered practices covering over 15 million registered patients across practices and being a representative network, there are only small differences with the national population [27].

The RSC uses pseudonymised information extracted from computerised medical records (CMRs) for disease surveillance and is compliant with General Data Protection Regulation (GDPR) Article 6 in the use of personal data and Article 9 in the use of sensitive data (such as health data). The RSC works within all relevant governance frameworks including NHS Digital and is compliant with all existing legislation and national guidance on the use of patient level data. Patients also have an 'opt out' option if they do not wish to share their data [28]. The RSC's pseudonymised data extracts are either daily or twice-weekly and capture information about demographics, diagnoses and symptoms, drug exposures, vaccination history, laboratory tests and referrals to hospital and specialist care [25].

2.2 Variable Curation

Clinical coding in CMRs is standard practice in UK primary care and has been used for over three decades [29]. Since 2016, NHS Digital, the national information and technology partner to the English NHS, has governed the transition of English primary care coding from traditionally deployed terminologies, such as Read codes and Clinical Terms Version 3 (CTV3), to the contemporaneous Systematized Nomenclature of Medicine Clinical Terms (SNOMED CT) terminology.

SNOMED CT is an international, polyhierarchical human- and machine-readable clinical terminology which contains more than 350,000 concepts permitting recording of all necessary patient-related events, from diagnoses and symptoms through to clinical measurements, procedures and medications. Previous efforts have been made to fit the SNOMED CT terminology to a standardised ontology format [30, 31]. Within the SNOMED ontology, concepts are grouped into a top-level hierarchy of concept classes or domains known as "semantic tags". These semantic tags provide information about the type of concept represented and consist of groupings such as clinical findings, procedures, observable entities and substances, amongst others. These semantic tags serve to disambiguate concepts which contain the same or similar commonly used words or phrases to create vertical division across the concept hierarchy.

Within the UK, SNOMED CT is maintained by NHS Digital, which permits local extension of the library of SNOMED CT concepts accessible within CMR systems relevant for NHS-specific service provision, as part of the overall SNOMED CT UK Edition [32]. As part of efforts by NHS England to bring social prescribing into mainstream primary care clinical workflows, local SNOMED CT extensions related to social prescribing referral and declined have been developed and activated in CMR systems. Previous work by the authors has investigated patient-level factors and regional variation related to the use of these social prescribing concepts [24].

2.3 Design and Development of the Social Need Ontology for CMHP

Ontologies are regularly used to model the semantics of medical concepts and to facilitate exchange of medical data between different health care service providers [33]. We have previously reported the process used to design the social need ontologies linked to social prescribing through the use of key principles derived from the five ways to wellbeing model proposed by the New Economics Foundation and Wilkinson and Marmot's work on social determinants of health [28].

Leveraging experience developing other application ontologies [34–36], we sought to create an ontology for CMHP, for use principally in extracting primary care CMR data. We implemented our established three-step method to develop the ontology, separating ontological concept development from mapping to SNOMED CT and data extraction and validation. These categories and variables were then used against data from health systems utilising SNOMED CT or mapped to other coding terminologies such as Read V2 and CTV3. The ability to map to Read V2 and CTV3 was particularly relevant for this analysis because data from 2017–2020 was used and these two coding terminologies were used prior to the national transition to SNOMED CT in 2020.

To develop our CMHP indicators in SNOMED CT, we integrated domain-level expertise from the fields of primary care, clinical informatics and database management expertise. Variables were generated comprising all SNOMED CT concepts across the top-level hierarchy followed by incorporation of concepts related to clinical findings, procedures and situations that would indicate an individual patient had a CMHP (Table 1). Algorithms which defined the overarching variables were developed to capture as wide a reach for issues related to CMHP. The entirety of CMHP were then catalogued within the RSC variable library under the heading of 'Common Mental Health Problems' to allow visibility to external researchers and stakeholders while also facilitating updating with new releases of SNOMED CT [37].

2.4 Data Validation and Analysis

Validity of our ontology was tested by running data extracts of the variables listed in Table 1 against the RSC database as part of a wider logical data extract framework. This step systematically tests the variables developed to ensure outputs are consistent with the requirements of the use case. Data extraction was undertaken in SQL server management studio. Extraction queries were developed, permitting the identification of

Table 1. Key SNOMED CT categories and themes linked to the 'Common Mental Health Problems' ontology

Social need indicator	Category	Theme Variable
Common Mental Health Problems	Depression	Mild Major Depression Single Episode Moderate Major Depression Single Episode
		Moderately Severe Major Depression Single Episode
		Mild Recurrent Major Depression
		Atypical Depression
		Premenstrual Dysphoric Disorder
		Mild Recurrent Major Depression
		Moderate Recurrent Major Depression
		Cyclothymia
		Dysthymia
		Disruptive Mood Dysregulation Disorder
		Postpartum Depression
	Neurotic Disorders	Agoraphobia
		Social Phobia
		Acrophobia
		Zoophobia
		Natural Environment Type Phobia
		Blood InjuryInjection Type Phobia
		Androphobia
		Claustrophobia
		Gynephobia
		Simple Phobia
		Panic Disorder
		Generalised Anxiety Disorder
		Acute stress disorder
		Posttraumatic Stress Disorder
		Adjustment Disorder

individuals within the dataset who presented to primary care with one of the mental health-related variables listed in Table 1.

To explore time trends of population-level presentation to primary care with a CMHP, data extracts using our ontology were disaggregated by different attributes (region, ethnicity, Index of Multiple Deprivation [IMD – an indicator of socio-economic status], sex, age), converted to mean weekly rates per 10,000 normalised for the attribute of interest and, finally, the mean weekly rates aggregated and averaged across the NHS-E financial year, which runs from April to March (e.g. '2017' indicates activity from April 2017 to March 2018).

The following calculation was carried out to estimate the eligible population with a CMHP that received a social prescription for mental health. The annual mean weekly rate/10,000 for a population with a given attribute (e.g. ethnicity) presenting to primary care with a CMHP was used as a proxy for the eligible population that could have received a social prescription for mental health. The annual mean weekly rate/10,000 for a population with the same attribute (e.g. ethnicity) that received a social prescription for mental health was divided by the proxy eligible population to determine the percentage of the population that received a social prescription for mental health that could have benefited from one. A SNOMED CT code, "Social prescribing for mental health" (semantic tag: regime/therapy), which also exists in Read V2 and CTV3, was used to extract data related to social prescriptions for mental health issues.

3 Results

3.1 Time Trends of CMHP in England from 2017–2020

Figure 2 presents mean weekly rates/10,000 of populations presenting to primary care with a CMHP (Table 1) based on different attributes: NHS-E region (Fig. 2A. Northeast and Yorkshire; Northwest; East of England; Midlands; London; Southeast; Southwest and All regions); ethnicity (Fig. 2B. Black, Asian, Mixed, White, Other, Unknown); Index of Multiple Deprivation quintile (Fig. 2C. IMD, an indicator of socio-economic status with IMD1 representing the most deprived quintile and IMD5 representing the least deprived quintile); sex (Fig. 2D. Female, male); and age group (Fig. 2E. 18–39, 40–64, 65 +) for different NHS-E financial years from 2017 to 2020 (NB: '2017' indicates the 2017–2018 financial year which ran from April 2017-March 2018).

Across all attributes (Fig. 2A-E), we see a general increase in the presentation of populations to primary care with a CMHP. Taking 'All Regions' as representative of the total population of England (Fig. 2A), we see a mean rate/10,000 of ~ 2.2 in 2017 versus a rate of ~ 3.1 in 2021 – a 1.4-fold increase over the 4-year period analysed.

We also see variation in the mean weekly rate/10,000 for sub-attributes with the relative positioning of these sub-attributes largely maintained over the 4-year period analysed, though the differences increase and decrease over time. For example, for NHS-E regions (Fig. 2A), we see that in 2017, the Northwest had the highest mean weekly rate/10,000 at ~ 3.4 while the East of England had the lowest rate at ~ 1.3 – a 2.6-fold difference. In 2020, the relative positioning of these two regions was maintained though the gap between them widened to a 2.8-fold difference (Northwest with a rate of ~ 4.8 and the East of England with a rate of ~ 1.7).

The largest difference between different ethnic groups (Fig. 2B) in 2020 was between White ethnicity (rate: ~ 2.9) and Asian ethnicity (rate: ~ 1.6) – yielding a 1.8-fold difference. The largest difference between IMD quintiles (Fig. 2C) in 2020 was between IMD1 (the most deprived IMD quintile; rate: ~ 4.2) and IMD5 (the least deprived IMD quintile; rate: ~ 3) – yielding a 1.4-fold difference. The difference between female (rate: ~ 4.4) and male (rate: ~ 2.6) sex (Fig. 2D) in 2021 was 1.7-fold. Finally, the largest

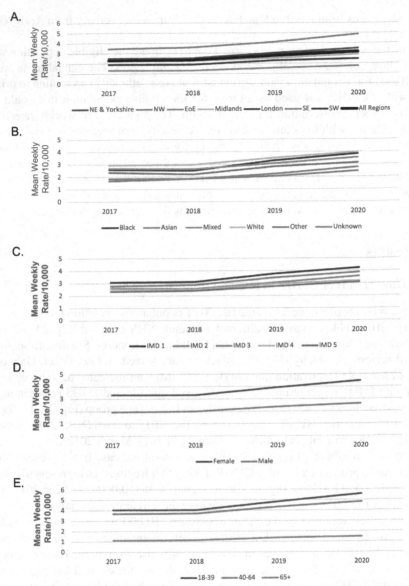

Fig. 2. Presentation of individuals with a CMHP presenting to primary care in England from the 2017 to 2020 financial years (e.g. '2017' indicates the 2017–2018 financial year which ran from April 2017-March 2018). A. Breakdown of presentations by NHS-E regions in England (NE & Yorkshire – Northeast and Yorkshire; NW – Northwest; EoE – East of England; Midlands; London; SE – Southeast; SW – Southwest and All regions). B. Breakdown of presentations by ethnicities. C. Breakdown of presentations by Index of Multiple Deprivation quintile (IMD – an indicator of socio-economic status with IMD1 representing the most deprived quintile and IMD5 representing the least deprived quintile). D. Breakdown of presentations by sex. E. Breakdown of presentations by age groups.

difference between different age groups (Fig. 2E) in 2021 was between the 18–39 age group (rate: ~ 5.5) and the 65 + age group (rate: ~ 1.4) – yielding a 3.9-fold difference.

3.2   Estimates of Eligible Population Subgroups Receiving Social Prescribing for Mental Health from 2017–2020

Figure 3 presents the estimated percentage of different population subgroups who could have benefited from a social prescription for mental health that received one. Population subgroups were defined by different attributes including: NHS-E region (Fig. 3A); ethnicity (Fig. 3B); Index of Multiple Deprivation quintile (Fig. 3C); sex (Fig. 3D); and age group (Fig. 3E) for different NHS-E financial years from 2017 to 2020.

Across all attributes we see marked underuse of social prescribing for mental health – for none of the attributes do we see the percentage rise above ~ 40%. For the regions, the highest percentage of use is seen in London in the 2019 financial year with ~ 40% use (Fig. 3A); for ethnicities, the highest percentage of use is ~ 14% for mixed ethnicity in 2020 (Fig. 3B); for IMD, the highest percentage of use is ~ 11% for IMD1 in 2020 (Fig. 3C); for sex, the highest percentage of use is ~ 11% for males in 2020 (Fig. 3D); and for age groups, the highest percentage of use is ~ 31% for the 65 + age group in 2019 (Fig. 3E).

We see a general increase in the use of social prescribing for mental health across all attributes over the 4-year period analysed. The exceptions to this are the London region, which decreased from ~ 40% in 2019 to ~ 11% in 2020 (Fig. 3A); IMD 4, which decreased from ~ 12% in 2019 to ~ 10% in 2020 (Fig. 3C); and the 65 + age group which decreased from ~ 31% in 2019 to ~ 10% in 2020 (Fig. 3E).

We also find interesting variation-linked trends over time that are not mirrored in the presentation of individuals to primary care with a CMHP (Fig. 2 vs Fig. 3). The most striking examples are the spikes we see in social prescribing for mental health in London and the 65 + demographic in 2019 and their subsequent decreases in 2020 (Fig. 3A, 3E). The slopes of increase in the use of social prescribing for mental health noticeably varied between different ethnic groups with Mixed, Unknown and Other ethnicities increasing more between 2019–2020 than White, Asian and Black ethnicities (Fig. 3B). Similar variation between sub-attributes is seen for IMD quintiles but the trends reveal a plateauing for IMD4 and IMD5 between 2019 to 2020 while a rise is seen for IMDs1–3 (Fig. 3C). Finally, the need versus use trends are reversed for sex (Fig. 3D) and age (Fig. 3D) where we see males and 65 + proportionally getting more social prescriptions for mental health despite their lower mean weekly rates/10,000 presenting to primary care with a CMHP (compare Fig. 2D to Fig. 3D and Fig. 2E to Fig. 3E).

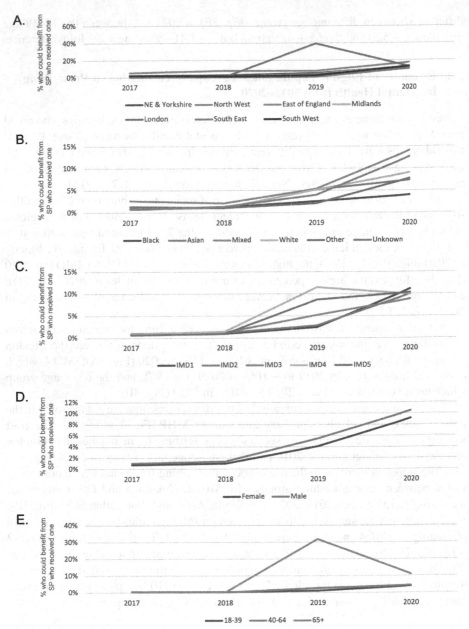

Fig. 3. Estimated percentage of population subgroups with a CMHP who received a social prescription for mental health. Attribute breakdown and financial year representations are the same as described in Fig. 2. SP stands for 'Social Prescription'. A. Breakdown by NHS-E regions. B. Breakdown by ethnicities. C. Breakdown by Index of Multiple Deprivation quintile D. Breakdown by sex. E. Breakdown by age groups.

4   Implications

In this manuscript we present a novel ontological approach to estimate the population of individuals, disaggregated by different attributes, that could be eligible to receive a non-medical intervention such as a social prescription. Given the lack of granular information emanating from the recording of information recommended by NHS-E's COF, it is impossible to know what gaps exist in service provision of social prescriptions for those with a CMHP. Utilising routine primary care data, we investigated trends across a four-year period related to CMHP, for which a social prescription for mental health is recommended [19, 22, 23]. Though only an estimate, our novel approach provides important insights that can be used to inform both policy and practice.

4.1   Implications for Policy and Practice

Two general trends across our analyses include:

1. A general increased presentation of individuals, across all attributes, to primary care with a CMHP across the four-year period analysed
2. Despite an increase in the use of social prescribing for mental health in the four-year period analysed, there was substantial underuse of it across all attributes in England

The first finding points to the need to gain a better understanding of the aetiology of the increase in presentation to primary care in England with a CMHP. The effects of the COVID-19 pandemic and the general increase in exposure to factors that can negatively impact mental health, such as unemployment and social isolation, can explain some of this increase but it is important to note that the slope of increase seen in Fig. 2 is fairly even – i.e. there isn't a sudden jump between 2019 and 2020. Considering the reports of the incidence of depression increasing in adults during the first lockdown in England in the second quarter of 2020 [10], this might suggest that even the increase seen in Fig. 2 is an underrepresentation of the true incidence of CMHP in England. This is corroborated by findings that during the pandemic, presentations of individuals to primary care with a CMHP decreased but prescriptions for anti-depressants actually increased [38]. This underrepresentation could be due to individuals seeking help elsewhere (e.g. local authorities or local voluntary sector organisations) and/or it could represent unmet need. In either case, it is important to get a better understanding of the root cause of this trend and to explore whether there is unmet need in the population and to take approaches to address this unmet need accordingly. With NHS-E's recent shift towards integrated care across health and care organisations, triangulation of information across these different organisations could help to shed light on the true incidence and aetiology of CMHP in England.

Regarding the second point, despite being recommended by NICE in their stepped care model as well as the Royal College of Psychiatrists [19, 22, 23], we found marked underuse of social prescribing for mental health in primary care in England. There could be a variety of non-mutually exclusive reasons for this finding. For example, this could represent an issue with recording in the electronic health record – it could be that an individual is referred to a source of support, but it is done using a code other than the one used in our analyses or it could be that despite an individual being referred, it was not coded at all. It could also be the case that a primary care professional may have wanted to refer an individual to a social prescription for mental health but there were no appropriate local options available, which is an issue that has been highlighted for social prescribing generally [19]. An individual may also have found support through other organisations like local authorities or local charities, precluding the need for a referral from primary care.

Beyond these two general trends, we also find variation in the use of social prescribing for mental health over time for different population groups across all attributes examined. The variation between different subgroups changes over time and points to potential inequalities and unmet need in the provision of social prescriptions for mental health. The same reasons as highlighted above could apply for the variation seen for these different population subgroups. Whatever the reason may be for the underuse and variation we see, these findings point to the need for changes in practice linked to clinical coding, better design/support for appropriate local services based on population need and/or better coordination with other local organisations that provide support for individuals with a CMHP.

4.2   Further Developments and Considerations

Despite the promise of the ontological approach, there are some important considerations that must be taken into account that impact the results presented in this manuscript.

Firstly, the ontology for CMHP only provides an estimate of the eligible population that could benefit from a social prescription for mental health. Through our approach of engaging relevant expertise, we aimed to compile a comprehensive set of codes that could capture CMHP but we may have missed some codes. Furthermore, there is heterogeneity in the quality and accuracy of coding across different clinical contexts, which will inherently limit the ability to accurately capture clinical activity. Taking account of both of these considerations, however, would mean that our ontological approach would have underestimated the total eligible population that could have benefited from a social prescription for mental health - which would mean that our general findings of underuse underestimated the true situation. The findings on variation would be more complex to generally interpret because we know that the proactive recording of some of these attributes, like ethnicity, is very heterogeneous in clinical practice and this could significantly affect the results seen [39]. Emerging approaches like computer-assisted clinical coding could help to resolve some of these issues but it will take time to implement this systematically across healthcare settings [40].

Secondly, the 'social prescribing for mental health' code we used for our analyses is very general. While this code implicitly indicates that the presenting complaint was related to mental health, it does not actually indicate the specific intervention delivered – for example, a referral to employment support, talking therapy, a gardening club, etc. Without more granular information on the specific type of service an individual was referred to, it will be difficult to understand the true gaps in service provision as well as the areas for improvement.

Finally, without knowing the actual service delivered, we will also be unable to explore the quality of the service delivered and the outcomes we could reasonably attribute to it. Though some clinical trials have demonstrated the efficacy of non-pharmaceutical interventions, their effectiveness in real-life clinical settings remains unknown. More granular and accurate information on the interventions that are being prescribed could facilitate the use of real-world data, coupled with quasi-experimental methods, to establish the evidence of the value of these types of interventions [19].

Whilst our ontological approach only provides estimates, the general trends revealed through our analyses provide valuable insights that can help to inform both policy and practice to address variation, health inequalities as well as to proactively design and implement services that meet the needs of groups with different attributes.

References

1. Barton, J., Rogerson, M.: The importance of greenspace for mental health. BJPsych. International **14**(4), 79–81 (2017). https://doi.org/10.1192/S2056474000002051
2. National Institute for Health and Care Excellence. Depression (2020). Available at: https://cks.nice.org.uk/topics/depression/
3. Barton, J., Rogerson, M.: The importance of greenspace for mental health. BJPsych. International **14**(4), 79–81 (2017). https://doi.org/10.1192/S2056474000002051
4. Mind: Depression (2020). Available at: https://www.mind.org.uk/information-support/types-of-mental-health-problems/depression/causes/
5. de Lusignan, S., Chan, T., Parry, G., Dent-Brown, K., Kendrick, T.: Referral to a new psychological therapy service is associated with reduced utilisation of healthcare and sickness absence by people with common mental health problems: a before and after comparison. J Epidemiol Community Health. **66**(6), e10 (2012). https://doi.org/10.1136/jech.2011.139873. Jun
6. The World Bank: World Bank Education COVID-19 School Closures Map. See: https://www.worldbank.org/en/data/interactive/2020/03/24/world-bank-education-and-covid-19. Last checked 19 April 2021
7. Grzegorczyk, M., Wolff, G.: The scarring effect of COVID-19: youth unemployment in Europe. Bruegel Blog (28 November 2020)
8. Bambra, C., Riordan, R., Ford, J., Matthew, F.: The COVID-19 pandemic and health inequalities. J Epidemiol Community Health **74**, 964–968 (2020)
9. Hensher, M.: Covid-19, unemployment, and health: time for deeper solutions? BMJ **371**, m3687 (2020)
10. Office for National Statistics: Coronavirus and depression in adults. Great Britain (June 2020). See: https://www.ons.gov.uk/peoplepopulationandcommunity/wellbeing/articles/coronavirusanddepressioninadultsgreatbritain/june2020. Last checked 19 April 2021
11. National Institute for Health and Care Excellence. Improving Access to Psychological Therapies (IAPT) (Jan 2022). See: https://www.nice.org.uk/about/what-we-do/our-programmes/nice-advice/iapt
12. Rose, G.: Sick individuals and sick populations. Int J Epidemiol **14**, 32–38 (1985)
13. Rose, G.A., Khaw, K.-T., Marmot, M.G.: Rose's strategy of preventive medicine: The complete original text. Oxford University Press, Oxford, UK (2008)
14. WHO: Social Determinants of Health: the Solid Facts, 2nd edn. WHO, Geneva (2003)
15. Jani, A., Kawazura, Y.: Policy responses to the nonlinear future of COVID-19's aftermath. COVID: A complex systems approach. In: Morales, A.J. (ed.) COVID-19 A Complex Systems Approach Papers and Commentaries, pp. 209–221. STEM Academic Press, New York
16. NHS England: Population Health and the Population Health Management Programme (2020). See: https://www.england.nhs.uk/integratedcare/what-is-integrated-care/phm/

17. NHS England: Core20PLUS5 – An approach to reducing health inequalities (2021). See: https://www.england.nhs.uk/about/equality/equality-hub/core20plus5/
18. NHS England: Social prescribing and community-based support: Summary guide (2019). https://www.england.nhs.uk/wp-content/uploads/2019/01/social-prescribing-community-based-support-summary-guide.pdf. Accessed June 2 2021
19. Royal College of Psychiatrists: Social prescribing (2021). See: https://www.rcpsych.ac.uk/docs/default-source/improving-care/better-mh-policy/position-statements/position-statement-ps01-21---social-prescribing---2021.pdf?sfvrsn=2b240ce4_2
20. NHS England: NHS Long Term Plan (2019). https://www.longtermplan.nhs.uk/. Accessed June 2 2021
21. NHS England: What is personalised care? (2021). https://www.england.nhs.uk/personalised care/what-is-personalised-care/. Accessed June 2 2021
22. National Institute for Health and Care Excellence: Depression in adults: recognition and management (2009). See: https://www.nice.org.uk/guidance/cg90/chapter/Recommend ations
23. National Institute for Health and Care Excellence: Generalised anxiety disorder and panic disorder in adults: management (2019). See: https://www.nice.org.uk/guidance/cg113/cha pter/1-Guidance#principles-of-care-for-people-with-generalised-anxiety-disorder-gad
24. Jani, A., et al.: Using an ontology to facilitate more accurate coding of social prescriptions addressing social determinants of health: Feasibility study. J Med Internet Res (2020). https://doi.org/10.2196/23721
25. RCGP RSC: RCGP Research and Surveillance Centre (RSC) (2021). https://www.rcgp.org.uk/clinical-and-research/our-programmes/research-and-surveillance-centre.aspx. Accessed June 2 2021
26. HDI: ORCHID - Health Data Research Innovation Gateway (2021). https://web.www.health datagateway.org/collection/5626663352808625. Accessed June 2 2021
27. Oxford-RCGP RSC: ORCHID-RCGP RSC Practice Map (2021). https://orchid.phc.ox.ac.uk/index.php/orchid-practice-map/. Accessed June 2 2021
28. Jani, A., et al.: Use and impact of social prescribing: a mixed-methods feasibility study protocol. BMJ Open (2020). https://doi.org/10.1136/bmjopen-2020-037681
29. Benson, T.: Why general practitioners use computers and hospital doctors do not—Part 1: Incentives. BMJ (2002). https://doi.org/10.1136/bmj.325.7372.1086
30. El-Sappagh, S., Franda, F., Ali, F., Kwak, K.S.: SNOMED CT standard ontology based on the ontology for general medical science. BMC Med Inform Decis Mak (2018). https://doi.org/10.1186/s12911-018-0651-5
31. Unified Medical Language System: SNOMED CT BioPortal Ontology (2021). https://biopor tal.bioontology.org/ontologies/SNOMEDCT. Accessed June 2 2021
32. NHS Digital: SNOMED CT UK Edition (2021). https://isd.digital.nhs.uk/trud3/user/guest/group/0/pack/26. Accessed June 2 2021
33. Liyanage, H., Krause, P., De Lusignan, S.: Using ontologies to improve semantic interop-erability in health data. J Innov Heal Informatics (2015). https://doi.org/10.14236/jhi.v22 i2.159
34. Liyanage, H., Williams, J., Byford, R., De Lusignan, S.: Ontology to identify pregnant women in electronic health records: Primary care sentinel network database study. BMJ Heal Care Informatics (2019). https://doi.org/10.1136/bmjhci-2019-100013
35. Cole, N.I., et al.: An ontological approach to identifying cases of chronic kidney disease from routine primary care data: a cross-sectional study. BMC Nephrol (2018). https://doi.org/10.1186/s12882-018-0882-9
36. de Lusignan, S., et al.: COVID-19 surveillance in a primary care sentinel network: In-pandemic development of an application ontology. JMIR Public Heal Surveill (2020). https://doi.org/10.2196/21434

37. Oxford-RCGP RSC: Using Oxford-RCGP RSC for observational studies (2021). https://orc hid.phc.ox.ac.uk/index.php/orchid-data/
38. Lemanska, A., et al.: Study into COVID-19 crisis using primary care mental health consultations and prescriptions data. Stud Health Technol Inform. **27**(281), 759–763 (2021). https://doi.org/10.3233/SHTI210277. May
39. Nuffield Trust: Ethnicity coding in English health service datasets (2021). See: https://www.nuffieldtrust.org.uk/research/ethnicity-coding-in-english-health-service-datasets
40. Campbell, S., Giadresco, K.: Computer-assisted clinical coding: A narrative review of the literature on its benefits, limitations, implementation and impact on clinical coding professionals. Health Inf Manag (2020). https://doi.org/10.1177/1833358319851305

FinTech and Its Implementation

Suzana Stojakovic-Celustka (ID)

InfoSet d.o.o., Zagreb, Croatia
owner@infoset-world.com

Abstract. The article presents an overview of current implementations in the FinTech field. FinTech is an abbreviation for the term Financial Technology. This article shows the general characteristics of some of the most popular FinTech technologies and their implementation. FinTech has no implications only for the financial industry. It includes virtually all forms of e-commerce and spreads to other industry fields, especially in blockchain technology. The article presents four significant areas of FinTech such as insurance, banking services, trading on capital markets, and risk management. It also covers key technologies in use in FinTech, such as artificial intelligence (AI), Big Data, advanced analytics, robotic process automation (RPA), and blockchain technology. There are two case studies of FinTech implementation presented in the article. The first case study discusses applying artificial intelligence and advanced data analytics in payment fraud prevention and detection. Blockchain implementation is illustrated in more detail in the Dubai Government's Blockchain Strategy case study. The connection of FinTech to ontology theory is given at the end of the article.

Keywords: FinTech · Artificial intelligence · Big data · Blockchain · FIBO · UMF

1 Foreword

FinTech is an abbreviation for "Financial Technology." It is a collective name used for all disruptive technologies which have appeared in the financial industry of the 21st century. The term is used both for products and services.

Traditional banking is the first financial industry sector deeply affected by FinTech, which some consider a threat to conventional banking. In a broader sense, especially regarding some specific technologies arising from FinTech but not implemented only in the financial sector, such as blockchain, these innovative technologies can threaten all intermediary institutions. Blockchain, for example, reduces the need for a central authority or any intermediator between two parties willing to perform any transaction.

Customers of FinTech services tend to prefer their ease of use and faster service, report better experience, and be more satisfied with FinTech services than traditional financial services [1]. There is, undoubtedly, occasional embracing of FinTech services as a kind of "fashion" by part of customers who want to be "trendy," but, in general, it is genuine interest in better user experience that drives demand for FinTech products and services.

© Springer Nature Switzerland AG 2022
R. Polovina et al. (Eds.): MOVE 2020, CCIS 1694, pp. 256–277, 2022.
https://doi.org/10.1007/978-3-031-22228-3_12

This article will show the general characteristics of some of the most popular FinTech technologies and their implementation. As blockchain is one of these technologies that rapidly enters every aspect of daily life, the case study will present its application in the government sector of the city of Dubai in the UAE.

The paper is written in an ontology-like manner presenting the main aspects of FinTech fields. It discusses the possibility of establishing a unified FinTech ontology at the end of the main presentation.

If we confine to a specific ontology definition, it is possible to start resolving current ontology problems in this area. According to ontology definitions, one definition is: "It provides a common background and understanding of a particular domain, or field, of study, and ensures a common ground among those who study the information." [19] Therefore, this article aims to provide that "common ground" for various topics inside the growing FinTech field. It forms a basis for future improved and better-organized categorization in an attempt to approach another definition of ontology: "Ontology is an organizational system designed to categorize and help explain the relationships between various science concepts in the same area of knowledge and research." [19]

2   Introduction

The FinTech industry is very friendly to the end-user, unlike the traditional finance industry. It also has its effects on the global economy. It affects banking jobs in a way that can eliminate many of them. FinTech allows customers the possibility to make financial transactions without the need to visit physical branches. They can perform them now very quickly from their mobile phones.

FinTech has no implications only for the financial industry. It includes virtually all forms of e-commerce. It also cuts jobs in the retail industry because it is much easier to purchase some items online and get the shipment home than to visit a physical shop.

On the other hand, while finance and retail industries lose jobs, technology sectors gain new jobs as innovations in FinTech appear every day. It also changes the way of sales. People return to selling to each other directly through services such as, e.g., Paypal. It enables many small and micro businesses to flourish.

New online jobs are also appearing that use all conveniences of the Internet, including the possibility of online payments. FinTech significantly affects the global economy in many ways, and we cannot neglect its importance.

2.1   History of FinTech

We often think that FinTech appeared only recently in the 21st century. Its history is somewhat longer and dates to the 1950s [2]. Those early years brought credit cards to customers of financial institutions. In the 1960s, customers got ATMs that replaced tellers and branches. Electronic stock trading began in the 1970s. In the 1980s, banks adopted mainframe computers for data processing and record keeping. In the 1990s, Internet use got wider and enabled e-commerce. Since 2000 many new applications of FinTech appeared, such as mobile apps for payments, electronic wallets, e-banking, m-banking, robots-advisors, etc.

2.2 FinTech Today

We can see the progress of FinTech the best by looking into investments in the FinTech industry. Global investments in FinTech raised more than 2200% in less than ten years [3]. They increased from $930 million in 2008 to more than $22 billion in 2015 and remained growing. In 2018, total global investments into FinTech doubled from the previous year.

Piyush Singh, senior managing director of financial services for Africa, Middle East & Turkey, and the Asia Pacific at Accenture, said about this amazing trend [4]: "Even if you discount the massive Ant Financial transaction[1], we'd still have a record year for global FinTech fundraising, with strong activity in many corners of the world, so these are broad-based gains.

It's hard to tell whether we'll be able to keep up with this pace of torrid growth. Still, one thing is for sure: many investors have woken up to the fact financial technology can add a lot of benefits to businesses and consumers alike both in developed and developing markets, which is why we keep seeing an increase in FinTech activity." (Quoted from [4]).

2.3 FinTech Key Areas

Four significant areas of FinTech are [3]:

- Insurance
- Banking services
- Trading on capital markets
- Risk management.

Insurance Industry – InsurTech. FinTech in the insurance industry (InsurTech) assures a more customer-centric approach. The insurance industry applies InsurTech to attract a younger population of customers by providing its services through mobile apps. Younger customers are more willing to adopt new technologies, so InsurTech offering new technical inventions appears more attractive to younger generations.

By using InsurTech products and services, customers get [5]:

- Enriched connectivity (by using chatbots that can understand and act on customer queries at any time)
- Personalized product offerings (by using, e.g., Buzzvault for the digitized inventory of their possessions or Slice for users renting their homes or cars)
- End-to-end automation (e.g., Shake and Go to report car insurance claims).

Banking Services. Banks started to adopt FinTech applications in payments first. Soon the banks realized that the potential of using FinTech was much more significant. They began to use FinTech in various fields of their business activities. The banks are now

---

[1] Ant Financial, the digital payments arm of China's Alibaba, raised $4.5 billion in a single funding round.

replacing their incumbent value chains with new FinTech products and services. The main challenge for banks remains to be the way of choosing the right FinTech partner. EY explained in their 2017 Report [6] the best practices for banks to cooperate with FinTech companies. Table 1 summarizes the main points from the EY Report.

The most used features of FinTech that both banks and individual users are adopting are [7]:

- Money transfers and payments,
- Savings and investments,
- Borrowing,
- Financial planning.

All traditional banking services are transferring into the FinTech sphere. The merging of conventional banking and FinTech might end the banking industry we know. Some experts argue that banks need to rethink how they work thoroughly to keep pace with technology and societal changes that FinTech has brought about lately [8].

Table1. The partnership imperatives and opportunities for banks and FinTechs (adjusted from [6])

Banks	FinTechs
Develop a FinTech innovation framework	Articulate value proposition
Choose an innovation operations model	Differentiate with regulatory prowess
Assess FinTech engagement strategies	Are prepared and well-networked
Manage talent and architectural change	Build a robust business case

Trading on Capital Markets. FinTech brings many improvements to trading in capital markets (CM). The benefits are significant for the CM sector. FinTech improves the following areas of CM [9]:

- IT architecture by making it much simpler
- Industry standards by accelerating the development of new standards for new technologies in CM
- Collaboration among industry players by promoting goodwill
- Risk mitigation by including reliability and security in their products and services.

FinTech in CM enables the creation of new values primarily. It helps CM be more user-friendly by building capabilities to enhance their client relationships. FinTech improves CM's overall performance by reducing costs through automation and simplifying business processes. It also facilitates regulatory compliance of CM.

About 310 FinTech companies helped the CM industry in the post-crisis wave, starting in 2008, to fix post-crisis challenges, such as falling revenues and decreasing liquidity.

Given the size and growth of these two industries, their successful merger can make an attractive market for both technology investors and new FinTech entrepreneurs. Most FinTech players in CM sectors have lower costs than traditional technology providers have. In this way, the FinTech industry enables significant savings to the CM sector while adopting cutting-edge technology.

Risk Management. The main risks that financial institutions are dealing with are credit, market, and operational risks. Credit risk means that the borrower will not be able to repay his debt. Market risk happens because of the unpredictability of markets. Operational risk includes human errors, fraud, cybercrime, etc.

When dealing with these three types of risks, FinTech can help in the way to include additional intelligence, such as social media behavioural analysis, to approach credit risk [10]. Some advanced FinTech analytics tools, such as predictive analytics and machine learning, can prevent fraud in financial transactions. Blockchain technology also improves the security and integrity of all kinds of transactions.

Figure 1 shows the elements of credit risk where FinTech can improve credit risk management [11].

The developments in artificial intelligence (AI), blockchain technologies, advanced analytics, biometrics, and similar technologies will improve finance institutions' overall risk management in the future. Dealing with all types of risks often requires analyzing a significant amount of data. It is a Big Data problem. Advanced FinTech analytics tools can significantly help analyze Big Data and optimize the whole risk management process by automation.

The future of financial risk management will depend on further developments in FinTech. Only the synthesis of classic risk management techniques and FinTech advanced technologies can bring improvements in this field in the future.

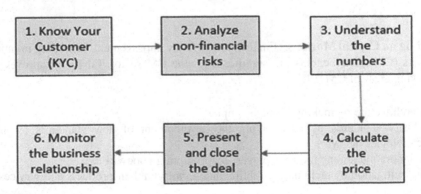

Fig. 1. Six elements of credit risk management (redrawn from image source [11])

2.4 FinTech Key Technologies

Key technologies in use in FinTech are the following [3]:

- Artificial intelligence (AI)
- Big Data
- Advanced analytics
- Robotic process automation (RPA)
- Blockchain

FinTech experts use AI algorithms for various purposes, such as analyzing customers' behaviour (e.g., spending habits) or predicting changes in financial markets (e.g., the stock market). Chatbots are AI tools to improve customer service.

Financial transactions include enormous amounts of data, so-called Big Data. Various tools for collecting, researching, and analyzing Big Data are in use for daily optimizations of financial operations.

Related to Big Data are tools for advanced data analytics, such as predictive analytics or machine learning (ML). These analytic tools help financial institutions to adjust their strategies and portfolios in an environment of frequent changes.

Robotic process automation (RPA) serves to automate repetitive manual tasks. RPA can complete such tasks (e.g., accounts payable and receivable) more efficiently than human workers.

Blockchain is a digital, distributed, decentralized, public, or private transaction ledger. It records transactions across many networked nodes using a peer-to-peer network. The primary use of blockchain was to be a digital, distributed ledger for financial transactions with cryptocurrencies. Its use soon went out from the financial sector to many other industries, such as, e.g., government or transport sectors.

3 FinTech Implementations

Implementations of FinTech are numerous and very various. We will limit our presentation of FinTech use to two examples of its application. The first example will present predictive analytics, machine learning, and AI techniques to prevent payment fraud. The second example will introduce blockchain technology and go outside the finance sector to show how financial technology initially became widely used in other areas. The case study will show the Dubai Government's Blockchain Strategy.

3.1 Using Advanced Technology in Payment Fraud Prevention

Fraud in payments is any fraudulent or illegal transaction completed by a cybercriminal. The perpetrator deprives the victim of funds, personal property, interest, or sensitive information via the Internet.

These days fraud goes international. International fraudsters perpetrate this fraud by knowing how to work the payment system to their advantage, to the detriment of the business. The aim is to extort products and money from the company, and they have many elaborate scams associated with their international fraud activities [12].

Utilizing predictive analytics to anticipate and combat fraud in a digital world. Looking at various companies' experiences across all industries, we can observe that fraud attacks often do not come from where one would expect. Companies still rely too much on guesswork and empiric methods while investigating potentially fraudulent transactions.

Fraud patterns evolve quickly and continuously. Companies put in place various measures to prevent fraud, but perpetrators rapidly adapt and find ways to circumvent them. There is a need for better processes and tools to enhance fraud detection and investigation.

To analyze and understand how and where fraud happens, one cannot just rely on the experience and intuitions of even the best investigators or the analysis of standard fraud reports and underlying metrics. Besides, the more common analytical tools appear ineffective for scanning very high and fast-growing volumes of data that bury critical information to understand fraud patterns and hidden paths.

Identifying fraud patterns means finding out:

- Where fraud comes from
- How it happens
- Who is involved
- What areas of the business it impacts

Fast-developing predictive analysis technologies offer great potential for improving fraud detection and prevention. They can help companies get deep insights into how and where fraudulent transactions originate and analyze changing fraud patterns to enhance their fraud detection strategies and adapt faster to new types of attacks [12].

Rolling out data mining and predictive modelling to manage risk proactively. The data to examine to identify the fraud trends is increasingly diverse. The data are structured and unstructured. Fraud detection is a Big Data problem.

To proactively manage the risk of fraud, we use data mining techniques to obtain useful data, and then we use predictive modelling to understand the collected data (Fig. 2).

In data mining, we use two types of learning – supervised and unsupervised. In supervised learning, there exist historical records with known patterns of fraud. The analysis consists of finding similarities to known recorded patterns. The disadvantage of this type is that it does not recognize unknown patterns. Unsupervised learning searches for behavioural patterns, which may lead to fraudulent actions (heuristics). Its advantage is that it can recognize new patterns of fraud (Table 2).

Data mining techniques aim to obtain meaningful data for predictive models. After obtaining useful data from data mining, we use predictive models to find patterns (Table 3).

Predictive models aim to find useful relationships in large data sets.

Preventing and predicting fraud in real-time without affecting the experience of the customer. To deter and predict fraud in real-time without affecting the experience of the customer, we need an intelligent system capable of (Fig. 3):

- learning or understanding from experience
- acquiring and retaining knowledge

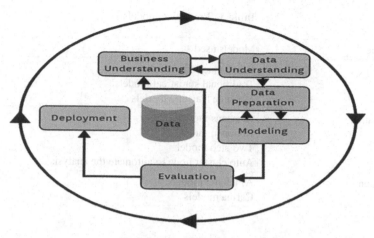

Fig. 2. Cross Industry Standard Process for Data Mining – CRISP-DM Methodology (image source [36])

Table 2. Data mining techniques

Technique	Usage	Algorithms
Classification (or Prediction)	Predict group membership or a number (Example: recognizing known patterns of fraud)	(Supervised learning) Auto classifiers, Decision trees, Logistic, SVM, Time series, etc.
Segmentation	Classify data points into groups that are internally homogenous and externally heterogeneous Identify unusual cases (Example: searching for new patterns of fraud)	(Unsupervised learning) Auto clustering, K-means, etc. Anomaly detection
Association	Finds events that occur together or in sequence (Example: searching for new patterns of fraud)	(Unsupervised learning) APRIORI, Carma, Sequence

- responding successfully and quickly to a new situation
- making proper decisions, etc.

An intelligent system for fraud detection and prevention has to be [13] (Table 4):

- "Invisible" to customer
- Fast
- Reliable

Table 3. Predictive models

Technique	Models used
Classification	Rule induction models Traditional statistical models Machine learning models
Segmentation	K-means model Kohonen model Two-step model Auto cluster node to automate the analysis
Association	APRIORI models Carma models

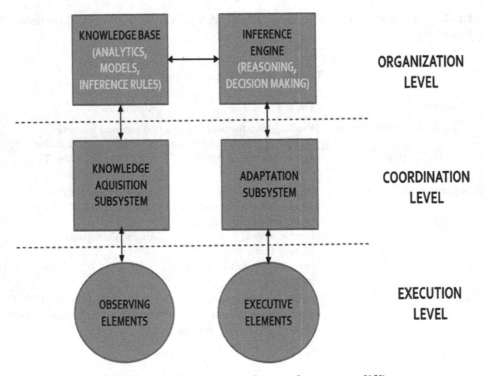

Fig. 3. An Intelligent System Concept (image source [13])

- Precise (small number of false positives or negatives)
- Small
- Adaptive
- Distributed

Table 4. How an intelligent system works

Part of IS	Level	Function	Needed capabilities
Observing elements	Executive	Collect data	Speed, Accuracy
Knowledge acquisition subsystem	Coordination	Data mining, preparing meaningful data for the next level	Speed, Reliability, Obtaining "clean data."
Knowledge base	Organization	Predictive modelling and analytics stores inference rules	Algorithmic diversity, ability to deal with data complexity, Precision
Inference engine	Organization	Select inference rules to perform	Cognitive abilities
Adaptation subsystem	Coordination	Adapt and transfer inference rules to execution elements	Speed, Accuracy
Executive elements	Executive	Execute rules	Speed, Accuracy

Analyzing past failures of data to forecast and handle uncertainty. An intelligent system has to be reliable and have the ability to learn from experiences and past failures. This characteristic is required for the knowledge database (predictive models and analysis) and the data acquisition subsystem (data mining techniques).

Even the best predictive models can fail due to the data's low quality and uncertainty in collected data. Data is typically far from complete, frequently ambiguous, and often scattered over many different data sources.

We use entity analytics to improve the reliability of data. Whereas predictive analytics attempts to predict future behaviour from past data, entity analytics focuses on improving the coherence and consistency of current data. It resolves identity conflicts within the records themselves.

An identity can be that of an individual, an organization, an object, or any entity for which ambiguity might exist. Identity resolution can be vital in fraud detection.

We can obtain the learning capabilities of an intelligent system by using AI (Artificial Intelligence) techniques, e.g., Machine Learning (ML).

The process of machine learning looks very much like the process of data mining. Both techniques use searching through significant amounts of data to discover patterns. Machine learning, however, is not entirely like data mining, which merely extracts data for human understanding because it uses the data to detect patterns in them and adjust programmed actions accordingly.

ML algorithms can be supervised or unsupervised. Supervised algorithms can apply learned patterns and end occurrences from the past to new data. Unsupervised algorithms can draw inferences from datasets.

Developing analytics to uncover the identity of individuals and groups. We use entity analytics also to discover the identity of individuals and groups (Table 5).

Table 5. Entity analytics in Fraud Detection

Characteristic	Predictive analytics	Entity analytics
Fraud detection	Records are flagged as potentially fraudulent if they have typical characteristics of fraudulent action	Records are flagged as potentially fraudulent if related to known fraudulent records or originating from the same individuals but with different identities

One of the more critical data preparation activities involves recognizing when multiple pointers to the same entity are the same entity (within the same data source and across different data sources). It is vital to differentiate the cases where multiple transactions are carried out by various people from when one person carries out all operations.

We achieve an even deeper understanding when we determine that entities are identical (resolved). We can, therefore, recognize when these resolved entities are related to each other (such as sharing the same home address).

Diminishing the chance of data breaches with intelligent analytics. Today's best fraud management and intelligent analytics solutions have many benefits. They:

- Identify fraud patterns and trends more precisely,
- Enable finding the less known and more complex patterns and networks,
- Enable earlier detecting of fraud, minimizing the damage from cleverly hidden suspicious transactions,
- Provide the needed capabilities to analyze very variable data and a very high volume of data in a very fast way, relying on fast computing technology,
- Help fraud investigators reduce false alerts resulting from inadequate fraud detection mechanisms.

The innovation brought by predictive and intelligent analytics also touches many other business areas. The use of predictive analytics will develop further to enable better predictability of risk in areas such as governance, risk, and compliance (GRC).

New predictive technologies must also become approachable for non-experts and more readily consumable by their most interested audience.

Concluding remarks about intelligent analytics in fraud prevention/detection. The combination of predictive and intelligent analytics with traditional fraud management solutions enhances investigators' capabilities to detect fraud and better prevent potential future fraud attempts.

It enables a more in-depth and better forensic approach against fraud. Intelligent analytics is helping users to improve the effectiveness of their investigations by better focusing on new types of fraud risks. It is also continuously updating and refining its fraud detection strategies using the data from predictive analytic tools.

However, with the growing complexity of analytical tools, the required levels of expertise to work with them are changing. Finding the right experts for sophisticated fraud pattern analysis will undoubtedly be one of the biggest challenges in the future of digital payment fraud prevention.

3.2 Blockchain Technology

Blockchain appeared for the first time in 2008. Since then, a lot of public attention has been dedicated to the importance of its role in modern society. There were numerous public forums and other media discussions, and they are still active. Many technology fans praise the blockchain as the most important invention on the Internet of today.

Why People Need Blockchain? One of the persistent human needs is the desire for trust, autonomy, and safety in every environment. The same is valid for the integrity of the data in financial transactions on the Internet. The appearance of blockchain is following the quest for solutions to the significant human problems related to the safety of data and money on the Internet.

The Problems. We create, every second, an enormous amount of data on the Internet. The pace of this creation is ever-growing. We upload just about everything to cloud storage places connected to the Internet: our photos, various documents, notes, memos, identity information, financial records, etc. We move a significant portion of our lives to cyberspace.

As soon as we upload our data to the Internet, we give control over them to the administrators of storage places on the Internet. We trust experts to keep our data secure, but there is no way for us to verify who else is accessing our data online.

However, our data are valuable merchandise. They have value not only to us but also to many legitimate or illegitimate pursuers of our data. For example, marketing houses are very interested in our data as they continually look for new potential customers for their clients. Whoever wants to sell us something will have use of our data.

Data hunters pursuing our data can use legal or illegal ways to acquire them. There are black markets for the illicit trade of personal and financial data of Internet users. Cybercriminals use those data to commit frauds and thefts.

We need somebody or something to ensure the security and privacy of our data on the Internet because we do not want to be victims of cybercrime. At the same time, we do not wish everyone who wants to sell us some product or service to bother us excessively.

Financial transactions are ubiquitously running through the Internet. There are millions of them travelling in all directions every day. If not secured, these transfers can cause enormous monetary losses. Therefore, the money transfer through the Internet has to be secure too.

We need to trust the Internet with our data and our money. Nevertheless, many breaches of security and privacy, as well as money thefts, happen daily on the Internet. If we are not safe on the Internet, our reliance on it will diminish significantly. Therefore, we need credible solutions to these problems.

The Solutions. One solution is using peer-to-peer systems for any transactions of data, financial or otherwise. Peer-to-peer networks are distributed systems, meaning there is no central point of coordination governing the activities of individual nodes in the network. All resources of individual network members are directly available to all other members in the network. All nodes in the network are suppliers and consumers of resources, having equal rights and roles in the system.

Peer-to-peer networks have the potential to reshape whole industries by replacing intermediaries with peer-to-peer interactions. Banks and many other financial institutions are intermediaries in lending or transferring money to end-users. Using peer-to-peer systems instead reduces processing costs and transaction fees (Fig. 4).

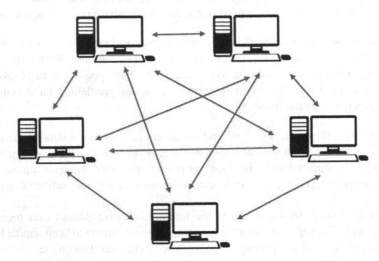

Fig. 4. Peer-to-peer network (redrawn from image source [37])

However, although a more efficient, peer-to-peer system itself does not automatically ensure the integrity of data, the tool for achieving and maintaining integrity in such systems is blockchain.

Threats to integrity in peer-to-peer networks are technical failures and malicious peers. Blockchain must ensure resilience to both threats to integrity in peer-to-peer systems. Therefore, peer-to-peer networks change the paradigm of the need for an intermediary in financial or other data transactions on the global network, such as the Internet, and blockchain is a mechanism to enable the integrity of such a system so that the users can trust it.

How Blockchain Works? Peers in the peer-to-peer network are called "nodes." Nodes in the blockchain peer-to-peer network usually have one or two different roles. They can be "miners" that create new blocks in blockchain (e.g., producing "coins" of some cryptocurrency). On the other hand, they can be "block signers" that validate and digitally sign the transactions [14]. The main decision in the blockchain network is about which node will append the next block to the blockchain.

"Block" is a fundamental element of blockchain and carries information about "transactions." A "transaction" is any event in blockchain, e.g., transferring some value (financial or other) from one network account to the other. Block contains records of such transactions. "Chain" is the way blocks are connected in the blockchain. Blocks are "chained" to each other by using "hash" [14]. Hash is a cryptographic digital fingerprint of data contained in the block. Each block in chained blocks includes the hash of the previous block in the chain. The first block in the chain of blocks has the name "genesis block." It is hardcoded at the time when a particular blockchain has started for the first time [14]. Figure 5 shows the generic structure of the blockchain.

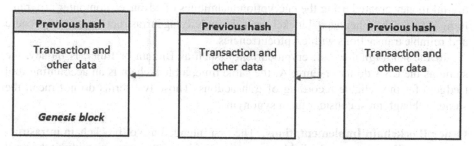

Fig. 5. Generic structure of blockchain (redrawn from image source [14])

Blockchain transactions use unique identifiers called "addresses" to denote senders and recipients. The transaction itself represents sending some value from one address to another. A node in the peer-to-peer network starts a transaction by first creating it and then digitally signing it. The node then propagates transactions to other peers in the network. Other peers then validate the transaction according to predefined criteria. The process of confirming a transaction usually requires more than one node. When the transaction is validated, it is included in the block, which further propagates through the network. The transaction is considered confirmed at that point.

The newly created block becomes a constitutive part of the blockchain. The next created block in the blockchain links itself cryptographically back to this previous block. The link is before the mentioned hash. In that way, the transaction gets its second confirmation. The block containing data about the transaction gets its first confirmation. Every time a new block is created, the transactions are reconfirmed.

Once the data about a transaction enter the blockchain by adding new blocks, it is very complicated to change it back due to cryptographic methods. Therefore, a blockchain is an immutable ledger of all transactions propagating through it. All transactions are also cryptographically secured, providing in this way the integrity of data.

Because blockchain infrastructure is a peer-to-peer network, it is also highly available. Even if some nodes in the network become inaccessible, the network as a whole can continue its work. The blockchain is usually transparent. Every transaction is visible, and the history of transactions is traceable. Therefore, blockchain is a trustful tool for performing all kinds of transactions.

Blockchain and Cryptocurrencies. Many people connect the term blockchain with cryptocurrencies, such as Bitcoin. The blockchain structure was, indeed, for the first time described and used when Bitcoin appeared. Its author (or authors), known by the name Satoshi Nakamoto has implemented a blockchain structure to serve as the public ledger for all transactions with the cryptocurrency Bitcoin. The first Bitcoin was minted or "mined" in January 2009 [15].

The early success of Bitcoin led to the creation of other cryptocurrencies. Some of them use the Bitcoin blockchain, and others use their own blockchain (for example, the Ethereum blockchain is used as a ledger for transactions with cryptocurrency Ether).

However, not all cryptocurrencies use a blockchain structure. Therefore, it is not correct to equate the blockchain system with cryptocurrencies. Cryptocurrency is essentially digital money created using the encryption techniques of advanced computer programming [16]. On the other hand, blockchain is the underlying infrastructure enabling secure and reliable transactions with cryptocurrencies.

In the non-digital world, cryptocurrency, such as Bitcoin or Ether, is money, the same as the USA dollar or Euro. At the same time, a blockchain is an accounting tool (ledger) for the reliable recording of transactions. Those two terms do not mean the same, although most consider them synonyms.

Other Blockchain Implementations. The first intended use of blockchain infrastructure was to allow secure and reliable transactions with cryptocurrencies without the need for central authorities or intermediates, such as banks.

While blockchain use in payment processing of digital money is the most known and arguably its most logical implementation, it is not the only one. We can use blockchain for many other purposes, where we need a reliable distributed recording of transactions.

The other implementations of blockchain include (but are not limited to):

- Monitoring supply chains
- Controlling digital identities
- Digital voting
- Medical recordkeeping
- Managing the Internet of Things (IoT) networks
- and many others.

The fields where we can use blockchain technology are very various. They include:

- Government
- Energy production
- Advertising industry
- Insurance industry
- Music Industry
- Healthcare
- Agriculture
- and many others.

Therefore, blockchain is becoming a ubiquitous part of our daily life increasingly.

Case Study – Dubai Blockchain Strategy. Dubai is one of the seven emirates that constitute the United Arab Emirates (UAE). In the last 40 years, the Dubai emirate experienced significant economic growth. It achieved this success by diversifying its gross domestic product. The Emirate made vast real estate, tourism, travel, retail, and logistics developments. The city of Dubai got an international reputation as an economic and investment centre for various businesses [17].

The strong and productive government sector was an enabler of this remarkable economic growth. The city of Dubai adopted advanced technology very early in this process. It announced its first ICT strategy in 1999. This strategy was followed by the launch of Dubai Internet City, Dubai Smart Government, and the Dubai Smart Office.

Dubai launched its Blockchain Strategy in October 2016 [18]. The objective was to become the first blockchain-powered city by 2020. The Dubai government's needs to start this ambitious project were:

- Improving government effectiveness
- Strengthening controls over permissions
- Improving control in transaction verification and tracking.

To resolve these issues successfully, the Dubai government adopted blockchain technology.

Dubai Blockchain Strategy is based on three pillars:

1. Government efficiency
2. Industry creation
3. International leadership

The first pillar, "Government efficiency," aims to improve government efficiency by enabling a paperless digital layer for all city transactions. It supports Smart Dubai initiatives in the public and private sectors. Blockchain technology is used across various city sectors, such as municipal and land works, transport and logistics, economic development, energy, social services, etc. The estimated savings by using blockchain infrastructure are up to 114 MT of CO_2 emissions from trip reductions and up to 25.1 million hours of economic productivity in saved document processing time.

The second pillar, "Industry creation," introduces the system for enabling the creation of new businesses using blockchain technology. Industries to draw benefit from it may be FinTech and traditional banking, transport, real estate, healthcare, tourism, digital commerce, and smart energy. The pillar will apply four key action areas:

- Policy development
- Blockchain accelerator to engage startups
- Global blockchain startup competitions.

Under the third pillar, "International leadership," Dubai will open its blockchain platform to global partners through Global Trust Network. In this way, Dubai will enhance security and convenience for international visitors to Dubai through faster security clearance and mobility that is more comfortable, as well as other services. This pillar will apply five key action areas:

- Skill development
- Intellectual capital
- Blockchain speaker series
- International Blockchain Award
- Academic sector activation.

With the adoption of blockchain technology, Dubai commits itself to provide a prosperous ecosystem for businesses and startups to thrive, thus enabling further advancement of economic growth. Dubai also aims to improve its tourist sector by allowing tourists a more relaxed and pleasant visiting experience. The city is also ready to share its knowledge and expertise related to the blockchain with the rest of the world. Dubai aims to establish itself as a leading international centre for developing and improving blockchain technologies. It is a very ambitious goal for still novel technology. However, it is a necessary step in the world of fast-developing innovations where being a leader in adopting the newest technologies means having a competitive advantage.

4   Connection of FinTech with Ontology Theory

One may ask what FinTech implementation has to do with ontology theory. It would be usual to understand that where there is "Fin" in the name, the topic should be related to the field of finance. However, as we have seen through the article, when considering some cases based initially in the finance field, we can soon step out to other areas, such as artificial intelligence, Big Data, etc. Furthermore, the implementation of blockchain technology spreads to very different use cases, as we have seen in Dubai Government's Blockchain Strategy case study.

Therefore, there is an urgent need to find an appropriate way to categorize such a multidisciplinary field. However, the ontology theory of FinTech is in its early stage and has not been researched enough.

One of the ontologies applicable to the FinTech area is FIBO (Financial Industry Business Ontology) [38, 39]. It defines a set of entities related to financial business applications and their mutual relations. FIBO is sponsored and hosted by the Enterprise Data Management Council (EDMC). FIBO is an EDM Council, Inc. Trademark standardized by the Object Management Group (OMG). Various FIBO publication formats are available for business definitions and operational implementation.

FIBO is developed in the Web Ontology Language (OWL). The OWL is codified by the World Wide Web Consortium (W3C), and it is based on Description Logic. Using this specific logic ensures that each FIBO concept is categorized in a way that is unambiguous and readable by humans and machines.

Financial institutions use FIBO for [38]:

- Data harmonization
- Standardized data integration
- Flexible analysis
- Blockchain implementation

- Machine Learning implementation.

FIBO's technical expression is the RDF/OWL – the triplestore language of the World Wide Web for machine-readable inference processing. A triplestore is a method of organizing data into groups of three that contain subjects and objects linked together by predicates. By taking advantage of the RDF/OWL Web standard, FIBO uses machine intelligence and network graph capabilities to express, classify and connect data in ways that were not previously possible [38].

An interesting ontology framework is given in [40] and applied to the AI field. Upper Modelling Framework (UMF) is a modelling tool that uses an intuitive approach to explain domain complexity. It seems suitable to use in a complex domain such as FinTech.

The UMF concept is presented in Fig. 6. This framework includes four spheres or levels of the model's existence: principal, conceptual, formative, and manifestation spheres/levels. In addition to the four spheres or levels of the model's existence, ten main modelling principles are observed within the spheres: object essence, contrasted object, relationship, system, time, memory, bliss, thought, being, and reality. These principles may represent views or modelling dimensions.

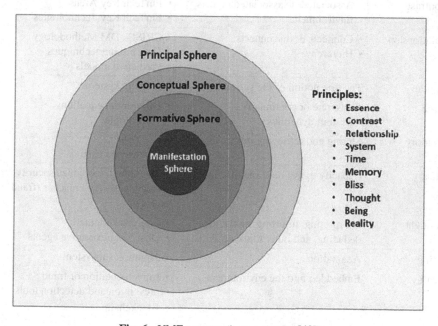

Fig. 6. UMF concept (image source [40])

The principle sphere/level modelling focuses on differentiating ideas. The modellers choose only those ideas they believe to be relevant to the model. Modellers construct their visions of the future reality in the conceptual sphere. The conceptual sphere contains prototypes and all methodologies, methods, paradigms, formalisms, or other patterns that modellers have at their disposal. In the formative sphere, modellers produce a palpable form of the system. This form receives characteristics in quantities, dimensions, and design, establishing it as a specific system. A form will be manifested in the manifestation sphere when it is produced in a reality where modellers build models by perceiving the physical world.

The ten modelling principles may be used as dimensions to classify models and modelling paradigms. Based on these ten principles, we performed the modelling of the main aspects of FinTech fields presented earlier in this article. The model's presentation can be seen in Table 6.

Table 6. The main modelling principles of the UMF concept

Modelling principles	Description	Examples of cognitive processes and formal paradigms
Essence	• Object recognition • Determining the essence	• Main objects in FinTech - money, financial transactions, people, • Need for technical solutions
Contrast	• Associated/disassociated objects • Environment	• FinTech Key Areas • FinTech Key Technologies
Relationship	• Connects or disconnects • Hierarchy	• CRISP _DM Methodology • Data mining techniques • Predictive models
System	The first notion of the system	Intelligent system
Time	• Discrete or continuous • System dynamics	• Differential equations • Fuzzy logic
Memory	Storing and retrieving information	• Big Data • Knowledge base
Bliss	Capacity to evaluate and discriminate	Being able to recognize security, privacy, or safety breaches (fraud issues)
Thought	Interpreting, inferring, analyzing, deducing, and other thinking skills	• Inference engine • Observing/executive agents
Being	Adaptation	Adaptation subsystem
Reality	Embedded into the environment	• Implementation of fraud prevention and detection tools • Blockchain

5   Conclusions

We started this discourse through FinTech in the finance industry and ended in the government sector. How is that possible? As we initially said, FinTech is an abbreviation for Financial Technology. Therefore, the narrative should be mainly about the finance industry. However, it is not always the case.

FinTech is a highly complex mix of various technologies. Many of those, such as artificial intelligence (AI), also have applications in other areas of the financial industry. It was inevitable that including these technologies in the finance industry would blend it with other sectors too.

This issue is the most visible in the examples of blockchain implementation. The technology, primarily designed for ensuring transactions with cryptocurrencies, spread very fast into all other areas of daily life. Its further development is still unknown.

We can conclude that FinTech is a fascinating and unpredictable field. Although FinTech was in the first period of its existence aiming to improve the traditional finance industry, mainly banking, it developed unexpectedly into its opposite. Many people today wonder if the conventional banking industry will survive as we know it or evolve into something completely different. It is possible that traditional banking will disappear entirely, as numerous blockchain technology fans predict. The future of the insurance industry is also uncertain.

FinTech brings an exciting future to the finance industry and all other sectors. Its further development will undoubtedly be very interesting.

Equally challenging is the ongoing problem of categorizing such a complex field as FinTech through unified ontology theory. We discussed two potentially usable ontology frameworks: FIBO (Financial Industry Business Ontology) and UMF (Upper Modelling Framework). While FIBO is an existing EDM Council, Inc. Trademark standardized by the Object Management Group (OMG) and used in some financial institutions, it might be too cumbersome for ubiquitous implementation. UMF is, at the moment, only a research ontology project, but it is much more straightforward and intuitive for implementation while covering a broader universe of concepts. We have demonstrated its usability to cover various FinTech concepts presented in this paper and will follow its further development.

References

1. Hayen, R.: FinTech, the Impact and Influence of Financial Technology on Banking and the Finance Industry. Kindle (2016)
2. Desai, F.: The Evolution of Fintech. Forbes online article. https://www.forbes.com/sites/falgunidesai/2015/12/13/the-evolution-of-fintech/#2bd1790c7175 (2015). Accessed 22 Sep 2022
3. Financial technology, Wikipedia. https://en.wikipedia.org/wiki/Financial_technology. Accessed 22 Sep 2022
4. Mallis, A.: Global FinTech Investments Doubled in 2018: Report, 2019, online article. https://which-50.com/global-fintech-investments-doubled-in-2018-report/. Accessed 22 Sep 2022
5. Dossey, A.: How FinTech is Transforming the Insurance Industry. https://clearbridgemobile.com/how-fintech-is-transforming-the-insurance-industry/ (2018). Accessed 22 Sep 2022
6. EY: Unleashing the potential of FinTech in banking. EYGM Limited (2017). https://www.ey.com/Publication/vwLUAssets/ey-unleashing-the-potential-of-fin-tech-in-banking/$File/ey-unleashing-the-potential-of-fin-tech-in-banking.pdf. Accessed 22 Sep 2022

7. Perzhanovskiy, N.: How FinTech Affects Banks and Financial Services? https://justcoded.com/blog/the-impact-of-fintech-on-banks-and-financial-services/ (2019). Accessed 22 Sep 2022
8. Haycock James, Bye Bye Banks? Adaptive Lab. Kindle (2015)
9. BCG Authors: FinTech in Capital Markets: A Land of Opportunity. https://www.bcg.com/publications/2016/financial-institutions-technology-digital-fintech-capital-markets.aspx (2016). Accessed 22 Sep 2022
10. Lazarova, D.: FinTech Trends: Risk Management. https://www.finleap.com/insights/fintech-trends-risk-management/# (2016). Accessed 22 Sep 2022
11. Actico Authors: The Six Elements for A Successful Credit Risk Management Process. https://www.actico.com/blog-en/elements-successful-credit-risk-management-process/ (2018). Accessed 22 Sep 2022
12. Sepahvan, M.: Iranian banks need tech to face growing cyber threats, an interview with Mrs Suzana Stojakovic – Celustka for Trend News Agency. https://en.trend.az/iran/business/2694498.html. Accessed 22 Sep 2022
13. Stojakovic – Celustka Suzana, Raeisi Reza: Advanced Analytics in Payment Fraud Prevention. https://www.researchgate.net/publication/336988636_Advanced_Analytics_in_Payment_Fraud_Prevention (2019). Accessed 22 Sep 2022
14. Bashir, I.: Mastering Blockchain, 2nd edn. Packt Publishing, Kindle (2018)
15. Tiana, L.: Blockchain For Dummies. John Wiley & Sons Inc., Kindle (2017)
16. Horsley, M.: CRYPTOCURRENCY: The Complete Basics Guide For Beginners: Bitcoin, Ethereum, Litecoin and Altcoins, Trading and Investing, Mining, Secure and Storing, ICO and Future of Blockchain and Cryptocurrencies. Cryptocurrency, Kindle (2017)
17. Al Faris, A., Soto, R.: The Economy of Dubai. Oxford University Press, Kindle (2016)
18. Smart Dubai Office, Case Study: Dubai – The First City on Blockchain. https://www.smartdubai.ae/docs/default-source/publications/dubai---the-first-city-on-blockchain_jan-2017.pdf?sfvrsn=d537e1a6_0 (2017). Accessed 22 Sep 2022
19. Ontology definitions: https://www.yourdictionary.com/ontology. Accessed 22 Sep 2022
20. Mehta, N., Agashe, A., Detroja, P.: Blockchain, Bubble or Revolution?, 1st edn. Paravane Ventures, Kindle (2019)
21. Drescher, D.: Blockchain Basics. Apress Media, Kindle (2017)
22. Reed, J.: Financial Technology: FinTech. Blockchain. Smart Contracts, Kindle (2016)
23. Swan, M.: Blockchain. O'Reilly Media Inc., Kindle (2015)
24. Malekan, O.: The Story of the Blockchain. Amazon (2018)
25. Antonopoulos Andreas, M.: The Internet of Money. A Collection of Talks 2013–2016, Amazon
26. Horsley, M.: Blockchain Guide for Beginners. Amazon (2017)
27. William, J.: Blockchain, the Simple Guide to Everything You Need to Know. Amazon (2016)
28. Tapscott, D., Alex, B.: Revolution. Penguin Random House LLC, Kindle (2016)
29. William, J.: FinTech, the Beginner's Guide to Financial Technology. Amazon (2016)
30. Bruce, K.: The Bitcoin Tutorial. FSVpress, Kindle (2016)
31. Nicoletti, B.: The Future of FinTech. Palgrave Macmillan, Kindle (2017)
32. Richblood, J.: Cryptocurrency for Dummies. Amazon (2018)
33. Augustin, R.: FinTech in a Flash. Simtac Ltd., Kindle (2017)
34. Susanne, C., Janos, B.: The FinTech Book. John Wiley & Sons Ltd., Kindle (2016)
35. Flynt, O.: FinTech: Understanding Financial Technology and its Radical Disruption of Modern Finance. Amazon (2016)
36. Dylan: The Data Mining Process (CRISP-DM). https://www.nimblecoding.com/data-mining-process-crisp-dm/ (2019). Accessed 22 Sep 2022
37. Quora discussion: https://www.quora.com/What-is-peer-to-peer-communication. Accessed 22 Sep 2022

38. About FIBO: https://edmcouncil.org/page/aboutfiboreview. Accessed 22 Sep 2022
39. FIBO: https://spec.edmcouncil.org/fibo/. Accessed 22 Sep 2022
40. Polovina, R.: On Understanding and Modeling Complex System: Pandemic Use Case, to be published in Aligning Computing Productivity with Human Creativity for Societal Adaptation. Springer (2022)

Author Index

Baxter, Matt 101

Caine, Jamie 114

de Lusignan, Simon 227, 241
de Moor, Aldo 171, 203

Ferreira, Filipa 227, 241

Graf, Simon 86
Groza, Adrian 57, 73

Hoang, Uy 227, 241

Jakobsen, David 86
Jani, Anant 227, 241

Kemp, Neil 101
Knutas, Antti 171, 203

Laurier, Wim 101
Liyanage, Harshana 227, 241

McGagh, Dylan 227, 241
Mulder, Ingrid 203

Okusi, Cecilia 227, 241

Papalioura, Evi 171, 203
Polovina, Rubina 3, 21
Polovina, Simon 21, 101
Pomarlan, Mihai 73

Rapti, Dora 171, 203

Sherlock, Julian 227, 241
Stojakovic-Celustka, Suzana 256

Taka, Evi 171, 203

Velde, Tomas te 171, 203

Williams, John 227, 241
Wolff, Annika 171, 203

Yonova, Ivelina 227, 241

Author Index

Printed in the United States
by Baker & Taylor Publisher Services

Printed in the United States
by Baker & Taylor Publisher Services